THE BATTLEFIELD AND BEYOND

CONFLICTING WORLDS

NEW DIMENSIONS OF THE AMERICAN CIVIL WAR

T. Michael Parrish, Series Editor

THE
BATTLEFIELD
xxxxxxxxxxxxxxxxxxx AND xxxxxxxxxxxxxxxxxxx
BEYOND

ESSAYS ON THE AMERICAN
CIVIL WAR

EDITED BY
CLAYTON E. JEWETT

LOUISIANA STATE UNIVERSITY PRESS)|(BATON ROUGE

Published by Louisiana State University Press
Copyright © 2012 by Louisiana State University Press
All rights reserved
Manufactured in the United States of America
First printing

DESIGNER: Michelle A. Neustrom
TYPEFACE: Whitman
PRINTER: McNaughton & Gunn, Inc.
BINDER: Acme Bookbinding

LIBRARY OF CONGRESS CATALOGING-IN-PUBLICATION DATA

The battlefield and beyond : essays on the American Civil War / edited by Clayton E. Jewett.
   p. cm.
   ISBN 978-0-8071-4355-1 (cloth : alk. paper) — ISBN 978-0-8071-4356-8 (pdf) — ISBN 978-0-8071-4357-5 (epub) — ISBN 978-0-8071-4358-2 (mobi)
   1. United States—History—Civil War, 1861–1865. I. Jewett, Clayton E.
   E464.B38 2012
   973.7—dc23

2011037860

The paper in this book meets the guidelines for permanence and durability of the Committee on Production Guidelines for Book Longevity of the Council on Library Resources. ♾

Dedicated to
JON L. WAKELYN

On any given evening in the 1980s and 1990s, one could walk into Colonel Brooks' Tavern across the street from the Catholic University of America and spot a man, sporting a bow tie and devilish grin, sitting in a booth with his graduate students. Everyone knew it was Jon L. Wakelyn holding court after class. I happened to be one of the honored few along with Kenneth Nivison, Michael J. Connolly, John O. Allen, and others who had the privilege of sitting with Professor Wakelyn as he dispensed pearls of wisdom long after class had ended. We talked about the assigned readings for the week, our research projects, politics of the day, solved many of the world's problems over a pint or two, and sometimes we even talked about personal matters. Wakelyn took pride and joy in being our mentor in and out of the classroom. The relationship he fostered with us during our graduate school years did not end there. Long after walking down the aisle in our caps and gowns, he continues to exert his influence in our lives. Wakelyn includes us in his research projects, still teaches us, and persists to inform us of his opinion regarding our academic path and progress. When we do not keep him informed we will receive a one-line email from him saying "Why have I not heard from you?" or "You need to let me know what you are doing!" or "What are you working on?" He cares more than a professor is required to. I think I speak for all of his students when I say that Jon L. Wakelyn is more than just a professor, he is a father figure and he is a friend—a mentor in the truest sense. Wakelyn's influence transcends the impact he has on scores of students. The all-star cast of his colleagues who took time to contribute an essay or provide advance words for this collection speaks for itself regarding his friendships and influence in the field of southern and Civil War history. Professor Wakelyn, this is for you.

CONTENTS

XXXXXXXXXXXXXXXXX

CONTENTS

THE BATTLEFIELD AND BEYOND

INTRODUCTION

XXXXXXXXXXXXXXXXXXXXXXXX

CLAYTON E. JEWETT

The inspiration for this collection of essays on the American Civil War came about from historian Jon L. Wakelyn's years of influence not only on my career, but also that of countless students and colleagues engaged in the field of southern and Civil War history. Mere mention of the Civil War conjures thoughts of guns and blood, destruction and death, glory and honor. The military aspect has always garnered more attention from the masses and publicists than any other facet of the sectional conflict. It grabs people's attention, it sells books. In turn, it elevates certain figures, deserving or not, to fame. It was planned this way, a product of the southern Civil War military commanders who perpetuated the myth of the "Lost Cause." Even before the Civil War ended, southerners began to support a romanticized memory of the Confederacy. Such organizations as the Southern Historical Society, under the leadership of Jubal Early, catapulted military leaders, such as Robert E. Lee, Braxton Bragg, and Stonewall Jackson, to fame.[1] To grasp the Civil War, however, we must move well beyond the myths of the "Lost Cause" and better understand the critical issues that encompass society and the larger context of war. If we have learned anything from the decades of scholarship, it is that the Civil War is not confined to the bloody battlefield and has much to do with issues of race, gender, politics, the press, the economy, memory, and more; the essays in this collection testify to that. At first glance it might appear that this is simply a potpourri of pieces on the Civil War. Taken together, however, the collection provides the reader with an encompassing view of the critical issues surrounding the Civil War and its aftermath, and the original scholarship makes a serious contribution to the field of southern and Civil War history.

In our nation's past, race and warfare have gone hand in hand. Prior to the birth of this nation, southerners laid the foundation of their rule on the grounds of slavery. Leaders used slavery to place the colonies on equal economic footing in the world in order to purchase French assistance in the revolution against Great Britain. In other words, the United States bought its freedom on the backs of slaves. It was slavery that allowed the southern states to control the world supply and price of cotton from the 1790s to 1860 and provided the impetus for secession from the Union. It was the issue of slavery that built this nation, defined its growth, and allowed a minority of the southern population to control the social, economic and political sphere.[2] In this collection of essays, Orville Vernon Burton examines the topic of slavery. In "The Silence of a Slaveholder: The Civil War Letters of James B. Griffin," Burton analyzes the Civil War letters of a prominent South Carolina slaveholder. Burton's astute analysis reveals that, although apparently silent on the issue of slavery, Griffin's letters contain a wealth of information regarding African American life during the Civil War. Burton sheds further light on the war's disruptive influence on the slave family and southern racial relations, eroding the paternalistic system of slavery. As Burton points out, it was the Civil War, the most seminal event in American history, that began to alter those racial relationships.

While Burton emphasizes the nature of slave life and changing racial relationships, Leonne M. Hudson focuses more on the internal struggles of race facing the Confederate government and military—the arming of black men. Most northerners and southerners believed, or at least wishfully thought, that the military conflict would last only a matter of months. When this proved to be untrue, slaveholding Confederates eventually faced the difficult question of what to do with their slaves, and as the gears of war slowly continued to grind, Confederates readdressed issues of racial and gender relations. In "Robert E. Lee and the Arming of Black Men," Hudson examines the Confederate dilemma of being outnumbered and questioning the possibility of arming slaves to counter that Union strength. The predicament lay in the conflict between arming slaves for a better chance of winning the war or holding steadfast to a racist political ideology and hope for a military miracle. Slaves already were impressed as cooks, musicians, miners, mechanics, and more. Placing a gun in their hands, though, was quite a different matter. Offering them freedom for their participation in battle too was unthinkable to most for it would reveal the total folly of the war. Some pragmatists, however, not bound by the ideological or moral implications of slavery and freedom, supported the arming of slaves with the promise of emancipation. For those leaders, such as Robert E. Lee, more was at stake. The war was a matter of principle, a matter of honor, and a victory must be had at all costs. Hudson reveals that the mere suggestion of including slaves in the Confederate army negatively impacted loyalty and served as one of the internal factors in Confederate demise.

Military enlistment was a fatal dilemma. Not only did authorities face the predicament of arming slaves, but also the white population proved difficult enough to recruit. The Conscription Acts caused white southerners to shirk any responsibility they might have had for serving the Confederacy. In many states men chose to serve in the state militia so they could remain close to home. For those that did wear the gray, many deserted to serve family and county over country. To make matters worse, the complexity of issues surrounding military enlistment carried over into actual fighting. In his seminal article, "Guerrilla Warfare, Democracy, and the Fate of the Confederacy," Daniel E. Sutherland examines the issue of guerrilla warfare and its impact upon the fate of the Confederacy. This grassroots style of fighting that existed throughout the Confederacy exposed a great deal about ordinary citizens and Confederate leaders. Military commanders in the Confederacy, most trained at West Point, were not accustomed to this brand of fighting, finding it too democratic. Thus, Confederate leaders underestimated its potential and failed to "harness its passionate energy." For the Confederacy, issues of democracy, local identity, and failed leadership were more nails in its coffin.

When dealing with the internal struggles of the Confederacy, many historians and military buffs automatically point to the conflicts within the military since that aspect of the struggle has garnered the most attention. Supporting military leaders not associated with the "Lost Cause" is a risky undertaking due to its legacy and the place that the Confederacy holds in the southern mind. From the beginning, those who did not support fully the effort of Jubal Early and his followers to perpetuate the memory of the Confederacy found themselves on the losing side, regardless of their wartime accolades or reputation. This in turn has had a negative impact on Civil War scholarship with historians hesitant to veer from the popularly accepted view of the conflict. It is only in the current generation that this attitude has begun to change, as is apparent in Herman Hattaway's essay, "Jefferson Davis and Stephen D. Lee." Hattaway scans the military contribution of Stephen D. Lee and finds him an excellent commander who reaped the praises of Jefferson Davis. Lee outperformed his peers, and his superiors widely recognized him as an extraordinary leader. Hattaway reveals that it was Lee and his men that ultimately saved the Confederacy from complete destruction. Nevertheless, because Lee was not one of the famous generals and he defended Jefferson Davis after the Civil War, his place in southern memory and scholarship suffered much the same fate as that of Davis.

Paul D. Escott's essay, "Evaluating Jefferson Davis as President of the Confederacy," is an excellent follow-up to Hattaway's contribution. Escott points out that history and historians have clouded our view of Jefferson Davis. The Confederacy stood for slavery and militarily lost the Civil War, placing Davis on the losing side of history. In addition, the perpetrators of the "Lost Cause" had no room for Davis in their view of history, which any real assessment of the Confederate president must take into consideration. In his analysis, Escott finds that, on one hand, the president had personality flaws, made bad military appointments, was too respectful of departmental commanders, and failed to deal with the common people. On the other hand, Davis's strengths included being innovative, flexible, and a political risk taker. Nevertheless, whatever strengths he might have possessed ended up as weaknesses since in the eyes of many he appeared as nothing more than a despotic ruler who failed in his attempt to unite the South, revealing that the Confederacy suffered defeat more from internal than external causes.

The internal complexities of the Confederacy are further revealed in the essay "Edmund Kirby Smith's Early Leadership in the Trans-Mississippi" by Judith F. Gentry. One of the most intriguing aspects of the Confederacy is that it contained two military and civilian command centers. In 1861, Ulysses S. Grant began his assault down the Mississippi River. Taking control of the mighty river was one of the major Union goals of war, and on July 4, 1863, Grant and his seventy thousand troops succeeded in taking Vicksburg, severing the Confederacy. In turn, the Confederate government established the Trans-Mississippi Department with Lieutenant-General Edmund Kirby Smith at its helm to control the western Confederacy in all aspects. Although Edmund Kirby Smith has been denigrated throughout much of history, Gentry seeks to salvage his historical reputation. She examines Kirby Smith's efforts to carry out instructions from his superiors, his relationship with state political leaders, his military strategy, and the decisions he made relating to supply issues. One thus becomes acutely aware of the political, military, and economic quagmire in the western Confederacy. It is a wonder that anyone could have been partially successful in governing that region during the Civil War, and Gentry reveals that Kirby Smith deserves more credit than history and historians have given him. Nevertheless, whatever good Kirby Smith might have achieved for the Confederacy as leader of the Trans-Mississippi Department, the chaos that existed proved the further undoing of the Confederacy.

During times of military conflict, there often appears a specter of despotism. During the Civil War conflict this specter was not limited to the Confederate States; nor was it confined to political and military leaders. Amidst the turmoil of war, southerners struggled to preserve the status quo by maintaining their racial relationships. So important was this situation to slaveholders specifically and society in general that even in the North there existed no short supply of southern sympathizers. In his essay, "'Irresistible Outbreaks against Tories and Traitors': The Suppression of New England Antiwar Sentiment in 1861," Michael J. Connolly, an honorary southerner, examines the inherent difficulties surrounding the parameters of freedom and liberty during a national crisis and finds that southern society did not have a market on despotism; it was alive and well in northern society as well. Examining the New England region's dissent against the Civil War, he reveals a complexity to the region and war that prior historians have not fully appreciated. The Civil War, argues Connolly, tested the boundaries of freedom, revealed the difficulties of northern despotism (real and perceived), and shaped the future of northern Democrats. With the suppression of northern "doughfaces," the South was left without a northern sympathetic voice that could possibly broker peace between the two sections. Thus, Confederate difficulties and defeat had as much to do with outward issues as they did with internal struggles. Examining the issue of despotism and Confederate defeat, Clayton E. Jewett reveals the fallout from the centralizing tendencies of Confederate leaders like Jefferson Davis and Edmund Kirby Smith by examining Williamson Simpson Oldham, the Confederate senator from Texas, and his criticism of the Confederate government and military machine. In his essay, "Williamson S. Oldham and Confederate Defeat," Jewett reveals that Oldham was concerned most about the Confederate government trampling on individual rights and liberties. In addition, Oldham criticized Jefferson Davis, military commanders, and the government for interfering in the market—especially the cotton trade, conscripting men into service, and suspending the writ of habeas corpus. Military commanders abused their powers, and political leaders failed to legislate for the good of the people. In Oldham's mind, the Confederacy died of civil and military despotism.

The previous articles point to the complexity of issues that plagued the South and the newborn Confederacy. When it comes to Confederate defeat, it seems apparent that the Confederacy died of despotism and the internal struggles that the new southern nation faced. Racial relationships between masters and slaves that persisted for more than six decades suddenly were disrupted, voices of sympathy for those in the South were quieted, and there existed a general failure of leadership, both military and political. Leaders failed to address adequately the concerns of the civilian population, failed to utilize the manpower (white and black) in the South, failed to mobilize sufficiently the necessities of war that would engage continued popular support for the war effort, and failed to protect the freedoms and liberties of the people.

Ironically, it was the defeat of the Confederacy and the end of the Civil War that would usher in the most significant changes regarding freedom and liberty, not specifically for southern white society, but for the nation as a whole. The Civil War and its aftermath had the most profound impact upon our nation. In his essay "Transforming Original Intent: The U.S. Constitution in the Civil War and Reconstruction Era," David E. Kyvig examines the power of an amendment to fundamentally alter the Constitution, its original intent, and the nation. He reveals that the amendment-making process during the Civil War and Reconstruction impacted the meaning of American citizenship and our rights to life, liberty, and property and thus profoundly changed our traditional notions of federalism. Kyvig reveals that the Civil War would render Constitutional reform effective for solving the fundamental problems facing our society, thus disclosing the unique characteristic of the Constitution to change and meet our nation's needs, which would further reveal its significance over time. Not only did the defeat of the Confederacy and the resulting Reconstruction amendments irrevocably affect our nation, but also the attempt of southerners to remake their society and usher in a "new South" would profoundly and positively impact our nation. Alan M. Kraut reveals in his essay "Goldberger and Gershwin: Two New York Jews Encounter the American South in the Early Twentieth Century" that it was this effort of the South to remake itself, to embrace the progressive spirit of reform, that enabled two northern Jews to not only encounter southern society, but also help remake it, playing a significant role in the prolonged effort to reunify the sections. While Dr. Joseph Goldberger identified with southerners through socio-economic tragedy, George Gerschwin did so culturally, especially with African Americans who, like Jews, were always seen as outsiders. In his attempts to aid the South with its pellagra plague, Goldberger revealed the negative impact of land-ownership patterns in the South and how the persistent socio-economic patterns literally plagued the region by reinforcing patterns of poor diet among the less fortunate, which brought on pellagra. While his efforts shed light on the darker side of the post-Confederate era, Gerschwin's identification with the richness of African American culture reveals a part of the plagued South which he believed should be saved and sewn into the larger fabric of American culture. Taken together, Kraut's subjects reveal the complexity of the South as it grappled to find a new place in the larger schema of America society.

Historians will continue to debate the central question of Confederate defeat and exactly where to place the emphasis; we will continue to debate the positive and negative aspects of postwar southern society. In doing so, we raise another serious issue for scholars and enthusiasts alike—memory. What place do events, people, and institutions hold in the southern mind and memory? How has memory affected our understanding of the past? How have individuals changed our perception of the past?

In this regard, one of the significant events of the American past is the assassination of President Abraham Lincoln. Historians of the 1940s and 1950s applied psychological analysis to John Wilkes Booth's killing of Abraham Lincoln. In "The Psychology of Hatred and the Ideology of Honor: Current Parallels in Booth's Lincoln Conspiracies," Bertram Wyatt-Brown dismisses the various theses within this school of thought to argue that Shakespearean tragedy ultimately led Booth to pull the trigger. In promoting his thesis, Wyatt-Brown examines the ideology of assassination, the implementation of terror, and the public reaction to Lincoln's death. He attempts to place Booth and his colleagues within the mainstream of southern society by arguing that Booth reflected the ideals of slaveholding elites and may have viewed himself as an instrument of southern honor by upholding the ideals of southern masculinity. When it comes to the matter of terrorism, Wyatt-Brown points out the numerous terroristic plots against the president, identifying Booth's plan as simply one of many originating from the South, which was generally good at strategizing Lincoln's assassination but failed in its implementation, save Booth and his conspirators. Finally, by examining the northern and southern reaction, and the long-term consequences of Lincoln's death, Wyatt-Brown argues that Booth's actions were not a solitary act, but rather part of a larger ongoing schema of southern and Confederate identity.

Also dealing with identity and memory, Kenneth Nivison, in "Field of Mighty Memory: Gettysburg and the Americanization of the Civil War," focuses on the Battle of Gettysburg and examines the gradual effort to construct a national narrative about the Civil War. This process began with shared (Union and Confederate) Civil War reunions as men distanced themselves from the actual battlefield. Non-veterans too had a hand in creating a national narrative, especially when it came to Gettysburg. Over time, with the rise of mass consumption in the late nineteenth century, Gettysburg took its place in America as a national commodity. Throughout this process the national identity that individuals forged from the remembrance of the Civil War conveniently left African Americans out of the equation. As a result, argues Nivison, the Civil War became Americanized, fitting squarely into the larger pattern of white racist attitudes, affecting not only our memory of the Civil War but also serving to keep race at the center of our national identity.

As graduate students under Frank E. Vandiver, Emory Thomas, Judith Gentry, and Jon L. Wakelyn shared many ideas, discovered the importance of history together, and had fun in the process. Emory M. Thomas's essay "Of Health and History: The Museum of the Confederacy" is a reflection of just that. It is about the Museum of the Confederacy, its history, and the place it holds in the southern mind. He discusses the role of gender in running the museum; the role of curators and general happenings; the high points, transitions, and low points of the museum; and its present state. In doing so, Thomas reminds us of the importance of history—not the "stuff" that exists in the dusty enclaves of archives, but the history that is alive and present today. We as patrons of the past, he argues, should take an active role in its survival and presentation. How we treat the past speaks volumes about us today—as individuals and as a society.

From the battlefield to beyond, it is clear that the Civil War is the most seminal event in our nation's history. The war was not simply a matter of guns, blood, and death; it involved the critical issues of race, gender, leadership, politics, and memory. The historians contributing to this collection remind us of that fact, and the importance of continuing to understand the conflict, not only as a matter of discovering the past, but also for understanding the present. The failure and military defeat of the Confederacy is still the most relevant issue facing Civil War historians. For the history buff, Civil War enthusiast, and professional scholar, it remains important to understand since it sheds light on our nation, its development, and our current predicaments, especially at the time of this writing with the sesquicentennial of the Civil War. As we remember the war, we are reminded that our nation continues to face issues of race as revealed in the recent presidential election, issues of government circumscribing individual rights as evidenced by controversies surrounding the war on terror and the Patriot Act, issues of war as seen in the fight against suspected terrorists in Iraq and Afghanistan, and issues of government involvement in the marketplace with stimuli and bailouts of our nation's broken economy. One hundred and fifty years ago, these core issues tore the United States apart and led to Civil War. As we confront the anniversary of the Civil War and again consider the fundamental question of southern defeat, we must ask ourselves if the United States has learned from its history or has avoided a careful consideration of its troubled past.

NOTES

1. Initial works perpetuating the myth of the "Lost Cause" include Edward Pollard, *The Lost Cause: A New Southern History of the War of the Confederates* (New York: E. B. Treat & Co., 1866); Albert Taylor Bledsoe, *Is Davis a Traitor?* (Baltimore: Innes & Co., 1866); Robert L. Dabney, *A Defense of Virginia* (New York: E. J. Hale, 1867); and Alexander Stephens, *A Constitutional View of the Late War Between the States* (Philadelphia: National Publishing Co., 1868). For more information, see Gaines M. Foster, *Ghosts of the Confederacy: Defeat, the Lost Cause, and the Emergence of the New South, 1865–1913* (New York: Oxford University Press, 1987).

2. For works on slavery and its place in American society, see Edmund S. Morgan, *American Slavery, American Freedom: The Ordeal of Colonial Virginia* (New York: W. W. Norton, 1975); Peter Kolchin, *American Slavery 1619–1877* (New York: Hill and Wang, 1993); and Clayton E. Jewett and John O. Allen, *Slavery in the South: A State-by-State Analysis* (Westport, CT: Greenwood Press, 2004).

PART I

RACE

xxxxx AND xxxxx

WARFARE

xxxxxxx IN THE xxxxxxx

SOUTH

THE SILENCE OF A SLAVEHOLDER

XXXXXXXXXXXXXXXXXXXXXXXXXXXXXXXXXXXXXXXXXXX

The Civil War Letters of James B. Griffin

ORVILLE VERNON BURTON

When I first learned about a set of some eighty Civil War letters by James B. Griffin, an Edgefield slaveholder and second in command of the celebrated Hampton Legion, I realized the importance of this treasure trove for learning about the unstudied middle officer ranks of the Confederacy and white southern life and community. When I inquired about what Griffin had to say about slavery and African Americans, however, I was informed that he was silent about slavery, that he never discussed the institution. Now, having studied the letters, I see that Griffin did indeed ignore the dynamics of the slave community on his plantation. Nevertheless, although Griffin was not particularly observant or talkative, he told more than he even knew about his slaves. Thus can we squeeze African American history out of white sources. The letters hold specific references by name to eighteen of his enslaved people, and his various personal comments offer an intriguing view of those slaves and their lives. By an intense study of this one slaveholder's correspondence, we learn something about the world the slaves created and how that world changed over the course of the Civil War. Other sources, such as the census, newspapers, and church records, when put together with the letters, fill out the picture of slave life. The supposed silence of this white slave-owner speaks volumes about the life and culture of African Americans on this Edgefield, South Carolina, plantation. This essay looks at this set of letters, what they do and do not say, to give a voice to African Americans.[1]

In 1860, James B. Griffin was thirty-five years old, a wealthy planter, and the owner of sixty-one slaves. When he joined Wade Hampton's elite legion as a major of cavalry, Griffin left behind seven children, a pregnant wife, and an overseer in charge of his enslaved people. He took with him two slave valets, Abram and Ned, and a prized hunting dog. African Americans outnumbered the whites on Griffin's plantation by more than five to one. They provided Griffin with his livelihood and his wealth. They influenced his disposition toward the world and himself. Yet Griffin, like most other whites, was unconscious of their influence over him, inattentive as he was to this culture that existed around him.

Griffin's silence is particularly noticeable on the cause of the Civil War. Griffin clearly did not see the Civil War in terms of preserving slavery. Nor did it occur to him that his enslaved people might be hoping for an end to the old hierarchical and patriarchal order holding them in bondage. He was totally mute about African American freedom. He expected the people he held in slavery to continue to carry out their "duties" just as he was performing his. When meat became so expensive in the spring of 1862 that he instructed his wife Leila to halve rations, he assumed the slaves would identify with his interests and view war hardships as shared sacrifice. Acting the paternal role, he expected the slaves to respond as obedient children, the only capacity in which he could see them: "Tell them it is very painful for me to have to shorten their alowances in this way—but I am forced to do so by the press of circumstances. Talk to them reasonably this way. And tell them I shall expect them to submit to it without a murmer. I will put them back on full allowance as soon as I can." After explaining the necessity of it to the slaves, Leila Griffin was to instruct them all to plant large gardens; she was to buy the seed for them, and ensure that the overseer allowed them time off to cultivate the plots. "Tell them to remember what I am going through. And what the country is now suffering. Many People havent enough bread to eat and doubtless some have no meat at all. If you can buy any beeves do so and feed them to them. Make every possible effort to feed them as well as you can, and that ought to satisfy them."[2]

Griffin's silence on the issue of slavery itself points to the paradox throughout American history that republican ideology would arise amidst a slaveholding society, that the tradition of liberty grew alongside African slavery.[3] Griffin failed to see any contradiction, and his remarks do not indicate any guilt over slavery.[4] These letters show Griffin to be perfectly serious in his conception that a struggle for liberty was the basis of the Civil War. Nevertheless, Griffin's way of life equated with the slave economy, and Griffin's assertion of "battling for Liberty and independence" meant the liberty to own slaves.[5]

Griffin is also completely silent regarding President Lincoln's Emancipation Proclamation, issued in September 1862 to take effect on 1 January 1863. South Carolina had not given the proclamation much attention when it was announced. The Edgefield *Advertiser* wrote: "We have expressed our opinion that Lincoln's Proclamation should be met in the South, by Proclamations from the Southern Governors announcing their intention to enforce strictly the existing State laws against negro thieves and insurrectionists."[6] After the Emancipation Proclamation took effect, the *Advertiser* printed the full text and noted that, while some in the North supported the measure, others condemned it. The paper characterized the proclamation as "unwise, illtimed, impracticable, outside of the Constitution. . . . It will assuredly do no good as a war measure." The editor observed that, as long as Jefferson Davis's government in Richmond was secure, such proclamations were useless, "as ridiculous as the Pope's bull against the comet."[7] The whole article took up only one-half of one column. It offered no analysis on its effect on the black community nor on the local economy.

In fact, the local economy would never be the same, based as it was on slave labor. Back in 1793, the invention of the cotton gin in the United States, together with the textile revolution in England, produced a boom in short-staple cotton that transformed the economy of the interior during the opening decades of the nineteenth century. With high profits, even fortunes, that could be made in upland cotton, cultivation of the fleecy staple spread across the South, expanding the plantation system upon the backs of the enslaved African Americans. At the turn of the century, only a quarter of white households in upcountry South Carolina owned slaves; by 1820 almost 40 percent did. In the lower Piedmont of South Carolina, the incidence of slaveholding was higher than in the region as a whole: it rose from 28 percent to almost 45 percent between 1800 and 1820. In Griffin's home of Edgefield District, the black population was almost equal to the white by 1820; by 1830 whites were outnumbered, and the black majority grew proportionally larger with each successive decade. By 1860, 61 percent of the population was African American.[8]

In 1850 J. B. Griffin owned 340 acres of land worth $3,000, almost in the top quarter of all local property owners (about 40 percent of all households held no property).[9] He owned 26 slaves, which placed him almost in the top decile of all slave-owners. J.B. lived and farmed beside his father, and most likely in 1850 twenty-four-year-old J.B. was also helping his sixty-seven-year-old father farm. A striking disparity in the demography of the two slave populations supports the supposition that father and son pooled their labor and their agricultural resources. In 1850 the father had a much older slave population (average age 21.9 years to J.B.'s 13.6) with a low child-to-woman ratio (1.6, nearly half of J.B.'s 3.0). J.B., starting a new farm, had virtually all younger slaves.

By 1860 J.B. had inherited his father's slaves and land; he owned 36 adults and 25 children and a total of 1,500 acres, of which 700 were improved. His personal property was assessed at $56,000 (only 77 people in Edgefield, South Carolina had a greater personal estate), much of it accounted for by his 61 slaves. Griffin was in the top 4 percentile of slave-owners; only 47 people in Edgefield owned more slaves in 1860.[10] In Edgefield, South Carolina, at this time 46.1 percent of household heads held at least one slave, and an additional 158 non-household heads owned one or more slaves. Less than one-fourth of the slave-owners held 20 or more, and only 5 percent owned between 50 and 99 bondsmen. Only 12 individuals in Edgefield owned 100 or more slaves.[11]

Griffin's letters suggest that his 61 slaves lived and worked together as a community and, quite likely, lived in family arrangements. Several things also suggest that families with male heads were the norm. Griffin mentions in an 1865 letter, for instance, that one of his former slaves had gone to Augusta, Georgia, to look for his teenage son.[12] Census records support this suggestion. The sex ratios balance remarkably well, especially for slaves fifteen years and older. In 1850, J.B.'s father had 9 male and 9 female slaves fifteen years of age or older, and J.B. had 5 male and 4 females of that "marriageable" age. In 1860, there were 20 males and 19 females. J.B.'s workforce suggests a stable slave population. This persistence rate is speculative, of course, based upon the age, gender, and color of slaves in the 1850 manuscript slave census compared to the 1860 slave census. In 1850 only 3 of James Sr.'s slaves were mulatto and none of J.B.'s, and in 1860 only 2 mulattoes are listed among J.B.'s slaves. In 1860, 44 slaves were ten years or older; most of these could have been one of either J.B.'s or his father's slaves in 1850. He purchased few, if any, slaves.

The stable work force with natural increase substantiates family arrangements on the plantation. Living accommodations also suggest families. In 1860, Griffin reported 12 slave houses as homes for his 61 slaves; that averaged out at about 5 slaves a house, probably a family.[13] Inferences from census data can be risky, but in the 1850 slave census many of the slaves appear to follow what would logically be a family order of a father, mother, children. Some of these listings, however, look like groupings of mother and children only.[14] Church records also attest to family relationships; members were listed as father, mother, wife, brother, etc. Naming patterns, which we learn from the letters and from other sources, reflect both African heritage and Biblical names. Enslaved people took names from their slave parents and relatives.

Another source of information is the mortality census. In 1859 Henry Griffin, a thirty-year-old farm laborer, and Kissy Griffin, a four-year-old, died of typhoid, each after a month-long illness. Also a Silva Griffin, fifty-seven years of age, died of dropsy after being sick half a year. The death of three slaves in a year is certainly tragic; whether it was typical is unknown. Another death was recorded in the Coroner Book of Inquisition. The coroner inquired into the death of "Abram a man slave of the said Jas B. Griffin." This Abram was father to the Abram who would go with J.B. to the war in 1860. The elder Abram had been cutting the tops of corn when a poisonous snake bit him on the arm and leg. Two other of Griffin's slaves testified at this inquiry.[15] Reports such as these confirm that farming had its dangers, and that slaves testified at a coroner's inquest.

Griffin speaks to illness at various times in his letters: "Sure enough I did receive your letter to day bringing the unwelcomed intelligence of the exposure of the negroes to the Small Pox. I hope it will turn out to be a false alarm. Where could old man Sib, have contracted the disease? If it is really so, you have made the best arrangement you can. In the mean time have all hands vaxcinated, especially those negroes at the plantation and tell Spradley [the overseer] to be scrupulously particular in not allowing any intercourse between the negroes at home and those at the plantation."[16]

Along with an examination of Griffin's letters, we can discover something of African American life from church records. Records at Antioch Baptist Church contain references to several Griffin slaves; actually, the only references to James B. Griffin is as the owner of slaves. Physically segregated by seating arrangements, whites and blacks worshipped together in the same building. In September 1832, at the same time that J.B.'s sister was "received by experience into the church," James Sr.'s slave Bob was "received by experience into the church." In 1843, another Griffin slave Kejiah went before the church, related her conversion experience, and was baptized. After James Sr.'s death in 1853, these people were referred to as the slaves of J. B. Griffin. In September 1856, J.B.'s slave Olive joined the church, and in May 1857 Olive's brother, Charles, was received by experience into the church. In August of 1861, both Charles and Olive, "the property of Mr. James B. Griffin," asked for letters of transfer.

Interestingly, beginning in 1860, the church clerks stopped referring to slaves in quasi-familial terms, that is, "James Griffins Bob" or "Griffins boy Peter," and used designations such as "Kizziah the property of Mrs. Eliza Harrington" (J.B.'s sister). The escalating sectional tension may have encouraged a more legalistic view of relationships between masters and slaves.[17]

Some of the church records suggest a hegemonic function of the law and planter paternalism. A slave is sometimes cited as one of somebody's "boys" or "girls." Masters often brought to the church charges against their slaves for lying, stealing, or disobedience. In January 1832, the senior "James Griffins Peter" joined the Antioch congregation. In August of that same year, James Sr. "informed against his servants Peter and Peggy for theft." In September an investigating committee found that Peter and his wife Peggy were guilty, and the church declared nonfellowship with the slaves; in 1839 the couple were restored to church membership. Years later, in March 1850, James Sr. again reported Peter for stealing and lying. Peter admitted his sins to the church and declared himself unfit for church membership; he was expelled. And yet the master's word did not hold absolute sway. Slaves were allowed to defend themselves before the church disciplinary committee; committee members (excluding the slaveowner) were sent to investigate the charges, and the slave's cause was sometimes upheld. For example, in June 1844 James Sr. charged Bob, "one of his boys," as "out of the way" (drunk). A church committee investigated the allegations and reported back favorably on Bob, who was restored to full membership in the church in July. In disciplinary matters both whites and blacks were charged with drunkenness and fighting, but at Antioch some blacks (but no whites) were charged with adultery (at other churches both whites and blacks were so charged). Churches gave an air of legitimacy to slave-owners' paternalist ideology and allowed them to see themselves as rightful and righteous guardians. Since churches were supposed to inculcate Christian morality, charges brought to the church against slaves gained a moral sanction and puffed up the slave-owner's self-image. Records for this church in this period are silent about the evils of slavery as a system.

The silence in Griffin's letters is not absolute. Griffin offers a few tantalizingly references to African Americans, and each of these allusions opens up a window to view a larger picture. For instance, from the letters we learn that a social and occupational hierarchy existed within the slave workforce. In June 1865 Griffin referred to "Jim who has been my *Foreman*."[18] Jim was also a skilled carpenter.

Griffin's slave carpenters fashioned plow stocks and shovel handles for neighboring farmers and planters, and his blacksmith shop made plow sweeps and shod horses. London was the plantation cobbler and, when away during the Civil War, Griffin wrote, "Do get London to make a pair of shoes for Ned and a pair for Jackson."[19] J.B.'s account ledger reveals that his slave artisans frequently built or repaired plows and tools for other farmers. He also hired his slaves out at $1.25 a day. These slaves were probably skilled workmen, for the same few names recur. In 1860, for example, he hired out Jim to B. P. Tillman on five separate occasions at $1.25 a day (Tillman's account was "by settlement in full" in 1864 though in kind, not cash), to Philip Eichelberger two days (paid in cash in 1863), to Bennet Holland for two days (paid in cash that year), to M. B. Wever for four and a half days (paid by cash in 1863).[20] In 1859 J.B.'s slaves shod two of S. B. Ryan's horses. In 1860 he hired Smith to S. S. Tompkins at $1.25 a day for nine days in February and two days in June. In March he hired Smith to Daniel Holland for four days, and immediately afterwards for three days to neighbor Benjamin F. Mays. He also sold Mays 243 pounds of iron, suggesting that the slave, "Smith," was a blacksmith or ironworker. While at the Virginia front, Griffin would write to his wife Leila about the slave Peter who was helping Leila with the garden and cotton. "Tell your man Peter, that he knows my plan for planting, and he must pursue it just as if I were there to attend to it."[21]

Griffin's letters tend to be more silent with regard to slave women, who worked various tasks in the fields and in the household. Griffin writes of one slave, Rachel, whom he was giving to Leila's sister to aid her with increased household responsibilities on the home front.[22] No mention is made of slave wet nurses, but Griffin's wife, Leila, bore eight children (including twins) in nine years. None of the first three births were more than fifteen months apart; the next two came at intervals of roughly seventeen months. Since nursing women tended to experience delayed ovulation and might have been expected to give birth about every two years, the close spacing of the Griffin children suggests that Leila may have weaned her infants within a few months of birth or used slave wet nurses.[23]

Griffin's attitude toward slaves was classic paternalism. Whereas some slaveowners raped slave women, took slave mistresses, fathered mulatto children, and exploited or abused male and female slaves abhorrently, J.B. lived up to a higher ideal.[24] He did not sell slaves. He had no mulatto children. He passed along messages for Leila to the slaves at home, "Tell all the negroes howdy for me and tell them not to forget what I told them when I left."[25] He wrote that he was pleased to hear of their good behavior, fully expecting that his distant approval would gratify them. He often sent greetings from Ned and Abram and reported on their health. He ended one letter, "Abram is well and sends his love to all," and another, "Abram and Ned beg to be remembered to all."[26] He informed his wife not to "let the negroes know when to expect me, or rather let them expect me at any time. I do hope they will behave themselves and give you all no trouble."[27] On another occasion he reported: "I am also delighted to hear that the Negroes are behaving so well—Do say to them that I hear with pleasure of their good behaviour, and hope they will continue to behave well—tell them they shall not loose [sic] anything by keeping it up."[28] Griffin reveals some of the complexities of slavery in his use of a mixture of familial, paternalistic, and prison terminology when referring to his bonds people. He regarded it his duty to train and direct slaves, to reward them for good performance and correct them—physically if necessary—for improper behavior. He is silent on their reaction to such correction.

The letters point out that the Griffin slaves also had some leeway to work for themselves. They were permitted to cultivate private garden plots, and in slack periods they had access to his unimproved acres of woodland from which they were allowed to sell for their own money whatever they produced or manufactured. Some apparently had a regular enterprise of making charcoal from firewood and selling it in town.[29]

The war immediately affected the slave community on Griffin's plantation. Some slaves were impressed into Confederate service, all having to leave home and family. Griffin asked his wife to "write me what has become of the Boys who were working on the fortifications—Have they returned home and when— Have you sent off any more if so who?"[30] Ned and Abram left immediately with Griffin to the Virginia front; later Peter, Jackson, and Bob would join Griffin and run errands between the South Carolina front and Griffin's Edgefield home. Union reports of the first South Carolina troops to move into Virginia noted the soldiers had "Negroes with them, as servants." Officers and privates alike brought slaves to camp to cook, wash, and tend their horses. Col. Thomas G. Bacon of the Seventh South Carolina Volunteers reported home to Edgefield that food prepared by some of these slave cooks was abominable (one wonders if this was done deliberately).[31] Griffin's fellow officer and friend James Conner wrote that his own slave, Edward, in contrast to the above report, "cooks capitally."

Conner was amused that Edward "stands up for my rights in the most glorious manner. He and the company are always quarreling about what belongs to
'Cap'n.'" Edward even politely refused Griffin's offer to deliver Conner's dinner
when the latter was out of camp positioning men to meet an expected attack;
despite the danger of anticipated fighting, he took it himself.[32]

The increased freedom that slaves experienced in camp worried masters.
Private Charles Hutson of the legion's Washington Light Infantry, for instance,
declined his uncle's offer to send him a valet because "one who has not seen
the workings of camp-life cannot conceive how thoroughly a servant is spoiled
by camp service. The very best are necessarily injured."[33] When Edgefieldian
Emmett Seibels wrote home from the Seventh South Carolina Volunteers to
ask for a camp slave, he specified that he did not want Bob: "he would be in
Lincoln's army before you could say Jack Robinson."[34] Some slaves obviously
saw federal lines as an open invitation to freedom, a fact of which some masters
were keenly aware, and others, like Griffin, chose to ignore.

Griffin wrote home that he was pleased with Abram's adjustment to military
life. When both Abram and Ned had colds, but Abram stayed up working, Griffin wrote, "He is a very fine boy, a general favourite with all the staff."[35] Griffin
relied on Abram, who always camped in a tent directly behind Griffin. Abram
supervised Griffin's tent and gear, and they shared many experiences. Abram
and Griffin were both struck by lightning when they tried to hold a tent pole in
place during a violent storm. "The shock knocked down both myself and Abram
in a pile."[36] Griffin depended upon Abram to get food supplies. "The way I manage, is to give Abram money and he provides for us. He is a first rate Boy—I
think more of him than I ever did."[37]

Griffin was utterly disbelieving when his slave Abram ran away to enemy lines
late in the spring of 1862. Griffin explained to his wife in great detail that Abram

has been a good boy and a faithful one to me most of the time, since I have
been in service. And only gave me cause of complaint a few times after he
commenced to cater for our Mess. . . . I gave him money and made him buy
provisions for us. He seemed to like it well at first. but grew tired before
long, as provisions became scarcer. I had to scold him on two or three occasions, and once while at Ashland gave him a light flogging which was the
only time I had struck him since he left home. . . . He went out as usual to
buy provisions, and got a pass to cross the York river, said he saw negroes

coming from over there, with poultry and such things as could not be bought where we were. This is the last I heard of him—I think he was decoyed off by some one, after he left—for I offered him a $20.00 bill that morning, but he declined, saying he had as much money as he would need for that day—I have never informed you of this before, because, I have always believed he would turn up again—and indeed I think so still—but he may not. I am sorry he was such a fool—I'll bet he will always be sorry for it. I have been pretty hard up lately for a servant—for since he has been gone, Ned has had the Measles, another singular fact—and he isnt well of them yet.

Griffin "had to hire a boy to attend to my horses—Ned will soon be well however."

Griffin mentioned a "light flogging," but has no perception what that meant to Abram. He had to convince himself that the Yankees had lured Abram away. Apparently Griffin thinks that if Abram had been planning an escape, he would have taken the twenty dollars. Just as likely, Abram wanted no suspicion. Finally, like thousands of other slave-owners whose bondsmen ran away during the war, he dismissed the matter by concluding that the former slave would always regret having been foolish enough to leave.[38]

The desertion of Abram to the Yankees did not alter J. B. Griffin's continued trust in his enslaved people. He still sent large sums of money by them and trusted them with jobs and traveling unescorted from the coast to his home in Edgefield, and even more importantly, trusted them with his family.[39] "I hope you recd the two hundered dollars I sent you by Peter. . . . I told Peter to buy a few apples and carry up to you for the children."[40] Very near the end of the war, Griffin wrote Leila with some advice "in case Sherman honors Edgefield with a visit." He trusted his slaves to hide foodstuffs although slaves throughout the area were giving provisions to the Union army, and he still maintained that the slaves who chose freedom, as Abram had done, would rue it. "If you do have to leave—You had better make the negroes hide out the bacon and as much corn and wheat as they can, and take as much with you as you can have hauled—Load both wagons with provisions and take all the Mules and horses— Tell the negroes to drive off from about the house all the cattle and hogs—as they will destroy every thing of the kind. Tell the negroes they can go if they choose, of course—But to remember they will always regret it. They know that I have never deceived them—and the men will be immediately placed in the army—The Women and Children they dont want."[41] He sincerely believed and still maintained that the slaves who chose freedom, as Abram had done, would regret it.

Many whites were desperately fearful about the freedom experienced by slaves on the home front during the war. As early as September 1863, James Henry Hammond, in a petition requesting a magistrate for the southwestern section of Edgefield, wrote, "The country around there is without exaggeration in a desperate condition. Negroes are uppermost, openly keeping white, & some very pretty, girls, & getting children by them. They do not conceal that they steal corn, meat & everything they can to support the fathers & mothers of their Sweet heart. There is not a Magistrate any [where] in reach."[42] This startling postscript sounds like the ravings of a paranoid man, but others too were worried about being so outnumbered by the slaves. Mary Chesnut wrote of slaves during the Civil War, "they go about in their black masks, not a ripple or an emotion showing." Griffin seems to have lacked any awareness that his slaves might have secret inner lives and concealed aspirations.[43]

During the last months of the war, when Sherman's troops were marching through Georgia, people opposed to the Confederacy were growing bolder. A spate of homes burned down, and rumors of slave arsonists abounded. Between the end of November and the middle of January, the Edgefield *Advertiser* reported the destruction of houses, a barn full of grain, and a cotton warehouse, all attributed to incendiaries.[44] On 6 December 1864 Griffin's plantation house burned to the ground, and although the newspaper reported a suspected slave arsonist, Griffin's letters are silent on such a suggestion. He wrote nearly two months later simply, "Has anything developed about the burning of the house?"[45] Having no home, Leila and the younger children moved into town. On 28 January 1865 Leila Griffin applied for an exemption for sixteen-year-old William Griffin as the "only white person" on the plantation with "over Fifty negroes." Noting that her husband was away serving the state, Leila explained that "we have had the misfortune to have our dwelling house destroyed by fire . . . & I am necessarily compelled to reside away from the place, as there is no building that I can occupy on the premises."[46] She left over fifty slaves on the plantation under the supervision of then fifteen-year-old son Willie. Quite likely some of these slaves had taken care of Willie as a younger boy, hunting and fishing with him, and they might have wondered who was supervising whom.

Indeed, the African Americans were left in de facto charge of the Griffin plantation. Griffin wrote, "How do the negroes behave And how are they getting along with the farm—."[47] Although Griffin continued to think of himself as master, one must question whether these African Americans were in fact still "enslaved." Certainly the system of slavery had changed dramatically from the beginning of the war.

This set of letters was from a white man the community deemed a gentleman. He was a competent businessman, not a stupid person. Yet he was ignorant regarding the tragedy of forced servitude, blind to his participation in an evil system. Although he was supposedly silent on the subject of slavery, his letters actually offer a glimpse into slave life on one plantation. With added information from other letters at this time, from the census (including the slave census), from church records, and from newspapers articles, the historian may fill in the picture with more detail. The silent African American majority can then be heard.

NOTES

1. The letters are reprinted and annotated in Judith N. McArthur and Orville Vernon Burton, "A Gentleman and an Officer": A Military and Social History of James B. Griffin's Civil War (New York: Oxford University Press, 1996). All letters cited to J. B. Griffin are in the James B. Griffin Papers, originally in the possession of Jack Gunter Sr., Dallas; a copy now deposited at the Center for American History, University of Texas at Austin.

2. In the Edgefield area that spring, bacon cost forty cents a pound, while beef on the hoof could be had for thirty. Carol Bleser, ed., Secret and Sacred: The Diaries of James Henry Hammond (New York: Oxford University Press, 1988), 286. J. B. Griffin to Leila Griffin, 2 April 1862.

3. The classic discussion of liberty and slavery is Edmund S. Morgan, American Slavery, American Freedom: The Ordeal of Colonial Virginia (New York: W.W. Norton & Co., 1975); also on the paradox of revolutionary slaveholders see John C. Miller, The Wolf by the Ears: Thomas Jefferson and Slavery (New York: The Free Press, 1977). On republicanism in South Carolina see Lacy K. Ford, Origins of Southern Radicalism: The South Carolina Upcountry, 1800–1869 (New York: Oxford University Press, 1988), and on Edgefield see J. William Harris, Plain Folk and Gentry in a Planter Society: White Liberty and Black Slavery in Augusta's Hinterlands (Middletown, CT: Wesleyan University Press, 1985), and Orville Vernon Burton, In My Father's House Are Many Mansions: Family and Community in Edgefield, South Carolina (Chapel Hill: University of North Carolina Press, 1985), 37–38; on the sectional conflict see Michael F. Holt, The Political Crisis of the 1850s (New York: John Wiley & Sons, 1978). A good review of the literature on Republicanism is Daniel T. Rodgers, "Republicanism: The Career of a Concept," Journal of American History 79, no. 1 (June 1992): 11–38, esp. 31 on the South.

4. For a summary of the literature on slavery and guilt, see Gaines M. Foster, "Guilt Over Slavery: A Historiographical Analysis," Journal of Southern History 56, no. 4 (Nov. 1990): 665–94.

However, one still cannot ignore the influential essay by Charles Grier Sellers Jr., "The Travail of Slavery," in *The Southerner as American,* ed. Charles Grier Sellers Jr. (Chapel Hill: University of North Carolina Press, 1960), 40–71.

5. J. B. Griffin to Leila Griffin, 26 February 1862.

6. Edgefield *Advertiser,* 5 November 1862.

7. Edgefield *Advertiser,* 14 January 1863.

8. Ford, *Origins of Southern Radicalism,* 7–12; Edgefield had 12,864 whites and 12,255 blacks in 1820. By 1860 the white population was only 15,653 while the black population had grown to 24,233. Burton, *In My Father's House Are Many Mansions,* 5, 19, 44–46.

9. The acreage listed in Schedule 1 of the manuscript agricultural census was less than the amount that Griffin's father deeded to him in 1848, suggesting that either his father was still farming it or the remainder was rented. In 1850, J.B. was in the 73rd percentile of all property owners and in the 87th percentile of all slave owners. For all household heads he was in the 74.2 percentile. When compared by household heads and by people his age (twenty-four) in 1850 he was well off. Of all the people twenty-four years and under who headed households, only 13 of the 239 were wealthier.

10. Only one person in the county younger than J. B. Griffin had more slaves, S. L. Shepperd, thirty-three years old, owned 69 slaves. A. L. Dearing, one year older than Griffin, had 205, which is the most listed in the district for one person. Francis Pickens, James Henry Hammond, and others owned more, but their slaves were in other districts, or even in other states on different plantations and were not all enumerated in Edgefield.

11. In 1860, the mean for slave owners was 14 slaves, median 8, mode 1 for the 1,552 slave owners recorded in the manuscript slave census.

12. J. B. Griffin to Capt. J. E. Bryant, 21 June 1865.

13. For the entire slave census of Edgefield in 1860, the mean number of slaves per slave house was 4.2, and in 1870 and 1880, the average African American household size was 4.9 persons.

14. The 1860 slaves were listed generally by age, and did not appear to follow any other groupings.

15. Coroner Book of Inquisition, 1844–1855, p. 27, South Carolina Department of Archives and History. Peter H. Wood informs me that one hundred years earlier South Carolina authorities had given a reward to an African who provided an effective cure for snakebite.

16. Sib is an older slave, the patriarch of his family. J. B. Griffin to Leila Griffin, 9 February 1963.

17. In May 1851 the Edgefield *Advertiser* noted that Antioch Baptist's new church had a large gallery for slaves. J.B.'s sister inherited Kizziah from her father, James Griffin. These references are all taken from the Records of the Antioch Baptist Church, January, August, September 1832, September 1838, February 1839, April 1843, June and July 1844, March 1850, September 1856, May 1857, May and August 1861.

18. J. B. Griffin to Capt. J. E. Bryant, 21 June 1865, Miscellaneous Griffin Papers, in possession of Jack Gunter Sr., Dallas.

19. J. B. Griffin to Leila Griffin, 29 January 1865. Ned and Jackson were Griffin's slave valets at this time.

20. Currency was highly inflated in 1863.

21. J. B. Griffin to Leila Griffin, 10 January 1862.

22. J. B. Griffin to Leila Griffin, 28 December 1862.

23. See Sally McMillen, *Motherhood in the Old South* (Baton Rouge: Louisiana State University Press, 1990), 32, 111–25.

24. See Burton, *In My Father's House Are Many Mansions,* 145–46, 168–80, 183–90.

25. J. B. Griffin to Leila Griffin, 11 July 1861 and 26 March 1862.

26. J. B. Griffin to Leila, 11 Aug 1861 and 10 January 1862.

27. J. B. Griffin to Leila, 2 January 1862.

28. J. B. Griffin to Leila Griffin, 10 January 1862.

29. J. B. Griffin to Capt. J. E. Bryant, 21 June 1865.

30. J. B. Griffin to Leila Griffin, 19 January 1865. The procurement of slaves to work on the coastal fortifications was a problem throughout the war and a source of public dissatisfaction with the government. Military commanders complained that they could get only a fraction of the necessary slave labor force to build and repair harbor defenses, while planters resisted complying with calls that drew workers away from the fields during the growing and harvesting seasons. After experimenting with various laws and amendments, the South Carolina legislature finally instituted systematic slave impressment on 23 December 1864. The Confederate bureau of conscription prompted the legislation by making known its intention in the fall of 1864 to impress slaves for twelve months' service with the army in accordance with state laws, where such existed, and targeting 20,000 impressments in South Carolina. The new South Carolina law authorized the impressment for twelve months of one-tenth of all slaves between eighteen and fifty ordinarily subject to road repair duty, but permitted the owners to make substitutions every three months. Those who failed to deliver slaves when called upon faced having the bondsmen arrested by the sheriff and the term of service doubled. Charles Cauthen, *South Carolina Goes to War, 1860–1865* (Chapel Hill: University of North Carolina Press, 1950), 178–183; *OR,* ser. 4, 3: 963–64; *Statutes at Large of South Carolina* 13: 211–15.

31. Edgefield *Advertiser,* 15 October 1862; Milledge Louis Bonham, "The Life and Times of Milledge Luke Bonham," 540, typescript, 1938, in Milledge Luke Bonham Papers, South Caroliniana Library, Columbia, SC. Hereinafter SCL.

32. Mary Conner Moffett, ed., *Letters of General James Conner, C.S.A.* (Columbia, SC: R. L. Bryan Co., 1950), 52, 71.

33. Hutson to Mother, 28 April 1862, Charles Woodward Hutson Papers, Southern Historical Collection (SHC), University of North Carolina at Chapel Hill. Hutson was from Charleston.

34. Emmett Seibels to Ed Seibels, 28 November 1862, Seibels Family Papers, SCL.

35. J. B. Griffin to Leila Griffin, 29 January 1862.

36. J. B. Griffin to Leila Griffin, 17 Sept 1861.

37. J. B. Griffin to Leila Griffin, 2 April 1862.

38. J. B. Griffin to Leila Griffin, 21 May 1862. Bell I. Wiley in *Southern Negroes, 1861–1865* (New Haven, CT: Yale University Press, 1953), 134–38, 142–43, has useful information on enslaved people at the front. According to Wiley, in 1861 numerous "elite" slaves went to the front with their masters, but as the war became more difficult in 1862–63, many were sent home to assist with crops and farm work. The duties performed by these slaves included barbering, errand running, cooking, cleaning, procuring extra food, and generally anything the master did not want to do. Many slaves used this work as an opportunity to make money for themselves, and masters seemed to tolerate this. Wiley claims that slaves begged milk and butter and then sold it to army personnel; camp slaves also performed errands or laundry for other soldiers besides their masters. Wiley

believes camp life was soft for slaves, offering leisure time for card playing and amusements. He argues that the presence of camp slaves raised the morale of white Confederates and that usually personal servants had long been associated with the master's family; therefore they were loyal to the master and to the Confederacy. He argues that the majority of runaway slaves were hired and thus lacking personal attachment to the master. See also Bell Irvin Wiley, *Plain People of the Confederacy* (1943; rpt. Gloucester, MA: Peter Smith, 1971), 99–100, for useful information pertaining to the intimate relations between master and slave. Although Griffin's slave, Abram, contradicted the model set forth by Wiley, more recent literature suggests that Abram was not atypical. See for example, Randall C. Jimerson, *The Private Civil War* (Baton Rouge: Louisiana State University, 1988), 50–87, for a more modern scholar's discussion of the loyalty of camp slaves.

39. For example see J. B. Griffin to Leila Griffin, 1 December 1864 on the slave Bob.

40. J. B. Griffin to Leila Griffin, 18 December 1862.

41. J. B. Griffin to Leila Griffin, 3 February 1865.

42. H. Howard et al. to M. L. Bonham, September 1863, Materials 1863–64, Papers of Governor Milledge Luke Bonham Papers, South Carolina Department of Archives and History (hereinafter SCDAH).

43. Mary Boykin Chesnut, *A Diary From Dixie,* ed. Ben Ames Williams (Boston: Houghton Mifflin, 1949), 293; C. Vann Woodward, ed., *Mary Chesnut's Civil War* (New Haven, CT: Yale University Press, 1981), 464.

44. Edgefield *Advertiser,* 19 December 1864.

45. J. B. Griffin to Leila Griffin, 29 January 1865.

46. Mrs. J. B. Griffin to Gen. A. C. Garlington, 28 January 1865, Petitions for Exemption, 1864–65, Administrative Records, Adjutant General, SCDAH.

47. J. B. Griffin to Leila Griffin, 29 January 1965.

ROBERT E. LEE AND THE ARMING OF BLACK MEN

XXXXXXXXXXXXXXXXXXXXXXXXXXXXXXXXXXXXX

LEONNE M. HUDSON

B y 1865, it was apparent to many southerners that the collapse of the Confederate States was imminent. To stave off the inevitable, the southern nation turned to a desperate measure to resuscitate the dying republic. The last hope of saving the government was to tap black men as a military resource. The plan to reinforce the Rebel armies with African American manpower generated a rancorous debate among politicians, military men, and civilians. The decision to elevate slaves to the rank of soldiers seemed to contradict the Confederacy's "cornerstone" doctrine of black inferiority. The fact that the drastic plan was anathema in many quarters did not dissuade General Robert E. Lee from putting his prestige and reputation on the line by supporting the freeing and the arming of slaves. The South had been driven by necessity to the point of no longer enjoying the luxury of an army consisting of white men only.

On January 2, 1864, General Patrick R. Cleburne, a superb divisional commander in the Army of Tennessee, announced his "Proposal to Make Soldiers of Slaves" as a plan of salvation for the Confederate nation. The Ireland native arrived in the United States in 1849 and settled in Helena, Arkansas, a year later. He penned his famous statement in support of black enlistment against the backdrop of the Rebel defeat at the battle of Missionary Ridge in Tennessee in November 1863. The death of so many soldiers weighed heavily on General Cleburne. The "long lists of dead and mangled" convinced him of the futility of trying to achieve political independence without the introduction of black soldiers into the Confederate army. Certain that the war would "exhaust the white race," Cleburne proposed that the Richmond government "immediately commence training a large reserve of the most courageous of our slaves, and further that we guarantee freedom within a reasonable time to every slave in the South who shall remain true to the Confederacy in this war."[1] The Irish general made it clear that any hope of European recognition and assistance hinged on freedom for the slaves. He believed that the implementation of his idea would solve the army's dire need for soldiers. The author declared that the time had come for the Davis administration to tap the manpower reservoir in the Confederate States, which contained approximately 680,000 slave men between the ages of seventeen and forty-five. Nonetheless, the Union possessed a significant numerical advantage over its adversary. According to one source, the United States had "approximately three times as many military-age white males as did the Confederacy."[2]

Upon learning of the proposal, which contained the signatures of several officers in the Army of Tennessee, Jefferson Davis ordered its suppression. The Irishman's statement struck some of his fellow officers as treasonous. Knowing that Cleburne's document would be controversial and divisive, the Confederate president did not want the public or the press to learn of its existence. Davis's success in preventing the circulation of the proposal would only delay what would become one of the most contentious debates in the history of the Rebel nation. The upheaval in political and military arenas caused by what Clement Eaton called an "eloquent document" reverberated from Virginia to Texas. The death of General Cleburne at Franklin on November 30, 1864, denied him the opportunity of knowing the outcome of his bold announcement. As historians Herman Hattaway and Richard E. Beringer have noted, Cleburne's "idea was far from dead. By now the issue had engaged the minds of many thoughtful Confederates."[3]

The debate over the recruitment and enlistment of the slaves did not escape the attention of Lee, whom one scholar calls "the single most prestigious and influential person in the Confederacy."[4] A few days after Virginia adopted an ordinance of secession the fifty-four-year-old soldier resigned his commission in the United States Army. The West Point graduate and Mexican War veteran's elevation to the position of commanding general of the Army of Northern Virginia coincided with the wounding of Joseph E. Johnston at the battle of Seven Pines. He accepted the responsibility of leading that army, knowing that the Union posed a formidable obstacle to southern autonomy. Lee's soldiers viewed him as the symbol of the Confederate cause. One private in the Army of the Northern Virginia described Lee as "that grand American Soldier and in all respects the perfect embodiment of a Christian Gentleman."[5] Lee proudly wore the labels of a Christian and gentleman in a world where black southerners struggled against the brutality of slavery.

Lee, like many of his contemporaries, knew that slavery was wrong; nonetheless he believed in the institution and the inferiority of black Americans. Lee, in a letter to his wife, Mary, in December 1856, acknowledged "that slavery as an institution, is a moral & political evil in any Country."[6] Lee grew up in a society, including his own family, where the acceptance of slavery was a natural fact of life. As the nation disintegrated, Lee embraced secession and joined the Confederacy in its fight to protect the social institutions of the South from outside interference. Although Lee did not believe in the expansion of slavery, he defended the system.[7] In January 1865, Lee expressed his views on slavery to State Senator Andrew Hunter of Virginia. Lee argued that slavery was the best arrangement to minimize problems between the races. He pontificated: "Considering the relation of master and slave, controlled by humane laws and influenced by Christianity and an enlightened public sentiment, . . . I would deprecate any sudden disturbance of that relation unless it be necessary to avert a greater calamity to both."[8]

Lee's stereotypical views of blacks did not end with his surrender at Appomattox. In February 1866, he told the Joint Committee on Reconstruction that African Americans lacked the intelligence to vote and that Virginia would be a better state without them. The institution of slavery, the defining characteristic of the American South, was inextricably tied to the ideology of the Confederacy. Many southerners believed that the destruction of slavery would be tantamount to the death of the republic itself. Therefore, they "simply could not conceive of breaking the bond between white liberty and black slavery."[9] The social implication of emancipation was of deep concern to poor whites. The expectation of having to compete with former bondsmen for work worried the nonslaveholding class.

From the start to the end of the war, the Confederate States of America was a paradoxical study regarding its black population. General Lee supported the idea of the Davis administration impressing slaves for duty as military laborers. In 1864, he requested five thousand slaves for the purpose of building roads and fortifications, thereby freeing white men from such tedious work so that they could fight. The South pressed the slaves into supporting the war as musicians, teamsters, cooks, mechanics, and coal miners. They also labored in the fields, munitions factories, and in railroad construction. The restriction of their freedom on one hand and their inclusion into the military apparatus of the Confederate government on the other presented an image that defied logic. The "divergence in policy" was a contributing factor in the decline of loyalty among southerners, which accelerated the fall of the republic.[10]

The debate over the enlistment of black soldiers raged in intensity with the precipitous demise of slavery, the severe shortage of manpower, and the deterioration of the military effort on battlefields across the South. The Confederacy's opposition to the employment of Negroes as soldiers was not new. The South was following a similar path of resistance to uniting blacks with guns to that which had been traveled by the North. The Lincoln administration had refused to consider the same proposal for the first two years of the war.[11] However, once committed to using United States Colored Troops, President Abraham Lincoln fully understood their value to the Union effort. "Take from us, and give to the enemy," the president declared, "the colored persons now serving as soldiers, seamen, and laborers, and we cannot no longer maintain the contest."[12]

Northerners realized that one of the practical advantages of African American enlistment was the sparing of white men from the deadly consequences of the war. White soldiers in the South believed that black slaves should perform the drudgery of military life and not fight.[13] Opponents of the drastic measure argued that slaves were inferior and should not be elevated to the status of arm-bearing men. Some of those who railed against the dangerous proposal were convinced that white troops would be offended by the sight of black men in gray uniforms. Other arguments against adding slaves to the ranks centered on their lack of experience with weapons. The large black population in the Confederate States and the fear of slave revolts reminiscent of Nat Turner's uprising caused southerners not to trust African Americans with arms.[14] Many southerners warned that the placing of weapons in the hands of slaves would hasten their push for liberation through servile insurrection.

The influential Georgian, General Howell Cobb, a staunch supporter of the Davis government, did not hesitate to condemn the plan. In a letter to Confederate Secretary of War James A. Seddon, the general remarked, "I think that the proposition to make soldiers of our slaves is the most pernicious idea that has been suggested since the war began." He added, "The moment you resort to negro soldiers your white soldiers will be lost to you." General Cobb concluded with a philosophical answer to the question of arming black men: "If slaves will make good soldiers," he said, "our whole theory of slavery is wrong." Cobb asserted that he was disillusioned "to see the name of that good and great man and soldier, General R. E. Lee, given as authority for such a policy."[15] Colonel Richard L. Maury opined that he hated "the idea of having to bring" African American men into the army.[16]

The Confederate defeat at Atlanta convinced Secretary Seddon to advocate for the use of black men as soldiers. However, he remained steadfast in his belief that whites were "better soldiers than negroes."[17] It was the opinion of the adversaries of the radical recommendation that black enlistment would signal the death knell of slavery. Abolition would, therefore, mean that both secession and the war were unnecessary.[18] The reluctance of southerners to embrace the idea diminished "once the North began recruiting black men. An enemy that stooped to such barbarism, they argued, deserved retaliation in kind."[19]

Confederate political and military leaders did not need to look into a crystal ball to comprehend the "crisis over manpower" facing their nation during the last months of the war. In between the fall of Atlanta and the fall of Savannah, the Confederates experienced devastating defeats at Franklin and Nashville.[20] The only lifeline that held out the possibility of saving the Confederate ship from sinking was to make slaves into full-fledged soldiers. Most southerners had come to the realization that it was better to sacrifice slavery than to lose the war. Only those who were blinded by a false sense of reality failed to see that the handwriting on the wall had spelled out what the outcome of the war would be. Robert E. Lee fully knew that the South did not have the luxury of replacing a lost soldier.

The concept of arming the bondsmen did not generate widespread attention until the Confederacy started its descent toward mortality in 1864. As the Richmond government spiraled toward death, more and more southerners found themselves preoccupied with the slave enlistment debate. Those who supported the proposition to arm black men reminded their detractors that they were being used as fighting warriors by the United States. Many of those who favored recruiting slaves believed they would make good soldiers because they had grown accustomed to obeying their masters. Two months before the death of General Cleburne, Governor Henry W. Allen of Louisiana added his voice to the chorus of southerners calling for the enlistment of African American men. On September 26, the governor advised Secretary Seddon "to put into the army every able-bodied negro man as a soldier." He added, "They will make much better soldiers with us than against us, and swell the now depleted ranks of our armies."[21] Allen's epistle was intercepted by the United States Army and subsequently published by the northern press. His letter represented "the first public appeal" to make soldiers of slaves "from a high ranking Southern official."[22]

The fall of Atlanta coincided with an increased presence of United States Colored Troops near Richmond and with Lee taking stock of the Confederate armies. Lee told Davis in a letter on September 2, 1864, that the combination of "battle and disease" had greatly diminished the numerical strength of the military. The general offered a solution to the manpower shortage that bedeviled the southern nation by then. Lee advised Davis to use black men wherever possible as replacements for whites, who were laborers, thereby freeing them for combat duty. General Lee reached the conclusion that "measures should be taken at once to substitute negroes for whites in every place in the army, or connected with it, where the former can be used."[23] Although Lee's advice fell short of officially endorsing the theoretical concept of black enlistment, he was leaning heavily in that direction.[24]

The debate raging over whether the Davis government should free and arm the slaves was nothing short of a convulsion. A public comment on the controversy from Lee, "the gallant, enigmatic Virginian [who] had captured the imagination and admiration of a war-weary people as had no one else" would doubtless give a measure of comfort to the southern nation.[25] An exchange of letters between William Porcher Miles of South Carolina, who chaired the Military Committee of the Confederate House of Representatives, and Lee, revealed that the general was ready to give more than tangential support to the controversial proposal. Prior to the war, Miles was mayor of Charleston, a member of the United States House of Representatives, and a leading secessionist. On October 24, 1864, he asked Lee for his opinion on the idea of "arming a portion" of southern blacks and then "making a regular military organization of them." He also took the opportunity to tell the Virginia general that the government needed to supply the cavalry "with more efficient weapons."[26] Lee's quick reply to Congressman Miles leaves no doubt that he had been thinking about the subject of military service for black men.

Although Lee's responding letter has not surfaced, his support for emancipating and arming the slaves was unmistakable, as indicated in subsequent correspondence from the Charleston native to Lee. Writing to Lee on November 3, Miles admitted to having "considerable misgiving as to the question of Negro troops, both as to their efficiency and the effect of such a measure upon our political and social system."[27] By the end of the year, Miles had reached the conclusion that it was better to sacrifice slavery than to suffer defeat at the hands of the North. Miles appreciated Lee's response to the question of arming the slaves, telling him that his voice carried "a weight of authority second to no one in the Confederacy. Your opinion seems mature and decided."[28] The correspondence between Miles and Lee made it plain that the latter supported the idea of permitting the slaves to bear arms. The public, clamoring for Lee to speak, had to be content with information from politicians who claimed to have had knowledge about his views on the creation of a black Confederate army.

The subject of manpower shortage came up for discussion at the last session of the Confederate Congress, which opened on November 7, 1864, the eve of the presidential election. The next day, Abraham Lincoln handed the peace Democrats a severe blow by soundly defeating George B. McClellan. As the politicians gathered in Richmond, Lee's famous army continued its occupation of the trenches at Petersburg. And General William T. Sherman and his huge Union army were on their way to Savannah, that "beautiful city by the sea." The southern president in a speech to the lawmakers proposed that the government use more slaves as army laborers and even suggested emancipation as a reward for faithful service. He called for the 20,000 black noncombatants provided for by the February 17, 1864, law to be increased to 40,000. Davis went on to say that he was against the "arming of slaves for duty of soldiers," maintaining that such a necessity would be neither "wise or advantageous." Before ending his message Davis, the Mississippi planter turned president, revealed a glimpse of his true feelings: "But should the alternative ever be presented of subjugation or of the employment of the slave as a soldier, there seems no reason to doubt what should then be our decision."[29] Historian Mark L. Bradley maintains that the head of the Rebel government "couched his endorsement of black soldiers in conditional terms to soften its impact on white Southern sensibilities."[30] Davis's position was a reflection of both political realism and ambivalence. The cautious nature of the Confederate leader could not mask the fact that his conversion to what he called "a radical modification of the theory of the law" was nearly complete.

Not surprisingly, an avalanche of criticism descended upon Davis following his appearance on the floor of the legislature. With increasing frequency, southerners questioned the Confederacy's willingness to put black men in gray uniforms. Responding to Davis's address, the editor of the *Richmond Examiner* called attention to the inconsistency of military service and slavery. "If a negro is fit to be a soldier," the editorial proclaimed, "he is not fit to be a slave."[31] A congressman from North Carolina observed, "The country was beginning to learn that all the abolitionists were not in the North, and our own President had proposed abolition in a way that created suspicion as to his soundness."[32] Early in the war, James Chesnut of Mullberry Plantation in South Carolina asked some of his slaves about their willingness to fight for the Confederacy. His wife Mary Boykin Chesnut recorded in her diary that at that time "they were keen to go in the army" if they could be guaranteed their freedom and a "bounty after the war." The enthusiasm of the Chesnut slaves on becoming soldiers evaporated with Union victories. With the nation in a downward spin by the fall of 1864, Mary Boykin questioned the wisdom of using black men as troops. She recorded in her Civil War diary on November 28 that "If we had only freed the negroes at first and put them in the army—that would have trumped their trick. No use now." Referring to the slaves on Mullberry, she concluded: "Now they say coolly they don't want freedom if they have to fight for it. That means they are pretty sure of having it anyway."[33]

As the military hopes for victory continued to fade, the *Richmond Sentinel* weighed in on the controversy by suggesting that Lee was the most qualified person to make the final decision on black enlistment. The paper said: "Gen. Lee knows better what the necessity is than we. . . . He and his council of officers know better, too, than civilians can, whether such recruits would be available. . . . We are disposed, therefore, to be very much guided in this matter by the opinions of the military men."[34] In an effort to fuel the discussion, Secretary of State Judah P. Benjamin of Louisiana called on Frederick A. Porcher of Charleston to stir up the debate in his home state. Porcher served in the South Carolina legislature and taught history at the College of Charleston during the antebellum years. Benjamin told the South Carolinian on December 21, 1864, that "the period was fast approaching when we should be compelled to use every resource at our command for the defense of our liberties."[35] The opinionated secretary of state affirmed his position on the freeing and the arming of the slaves. "I further agree with you," he stated, "that if they are to fight for our freedom they are entitled to their own." Benjamin did not pass up the opportunity to inform the Charlestonian where Lee stood on the issue. "It is well known that General Lee, who commands so largely the confidence of the people," he wrote, "is strongly in favor of our using the negroes for defense, and emancipating them, if necessary, for that purpose."[36] Benjamin ended his letter by asking Porcher to "write a series of articles" for the newspapers of his state in order to win support among South Carolinians for the famous proposal.

Lee did not share Davis's timidity on the proposition to enroll slaves as soldiers. He was a keen observer of the debate then raging in the South and the Confederate Congress. As if carried by the wind, rumors circulated for several weeks that Virginia's native son supported the recruitment and enlistment of African American soldiers. Numerous civil and military leaders were aware of Lee's favorable impression of turning slaves into soldiers. In the meantime, the public remained uncertain of the general's position. Supporters of the revolutionary measure realized that it would take the intervention of an extraordinary person to penetrate the wall of congressional opposition. They were mindful of the great confidence that the people of the South placed in Lee.

By the start of 1865, lofty oratory by Confederate leaders was insufficient to reverse the trend of the public's lack of support for the war. More than anyone else, "General Lee realized the significance of this loss" and the plain truth that "the great heart of the South with the opening of the last year of the war was no longer in the struggle."[37] On January 7, 1865, Andrew Hunter wrote to his fellow Virginian to find out where he stood on the important topic of employing slaves as soldiers. Lee answered State Senator Hunter's letter four days later. The man whom Emory M. Thomas calls "the patron saint of the American South" used unimpeachable logic when acknowledging that in all likelihood without some change in southern policy the Union army would achieve victory with the help of southern blacks and emancipation would follow. Lee knew that tens of thousands of black southerners had attached themselves to the various armies of the United States, and that many of those African American men had returned to the South donning blue uniforms.

General Lee did not equivocate in his belief that emancipation must follow military service for black Confederate troops. He told Hunter: "I think, therefore, we must decide whether slavery shall be extinguished by our enemies and the slaves be used against us, or use them ourselves at the risk of the effects which may be produced upon our social institutions. I believe that with proper regulations they can be made efficient soldiers."[38] With clouds of defeat descending upon the Confederacy, Lee had made it crystal clear that military necessity trumped the continuation of slavery. Lee was losing patience with the Southern Congress as it methodically debated adding slaves to the ranks. The general understood the effort that it would take to recruit, train, and equip the black army. In spite of the challenges of converting slaves into soldiers, Lee looked forward to the opportunity of experimenting with them in battle. He concluded his letter to Hunter with an endorsement of their freedom: "In addition to the great political advantages that would result to our cause from the adoption of a system of emancipation, it would exercise a salutary influence upon our whole negro population, by rendering more secure the fidelity of those who become soldiers."[39]

As soldiers continued their struggle on the battlefields, on February 3, 1865, a Confederate delegation consisting of Alexander Stephens, Robert M. T. Hunter, and John A. Campbell spent several hours aboard the Union steamer the *River Queen* at Hampton Roads in Virginia in peace talks with Abraham Lincoln and his secretary of state, William H. Seward. Finding President Lincoln intractable, especially on the "unconditional surrender" of the Confederate States, the three southern commissioners realized that a negotiated peace would not be reached. With the failure of the peace conference, the war would continue until one side was beaten into submission. The lack of success of the Hampton Roads meeting inspired the proponents of the audacious proposal to ratchet up their efforts to make black enlistment a reality. They were now more convinced than ever that the only lifeblood available was its slave population. An immediate response to the collapse of the peace conference was the convening of public meetings in several Virginia counties in which the citizens drafted resolutions imploring the Davis government to allow African American men to don the Confederate gray. These gatherings also served as important places for Virginians to stress the point that Robert E. Lee supported the arming of the slaves.[40]

Two weeks after the Hampton Roads conference the *Macon Telegraph and Confederate* printed a portion of an epistle from General Lee. In the letter, the "patron saint" affirmed his support for black men to be granted the legal authority by the Richmond government to take to the field as soldiers. Lee averred: "I am favorable to the use of our servants in the army. . . . I would hold out to them the certainty of freedom and a home, when they shall have rendered efficient service."[41] Congress was unyielding in its opposition to the introduction of slaves into the army during the early weeks of 1865. Responding to the pressure of public opinion the House of Representatives considered a motion on February 6 to make soldiers of able-bodied Negro men. The next day a bill was introduced into the Senate calling for the enrollment of 200,000 African American troops. The bill was defeated.

Lee and Davis, the most visible symbols of the Confederacy, were not immune to criticism. It appeared that President Davis, who attracted enemies in abundance, had to deal with a new controversy during the debate. Several congressmen who were dissatisfied with his military leadership wanted Lee to assume greater direction and authority over strategy. They believed that with Lee in charge of the military forces of the Confederacy as general-in-chief there would be a reversal of the low morale among both soldiers and citizens. A Richmond editor counseled the Davis administration to place Lee in "supreme control over the armies" as a way of restoring "public confidence" in the southern government.[42] On February 6, 1865, two weeks after Congress passed a law authorizing the president to appoint a general-in-chief, the Adjutant and Inspector General's Office issued General Order No. 3, announcing the appointment of Lee to that position.[43] Lee's confirmation as general-in-chief by the Senate did not alter his authority as commander of the Army of Northern Virginia. The president was aware that his enemies were calling for Lee to replace him in the government and be given dictatorial powers. George C. Rable maintains that, at this juncture, "Davis's political base, especially in Congress, was clearly eroding; more ominous, his power as commander in chief was in danger of evaporating."[44]

Secretary Benjamin, who was a strong advocate for the creation of black units, made his first public appeal for the enlistment of African American soldiers on February 9, 1865. Speaking before a huge crowd at the African Church in Richmond, which was home to the largest hall in the city, the Louisiana native made it clear that enrollment must be combined with emancipation. Benjamin "proposed that those slaves who might volunteer to fight for their freedom should be at once sent to the trenches."[45] Benjamin, as a political pragmatist, fully knew that the proposal needed the stamp of approval from the Confederacy's most accomplished military leader. At this moment, Lee's power of persuasion was in great demand.

On February 11, Judah Benjamin sent a letter to Lee, appealing to him to trumpet the call for the enlistment of the slaves. The secretary also hoped to influence public opinion on this matter because of the fierce opposition to the policy. He summarized one of the main arguments against black enrollment.

Benjamin said that "some of the opponents of the measure are producing a strong impression against it by asserting that it would disband the army by reason of the violent aversion of the troops to have negroes in the field with them."[46] After commenting on the position of the detractors, Benjamin finally got around to the purpose for writing to Lee. He wrote: "It occurs to me that if we could get from the army an expression of its desire to be re-enforced by such negroes as for the boon of freedom . . . we may yet be able to give to you such a force as will enable you to assume the offensive when you think it best to do so."[47] Benjamin concluded by telling Lee that his endorsement of the plan would be sufficient to curtail any "further effective opposition" from state assemblies and the Confederate legislature at Richmond. General Lee acknowledged that raising black regiments was extreme but necessary.

Following Benjamin's letter to Lee, endorsements from several units in the Army of Northern Virginia poured into newspapers calling on the Confederate government to create black units. These resolutions were one way in which the soldiers participated in the debate. The loyalty of Lee's soldiers to him was a powerful phenomenon. Many of them were certain that General Lee knew what was best for the Army of Northern Virginia and the Confederacy. Some Rebel troops were willing to accept slave men as soldiers. Private James B. Jones of the First Battalion North Carolina Sharpshooters noted: "The all absorbing topic here at present is whether to put negroes in the army or not nine tenths of the Army is in favor of it. I am for one if Genl Lee thinks he can use them to any advantage which he says he can."[48] A Texas soldier called on his comrades to "lay aside all prejudice" and support the arming of black men who were "available and necessary for the furtherance of our ultimate object—independence and separate nationality."[49] The widespread support for the plan was indicative of the soldiers' desire to strengthen their grip on southern independence even as it slipped away. Necessity rather than choice had driven them to give credence to the extreme measure of conscripting slaves.

There was, however, opposition in Lee's army to the notion of black Confederates. Some of his soldiers still believed that blacks would not fight and that their enlistment would lead to the demise of southern society. The possibility of slaves actually fighting with white soldiers in the Army of Northern Virginia was repulsive to many of them. That of course would mean that black troops would have the distinct honor of serving under Robert E. Lee, the preeminent soldier of the South. As defeat gripped the southern states during the last months of the war, discouragement held sway in many quarters. Some of Lee's soldiers viewed the recruitment of black men as solid proof that the Rebel cause was on its deathbed and no longer worth fighting and dying for.

Congressman Ethelbert Barksdale of Mississippi was the sponsor of the "Negro soldier bill" then under consideration in the Confederate legislature. Before the war, his chosen profession was journalism. After the hostilities, he served two terms in the House of Representatives as a Democrat. In a letter from Lee to Barksdale, dated February 18, 1865, the general presented a strong case for the freeing and the arming of slave men. "I cannot see the wisdom of the policy of holding them to await his arrival [Union army]," he said, "when we may, by timely action and judicious management, use them to arrest his progress."[50] One can not underestimate the importance of this letter in galvanizing support among ordinary southerners and Confederate legislators for the cause of black enlistment. With Lee's consent, his letter appeared in newspapers in Richmond and beyond. Doubtless, Lee had permitted the publication of his letter to Congressman Barksdale so that his views on the radical experiment would become public. Robert F. Durden acknowledges that Lee's letter to Barksdale "apparently turned the tide of opinion, in and out of Congress," on the issue of African American soldiers.[51]

Through Barksdale, Lee implored Congress to raise a black army. Time was running out in the South in its attempt to establish an independent nation. The large untapped reserve of black men was the only hope available to the Confederate States at this late point in the game. Desperation, which had been the constant companion of southerners for several months, became more deeply entrenched with each passing day. Lee realized that the war had taken a heavy toll on white southerners. They had shouldered the burden of fighting against an enemy whose army by then consisted of tens of thousands of United States Colored Troops. "I do not think that our white population can supply the necessities of a long war without overtaxing its capacity," he told Barksdale, "and imposing great suffering upon our people."[52] The *Richmond Whig* used Lee's name in an effort to persuade the Confederate Congress to enact the bill to employ black men as soldiers. The paper stated, "It is known that he urges—with a warmth he has not perhaps, exhibited in regard to any other matter of legislation— the passage of a law subjecting the negro element to military use. His opinion, at all times entitled great weight, becomes imperative as to such a matter."[53]

Lee did not subscribe to the notion that blacks were incapable of fighting. Evidence of their martial ability was made abundantly clear on numerous battlefields across the South. Lee believed that, with good leadership and proper training, slaves could be molded into effective warriors. The general was unequivocal in his opinion that enlistment must be accompanied by emancipation. He told Congressman Barksdale: "I think those who are employed should be freed. It would be neither just nor wise, in my opinion, to require them to serve as slaves."[54] On the same day that Lee wrote to Barksdale, the *Richmond Enquirer* announced its support for the arming of black men and turned its attention to the issue of discipline for them. The paper said that the promise of freedom would not make soldiers of black volunteers; only discipline could achieve that purpose. The paper counseled that discipline for African American recruits should be "sharp, severe, exacting, which teaches them their duty and then compels them to perform it." The *Enquirer* concluded that the threat of punishment was more effective in controlling Negro troops than the promise of reward.[55]

Lee's correspondence to Barksdale was published in the *Richmond Sentinel* on February 23. The prefatory statement to the general's letter appeared to have been speaking to the public at large. It stated that Lee's letter was all that was needed "to settle every doubt or silence every objection" to the drastic measure. "The opinion of Gen. Lee may be repudiated or it may be adopted," the *Sentinel* wrote; "it is too clear and unequivocal to be compromised or evaded."[56] During the uproar, the controversial proposal received the powerful endorsement of General Lee.[57] Indeed, the scheme gathered momentum, aided by his influential voice. Lee had broken his tradition of reticence on important political debates and spoken out forcefully in support of using black men as troops. For Lee, this was out of character. He had disliked politics during his adult life and tried to stay clear of it. His major complaint against politicians was that they were motivated by parochialism and selfishness. The famous general learned during the Civil War that the job of commanding the Army of Northern Virginia required both military and political skills.[58] The crisis that swept through the Confederate nation during the last few months of the war had forced Lee to take a political stand.

Lee's support of the audacious measure earned him the scorn of some southerners. Even the mighty Lee could not move the *Charleston Mercury*, which remained hostile to the infusion of male slaves into the army. Robert Barnwell Rhett Jr. suggested that Lee restrict himself to military affairs and leave civil matters to others.[59] Even with Lee's support, opposition to the "Negro soldier bill" remained strong. Confederate Senator Robert M. T. Hunter of Virginia was a powerful obstacle to congressional approval of the bill. This vocal opponent defended slavery as the pillar of the political and social system of the South. Hunter argued that the enrollment of slaves would not only be duplicitous, but detrimental to the economic survival of the Confederacy. Under heavy pressure from the state legislature of Virginia to support the bill, Senator Hunter finally acquiesced and voted in favor of raising a black army.[60]

On March 10, Lee wrote to Jefferson Davis to express his views on how the Confederacy should proceed with the recruitment of black soldiers upon the Negro bill receiving congressional and presidential approval. The general reminded his commander-in-chief that the recruiting of as many African American men as possible should begin without delay. Lee wrote, "In the beginning it would be well to do everything to make the enlistment entirely voluntary on the part of the negroes, and those owners who are willing to furnish some of their slaves for the purpose." Lee concluded that he had assurance from several plantation holders of their willingness to offer "the most suitable among their slaves" for military service.[61] However, when the hour came for them to deliver, they did not meet Lee's optimistic expectations.

In February, the Confederate House passed a bill authorizing Davis to enlist as many black men into the army as he deemed expedient. The Senate added an amendment to the House Bill, stipulating that the president could recruit an additional 300,000 troops regardless of color. With Davis's support, the "Negro soldier bill" became law on March 13, 1865. The close vote in the Confederate Congress, forty to thirty-seven in the House and nine to eight in the Senate, showed how divided the South was on the creation of black regiments. The decision to raise black units was the "last desperate measure" to introduce the "last untried resource" as a means of pumping life into a dying republic.[62] After much acrimonious debate, the president finally had the authority to call on each state for its quota of troops. Unlike the Union army, black Confederate enlistees from the beginning would be the recipients of the same provisions such as pay, clothing, and food as extended to white soldiers.

Although Lee had recommended emancipation for the slaves, the new Confederate law had left slavery intact. "That nothing in this act shall be construed to authorize a change in the relation which the said slaves shall bear toward their owners," declared section five of the statute, "except by consent of the owners and of the States in which they may reside."[63] The law did, however, empower Lee with the responsibility of organizing "the said slaves into companies, battalions, regiments, and brigades, under such rules and regulations as the Secretary of War may prescribe, and to be commanded by such officers as the President may appoint."[64] An immediate response to the law was a flood of petitions from military leaders to the War Department offering to recruit African American units. The process of recruiting slaves and Negroes immediately got underway. Elizabeth Brown Pryor asserts that military reversals finally convinced most southerners to accept "the cold logic that independence without slavery was better than suppression by the North."[65]

John B. Jones, the War Department clerk, believed that the creation of black units would become a reality. Writing in his diary four days after the passage of the Negro soldier law, Jones recorded: "We shall have a negro army. Letters are pouring into the department from men of military skill and character, asking authority to raise companies, battalions, and regiments of negro troops. It is the desperate remedy for the very desperate case—and may be successful."[66] Jones's optimism was no doubt dashed when he witnessed a small contingent of black Confederates marching in Richmond a few days later. The clerk was not impressed by the sight. "The parade of a few companies of negro troops yesterday," he said, "was rather a ridiculous affair. The owners are opposed to it."[67] The recruiting efforts of the Confederacy yielded meager results among both free blacks and slaves after March 13. In the words of Bruce Levine, the time had run out for the southern nation, and it was simply "too late to convince more than a handful of slaves that rallying to the Confederacy was a promising course of action for them."[68]

George C. Rable concludes that "General Lee favored enlisting slaves was enough to convince many reluctant Confederates, but others decided that his military genius did not extend into the political arena."[69] The politics and the military of the Confederacy met at the intersection of the peculiar institution during this memorable debate. General Lee's influence among political leaders and ordinary southerners combined with his performance in battle proved to be too powerful for the opposition to overcome during the South's winter of discontent. The decision of the Davis government to enlist black men revealed that the collapse of the southern experiment was imminent. "Intent on winning, the leaders of the Confederacy were willing to accept any expedient," observes one historian, "even to reverse themselves on the theories upon which the Confederacy had predicted its existence."[70] Although frustrated by the tepid response of the planter aristocracy to the recruitment initiative, Lee remained the consummate soldier to the bitter end. He never wavered in his belief that the law to "transform slaves into soldiers" was the proper course of action for the vanishing southern republic. Lee was convinced that, if only black regiments could take to the field, they would "remove all doubts as [to] the expediency of the measure" enacted by the Confederate Congress.[71]

The passage of the law was clear evidence that the Confederacy was on life support. By then, the outcome of the war was no longer in doubt. According to one scholar's incisive analysis of the statute, it "was the dying gesture of a crumbling nation."[72] The decision giving the slaves permission to engage in combat cast a revealing light upon the South and its peculiar institution. Many southerners conceded that black enlistment was a step toward the inevitability of total emancipation. This act represented a contravention of the very principles upon which the Confederate States had been established. Looking through the telescope of retrospect, Davis accurately recalled that "the passage of the act had been so long delayed that the opportunity was lost. There did not remain time enough to obtain any result from its provisions."[73] By the time that the government had settled the historic debate, the tentacles of defeat had enveloped the South. Nonetheless, many southerners remained loyal to the Richmond government during the intense debate because General Lee and his Army of Northern Virginia had emerged as "the preeminent symbol of the Confederate struggle for independence and liberty."[74]

The reaction of southern blacks to the new law was excitement tinged with caution and realism. The greatest enthusiasm for the law was shown by black Richmonders. For black southerners, the opportunity to fight for their freedom combined with the chance to prove their manhood was a powerful inducement. The euphoria that gripped blacks in Richmond, however, did not spread to other places. Many African Americans, who were insightful observers of the war, knew that, by the spring of 1865, the Confederacy was a beaten republic. Therefore, they saw no need to risk life and limb for a cause that was on its deathbed. Furthermore, they knew that they would have to live among whites once the war was over. Blacks did not want to do anything to add to the bitterness and humiliation of southern whites brought on by defeat. Reconciliation was around the corner.

Although the slaves did not have a voice in the debate, they were aware of the consternation it was causing for white southerners. By the time the debate reached a crescendo in political and military circles, southern blacks understood that the Confederacy had no real chance of winning the war. Their preference for a Union victory far outweighed a Confederate triumph under any circumstance. Therefore, the slaves had no real desire to attach their fortunes to a losing cause. Furthermore, many recognized the limitations of the law regarding their freedom. Both the owner and the state would have to consent to emancipation in order for a bondsman to receive freedom as a reward for military service. Lee and others understood the folly of not extending freedom to the families of black volunteers. Without the benefit of emancipation for their loved ones, the revolutionary law had no chance of success. During the acrimonious debate, which was one of the last major political crises to preoccupy the South, the lack of magnanimity and foresight on the part of Confederate leaders helped to doom their nation. As Paul D. Escott concludes, "The Confederate debate on emancipation revealed the limits of white Southerners' creative imaginations, crippled by racism and the desire to retain the benefits and privileges of slaveholding."[75]

A week before the adoption of the "Negro soldier bill," the State of Virginia passed legislation authorizing the recruitment of black men. There was no provision in the law for freedom for those who served. On March 24, Lee applied to Governor William Smith for the maximum number allowable under the statute. "The services of these men," he said, "are now necessary to enable us to oppose the enemy."[76] Other southern states did not follow Virginia's lead. In fact, they shied away from dabbling in the controversial and revolutionary experiment. Most of the governors staunchly opposed any attempt by the Davis administration to tamper with slavery. It was apparent that the influence Lee wielded in Virginia did not extend to other southern capitals. The sensational topic was the focal point of an earlier meeting of several governors in Augusta, Georgia. The state leaders discussed but decided not to endorse the raising of black soldiers.

General Lee cooperated in every way with the War Department in facilitating the recruiting of Negro troops after the bill's passage. On March 28, 1865, Lee told James Longstreet, "It will be necessary to send recruiting officers to the various counties" in order to create African American regiments.[77] When President Davis informed Lee on April 1, 1865, that he was experiencing difficulty recruiting black volunteers, the end of the Confederacy was already at hand. Lee telegraphed Davis from Petersburg the next day to tell him that Richmond would have to be evacuated. General Lee and his battle-tested Army of Northern Virginia were Appomattox bound. Lee and Joseph E. Johnston surrendered before the law could have an impact on the outcome of the war. The once vibrant Confederate republic was by then void of life with no hope of resuscitation in sight. Lee's prediction that the Union would prevail and the slaves would gain their freedom was on point. The Virginia general was a major actor in the drama to enlist African American men into the Confederate army. The end of the war denied southern black men the chance to prove themselves in battle. The military legacy of black Americans in the Civil War was marked by their participation as soldiers in the United States Army, not the Confederate States of America.

NOTES

1. U.S. War Department, *The War of the Rebellion: A Compilation of the Official Records of the Union and Confederate Armies* (Washington, DC: Government Printing Office, 1880–1901), ser. 1, vol. 52: 589.

2. Bruce Levine, *Confederate Emancipation: Southern Plans to Free and Arm Slaves during the Civil War* (New York: Oxford University Press, 2006), 17.

3. Herman Hattaway and Richard E. Beringer, *Jefferson Davis, Confederate President* (Lawrence: University Press of Kansas, 2002), 331.

4. William J. Cooper Jr., *Jefferson Davis, American* (New York: Alfred A. Knopf, 2000), 517.

5. Recollections of a Private of the Army of the Confederate States, William Robert Greer Papers, 1920–32, South Carolina Historical Society, Charleston.

6. Quoted in Emory M. Thomas, *Robert E. Lee: A Biography* (New York: W.W. Norton & Co., 1995), 173.

7. Brian Holden Reid, *Robert E. Lee: Icon for a Nation* (Amherst, NY: Prometheus Books, 2007), 62–63.

8. *Official Records*, ser. 4, vol. 3: 1012.

9. Cooper, *Jefferson Davis*, 517.

10. Charles H. Wesley, *The Collapse of the Confederacy* (Washington, DC: Associated Publishers, Inc., 1937), 144.

11. Charles H. Wesley, "The Employment of Negroes as Soldiers in the Confederate Army," *Journal of Negro History* 4, no. 3 (July 1919): 240.

12. Quoted in Gary L. Bunker, *From Rail-Splitter to Icon* (Kent, OH: Kent State University Press, 2001), 181.

13. Thomas Robson Hay, "The Question of Arming the Slaves," *Mississippi Valley Historical Review* 6, no. 1 (June 1919): 36.

14. Bell Irvin Wiley, *Southern Negroes, 1861–1865* (New Haven, CT: Yale University Press, 1938), 147.

15. *Official Records*, ser. 4, vol. 3: 1009.

16. Richard Launcelot Maury Diary, 1865, Virginia Historical Society, Richmond.

17. *Official Records*, ser. 4, vol. 3: 693–94.

18. William C. Davis, *Jefferson Davis: The Man and His Hour* (New York: Harper Collins, 1991), 541.

19. Ira Berlin, Joseph P. Reidy, and Leslie S. Rowland, eds., *Freedom: A Documentary History of Emancipation, 1861–1867*, ser. 2: *The Black Military Experience* (New York: Cambridge University Press, 1982), 22–23.

20. Hattaway and Beringer, *Jefferson Davis*, 327.

21. Henry W. Allen to James A. Seddon, September 26, 1864, Black Soldiers Collection, New Orleans Historic Collection, New Orleans.

22. Mark L. Bradley, "This Monstrous Proposition: North Carolina and the Confederate Debate on Arming the Slaves," *North Carolina Historical Review* 80, no. 2 (April 2003): 159.

23. Clifford Dowdey and Louis H. Manarin, eds., *The Wartime Papers of R. E. Lee* (Boston: Little Brown and Co., 1961), 848.

24. Ernest F. Furgurson, *Ashes of Glory: Richmond at War* (New York: Vintage Books, 1996), 280–81.

25. Quoted in Robert F. Durden, *The Gray and the Black: The Confederate Debate on Emancipation* (Baton Rouge: Louisiana State University Press, 1972), 134.

26. Copy of William Porcher Miles to Robert E. Lee, October 24, 1864, in William Porcher Miles Papers #508, Southern Historical Collection, Wilson Library, University of North Carolina at Chapel Hill.

27. Quoted in Durden, *The Gray and the Black*, 136.

28. Ibid.

29. James D. Richardson, ed., *A Compilation of the Messages and Papers of Jefferson Davis and the Confederacy, Including Diplomatic Correspondence, 1861–1865* (Nashville: United States Publishing Co., 1905), vol. 1: 493–96.

30. Bradley, "This Monstrous Proposition," 163.

31. John M. Daniel, *The Richmond Examiner During the War* (1868; rpt. New York: Arno Press Inc., 1970), 213.

32. Frank E. Vandiver, ed., *Southern Historical Society Papers: The Proceedings of the Second Confederate Congress*, vol. 52 (Richmond: Virginia Historical Society, 1959), 241.

33. C. Vann Woodward, ed., *Mary Chesnut's Civil War* (New Haven, CT: Yale University Press, 1981), 678–79.

34. *Richmond Sentinel,* November 24, 1864.

35. *Official Records*, ser. 4, vol. 3: 959.

36. Ibid., 959–60.

37. Wesley, *The Collapse of the Confederacy,* 170–71.

38. *Official Records*, ser. 4, vol. 3: 1013.

39. Ibid.

40. Philip D. Dillard, "What Price Must We Pay for Victory? Views on Arming Slaves from Lynchburg, Virginia, to Galveston, Texas," *Inside the Confederate Nation: Essays in Honor of Emory M. Thomas,* ed. Lesley J. Gordon and John C. Inscoe (Baton Rouge: Louisiana State University Press, 2005), 324.

41. Quoted in Philip D. Dillard, "The Confederate Debate Over Arming Slaves: Views from Macon and Augusta Newspapers," *Georgia Historical Quarterly* 79, no. 1 (Spring 1995): 137–38.

42. Daniel, *The Richmond Examiner During the War,* 217.

43. Confederate States of America, General Order No. 3, February 6, 1865, Abraham Lincoln Presidential Library, Springfield, Illinois.

44. George C. Rable, *The Confederate Republic: A Revolution against Politics* (Chapel Hill: University of North Carolina Press), 286.

45. *Official Records*, ser. 1, vol. 46, part 2: 1229.

46. Ibid.

47. Ibid.

48. Quoted in J. Tracy Power, *Lee's Miserables: Life in the Army of Northern Virginia from the Wilderness to Appomattox* (Chapel Hill: University of North Carolina Press, 1998), 253.

49. Ibid., 251.

50. James D. McCabe, *Life and Campaigns of General Robert E. Lee* (Atlanta: National Publishing Co., 1866), 574.

51. Durden, *The Gray and the Black,* 206.

52. McCabe, *Life and Campaigns of General Robert E. Lee,* 574.

53. *Richmond Whig,* February 20, 1865.

54. McCabe, *Life and Campaigns of General Robert E. Lee,* 575.

55. *Richmond Enquirer,* February 18, 1865.

56. *Richmond Sentinel,* February 23, 1865.

57. Levine, *Confederate Emancipation,* 5.

58. Elizabeth Brown Pryor, *Reading the Man: A Portrait of Robert E. Lee Through His Private Letters* (New York: Viking Penguin, 2007), 397.

59. Richard E. Beringer, Herman Hattaway, Archer Jones, and William N. Still, *Why the Confederacy Lost the Civil War* (Athens: University of Georgia Press, 1986), 373.

60. Furgurson, *Ashes of Glory,* 308.

61. Dowdey and Manarin, eds., *The Wartime Papers of R. E. Lee,* 914.

62. Wesley, *The Collapse of the Confederacy,* 134.

63. *Official Records,* ser. 4, vol. 3: 1161.

64. Ibid.

65. Pryor, *Reading the Man,* 397.

66. John B. Jones, *A Rebel War Clerk's Diary at the Confederate States Capital* (2 vols., Philadelphia: J. B. Lippincott and Co., 1866), 451.

67. Ibid., 457.

68. Levine, *Confederate Emancipation,* 140.

69. Rable, *The Confederate Republic,* 289–90.

70. Wesley, *The Collapse of the Confederacy,* 166.

71. Pryor, *Reading the Man,* 380.

72. James M. McPherson, *The Negro's Civil War: How American Blacks Felt and Acted During the War for the Union* (New York: Vintage, 2003), 248.

73. Jefferson Davis, *The Rise and Fall of the Confederate Government* (2 vols., New York: D. Appleton and Co., 1881), vol. 1: 519.

74. Gary Gallagher, *The Confederate War* (Cambridge, MA: Harvard University Press, 1997), 85.

75. Paul D. Escott, *"What Shall We Do With The Negro": Lincoln, White Racism, and Civil War America* (Charlottesville: University Press of Virginia, 2009), 196–97.

76. Richard Harwell, *Lee: An Abridgment in One Volume* (New York: Charles Scribner's Sons, 1961), 449.

77. Robert E. Lee to James Longstreet, March 28, 1865, John Walter Fairfax Papers, 1863–1937, Virginia Historical Society, Richmond.

GUERRILLA WARFARE, DEMOCRACY, AND THE FATE OF THE CONFEDERACY

XXXXXXXXXXXXXXXXXXXXXXXXXXXXX

DANIEL E. SUTHERLAND

O
ne of the most enduring explanations for why the Confederacy lost the
Civil War asserts that the Rebels were too democratic. First proposed
by David H. Donald as a variation on a theme by Frank L. Owsley, this
theory has survived, with some modification by recent scholars, as a
viable part of most multicausal explanations of Confederate defeat.
To date, the argument has rested largely on the supposed political blunders of
the central government, in its indelicate handling of issues that infringed on
personal liberties or that injured the sensibilities of powerful state politicians,
to demonstrate the disruptive effect of Confederate individualism. Occasional
references are also made to problems caused by the independent spirit of the
Confederate soldier, but these discussions tend to convey a greater sense of
pride or respect for this quality than rebuke. Little has been said about how
military policy might have been influenced by an underlying tension in Confederate society between democracy and authority, between individualism and
discipline, or between popular conceptions of the war and the government's
conduct of the war. Conscription, probably the most divisive issue involving
individual rights, cut across both social and military lines, but another pivotal
military issue eclipsed even conscription: guerrilla warfare. Indeed, guerrilla
warfare sparked sharp policy debates in both North and South that affected the
outcome of the war in no small way.[1]

Large numbers of common folk assumed from the earliest days of the Confederacy that guerrillas would be an important component of their nation's
military force. This is not to say they underestimated the role to be played by

conventional soldiers, for even the least militarily knowledgeable Rebels sensed that independence could not be won by fighting an exclusively irregular contest. Rather, they believed that guerrillas could help win the war, and many men wished to contribute to Confederate victory in that way. They saw guerrilla warfare as a freewheeling, unfettered, grassroots style of fighting that suited southern tendencies toward individualism and localism. Like the Europeans who had associated the guerrilla style with "natural man" since the eighteenth century, Rebel advocates also thought of it as "natural," almost primordial. For Confederates, guerrilla warfare was not democratic in any political sense, in that it was not based on philosophical musings about republican values, but it exemplified democracy in a social, Tocquevillian sense, whereby equality and individual action formed the impetus for a "people's war."[2]

Yet, for two reasons this popular enthusiasm for a democratic uprising ran amok almost from the start. First, the original guerrilla war produced a pair of nasty mutations—community vigilantism and outright outlawry—that made Rebel noncombatants the victims, rather than the beneficiaries, of this people's contest. Earlier advocates became disillusioned when the guerrilla struggle, feeding off its own excesses, began to hurt more than help those it was supposed to defend. Second, Confederate political and military leaders, tied to traditional, hierarchical forms of social and military organization, were suspicious of the guerrilla war's grassroots origins and feared the consequences of such an un-regulated mode of fighting. In a sense, the transformation of the original guer-rilla war from a useful means of local defense and voluntarism into a rapacious free-for-all justified their doubts and fears, but Confederate leaders added to the chaos by first underestimating and then failing to harness its passionate energy.[3]

None of this is to suggest, as have some historians, that the Confederacy fell because it failed to mount a more vigorous guerrilla contest. Yet the opposite position—that the guerrilla struggle was a mere "sideshow" that had little bear-ing on the outcome of the war—also misses the point. Scholars only began to appreciate the extensive social and political implications of the Confederacy's guerrilla war in the 1980s. Since then, they have presented increasingly sophis-ticated appraisals of the structure, organization, composition, and motivation of guerrilla bands, the roles of southern civilians in the irregular war, and the impact of guerrilla warfare on communities. The guerrilla war has emerged as a war unto itself, a war with its own rules, its own chronology, its own turn-ing points, and its own heroes, villains, and victims. At the same time, it also formed part of the wider war. It influenced the strategy and logistics of conventional campaigns, the political culture, the morale of soldiers and civilians, the southern economy, and ultimately, the very nature of the conflict. Insofar as it evolved in unexpected ways and lurched out of the control of leaders and civilians alike, the guerrilla war weakened the Confederacy and became an important factor in Confederate defeat.[4]

The guerrilla war began almost spontaneously, as befits a people's war. The guns in Charleston harbor had scarcely cooled before Rebels from the Atlantic coast volunteered to lead "guerrilla," "partisan," "ranger," and "independent" companies against the enemy. One Rebel urged Confederate Secretary of War Leroy Pope Walker to authorize "a guerrilla service" in western Virginia, where several bands of irregulars had already formed. "I am deeply interested not only in defeating the enemy," this man emphasized, "but in whipping him by any and all means and as speedily as possible." A Louisianan explained the advantages of posting "a regiment of mounted men, on the guerrilla order," in the southern parishes of his state." I can get the sturdy men of our State, besides 100 or 200 Indians," he declared. An Alabamian asked Walker's permission to raise a company that would wage war "without restraint and under no orders." He reasoned, "We have a desperate enemy to contend with, and if necessary must resort to desperate means." Governors got the message, too. A Tennessean urged Isham G. Harris to wage a "guerrilla war" by flooding the countryside "with armed men to repel the enemy at every point." A "more deadly and destructive antagonism," he stressed, "could not be raised to repel the invaders."[5]

Even in the farthest reaches of the country, areas too often ignored by Civil War historians, Rebels prepared for a guerrilla conflict. In Colorado Territory, irregulars hatched plans during the summer of 1861 to stockpile weapons and launch raids against vulnerable minting establishments and ranches—gold and horses being of nearly equal value to the new Confederate nation. As the war progressed, these westerners attacked Union mail trains and expanded their activities into New Mexico. In California, Unionists begged U.S. Secretary of War Simon Cameron for help in August 1861. Rebels—desperate men who were "never without arms"—controlled the state government, the petitioners wailed. The ruffians devoted all their energy to "plotting, scheming, and organizing," insisted the loyal citizens, and it would not be long before "[t]he frightful scenes . . . transpiring in Missouri would be rivaled by the atrocities enacted upon the Pacific Coast."[6]

Everyone knew about Missouri, where the most bitter of all guerrilla contests had already broken out. In fact, the instinctive way in which Missourians and other westerners grabbed their muskets and squirrel rifles helps to explain the popularity of the guerrilla war. Some people saw this irregular activity as a brand of western warfare that grew from the region's frontier heritage. Many westerners, even in 1860, still lived beyond the effective rule of courts and legislatures. They had grown accustomed to settling their own feuds, and they were not squeamish about resorting to vigilante justice. Much has been written about the tendency toward violence of southerners generally, but southerners on the frontier—especially unmarried young men—inhabited a world that exacerbated their aggressive tendencies. The Missouri-Kansas border war of the 1850s represented just one of the many "Wars of Incorporation"—including land wars, Indian wars, and open brigandage—waged west of the Mississippi River during the antebellum years. Indeed, this was one region where northern settlers, as demonstrated by the jayhawkers of Kansas, matched southern predilections for guerrilla fighting.[7]

Yet this spontaneous eruption of irregular warfare was not limited to the West. People all along the North-South border, in Kentucky, Tennessee, Maryland, and Virginia, embraced it. These states, like those beyond the Mississippi, had been up for grabs politically during the secession crisis. Virginia and Tennessee had been among the last states to join the Confederacy, while Kentucky and Maryland never did enter the fold. The border region thus came to represent a different sort of "frontier," unmistakably associated with the idea of guerrilla war in the eyes of new Confederates. Here is where they would have to rally and turn back the invading Federals: even guerrilla bands from the Deep South volunteered "for border service" during the spring and summer of 1861. A South Carolinian, for example, raised a hundred men "to be employed on the border" as "destructive warriors," and similar offers came from Alabama, Georgia, Louisiana, and Mississippi.[8]

Most wars begin without the opposing sides knowing what to expect. Neither citizens nor even the soldiers can fully anticipate how a contest will be fought or what their roles will be. As a result, the spontaneous, sometimes desperate border clashes in the early months of hostilities quickly defined the nature of the struggle for most southerners. Journalist Murat Halstead reported from Baltimore, "Occurrences so suggestive of assassins behind the bushes, gives a smack of the excitement of real war." Another citizen confirmed the determination of Marylanders to strike at the Yankees by whatever means possible. "As soon as they begin the retreat through Maryland the people will rise upon them," he pledged. In Missouri Thomas C. Reynolds, the pro-Confederate lieutenant governor, informed Jefferson Davis that he and other "Southern men" vowed to throw Missouri "into a general revolution" and oppose the Federals in "a guerilla war," until sufficient numbers of Confederate troops reached the state.[9]

As Union armies pushed the border farther south, threatening communities and citizens with immediate violence, more Confederate citizens resisted. Edmund Ruffin, the quintessential Rebel, who legend says fired the first shot of the war at Fort Sumter, wrote from Virginia in late June 1861, "Guerrilla fighting has begun, & with great effect, near Alexandria & also near Hampton. Some of our people, acting alone, or in small parties, & at their own discretion, have crept upon & shot many of the sentinels & scouts. It is only necessary for the people generally to resort to these means to overcome any invading army, even if we were greatly inferior to it in regular military force."[10]

When Federal troops menaced the coast of his beloved South Carolina, the novelist and poet William Gilmore Simms recommended that the army assign ten men from each company to guerrilla operations. "[H]ave them . . . painted and disguised as Indians," Simms urged the local Confederate commander, and arm them with "rifle, bowie knife & hatchet." Plenty of men in the army, he assumed, were familiar with Indian warfare. "If there be any thing which will inspire terror in the souls of the citizen soldiery of the North," reasoned the poet-strategist, "it will be the idea that scalps are to be taken by the redmen." The fifty-five-year-old Simms, too old and sedentary to embark on active service himself, nonetheless urged all Confederates to join the fray in some fashion. "Every body is drilling and arming," he observed with satisfaction on July 4, 1861. "Even I practise with the Colt. I am a dead shot with rifle & double barrel. . . . Our women practise, & they will fight, too, like she wolves."[11]

The widespread excitement had become palpable by that first summer of the war. "All persons that feel inclined to go into guerrilla or independent service," declared an Arkansas newspaper in July 1861, "will rendezvous at Little Rock." Volunteers should be prepared for immediate action, with "a good horse, a good double-barrel shot gun, and as well supplied with small arms as possible." That same month, recruitment posters went up in Hanover County, Virginia, for the Virginia and North Carolina Irrepressibles. "We are to WEAR CITIZENS' CLOTHES and to use such arms as we can furnish ourselves," promised the notice, "to serve during the war . . . without pay." *De Bow's Review* predicted that, in addition to its magnificent armies, the Confederacy must be prepared "on proper opportunities to pursue that desultory partisan method of warfare before which invading armies gradually melt away." Indeed, *De Bow's* insisted that, should the war prove to be a long one, with the enemy gaining ground in the South's interior, the nation's "chief reliance must be on irregular troops and partisan warfare."[12]

American history also shaped thinking about the type of war to expect. Southerners justified secession in 1860 by insisting that northerners had abandoned the governing principles forged in the American Revolution and the spirit of government defined in the U.S. Constitution. Similarly, the secession movement and the creation of a Rebel government inspired comparisons between the Confederate struggle for independence and the war waged by England's American colonies some fourscore years earlier. Confederate editorialists, orators, and pamphleteers used this theme time and again to rally the populace. "Who can resist a whole people, thoroughly aroused, brave to rashness, fighting for their existence?" asked a Virginian. "This revolution is not the work of leaders or politicians," elaborated a Tennessean. "It is the spontaneous uprising and upheaving of the people. It is as irresistible as the mighty tide of the ocean."[13]

For many Rebels the revolutionary heritage of a "People's War," as they were calling the current conflict by October 1861, included guerrilla fighting. Southerners, like most mid-nineteenth-century Americans, believed that their ancestors had defeated Great Britain not with the well-drilled, well-disciplined Continental Army, but with the ragtag, defiant militia that operated in critical situations as irregulars. Although modem historians have shown that this was not the case, ardent Rebels had their own version of the past. "The scenes attendant upon the retreat of the British army from Concord and Lexington in the days of the Revolution should be reenacted to the last degree," insisted one Confederate. "Every man, woman, and child should rise in arms along the line of the retreating foe, and enforce by terrible illustration the lesson to the frightened outlaws how fearful the vengeance of a people armed in the holy cause of liberty."[14]

American colonists had fought as "partizans"—the common name for guerrillas in the eighteenth century—in every theater of their war for independence but nowhere with more success or deadly effect than in the South. The exploits of Francis Marion, Thomas Sumter, Daniel Morgan, and Henry "Light-Horse Harry" Lee had become legendary by 1860. Both Yankees and Confederates saw themselves as the heirs of Revolutionary "minutemen," a tradition that most often played itself out, as it had during the War for Independence, with amateur soldiers forming conventional armies. As the South braced for an invasion by vastly superior numbers—again, just as in 1776—the intangible association of amateur minutemen with partisan resistance had a particularly dramatic impact on Confederate assumptions about how to fight.[15]

The spirit of those Revolutionary partisans entered southern mythology and shaped the region's consciousness, especially through the work of nineteenth-century authors, poets, and playwrights. Simms, the "representative writer" of the Old South, published both a biography of Francis Marion, the "Swamp Fox," and a series of historical romances in the 1830s and 1840s that celebrated the South's partisan war. Lesser-known works, like Mary Moragne's *British Partizan*, had a similar theme. When Nathaniel Beverley Tucker published *The Partisan Leader: A Tale of the Future,* a novel that predicted the creation of a southern confederacy, he selected a Virginia guerrilla chief as the story's hero. So striking was Tucker's apparent power of prophecy that his novel, originally published in 1836, was reprinted in both New York and Richmond after the war started. Poets, like Simms, Henry Timrod, and S. Teackle Wallis, paid tribute in verse to Confederate guerrillas and partisans during the war, and the first original Confederate drama performed on the Richmond stage was *The Guerrillas*, by James Dabney McCabe Jr.[16]

Many Confederates embraced their inheritance. "Would that the days of Sumter and Marion were come again!" exclaimed an anxious Georgian. Southerners proclaimed Meriwether Jeff Thompson, the earliest Missouri guerrilla leader to gain prominence, "the Marion of this Revolution." Later in the war a Confederate woman christened the dashing John Hunt Morgan, who would lead a series of raids through Kentucky and the Middle West, "our second Marion." A Louisiana guerrilla wished to serve the Confederacy "as Francis Marion did in the days of the revolution," and other would-be partisans christened their bands "Marion Men" and "Swamp Fox Rangers." It is likely that South Carolina–born Captain John W. Pearson, who led a band of guerrillas in the vicinity of Tampa, Florida, had been raised on the legends of Marion and Sumter, although he also witnessed a very practical application of irregular tactics when fighting against the Seminoles in the 1830s.[17]

Parts of the South more newly settled than the original coastal colonies called on more recent but no less powerful traditions. The Texas legislature passed a "Minute Men Law" just days after the state seceded, but military leaders also summoned recruits by exploiting images from their own revolution of the 1830s. "Remember the days of yore," came a typical appeal, "when your own red right hands achieved your independence." Texans must fight once again "to keep [their] soil free from the enemy's touch. . . . Let every man, then, clean his old musket, shotgun, or rifle, run his bullets, fill his powder-horn, sharpen his knife, and see that his revolver is ready to his hand, as in the trying but glorious days when Mexico was [his] foe." The Texas Ranger tradition also gained wide appeal across the South. The exploits of a band known as the "Red Rangers" in Kentucky caused a Louisville newspaper to hail its captain as "another Ben Mc-Culloch," a well-known Texas Ranger who had already applied "the partisan mode of warfare" to the Trans-Mississippi. Other Texans, like Benjamin F. Terry, volunteered to raise guerrilla units or offered companies to serve as "irregular cavalry on the northern border from Cairo [Illinois] to [the] mouth of the Potomac." In Louisiana, people found inspiration in the War of 1812 (the Second American Revolution), when Andrew Jackson's backwoodsmen had leveled "the veterans of the British army on the plains of Chalmette."[18]

Guerrilla service also appealed to Confederates in several ways at a very personal level. Most important, it permitted the sort of "self-organized combat," as one historian has called it, favored by many southerners. Rebel irregulars detested the conventional, or paper, army with its discipline, rules, and regulations. "That kind of warfare did not suit me," explained an Arkansan in justifying his desertion from the volunteer forces to enter guerrilla service. "I wanted to get out where I could have it more lively; where I could fight if I wanted to, or run if I so desired; I wanted to be my own general." He and his friends were fighters, not soldiers, and they acknowledged no formalities of war or restrictions on how, when, or where they might strike the enemy. Another Confederate found the guerrilla style of warfare exhilarating. "It is very exciting to be in the enemy's country not knowing what moment we will be attacked," he cavalierly informed his worried wife. "When we camp, we hunt for a swamp and then move before day."[19]

The independence of irregular service also allowed men to fight where it most mattered to them, near their homes. Although President Davis pledged himself publicly to local defense, preservation of territory, and maintenance of the geographical integrity of the Confederacy, the government could not possibly provide the blanket of security implied by his rhetoric. Consequently, thousands of Rebels had either to flee their homes or live under Union occupation. Rebel soldiers serving in places distant from their own troubled neighborhoods became convinced that they could not rely on the government to protect their families while they were away; if they deserted official service, they could defend hearth and home by organizing local guerrilla bands. This line of reasoning gained credence as more communities fell prey to invading armies and enemy marauders. The governor of Arkansas saw fit to remind Jefferson Davis, "[S]oldiers do not enter the service to maintain the Southern Confederacy alone but also to protect their property and defend their homes and families." Both local defense and independent service seemed to be on the minds of some Texans who rebelled when the local Confederate commander tried to convert their irregular band into a formal cavalry regiment. "This created a great deal of dissatisfaction amongst the boys," recalled one man; "for service in a local Partizan Regiment, for which they had enlisted, was very different from that in a regular corps."[20]

Unfortunately, local defense had another, more troublesome connotation. The initial enthusiasm for guerrilla warfare reflected a desire to catch the Federals on the border, thump them soundly, and end the war. Guerrillas, reasoned their advocates, could function in this capacity as a valuable military tool. Had this remained the only role played by Rebel guerrillas, they would have rendered valuable service to the Confederate cause; but early in the war—virtually from the beginning in places like Missouri and western Virginia—guerrillas also operated as something other than organized military forces, and the value of the guerrilla system broke down accordingly. This second function of guerrilla warfare, inherent to yet at odds with the first, turned neighbor against neighbor and destroyed the unity of the border region's home front.

Some scholars have suggested that the North's determination to preserve the Union derived in no small part from a desire to maintain the rule of law and order. Southerners embraced guerrilla warfare in similar fashion, as a means of community control. In addition to protecting homes against rampaging Union armies, local defense also meant preserving the peace against internal enemies. Divisions between Unionists and secessionists ran deep in some parts of the Confederacy, and long before conventional troops collided in those regions, irregular bands formed to keep wrongheaded neighbors in check. Both sides considered themselves arbiters of justice whose mission it was to restore order to communities in chaos by forcing the "enemy" either to submit or to flee. It had all happened before. During the American Revolution, Tories and patriots had squared off in the same way, and at least some Confederates recognized this type of conflict as another part of their revolutionary heritage: "The tory Bushwhackers from East Tenn, and some from the county and neighboring ones, are doing a great deal of mischief. . . . [T]hey are going to have such a state of things as existed during the Revolution, when the Tories and Indians were so mischievous."[21]

Border warfare in Missouri, Kentucky, Tennessee, and Virginia became such a brutal business because Rebel guerrillas, in addition to disrupting Union communications and bushwhacking enemy troops, preyed on Lincolnite noncombatant neighbors. Tennessee was "alive" with "Wild Gorillas," testified a Yankee officer, "& Union men have to keep very quiet, & soldiers are not safe out of camp." The Rebels in western Virginia, a horrified northern journalist reported, had "degenerated into assassins. . . . Not only the Union volunteers, but their own neighbors, who peaceably and quietly sustain the cause of the Union, are the victims of their malice and blood-thirsty hate. . . . They shoot down their neighbors, daytime and at night, and bum their property to ashes." Confederate guerrillas had committed to fight a war for national independence and for states' rights, too, but they would also protect their homes and families. Had conventional armies never entered this border region, its people would still have waged a guerrilla war against each other.[22]

As the war spread, bands of Unionist and Rebel guerrillas faced off wherever southern civilians had divided over secession or had grown ambivalent about the wisdom of the war. The bloodletting started even before the armies arrived, and it persisted after the armies had passed, or overflowed into places where armies never appeared. Much of the violence was gratuitous and mean-spirited, what one historian has termed "blood sport," and it often led to the sort of personal vendetta that can make the guerrilla war appear to be little more than banditry. Yet much of the mayhem had a purpose. As guerrillas, they struck back at neighbors who had chosen the wrong side in the war or waged family feuds that had nothing to do with patriotic issues like "union" or "independence." "The large majority of these who joined the guerrilla bands," explained one of their officers, "had deadly wrongs to avenge and this gave to all their combats that sanguinary which yet remains part of the guerilla's legacy [sic]."[23]

The dual—and very conflicting—dynamic of the guerrilla war put Confederate political and military leaders in a quandary. On the one hand, as a strategic military force, guerrillas had proved quite effective in disrupting Union communications, destroying railroads, and plundering supply trains; and most leaders eventually recognized the popularity of this style of fighting. As a result, some of them even turned a blind eye when it suited their interests, or when, as became the case in some places, they simply lacked the influence to control independent local bands. On the other hand, the Confederate leadership, who had always worried about the potentially negative effects the individualistic character of guerrilla warfare had on the morale of the armies and on the conduct of military operations, became equally aware of the havoc guerrillas played on the home front. By the spring of 1862 the leaders faced a much broader set of problems, defined largely by their own perceptions of guerrilla warfare and the Union's reaction to the irregular war.[24]

Central to their dilemma was the fact that many of the Confederacy's leaders had been educated in military academies, most notably West Point, but also the Virginia Military Institute, the Citadel, and similar southern state schools. As these men organized the Confederate nation's armies and reviewed its strategic options, their formal military training—all of it aimed at winning wars with grand, climatic battles—dictated that they think in terms of conventional armies and traditional tactics. Everything they knew about victorious generals, from Julius Caesar to Napoleon Bonaparte, forced them to this position, which was far removed from the partisan combat favored by their untutored countrymen. Military doctrine positively discouraged the use of guerrillas, or even militia, as an independent force. The standard manuals stressed that armies should be disciplined and trained in conventional tactics.[25]

At West Point, for example, cadets had been much influenced by the tactical doctrines of Swiss military theorist Antoine Henri de Jomini; but Jomini, who had fought with Napoleon against Spanish guerrillas in 1808–13, disapproved of guerrilla warfare. "The spectacle of a spontaneous uprising of a nation is rarely seen," he cautioned; "and, though there be in it something grand and noble which commands our admiration, the consequences are so terrible that, for the sake of humanity, we ought to hope never to see it." Any cadet who happened upon William Napier's magisterial account of the Peninsular War would have been just as impressed by that British officer's disdain for guerrillas, even despite the fact that the Duke of Wellington had shown the value of properly utilized irregulars. Most other post-Napoleonic military manuals that discussed partisan warfare, including Carl von Clausewitz's *On War*, had been published only in German, French, Italian, and Polish and therefore were largely inaccessible to the army's future Confederate leaders.[26]

Amateur soldiers, however, feared that the products of such an education could jeopardize the Rebel cause. Robert A. Toombs, the Georgia politician, moaned that the conventional army, led by such incompetents, might not survive the first winter of the war. The "epitaph" of the Confederacy, he predicted, would be "died of West Point." Toombs did not necessarily advocate a partisan war, but he did believe that anyone associated with the "old army" was incapable of developing a military strategy audacious enough to achieve victory. Similarly, an Alabama planter warned that the war would not be won by reading books and manuals. "[T]heir contents are known to military men," he pointed out wryly, "and but little good has been the result." *De Bow's Review* pleaded with young army officers not to become "martinets, adopting on all occasions the tactics of the schools, but [to be] ready . . . to pursue . . . [the] partisan method of warfare."[27]

Despite these jabs about book-learning, the West Pointers' theoretical concerns about guerrilla warfare had been validated by their experiences fighting Indians and Mexicans in the antebellum years. Native American warriors in Florida and Texas had long waged guerrilla wars of raids and ambushes on army posts and civilians alike. The Mexicans had fought a conventional war in 1846–48 on most occasions, but they had also used irregular troops. Freshest in memory was the "war" against Juan Cortinas and his Mexican bandits in 1859–60. The U.S. army had mixed success with these varied foes, but in every case American soldiers came to associate guerrilla combat not with the romantic knights of the American Revolution but with peoples thought to be uncivilized. The warlike Comanches and Kiowas of the Texas frontier might have been fierce and courageous, but they were also seen as heathen and barbaric. Robert E. Lee thought them "hideous" and less than human. Nor were "half-civilized" Catholic "greasers" much better in the eyes of many men. Mexican "Guerilleros" were nothing but thieves and cowards, said Lee, "who had not courage to fight . . . lawfully."[28]

Civilians and amateur soldiers, in contrast, warmed to this sort of fighting precisely because it was so ruthless. A no-holds-barred guerrilla contest was what pillaging Yankees and southern Unionists deserved, these Rebels insisted. But while the amateurs were out for blood, most professionals remained restrained by the "rules" and "laws" of war, especially as impressed upon them by their heroes and mentors. Chief among these was Winfield Scott. "He is a great man," Lee asserted during the Mexican War. "Confident in his powers & resources, his judgement is as sound as his heart is bold and daring." No wonder, then, that Lee's opinion of guerrillas closely reflected Scott's views. The "atrocious bands called guerillas or rancheros," who "violate[d] every rule of warfare observed by civilized nations," wrote Scott of Mexican irregulars, were no better than thugs and murderers and should be given no quarter when captured.[29]

Jefferson Davis, the central figure in determining Confederate military policy, shared Lee's prejudices. Davis, too, had been educated at West Point; and, while he had not followed the career of a professional soldier, he had been battle-tested in Mexico. The "guerilleros," Davis believed, were scavengers and thieves that no true soldier should emulate. The Confederate president had been influenced not by Scott but by his own father-in-law, Zachary Taylor: "Fuss and Feathers" had crossed military and political paths with "Old Rough and Ready" too often for Davis to think highly of Lee's hero. Yet on the issue of guerrillas, at least, the two older men agreed. Taylor also counted guerrilla warfare as "barbarism," and he had impressed upon Davis that no soldier's reputation could be enhanced by engaging in that lowly form of combat. To be honorable, insisted Taylor, war must be waged by organized armies. When one of Davis's nephews, Jefferson Davis Bradford, resigned from the Confederate army to raise a partisan band in Louisiana, the president regretted that Bradford had not followed a "path more likely to lead to professional distinction and future promotion."[30]

Conflicting notions of democracy loomed large in all this, from the popular enthusiasm for guerrilla warfare to the leadership's scorn for it. Historians of the Confederacy have long agreed that leaders in both the government and the army were, at the very least, ambivalent about the benefits of democracy. Many seceded states tried to eliminate democratic political and legal initiatives of the antebellum years, even white male suffrage. Some Rebels advocated a monarchy, and John C. Calhoun's fears about the tyranny of the majority had long been a cornerstone of southern political thought. Other Confederates feared the national government reined in democracy too forcefully. It used its considerable power, these critics charged, to bully plain folk and restrict personal liberties—creating the tensions that served as evidence for the original "died of democracy" thesis. Of course, some restriction of individual freedom is almost inevitable in wartime, even in democratic countries. Nations in arms tend to modify whatever democratic or republican tendencies they might otherwise champion, a situation that applied as much to Abraham Lincoln's government as to the one in Richmond. Whatever the depth of the aristocratic or elitist inclinations of Confederate officials, it could only be exaggerated by the threat of invasion and the exigencies of war. Yet Rebel leaders envisioned a Confederacy, even in peacetime, spared of the bumptious, chaotic political culture of the North. They instead would promote a limited democracy and an ordered liberty.[31]

A degree of "barracks-style democracy," as one historian has described it, nevertheless did creep into the army. Tocqueville saw this outcome as inevitable in "democratic armies," and American militia and volunteer soldiers, individualistic and republican to the core, had always insisted on carrying their civilian rights of self-governance into the military world. Most notoriously, the Confederate government allowed enlisted men to elect company officers, a practice that alarmed professional soldiers. "I have seen a company rendered inefficient for months because of the opportunity of exercising the elective franchise in the choice of a lieutenant," fumed one officer. Still, aristocratic principles eventually prevailed, just as they did in the political world. The officer corps insisted on order and discipline, largely as a matter of military necessity, but also because their social prejudices had conditioned them to keep a wary eye on the middle- and lower-class citizens who served in the ranks. And if men in the conventional armies had to be held in check, how much greater the need to control independent guerrilla bands.[32]

It has been suggested by some historians that southern elites, both in and out of the army, feared that to give too large a role to the guerrillas would undermine their own authority, damage the prestige of the ruling class, tarnish southern ideals of honor and manhood, and perhaps even permit backwoodsmen and crackers to take credit for Confederate victory. One need not accept the most extreme of these concerns to appreciate the general anxiety. Virginia's colonial gentry had voiced similar misgivings about the influence of "democratically organized 'Independent Companies of Volunteers'" on traditions of hierarchy and deference in 1776. Similarly, it could not be expected that someone like Robert E. Lee, who had been as appalled by the implications of Jacksonian democracy as by the treacherous military tactics of the Mexicans, would put much faith in a guerrilla-driven people's war. When Rebel leaders complained about the independence, lack of discipline, and unpredictability of guerrillas, they spoke in apprehensive voices.[33]

Despite such strong prejudices, the Davis administration responded belatedly to the spreading guerrilla war, evidently believing it could minimize the peril with no great effort. The government could not hope to—and perhaps did not really want to—prohibit spontaneously formed bands of bushwhackers from harassing Union pickets or ambushing small patrols, but it did intend to neutralize those bands that volunteered officially for Confederate service. Needing to muster as many able-bodied men as possible, the War Department accepted volunteer companies for guerrilla service as long as they had the minimum number of sixty-four men, furnished their own weapons, and enlisted for twelve months. These conditions alone, especially the last one, caused many potential units to disband. Even more importantly—and revealingly—the government nearly always refused to grant these companies the "independent" status they sought. Volunteers had to serve where and how they were needed, which precluded the sort of freewheeling operations envisioned by most of the men. Davis told a potential guerrilla captain in mid-June 1861 that his company would not be accepted "if the term guerilla implies independent operations." The War Department informed another group that they would be "attached to a command deemed proper by the Government. . . . [A]n Independent Company is altogether inadmissible."[34]

When the number of requests for guerrilla service became unmanageable, and as more bands sought permission to operate exclusively in their own communities, Congress passed an act "for local defense and special service" in August 1861. The act did not mention "guerrillas" specifically, but everyone understood its intent. President Davis would have the power to accept "volunteers of such kind" as might be needed "for the defense of exposed places or localities" and for "such special service" as he deemed "expedient." This and similar legislation gave cavalry regiments operating under men like Turner Ashby and John Hunt Morgan "large discretionary powers" to drive out Union invaders. Davis and the War Department hoped this endorsement would settle the matter. They would allow limited guerrilla activity without calling it such.[35]

Still, numerous local guerrilla bands continued to operate without the government's permission, and their rough-and-tumble style brought the issue to a head. Federal authorities soon protested the lawless behavior of guerrillas, in part because they, like their Confederate counterparts, genuinely abhorred this style of warfare, but also because Rebel irregulars could be terribly effective. Chaos reigned wherever they gained a foothold, and Federal commanders started to retaliate. Confronted with rampaging guerrillas in western Virginia in June 1861, General George B. McClellan ordered that they be "dealt with in their persons and property according to the severest rules of military law."[36]

While McClellan's threats remained somewhat vague, his counterparts in the Trans-Mississippi, including John C. Fremont, Henry W. Halleck, and John Pope, imposed martial law in Missouri. Here, announced the western generals, citizens would pay for any damage inflicted on Federal property by bushwhackers in their neighborhoods. People who assisted guerrillas would have their own property confiscated or be forced to house, clothe, and feed Unionists who had been driven from their communities. Suspected guerrillas would be courtmartialed; if found guilty, they would be shot. By the end of 1861 an exasperated Halleck finally declared that guerrillas were simply "murderers, robbers, and thieves," subject to execution without trial. The U.S. army had adopted similar policies when combating the "inconclusive, unpopular guerrilla combat" of Native Americans, and Taylor and Scott had used like measures in Mexico.[37]

Confederate leaders sputtered in amazement and pointed to the equally disagreeable activities of Kansas jayhawkers, but they could not help but be embarrassed. Enthusiasm for the cause and patriotic fervor were fine, even desirable, but the Confederate government sensed a clear danger in becoming too closely associated with its bushwhacking friends. Guerrilla warfare, if it continued as it had evolved, would undermine Confederate hopes for foreign recognition. The new government, which needed desperately to be accepted abroad as a legitimate state, would be perceived as barbaric rabble, no better than Mexicans or Comanches, and certainly not fit to be recognized as a civilized nation.[38]

Although the Davis government stubbornly refused to apologize for the excesses of Rebel guerrillas, it did reassert its disapproval of irregular operations during the last half of 1861. General Lee informed his subordinates that the recruitment of guerrillas was "not deemed advisable by the President." The War Department warned an Alabamian who had volunteered to raise a partisan company that his men "must conform strictly to the laws and usages of civilized nations." Davis himself declared in early December that, because the Union army was led "by men of military education and experience in war," southerners should anticipate that the conflict would be fought "on a scale of very different proportions than that of the partisan warfare witnessed during the past summer and fall." Secretary of War Judah P. Benjamin, hoping to discourage the flow of letters that still urged guerrilla operations, and perhaps seeking to placate the U.S. government, stated flatly toward the end of the year, "Guerrilla companies are not recognized as part of the military organization of the Confederate States."[39]

As Federal protests and retaliation against guerrillas mounted in early 1862, the Confederate Congress tried to remedy the problem by instituting the Partisan Ranger Act. Introduced in the Senate by Henry C. Burnett of Kentucky as a means of "raising . . . guerrilla companies for the war," this legislation sought to control irregular bands, to spruce up their image, and to eliminate the excesses of unrestricted guerrilla fighting. It gave President Davis exclusive power to commission officers and authorize partisan units. These units, composed only of "such numbers as the President" approved, would "be subject to the same regulations as other soldiers." To discourage indiscriminate looting of private property and to keep the men focused on legitimate military targets, partisans would also receive the monetary value of all "arms and munitions of war captured from the enemy."[40]

But even this proposal, the firmest endorsement given by Confederate leaders to guerrilla warfare, went farther than Davis wanted it to go, and his allies in Congress resisted its passage. Normally a friend of Davis, Burnett broke ranks on this issue because his state teetered dangerously toward total Union domination by April 1862. Anticipating the arguments of opponents, supporters of the bill promised that their government-sponsored partisans would be strictly controlled, "mustered into the regular service," and "held for detached service," but that was not good enough for opponents. Edward Sparrow of Louisiana, who had consulted with Davis about the bill, insisted that the salvation of the nation rested in a large traditional army. Walter Preston of Virginia, a timid legislator who shunned precipitous or radical action, suggested that "[t]he law regulating local defence," under which officers like Ashby and Morgan already operated, was "ample" for supplying irregulars. In any case, Preston added, "All the forces must be subject to the same military laws."[41]

The week-long debate reached its climax when Burnett, while again conceding that the "war must be always carried on by regular army system," insisted that "West-Pointism had already done great injury to the country." Applause erupted from the galleries in response to this challenge, which, in turn, prompted opponents of the bill to insist that the chamber be cleared of spectators. An angry Louis T. Wigfall of Texas, at this time in the war still a Davis supporter, led the opposition, but Alabama's old fire-eater William Lowndes Yancey, who had already become suspicious of the "military dictator" Davis, leaped up to defend the right of the people to voice their opinions. "I approve of the sentiment that 'something should be pardoned to the spirit of liberty,'" he proclaimed. John Bullock Clark, a Missourian who supported partisan bands, defused the situation with a lame joke. The bill passed in late April, although opponents successfully removed a provision that would have paid partisans a bounty of five dollars for every enemy soldier they killed.[42]

Unfortunately, Confederates did not respond to the Ranger Act in the proper spirit. The government had intended to limit the numbers and regulate the operations of guerrillas, but its legislation produced opposite effects. Congress erred by passing the bill at the same time that it established national conscription. Untold numbers of southerners objected to the draft. Men who had not yet joined the army insisted that family or professional considerations compelled them to remain near their homes; volunteers who had already suffered the dangers and hardships of active campaigning resented the fact that conscription extended their enlistments. Both groups saw the Ranger Act as the solution to their woes. While partisans would be governed by the same "regulations" as the rest of the army, potential recruits assumed that they would retain some latitude in how, when, and where they served. Such flexibility made guerrilla service very attractive to conscripts, who joined irregular units rather than serving in the conventional army, and to men already in service whose original enlistments had expired. The government listed the latter group as deserters when they left their old regiments to become partisans, but in truth, these men had only gone off to fight the enemy as they had always wished to engage him. The army reacted in June and July 1862 by prohibiting transfers from volunteer service to partisan units, forbidding eligible conscripts from joining the rangers, and setting the minimum age for partisan service at thirty-five years, but the inherent problems continued.[43]

This old passion for local defense, becoming pervasive in 1862 and 1863, confounded the government's hopes of coordinating the irregulars and employing them as it chose. At the start of the war, with all attention focused on the border, even men from the Deep South had been eager to operate as guerrillas in Virginia and Kentucky. As the war now threatened their own neighborhoods, priorities changed. Colonel William C. Falkner (great-grandfather of the twentieth-century novelist William Faulkner) enlisted an entire regiment of partisans in less than a month to operate in northern Mississippi. Another Mississippian, whose neighborhood was "nearly in the hands of the Federals," announced that he would "abandon the Army" to operate as an independent guerrilla if not allowed to form a partisan band. A Floridian sought permission to organize partisan rangers in defense of Nassau County. "The enemy," he explained, "can at any time come . . . & plunder, steal our . . . cattle & insult our women." General Thomas C. Hindman, when recruiting partisans in the Trans-Mississippi, specified that all his companies would "serve in that part of the district to which they belong[ed]."[44]

The expanding home-front struggle between Unionists and secessionists also heightened concern over local defense. Again, unlike guerrilla companies that had formed in 1861 to confront Federal troops on the border, bands of partisan rangers rallied in 1862 and 1863 to defend their neighborhoods against armed Unionists. A resident of Tazewell County, Virginia, informed the War Department, "[A] guerrilla company [is needed] for the protection of the county, and more particularly for chastising the Union bands, who have become very daring, insolent and troublesome." A North Carolinian reported that the entire western end of his state—an area covering thirteen counties—was "dangerously infested with marauding bands of Tories & Bushwhackers." He volunteered to form a partisan company "to range this particular locality, & keep on the heels of the Bushwhackers." Georgians told Governor Joseph E. Brown that they must be allowed to protect themselves against the "[i]nsurrection or insubordination" of neighborhood tories. "[G]ive us the right of reprisal," urged one man.[45]

By 1863 the Davis government had a real mess on its hands. Efforts to restrict guerrilla service only drove more men to it. Lee complained to the president that the number of men deserting to become partisans "endangered" the future success of his army. The Ranger Act also angered and alienated Lee's men, who resented the license enjoyed by partisans and believed that the government, in limiting access to partisan ranks, had denied them an opportunity to defend their communities. What was more, the supposedly disciplined rangers often behaved as outrageously as common bushwhackers—"more formidable and destructive" to the Confederate people, as an alarmed Secretary of War James A. Seddon decided, than they were to the enemy. The citizens of a Georgia county, for example, petitioned for protection from "so caled Partizan rangers [sic]" who, having organized "in order to keep from the conscript law," were stealing horses and corn from local farmers.[46]

Worse still, the partisan and conscription acts in combination soon produced a third, unanticipated form of guerrilla warfare, perhaps the most destructive of all: outlawry. The original hope of Rebel guerrillas—to injure enemy soldiers and retard the invasion of the South—had been at least partially realized. Even a guerrilla war for community control, while betraying a worrisome tendency to get out of hand, had generally benefited Rebels because of their superior numbers in these local contests. But as guerrilla bands proliferated, as the collapse of law and order affected ever more communities, and as more men deserted the armies or turned against the war, many malcontents—army deserters, genuine outlaws, thieves, and bullies—exploited the upheaval to loot, pillage, murder, and destroy. "The whole country is infested with small squads of these miscreants," reported a Union cavalryman from Tennessee, "belonging to no regular organization & living by plunder." Such bands often claimed to be in service to either the Union or the Confederacy, but that was all a dodge. They subverted the legitimate use of the irregular war and sent the relatively contained pre-1862 guerrilla contest careening out of control.[47]

Some of the most dramatic evidence of the rapidly deteriorating situation could be found in communities where Unionist and secessionist "noncombatants" did battle. Confederate deserters who had become disillusioned by the war, as well as "outliers" who "took to the bush" to avoid conscription, joined existing bands of Unionists or formed their own guerrilla enclaves. Many of these groups only wanted to be left alone, but others aimed brutal attacks at Confederate troops and civilians. In Alabama, as loyal Rebel Thomas B. Cooper complained, bands of tories and deserters who claimed to be "Confederate scouts" scoured the countryside, "stealing horses, driving off cows and calves, robbing, burning & stealing whatever they find valuable." In Virginia one hundred citizens of Lee County reported in October 1862 that a new "species of warfare" had descended upon them. They had become accustomed early in the war to warding off Tennessee and Kentucky Unionists who invaded their county, but now they also faced raids by "bandits." "These marauders are in the mountains all along our border," read their petition for relief, "and they threaten to lay waste by fire & sword our county from Jonesville to Cumberland Gap."[48]

The entire South became infected by this new plague, but North Carolina, with the highest number of deserters from the Confederate army, may have suffered most. Rebel guerrillas in the state had actively engaged local Unionists and dealt with Union invasions from East Tennessee since the start of the war.

However, like the citizens of Lee County, they faced a new threat in the autumn of 1862. "[T]he Western Counties are in danger of being over run by deserters and renegades who by the hundred are taking shelter in the smoky mountains," William H. Thomas, who led a mixed band of Cherokee and white partisans, reported to Governor Zebulon Vance. A Confederate officer similarly observed, "[Deserters] organize in bands, variously estimated at from fifty up to hundreds. . . . These men are not only determined to kill in avoiding apprehension . . . but their esprit de corps extends to killing in revenge." Confederate troops arrived to reinforce home guards and local militia in apprehending or killing these desperadoes (the "massacre" at Shelton Laurel, where soldiers executed thirteen Unionist guerrillas in January 1863, being the most infamous such incident); but Governor Vance saw a larger problem: "The warfare between scattering bodies of irregular troops is conducted on both sides without any regard whatever to the rules of civilized war or the dictates of humanity."[49]

The final and most telling consequence of the Confederacy's people's war was the bitter mood of retaliation it instilled in the military policies of both North and South, beginning in the summer of 1862. Soldiers and the policies that governed them became less restrained and more vindictive, with both the Lincoln and Davis governments contributing to the deterioration. Historians have frequently noted this shift in policy, but they have not fully appreciated the extent to which the guerrilla war, in all its phases, inspired it. As explained earlier, the civility of the war began to sour quite soon in places like Missouri and western Virginia, where Federal commanders first protested the Confederacy's use of guerrillas. The words partisan and ranger in the Ranger Act, as opposed to guerrilla, bushwhacker, or some other pejorative variation, represented a bid for legitimacy by the Rebels, but the North would not buy it. Politicians and generals on both sides became embroiled in a ferocious debate about the rules of war that engaged in incredible flights of rhetoric and exaggeration. The debate eventually ranged far beyond guerrillas to address such issues as deprivations by the traditional armies and the treatment of noncombatants, but the guerrilla war remained the essence of the thing.[50]

The U.S. War Department tried to settle the issue in April 1863 with General Order No. 100, eventually known as the Lieber Code, for the Columbia University law professor—Francis Lieber—who drafted it at the army's request. The directive offered broad guidelines for the treatment of prisoners of war and of the persons and property of noncombatants. Yet it grew from a far more focused policy, recommended by Henry W. Halleck a year earlier, that sought to clarify existing laws governing guerrilla forces. The new rules avoided the word guerrilla altogether, referring to such men, instead, as robbers, pirates, armed prowlers, and war-rebels, and denying them the rights of legitimate soldiers if captured. The order acknowledged only partisans as a lawful part of the enemy's army, and it was extremely vague about their military role. In practice, the Union army acknowledged the right of partisan rangers to disrupt "lines of connection and communication . . . in the rear and on the flanks of the enemy," but this meant the Federals would continue to regard nearly all Rebel guerrillas, including government-sponsored partisans, as outlaws.[51]

Confederate leaders bristled at such arrogance. Did the Federals really think they could dictate how the war would be fought? It was an outrageous presumption, protested Jefferson Davis, as he cited instances where Union troops had behaved far more barbarously than the worst Rebel bushwhackers and irregulars. As the Federals dealt ever more harshly with both guerrillas and the citizens who harbored or assisted them, Davis found himself in the awkward position of defending the guerrilla war he had always deplored. Union retaliation against guerrillas only inspired more ferocious partisan resistance, which, in turn, brought new Federal reprisals, until the entire war—not just the Rebel "people's war"—became something ugly and brutish. "We find ourselves driven by our enemies by steady progress towards a practice which we abhor and which we are vainly struggling to avoid," Davis complained to Lee in July 1862. The Union's "savage war," he continued, fought under the black flag of "no quarter," was forcing the Confederacy to follow suit. The next month, Congress considered "retaliatory measures consistent with the law of nations and the usages of civilized warfare" against the "atrocities and brutal conduct perpetrated by the enemy . . . upon the property and persons of the citizens and soldiers of this Confederacy." The "soldiers" now included partisans.[52]

And so the sheer violence unleashed by this multifaceted guerrilla struggle became a crippling liability for the Confederacy in two ways. First, it injured public support for the government and the Confederate cause. By 1864, and far sooner in some places, people had lost confidence that the government could protect them against Unionist guerrillas, brigands, Federal soldiers, or even their own partisans. In Missouri, which had suffered the longest, one resident lamented, "I behold a fearful sight. People of every political opinion and all ages, fleeing from their homes. The guerillas prowling into the country and the

Federals ravaging towns. Murder, arson of daily occurrence. Fights rendered horrible by their ferocity. No quarter being given, no mercy shown. It is horrible." Elsewhere, people reflected that the entire South seemed in danger of becoming "one vast Missouri," with "a protracted guerilla war as the condition of final successes."[53]

Second, the Union army's new retaliatory policy against civilians, based to a significant extent on its experience against Rebel guerrillas, led to a sweeping Federal offensive strategy that devastated the South. The new policy has been characterized in many ways—as total war, absolute war, destructive war, hard war, relentless war, and Davis's "savage war" could apply as well—but by whatever name, it evolved into a coordinated strategy of exhaustion against Confederate armies and resources in 1864–65 that wore out the Rebels to the point of surrender. William T. Sherman's destructive Georgia campaign, David Hunter and Philip H. Sheridan's devastation of the Shenandoah Valley, and numerous deadly cavalry raids through Virginia, Alabama, and Mississippi formed part of the new design that bore a striking resemblance to the North's earlier counter-guerrilla operations. More than that, the new strategic policy was fashioned and directed by the same men who had retaliated during the first half of the war against Rebel guerrillas and the civilian communities that harbored them. Sherman, Hunter, and Sheridan, not to forget Ulysses S. Grant and Henry Halleck, who together directed all Union armies by 1864, were among those commanders who had faced formidable guerrilla opposition in Missouri, Kentucky, western Tennessee, northern Mississippi, and northern Arkansas, and along western rivers.[54]

By then, the Confederate government had already cut its losses in the partisan war. The possibility of reining in the rangers by placing them more directly under the control of local military commanders had been debated as early as August 1862, and Congress finally repealed the Ranger Act in February 1864. Lee and his generals played no small role in the latter action. In January 1864 they advised President Davis that even formal partisan bands lacked "order" and "discipline," and Lee told James Seddon point-blank, "I recommend that the law authorizing these partisan corps be abolished. The evils resulting from their organization more than counterbalance the good they accomplish." Seddon, who had been the administration's most vocal critic of the partisan system, drafted the legislation and had the influential South Carolina congressman William Porcher Miles, who always backed the president's military policies, submit it to

Congress. Some debate followed, but even most early congressional supporters of partisan warfare had come to fear its unpredictable tendencies. Lee expressed relief: "Experience has convinced me that it is almost impossible . . . to have discipline in these bands of partisan rangers, or to prevent them from becoming an injury instead of a benefit to the service."[55]

Not that abolishing the rangers did any good. Dozens of guerrilla bands ignored the edict. The internal war of neighbor versus neighbor, not to mention swarming bands of deserters and outlaws, disrupted the southern home front for the remainder of the war. Indeed, some of those bands would be the last Confederates to surrender. Some scholars have argued that Jefferson Davis finally intended to wage a guerrilla war when he announced in April 1865 that the Confederate nation had "entered upon a new phase" of its struggle; but given his wartime experiences, this seems doubtful. Virtually every member of his cabinet advised him against it. Besides, guerrillas cannot win wars single-handedly. Guerrilla movements—returning to where this discussion began—are born of the people they serve. Irregulars must have the active support of the civilian population to survive, and most Confederate civilians appear to have lost their stomach for war by the spring of 1865.[56]

So if it can be said that the Confederacy died of democracy, its death must be attributed in some part to the disruptive force of the guerrilla war. Whether or not the Rebel government could ever have controlled its lethal power is problematic. One authority believes that even within a single state, Missouri, the irregular war became so confused and contradictory that the government could establish no viable policy.[57] Many common folk decided early in the conflict that guerrilla warfare suited their inclinations and needs, but they ran up against the hard realities of military doctrine, class bias, and political priorities. Democracy ran amok when the guerrilla war, despite the government's efforts to control it, generated lethal mutations and inspired a Union policy of retaliation that helped to destroy the Confederacy from within and without.

NOTES

This article was previously published in the *Journal of Southern History* 68, no. 2 (May 2002): 259–92. The attention paid to Civil War guerrillas since the original publication of this essay has been extensive. The author himself followed up seven years later with the first comprehensive look at the guerrilla war in *A Savage Conflict: The Decisive Role of Guerrilla in the American Civil*

War (Chapel Hill: University of North Carolina Press, 2009). However, other scholars have also begun to look at ways in which irregular warfare shaped the course of events. Having previously focused largely on single states or communities, or on the activities of particular guerrilla bands and prominent leaders, they have, for the past decade, looked more often at regions of the South, or compared guerrilla operations in one state with those in other places. They have scrutinized more carefully the motivations of guerrillas and how the guerrilla conflict affected government policies, legislation, southern loyalties, the rules of war, the legal system, and a host of related issues. Guerrillas have even begun to receive their due in surveys of the war. Of course, Sutherland's essay alone did not produce this changed perspective, but it did contribute to a growing awareness that the full story of the war had yet to be told. The author would like to thank Stephen V. Ash, Benjamin Franklin Cooling, Michael Fellman, Noel C. Fisher, Perry D. Jamieson, and the anonymous reviewers for the *Journal of Southern History* for their helpful comments and suggestions. He also wishes to thank the National Endowment for the Humanities and the Fulbright College of Arts and Sciences, University of Arkansas, Fayetteville, for their financial support of his research.

1. David Donald, "Died of Democracy," in David Donald, ed., *Why the North Won the Civil War* (Baton Rouge: Louisiana State University Press, 1960), 77–90; Richard E. Beringer, Herman Hattaway, Archer Jones, and William N. Still Jr., *Why the South Lost the Civil War* (Athens: University of Georgia Press, 1986), 7–8, 356. Frank Lawrence Owsley, "Local Defense and the Overthrow of the Confederacy: A Study in State Rights," *Mississippi Valley Historical Review* 11 (March 1925): 490–525, which served as Donald's point of departure, actually hit close to the mark, but Owsley still saw the conflict between government and individual as largely political. Useful summaries of current historiographical thinking on this issue—although the epicenter of the debate has shifted from "democracy" to questions of social class and nationalism—may be found in Bradley G. Bond, "Southern State and Local Politics," 494–504, and Bill Cecil-Fronsman, "Southern Social Conditions," 530–43, both in Steven E. Woodworth, ed., *The American Civil War: A Handbook of Literature and Research* (Westport, CT: Greenwood Press, 1996); and in Emory M. Thomas, "Rebellion and Conventional Warfare: Confederate Strategy and Military Policy," 36–59, and James L. Roark, "Confederate Economy and Society," 201–27, both in James M. McPherson and William J. Cooper Jr., eds., *Writing the Civil War: The Quest to Understand* (Columbia: University of South Carolina Press, 1998).

2. Piers Mackesy, "What the British Army Learned," in Ronald Hoffman and Peter J. Albert, eds., *Arms and Independence: The Military Character of the American Revolution* (Charlottesville: University Press of Virginia, 1984), 197–99, discusses the eighteenth-century European fascination with "natural man" as the embodiment of *la petite guerre*, or "little war," an expression generally meant to imply guerrilla warfare. See, too, Michael Fellman, *Inside War: The Guerrilla Conflict in Missouri During the American Civil War* (New York: Oxford University Press, 1989), vi. This preference for guerrilla warfare was based largely on experience, as opposed to a scientific study of the issue. Yet the conduct of the Confederacy's guerrilla war—and Union responses to it—closely paralleled the strategies advocated by modern military writings on this subject, including those by such diverse authorities as Charles E. Callwell, T. E. Lawrence, Mao Tse-tung, and Che Guevara. Two good modern reviews of the literature are John Ellis, *From the Barrel of a Gun: A History of Guerrilla, Revolutionary and Counter-Insurgency Warfare, from the Romans to the Present* (Mechanicsburg, PA: Stackpole Books, 1995); and Anthony James Joes, *Guerrilla Conflict before the Cold War* (Westport, CT: Praeger Press, 1996). It should be stressed that not every "people's war" is necessarily waged

as a guerrilla war, and certainly not every one is based on democratic values. See John M. Gates, "People's War in Vietnam," *Journal of Military History* 54 (July 1990): 327–29. For the perspective of Alexis de Tocqueville, see *Democracy in America,* ed. by Phillips Bradley (2 vols., New York: A. A. Knopf, 1945), vol. 2, book 2, chap. 1.

3. Other scholars have pointed to this tug-of-war in Confederate thinking, but no one has fully explored its origins, complexities, and implications. See, for example, Robert L. Kerby, "Why the Confederacy Lost," *Review of Politics* 35 (July 1973): 326–45; Fellman, *Inside War,* 97–112; and B. Franklin Cooling, "A People's War: Partisan Conflict in Tennessee and Kentucky," in Daniel E. Sutherland, ed., *Guerrillas, Unionists, and Violence on the Confederate Home Front* (Fayetteville: University of Arkansas Press, 1999), 113–32. For the debate over guerrilla warfare as a viable Confederate military option see Gary W. Gallagher, *The Confederate War* (Cambridge, MA: Harvard University Press,1997), 120–27.

4. Our modern appreciation of the guerrilla war began with Phillip Shaw Paludan, *Victims: A True Story of the Civil War* (Knoxville: University of Tennessee Press, 1981), and Fellman, *Inside War.* For an analysis of this considerable literature see Daniel E. Sutherland, "Sideshow No Longer: A Historiographical Review of the Guerrilla War," *Civil War History* 46 (March 2000): 5–23.

5. *The War of the Rebellion: A Compilation of the Official Records of the Union and Confederate Armies* (70 vols. in 128, Washington, DC, 1880–1901), ser. 4, vol. 1: 415 (first and second quotations), 475 (third and fourth quotations), 505 (fifth quotation), 506 (sixth quotation); hereinafter cited as *Official Records*; A. O. W. Latter to Isham G. Harris, June 14, 1861, Isham G. Harris Papers, Papers of the Governors of Tennessee, Tennessee State Library and Archives, Nashville (seventh and eighth quotations).

6. Duane Allan Smith, "The Confederate Cause in the Colorado Territory, 1861–1865," *Civil War History* 7 (March 1961): 71–75; Daniel Ellis Conner, *A Confederate in the Colorado Gold Fields,* ed. Donald J. Berthrong and Odessa Davenport (Norman: University of Oklahoma Press, 1970), 145, 162–63; Morris F. Taylor, "Confederate Guerrillas in Southern Colorado," *Colorado Magazine* 46 (Fall 1969): 304–23; Leo P. Kibby, "Some Aspects of California's Military Problems During the Civil War," *Civil War History* 5 (September 1959): 253–57; *Official Records,* ser. 1, vol. 50, pt. 1: 590 (quotations).

7. Dickson D. Bruce Jr., *Violence and Culture in the Antebellum South* (Austin: University of Texas Press, 1979), 3–20, 89–113, 196–211; Elliott J. Gorn, "'Gouge and Bite, Pull Hair and Scratch': The Social Significance of Fighting in the Southern Backcountry," *American Historical Review* 90 (February 1985): 18–43; Grady McWhiney, *Cracker Culture: Celtic Ways in the Old South* (Tuscaloosa: University of Alabama Press, 1988), 146–70; David T. Courtwright, *Violent Land: Single Men and Social Disorder from the Frontier to the Inner City* (Cambridge, MA: Harvard University Press, 1996), 26–49; Richard Maxwell Brown, *Strain of Violence: Historical Studies of American Violence and Vigilantism* (New York: Oxford University Press, 1975), 98–103, and "Western Violence: Structure, Values, Myth," *Western Historical Quarterly* 24 (February 1993): 6–7 (quotation on 6); Gary L. Cheatham, "'Desperate Characters': The Development and Impact of the Confederate Guerrillas in Kansas," *Kansas History* 14 (Autumn 1991): 144–61; Albert Castel, *Civil War Kansas: Reaping the Whirlwind* (Lawrence: University Press of Kansas, 1997), 37–64; Kristen A. Tegtmeier, "The Ladies of Lawrence Are Arming! The Gendered Nature of Sectional Violence in Early Kansas," in John R. McKivigan and Stanley Harrold, eds., *Antislavery Violence: Sectional, Racial, and Cultural Conflict in Antebellum America* (Knoxville: University of Tennessee Press, 1999), 215–35. This tendency toward

violence should not be confused with the frequently mentioned "martial spirit" of the South. The two are not the same, and in any case, historians have fairly well qualified the supposed prevalence of southern militarism. See Bruce, *Violence and Culture in the Antebellum South*, 161–77, and R. Don Higginbotham, "The Martial Spirit in the Antebellum South: Some Further Speculations in a National Context," *Journal of Southern History* 58 (February 1992): 3–26.

8. Edward Conrad Smith, *The Borderland in the Civil War* (New York: Macmillan Co., 1927), 367; Benjamin Franklin Cooling, *Fort Donelson's Legacy: War and Society in Kentucky and Tennessee, 1862–1863* (Knoxville: University of Tennessee Press, 1997), 67–69; Noel C. Fisher, *War at Every Door: Partisan Politics and Guerrilla Violence in East Tennessee, 1860–1869* (Chapel Hill: University of North Carolina Press, 1997), 41–3; John F. Marszalek, ed., *The Diary of Miss Emma Holmes, 1861–1866* (Baton Rouge: Louisiana State University Press, 1979), 35; Levi W. Lawler to Leroy Pope Walker, June 17, 1861, in Letters Received by the Confederate Secretary of War, War Department Collection of Confederate Records, Record Group 109, Microform 437 (National Archives, Washington, DC), reel 4, frame 286 (first quotation), hereinafter cited as RG 109, M-437; William James Smith to Walker, June 3, 1861, RG 109, M-437, reel 3, frame 472 (second and third quotations). For other offers of service see I. W. Garrott to Walker, June 5, 1861, reel 3, frame 1110–11; J. T. Kirby to Jefferson Davis, June 7, 1861, reel 3, frame 1174; Stephen H. Rushing to Walker, May 30, 1861, reel 3, frame 1038; and D. M. Washington to Davis, May 19, 1861, reel 2, frame 1273; all in RG 109, M-437.

9. Donald Walter Curl, ed., "A Report from Baltimore," *Maryland Historical Magazine* 64 (Fall 1969): 281 (first quotation); Anna Bradford Agle and Sidney H. Wanzer, eds., "Dearest Braddie: Love and War in Maryland, 1860–61, Part 1," *Maryland Historical Magazine* 88 (Spring 1993): 83, 86 (second quotation); Lynda Lasswell Crist et al., eds., *The Papers of Jefferson Davis* (10 vols. to date, Baton Rouge: Louisiana State University Press, 1971–), vol. 7: 188 (Reynolds quotations).

10. William Kauffman Scarborough, ed., *The Diary of Edmund Ruffin 2: The Years of Hope: April, 1861–June, 1863* (Baton Rouge: Louisiana State University Press, 1976), 51–52 (quotation on 52).

11. Mary C. Simms Oliphant et al., eds., *The Letters of William Gilmore Simms* (6 vols., Columbia: University of South Carolina Press, 1952–82), vol. 4: 364 (first, second, and third quotations), 369 (fourth and fifth quotations). Interestingly, antebellum abolitionists sometimes invoked the image of the "savage" Indian warrior in their "war" against slavery. See John Stauffer, "Advent among the Indians: The Revolutionary Ethos of Gerrit Smith, James McCune Smith, Frederick Douglas, and John Brown," in McKivigan and Harrold, eds., *Antislavery Violence*, 236–73.

12. *Little Rock Arkansas True Democrat*, July 18, 1861, p. 2, col. 6; "Irrepressibles" notice in Folder 158, Ruffin, Roulhac, and Hamilton Family Papers #643 (Southern Historical Collection, Wilson Library, University of North Carolina at Chapel Hill; hereinafter cited as SHC); George Fitzhugh, "The Times and the War," *De Bow's Review* 32 (July 1861): 2–3.

13. Emory M. Thomas, *The Confederacy as a Revolutionary Experience* (Englewood Cliffs, NJ: Prentice-Hall, 1971), 1, 44–46; Robert F. Durden, "The American Revolution as Seen by Southerners in 1861," *Louisiana History* 19 (Winter 1978): 33–42; George C. Rable, *The Confederate Republic: A Revolution against Politics* (Chapel Hill: University of North Carolina Press, 1994), 44–48; William C. Davis, *"A Government of Our Own": The Making of the Confederacy* (New York: Free Press, 1994), 83; Jon L. Wakelyn, ed., *Southern Pamphlets on Secession, November 1860–April 1861* (Chapel Hill: University of North Carolina Press, 1996), 114, 177, 327; Dwight Lowell Dumond, ed., *Southern Editorials on Secession* (New York: Century Co., 1931), 505 (first quotation), 507 (second and third quotations), 515.

14. J. B. Jones, *A Rebel War Clerk's Diary at the Confederate States Capital* (2 vols., Philadelphia: Lippincott, 1866), vol. 1: 87 (first quotation; emphasis in original); Robert K. Wright Jr., "'Nor Is Their Standing Army to Be Despised': The Emergence of the Continental Army as a Military Institution," in Hoffman and Albert, eds., *Arms and Independence*, 50–74; Charles C. Jones Jr. to Mrs. C. C. Jones, April 8, 1862, in Robert Manson Myers, ed., *The Children of Pride: A True Story of Georgia and the Civil War* (New Haven, CT: Yale University Press, 1972), 872 (second and third quotations); Cooling, *Fort Donelson's Legacy*, 65–69. Cooling notes the mixed inheritance that pushed southerners toward a "people's war," although his starting point is Carl von Clausewitz's strategic framework of "the People in Arms" (xi–xv; quotation on xi).

15. Modem historians of British America have also stressed the democratic nature of the colonial minutemen's frequent clashes with the authoritarian elites that controlled the militia, as well as the negative British response to partisan warfare and the fragmentation of irregular war. The similarities of these aspects of the colonial story to the 1860s are striking. Mark V. Kwasny, *Washington's Partisan War, 1775–1783* (Kent, OH: Kent State University Press, 1996), xi–xv; Clyde R. Ferguson, "Functions of the Partisan-Militia in the South During the American Revolution: An Interpretation," in W. Robert Higgins, ed., *The Revolutionary War in the South: Power, Conflict, and Leadership: Essays in Honor of John Richard Alden* (Durham, NC: Duke University Press, 1979), 239–58; Charles Royster, *Light-Horse Harry Lee and the Legacy of the American Revolution* (New York: Knopf, 1981), 20–39; Don Higginbotham, "Military Leadership in the American Revolution," 84–105, esp. 90–91, "The American Militia: A Traditional Institution with Revolutionary Responsibilities," 106–31, esp. 114–15, 118–23, and "Reflections on the War of Independence, Modem Guerrilla Warfare, and the War in Vietnam," 153–73, all in Higginbotham, *War and Society in Revolutionary America: The Wider Dimensions of Conflict* (Columbia: University of South Carolina Press, 1988). For the rambunctious nature of colonial minutemen and the "internal" guerrilla war that erupted on the Revolutionary home front, especially in the South, see Hoffman and Albert, eds., *Arms and Independence*; Ronald Hoffman, Thad W. Tate, and Peter J. Albert, eds., *An Uncivil War: The Southern Backcountry during the American Revolution* (Charlottesville: University Press of Virginia, 1985); John Shy, *A People Numerous and Armed: Reflections on the Military Struggle for American Independence* (rev. ed., Ann Arbor: University of Michigan Press, 1990); and Michael A. McDonnell, "Popular Mobilization and Political Culture in Revolutionary Virginia: The Failure of the Minutemen and the Revolution from Below," *Journal of American History* 85 (December 1998): 946–81. Proslavery and antislavery forces in Kansas had similarly appealed to the traditions of the Revolution during their guerrilla war of the 1850s. See Michael Fellman, "Rehearsal for the Civil War: Antislavery and Proslavery at the Fighting Point in Kansas, 1854–1856," in Lewis Perry and Michael Fellman, eds., *Antislavery Reconsidered: New Perspectives on the Abolitionists* (Baton Rouge: Louisiana State University Press, 1979), 297–98, 301–7.

16. C. Hugh Holman, *The Roots of Southern Writing: Essays on the Literature of the American South* (Athens: University of Georgia Press, 1972), 16 (quotation), 76; William Gilmore Simms, *The Life of Francis Marion* (Boston, 1856); Simms, *The Partisan: A Tale of the Revolution* (New York, 1835); Karen A. Endres, "Mary Moragne's *The British Partizan*," in James B. Meriwether, ed., *South Carolina Women Writers* (Spartanburg: University of South Carolina, 1979), 27–39; Nathaniel Beverley Tucker, *The Partisan Leader: A Tale of the Future*, introd. C. Hugh Holman (Chapel Hill: University of North Carolina Press, 1971), vii–xxiii, esp. xix; Carla Waal, "The First Original Confederate Drama: The Guerrillas," *Virginia Magazine of History and Biography* 70 (October 1962):

459–67. For a few of the many examples of guerrilla-inspired poetry see Henry Timrod, "A Cry to Arms," 49–51, and S. Teackle Wallis, "The Guerrillas," 146–49, in William Gilmore Simms, ed., *War Poetry of the South* (New York: Richardson & Co., 1867); "The Mountain Partisan," in H. M. Wharton, comp., *War Songs and Poems of the Southern Confederacy, 1861–1865* (Philadelphia: John C. Winston Co., 1904), 275–76; and William Gilmore Simms, "The Guerrilla Martyrs," in Esther Parker Ellinger, *The Southern War Poetry of the Civil War* (1918; New York: B. Franklin, 1970), 102.

17. Mark Grimsley, *The Hard Hand of War: Union Military Policy Toward Southern Civilians, 1861–1865* (Cambridge, UK: Cambridge University Press, 1995), 18–19; Charles C. Jones Jr. to Rev. C. C. Jones, November 27, 1861, in Myers, ed., *The Children of Pride*, 804 (first quotation); Jay Monaghan, *Swamp Fox of the Confederacy: The Life and Military Services of M. Jeff Thompson* (Tuscaloosa, AL: Confederate Pub. Co., 1956); M. J. Solomons scrapbook, Rare Book, Manuscript, and Special Collections Library, Duke University, Durham, NC, p. 85 (second quotation); Marszalek, ed., *Diary of Miss Emma Holmes*, 164 (third quotation); E. E. Kidd to Jefferson Davis, June 1, 1861, reel 3, frames 1078–79 (fourth quotation), G. B. Latigue to Leroy Pope Walker, June 21, 1861, reel 4, frames 235–36 (fifth quotation), and H. V. Keep to Walker, July 15, 1861, reel 5, frames 623–24 (sixth quotation), all in RG 109, M-437; Zack C. Waters, "Florida's Confederate Guerrillas: John W. Pearson and the Oklawaha Rangers," *Florida Historical Quarterly* 70 (October 1991): 133–9.

18. David Paul Smith, *Frontier Defense in the Civil War: Texas' Rangers and Rebels* (College Station: Texas A&M University Press, 1992), 3–20, 57–58 (first quotation); *Official Records*, ser. 1, vol. 4: 115–16 (second and third quotations); Solomons scrapbook, p. 60 (fourth and fifth quotations); Thomas W. Cutrer, *Ben McCulloch and the Frontier Military Tradition* (Chapel Hill: University of North Carolina Press, 1993), 257–61; Scarborough, ed., *Diary of Edmund Ruffin* 2: 60, 62, 65; Crist et al., eds., *Papers of Jefferson Davis* 7: 219; B. F. Terry to P. G. T. Beauregard, July 2, 1861, reel 4, frame 1064, A. H. Cafiedo to Leroy Pope Walker, April 30, 1861, reel 2, frame 681 (sixth quotation), William D. O'Daniel to Jefferson Davis, June 17, 1861, reel 4, frame 513, all in RG 109, M-437; C. W. Raines, ed., *Six Decades in Texas, or Memoirs of Francis Richard Lubbock* (Austin, TX: B. C. Jones & Co., 1900), 314–17, 324–25; Dumond, ed., *Southern Editorials on Secession*, 513 (seventh quotation).

19. Fellman, *Inside War*, vi (first quotation); Robert L. Kerby, *Kirby Smith's Confederacy: The Trans-Mississippi South, 1863–1865* (New York: Columbia University Press, 1972), 46; George T. Maddox, *Hard Trials and Tribulations of an Old Confederate Soldier* (Van Buren, AR: Argus Office, 1897), 11–12 (second quotation); Joseph M. Bailey, "Memoirs of Captain J. M. Bailey," typescript, Special Collections Division, University of Arkansas Libraries, Fayetteville; Drury Connally to Ann Kilgore Connally, June 28, 1862, War Letters of Drury Connally, Trans-Mississippi Research Group Collection, Special Collections Division, University of Arkansas Libraries, Fayetteville (third quotation); Daniel E. Sutherland, "Guerrillas: The Real War in Arkansas," in Anne J. Bailey and Daniel E. Sutherland, eds., *Civil War Arkansas: Beyond Battles and Leaders* (Fayetteville: University of Arkansas Press, 2000), 136.

20. Crist et al., eds., *Papers of Jefferson Davis* 9: 10 (first quotation); R. H. Williams, *With the Border Ruffians: Memories of the Far West, 1852–1868*, ed. E. W. Williams (New York: Dutton, 1907), 303 (second quotation). This stated desire to defend homes and families supports the "relative deprivation" theory of Don R. Bowen, "Guerrilla War in Western Missouri, 1862–1865: Historical Extensions of the Relative Deprivation Hypothesis," *Comparative Studies in Society and History* 19 (January 1977): 30–51, although Bowen's emphasis on prosperous, slaveholding families would not fit all parts of the South. Stephen V. Ash, *Middle Tennessee Society Transformed, 1860–1870: War*

and Peace in the Upper South (Baton Rouge: Louisiana State University Press, 1988), 148–51, also stresses the role of guerrillas as protectors of their neighborhoods. Here, too, is where Owsley's emphasis on "local defense" provides some insight, although by stressing the efforts of the states to hoard arms and raise "regular" troops, Owsley misses the vital role assigned to individuals in irregular forces. For example, in looking at Arkansas, he cites the pages of a report that emphasized the struggle between Richmond and Little Rock over control of troops in the state, but he fails to consider the section of that same report devoted to the operations of Confederate guerrillas. Compare Owsley, "Local Defense and the Overthrow of the Confederacy," 501–2, to *Official Records,* ser. 1, vol. 13: 29–32 and 33–36.

21. Phillip S. Paludan, "The American Civil War Considered as a Crisis in Law and Order," *American Historical Review* 77 (October 1972): 1013–34; Sarah Ann Tillinghast to brother, July 31, 1863, Tillinghast Family Papers, Rare Book, Manuscript, and Special Collections Library, Duke University, Durham, N.C. (quotation). For the case of the American Revolution see the following essays in Hoffman et al., eds., *An Uncivil War*: Jeffrey J. Crow, "Liberty Men and Loyalists: Disorder and Disaffection in the North Carolina Backcountry," 125–78; Emory G. Evans, "Trouble in the Backcountry: Disaffection in Southwest Virginia during the American Revolution," 179–212; and Edward J. Cashin, "'But Brothers, It Is Our Land We Are Talking About': Winners and Losers in the Georgia Backcountry," 240–75. For a band of Unionist guerrillas who thought in similar terms see Kenneth C. Barnes, "The Williams Clan: Mountain Farmers and Union Fighters in North Central Arkansas," in Bailey and Sutherland, eds., *Civil War Arkansas,* 155–75.

22. Fellman, *Inside War,* 52–54, 62–65, 138–39, 184–92; Charles W. Andrews to Anna Robinson, June 23, [1861], Charles Wesley Andrews Papers, Rare Book, Manuscript, and Special Collections Library, Duke University, Durham, N.C. (first quotation); James E. Love to Molly, August 28, 1862, James Edwin Love Papers, Missouri Historical Society, St. Louis; *Cincinnati Times,* September 18, 1861, quoted in Richard O. Curry and F. Gerald Ham, eds., "The Bushwhackers' War: Insurgency and Counter-Insurgency in West Virginia," *Civil War History* 10 (December 1964): 418 (second quotation).

23. Fellman, *Inside War,* 176 (first quotation); Stephen V. Ash, *When the Yankees Came: Conflict and Chaos in the Occupied South, 1861–1865* (Chapel Hill: University of North Carolina Press, 1995), 125–27, 129–30; the several essays in Kenneth W. Noe and Shannon H. Wilson, eds., *The Civil War in Appalachia: Collected Essays* (Knoxville: University of Tennessee Press, 1997), and in Sutherland, ed., *Guerrillas, Unionists, and Violence on the Confederate Home Front*; "Discussion of Jayhawkers," Dandridge McRae Papers, Arkansas History Commission and State Archives, Little Rock (second quotation). The theme of community control is most consistently applied outside the border states by Jonathan Dean Sarris in "'Hellish Deeds . . . in a Christian Land': Southern Mountain Communities at War, 1861–1865," Ph.D. dissertation, University of Georgia, 1998.

24. Fellman, *Inside War,* 97–112, offers an insightful description of the ambivalence displayed by Confederate leaders about the war in Missouri.

25. William B. Skelton, *An American Profession of Arms: The Army Officer Corps, 1784–1861* (Lawrence: University Press of Kansas, 1992), 167–72; Russell F. Weigley, *The Age of Battles: The Quest for Decisive Warfare from Breitenfeld to Waterloo* (Bloomington: Indiana University Press, 1991), 538; Bruce Allardice, "West Points of the Confederacy: Southern Military Schools and the Confederate Army," *Civil War History* 43 (December 1997): 310–31; Higginbotham, "Martial Spirit in the Antebellum South," 16–19, 24–25; John K. Mahon, *History of the Militia and the National Guard* (New York: Macmillan Press, 1983), 78–96.

26. Antoine Henri de Jomini, *The Art of War*, trans. G. H. Mendell and W. P. Craighill (Philadelphia, 1862), 29 (quotation); W. F. P. Napier, *History of the War in the Peninsula and in the South of France* (6 vols., New York: F. Warne 1828–40); Jay Luvaas, *The Education of an Army: British Military Thought, 1815–1940* (Chicago: University of Chicago Press, 1964), 24–26; Beringer et al., *Why the South Lost the Civil War*, 39–52; Herman Hattaway and Archer Jones, *How the North Won: A Military History of the Civil War* (Urbana: University of Illinois Press, 1983), 12–14, 21–24. For samples of antebellum military manuals and memoirs that treated guerrilla warfare see Walter Laqueur, ed., *The Guerrilla Reader: A Historical Anthology* (New York: New American Library, 1977), 13–96; and Gerard Chaliand, ed., *The Art of War in World History: From Antiquity to the Nuclear Age* (Berkeley: University of California Press, 1994), 653–70. Christopher Bassford, *Clausewitz in English: The Reception of Clausewitz in Britain and America, 1815–1945* (New York: Oxford University Press, 1994), 50–57, challenges the old assumption that Clausewitz was unknown to antebellum Americans, but he acknowledges that the evidence is, at best, inconclusive. In any event, Clausewitz concluded his observations on guerrilla warfare, written in 1832, with this admission: "This discussion has been less an objective analysis than a groping for the truth. The reason is that this sort of warfare is not as yet very common" (*On War*, ed. and trans. Michael Howard and Peter Paret [Princeton, NJ: Princeton University Press, 1976], 483).

27. Ulrich B. Phillips, ed., "The Correspondence of Robert Toombs, Alexander H. Stephens, and Howell Cobb," in *Annual Report of the American Historical Association for the Year 1911* (2 vols., Washington, DC, 1913), vol. 2: 577 (first quotation), 628 (second quotation); Crist et al., eds., *Papers of Jefferson Davis* 9: 212 (third quotation); Fitzhugh, "The Times and the War," 2 (fourth quotation).

28. John M. Gates, "Indians and Insurrectos: The US Army's Experience with Insurgency," *Parameters: Journal of the U.S. Army War College* 13 (March 1983): 59–68; Emory M. Thomas, *Robert E. Lee: A Biography* (New York: W. W. Norton, 1995), 136–37, 167–68, 184 (first quotation on 167); Skelton, *An American Profession of Arms*, 306–12, 318–25, 331 (second quotation), 345–46; James M. McCaffrey, *Army of Manifest Destiny: The American Soldier in the Mexican War, 1846–1848* (New York: New York University Press, 1992), 194 (third quotation); Michael Fellman, *The Making of Robert E. Lee* (New York: Random House, 2000), 224–25; Gary W. Gallagher, ed., "'We Are Our Own Trumpeters': Robert E. Lee Describes Winfield Scott's Campaign to Mexico City," *Virginia Magazine of History and Biography* 95 (July 1987): 369 (fourth quotation), 371 (fifth quotation).

29. Gallagher, ed., "'We Are Our Own Trumpeters,'" 373–74 (Lee quotations); Winfield Scott, *Memoirs of Lieut.-General Scott.* (2 vols., New York: Sheldon & Co., 1864), vol. 2: 574 (Scott quotations); Grimsley, *Hard Hand of War*, 21–22. The most recent biography of Scott emphasizes the general's largely successful efforts to contain the guerrilla war by pacifying Mexican noncombatants, but it does not discuss Scott's retaliation against the guerrillas themselves. See Timothy D. Johnson, *Winfield Scott: The Quest for Military Glory* (Lawrence: University Press of Kansas, 1998), 167–69, 186–89, 194–95, 235.

30. William J. Cooper Jr., *Jefferson Davis, American* (New York: Alfred A. Knopf, 2000), 118–19; K. Jack Bauer, *The Mexican War, 1846–1848* (New York: Macmillan, 1974), 220–24 (second quotation on p. 221); Grady McWhiney, "Jefferson Davis and the Art of War," *Civil War History* 21 (June 1975): 105, 106, 108–9, 111–12; Crist et al., eds., *Papers of Jefferson Davis* 3: 203, 278 (first quotation), and 8: 114–15 (third quotation on 115).

31. E. Merton Coulter, *The Confederate States of America, 1861–1865* (Baton Rouge: Louisiana State University Press, 1950), 62–67; Rable, *Confederate Republic*, 112–13, 120–21; Thomas, *Confederacy as a Revolutionary Experience*, 16–17, 107–8; Emory M. Thomas, *The Confederate Nation:*

1861–1865 (New York: Harper & Row, 1979), 30–31; Fellman, *Inside War*, v–vi; Drew Gilpin Faust, *The Creation of Confederate Nationalism: Ideology and Identity in the Civil War South* (Baton Rouge: Louisiana State University Press, 1988), 32–40; Paul D. Escott, *After Secession: Jefferson Davis and the Failure of Confederate Nationalism* (Baton Rouge: Louisiana State University Press, 1978), 100–101; Mark E. Neely Jr., *Southern Rights: Political Prisoners and the Myth of Confederate Constitutionalism* (Charlottesville: University Press of Virginia, 1999), 7–10.

32. Thomas, *Confederacy as a Revolutionary Experience,* 109–10 (first quotation on 109); Tocqueville, *Democracy in America* 2, book 3, chap. 23 (second quotation); Ricardo A. Herrera, "Self-Governance and the American Citizen as Soldier, 1775–1861," *Journal of Military History* 65 (January 2001): 21–23, 35–39; Coulter, *Confederate States of America*, 329–30 (third quotation on 330n49).

33. George M. Fredrickson, *Why the Confederacy Did Not Fight a Guerrilla War after the Fall of Richmond: A Comparative View* (Gettysburg, PA: Gettysburg College, 1996), 27–29; McDonnell, "Popular Mobilization and Political Culture in Revolutionary Virginia," 950, 955 (quotation); Thomas, *Robert E. Lee,* 79–80, 109–10, 172–73; Fellman, *Making of Robert E. Lee,* 218, 224–25.

34. *Official Records,* ser. 4, vol. 1: 117, 249, 765–67; Crist et al., eds., *Papers of Jefferson Davis* 7: 201 (first quotation); A. T. Bledsoe to A. D. Prentiss, August 10, 1861, in Letters Sent by the Confederate Secretary of War, War Department Collection of Confederate Records, Record Group 109, Microform 522 (National Archives, Washington, DC) (second quotation), hereinafter cited as RG 109, M-522. Volunteers, such as Benjamin Terry, were occasionally allowed to operate as independent "scouts" but never as guerrillas or partisans. For the frustration these restrictions caused men who expected to be turned loose against the enemy, see the correspondence involving Boykin's Independent Company of Mounted Rangers of South Carolina: William Burdell and others to Alexander H. Boykin, July 28, 1861, and Alexander H. Boykin to wife, July 6, 1861, both in Folder 16, Boykin Family Papers #78, SHC.

35. *Official Records,* ser. 4, vol. 1: 579 (first five quotations); John Q. Winfield to wife, June 30, 1861, in John Q. Winfield Papers #1293, SHC (sixth quotation); James A. Seddon to Thomas Ball, June 15, 1863, RG 109, M-522.

36. *Official Records,* ser. 1, vol. 2: 195–97 (quotation on 196). See also Curry and Ham, eds., "Bushwhackers' War," 416–33.

37. *Official Records,* ser. 2, vol. 1: 234–35, 237, 242–43 (Halleck quotation); Skelton, *American Profession of Arms,* 318–25 (second quotation on 320); Bauer, *Mexican War,* 223–24, 269, 334–35.

38. Kerby, "Why the Confederacy Lost," 327–30, 340–43; Gallagher, *Confederate War,* 144–46. Some historians also suggest that the chaos attendant to a guerrilla war would have played havoc with slavery, and that for this reason, too, Confederate leaders rejected the strategy. However, as reasonable as this sounds, no one has produced any evidence to support the theory. See William L. Barney, *Flawed Victory: A New Perspective on the Civil War* (New York: Praeger, 1975), 18; Reid Mitchell, "The Perseverance of the Soldiers," in Gabor S. Boritt, ed., *Why the Confederacy Lost* (New York: Oxford University Press, 1992), 124–25; Gary W. Gallagher, "How Should Americans Understand the Civil War?" *North & South* 2 (March 1999): 16–17; and Gallagher, *Confederate War,* 148–50. Michael Fellman, the only historian to treat the subject in a substantial way, seems to agree that guerrilla warfare would have disrupted slavery, but he does not distinguish between the interaction of slaves and guerrillas and the fate of slavery in Rebel-occupied areas (*Inside War,* 65–73). Investigation of the subject warrants more attention than it can receive here, but one could argue that slavery was most seriously threatened when Union troops entered an area unopposed;

and some evidence suggests that guerrillas and local units, like home guards and militiamen, could serve as effective policing agencies. See Crist et al., eds., *Papers of Jefferson Davis* 8: 263, 451; 9: 320; and 10: 87; Thomas Ball to Jefferson Davis, May 28, 1863, RG 109, M-437, reel 82, frames 917–19; Armstead L. Robinson, "In the Shadow of Old John Brown: Insurrection Anxiety and Confederate Mobilization, 1861–1863," *Journal of Negro History* 65 (Autumn 1980): 286–87; John K. Bettersworth, *Confederate Mississippi: The People and Policies of a Cotton State in Wartime* (Baton Rouge: Louisiana State University Press, 1943), 64–65.

39. Carl E. Grant," Partisan Warfare, Model 1861–65," *Military Review* 38 (November 1958): 42 (first quotation); *Official Records*, ser. 4, vol. 1: 532 (second quotation); Crist et al., eds., *Papers of Jefferson Davis* 7: 434 (third and fourth quotations); Albert Castel, "The Guerrilla War, 1861–1865," Special Issue, *Civil War Times Illustrated* 13 (October 1974): 9 (fifth quotation).

40. "Proceedings of First Confederate Congress: First Session Completed, Second Session in Part," *Southern Historical Society Papers* 45, new ser., no. 7 (May 1925): 122 (first quotation); *Official Records*, ser. 4, vol. 1: 1094–95 (subsequent quotations on 1095). The Federal protest against "rebel barbarities" by guerrillas became complicated in spring 1862 by a U.S. congressional hearing into the mistreatment of Union prisoners and the wounded by Confederate soldiers and the desecration of the Union dead and graves after the battle of First Bull Run. Then, too, reports circulated after the battle of Pea Ridge that Cherokee Indians, fighting under the Rebel flag, had employed the "tomahawk, war-club, and scalping knife" against Union troops. *Senate Reports*, 37 Cong., 3rd sess., no. 108: *Report of the Joint Committee on the Conduct of the War* (3 vols., Serials 1152–54, Washington, DC, 1863), vol. 3: 449–57 (first quotation on p. 449); William L. Shea and Earl J. Hess, *Pea Ridge: Civil War Campaign in the West* (Chapel Hill: University of North Carolina Press, 1992), 320 (second quotation).

41. "Proceedings of First Confederate Congress," 122, 128–29 (quotations); Ezra J. Warner and W. Buck Yearns, *Biographical Register of the Confederate Congress* (Baton Rouge: Louisiana State University Press, 1975), 38, 195, 230.

42. "Proceedings of First Confederate Congress," 153, 160–61 (first, second, and fourth quotations); Warner and Yearns, *Biographical Register of the Confederate Congress*, 49–50, 256–57, 265 (third quotation).

43. *Official Records*, ser. 4, vol. 1: 1151–52; vol. 2: 26, 71–72, 113. Interestingly, Federal conscription sometimes contributed to the Rebel guerrilla force, too. A Federal naval commander complained that the number of guerrillas in eastern Kentucky mushroomed when the U.S. government attempted to conscript men in that region. "They . . . say if they must fight at all they will fight for Jeff Davis," he reported; "consequently they have run from the draft and gone into the guerrilla service." *Official Records of the Union and Confederate Navies in the War of the Rebellion* (30 vols., Washington, DC, 1894–1922), ser. 1, vol. 26: 384. Ash, *When the Yankees Came*, 48, believes deserters strengthened guerrilla bands in all parts of the South.

44. Andrew Brown, "The First Mississippi Partisan Rangers, C.S.A.," *Civil War History* 1 (December 1955): 375; W. S. Compton to George W. Randolph, June 7, 1862, reel 38, frame 1193–96 (first and second quotations), E. G. Clay to Randolph, September 24, 1862, reel 40, frame 333 (third quotation), John O. Sullivan to Randolph, August 17, 1862, reel 72, frame 313–14, all in RG 109, M-437; *Official Records*, ser. 1, vol. 13: 835 (fourth quotation). Ash, *When the Yankees Came*, 48, suggests that partisans were more firmly attached to the army than to their communities, but the strength of those ties seems to have depended heavily on the threat to those communities.

45. J. A. Cross to George W. Randolph, April 8, 1862, reel 38, frame 178–79, Samuel L. Graham to Randolph, April 20, 1862, reel 93, frame 107–8 (first quotation), B. M. Edney to James A. Seddon, December 8, 1863, reel 90, frame 874 (second and third quotations), all in RG 109, M-437; W. A. Campbell to Joseph E. Brown, February 26, 1863, G. C. Carmichael to Brown, August 3, 1862 (fourth and fifth quotations), both in Governor's Correspondence, Georgia Department of Archives and History, Atlanta.

46. James A. Ramage, *Gray Ghost: The Life of Col. John Singleton Mosby* (Lexington: University Press of Kentucky, 1999), 105–6. *Official Records*, ser. 1, vol. 12, pt. 3: 952–53; ser. 1, vol. 24, pt. 2: 649–50 (first quotation); ser. 4, vol. 2: 1003 (second quotation). [Citizens of Whitfield County, Georgia] to Joseph E. Brown, December 2, 1862, Governor's Correspondence (third and fourth quotations). A Texan urged his brother to resign from McNeill's Rangers, in part because of the low reputation of partisan bands. See Edward B. Williams, ed., *Rebel Brothers: The Civil War Letters of the Truehearts* (College Station: Texas A&M University Press, 1995), 131–32. Cooling, *Fort Donelson's Legacy*, 65, calls the failed Partisan Ranger Act "one of the Confederacy's missed opportunities."

47. Eugene Marshall diary, May 8, 1863, Eugene Marshall Papers, Rare Book, Manuscript, and Special Collections Library, Duke University, Durham, NC. For a similar phase in the South's partisan conflict during the American Revolution see Hoffman et al., eds., *Uncivil War*, especially Rachel N. Klein, "Frontier Planters and the American Revolution: The South Carolina Backcountry, 1775–1782," 37–69; A. Roger Ekirch, "Whig Authority and Public Order in Backcountry North Carolina, 1776–1783," 99–125; and Crow, "Liberty Men and Loyalists," 125–78. Grimsley, *Hard Hand of War*, 112, proposes four categories of Confederate guerrillas, three of which correspond roughly to the groups identified in this essay.

48. Ella Lonn, *Desertion during the Civil War* (1928; rpt. Lincoln: University of Nebraska Press, 1998), 62–76; Thomas B. Cooper to Thomas H. Watts, June 13, 1864, Alabama Governor Papers, Alabama Department of Archives and History, Montgomery; P. Hagan et al. [Citizens of Lee County, Virginia] to Jefferson Davis, October 22, 1862, RG 109, M-437, reel 53, frames 897–900. It is tempting to characterize this third guerrilla group as "social bandits," as defined by Eric J. Hobsbawm in *Primitive Rebels: Studies in Archaic Forms of Social Movement in the 19th and 20th Centuries* (2nd ed., New York: Praeger, 1963), 13–29, and *Bandits* (rev. ed., New York, 1981), 17–29, but the "primitive" aspect of Hobsbawm's social banditry, particularly its association with class conflict, is not a comfortable fit for the United States. The fact is that all three manifestations of southern guerrilla warfare could be brutish under the right circumstances. See Fellman, *Inside War*, 259–63, 308n49; Don R. Bowen, "Quantrill, James, Younger, et al.: Leadership in a Guerrilla Movement, Missouri, 1861–1865," *Military Affairs* 41 (February 1977): 42–48; Bowen, "Guerrilla War in Western Missouri," 30–51; and David Williams, *Rich Man's War: Class, Caste, and Confederate Defeat in the Lower Chattahoochee Valley* (Athens: University of Georgia Press, 1998), 141–50. A more likely framework might be found in Samuel Brunk, "'The Sad Situation of Civilians and Soldiers': The Banditry of Zapatismo in the Mexican Revolution," *American Historical Review* 101 (April 1996): 331–53, which, while dealing with a very different culture from that of the American South and a very different "revolution" from that of the American Civil War, does downplay Hobsbawm's class dimension, adds an element of political awareness, and suggests roughly the same three types of guerrilla activity—with the appropriate overlapping between groups—presented here. See, too, Richard W. Slatta, ed., *Bandidos: The Varieties of Latin American Banditry* (New York: Greenwood Press, 1987), esp. Miguel Izard and Slatta, "Banditry and Social Conflict on the Venezuelan Llanos," 33–47; Billy

Jaynes Chandler, "Brazilian Cangaceiros as Social Bandits: A Critical Appraisal," 97–112; and Gonzalo G. Sanchez and Donny Meertens, "Political Banditry and the Colombian Violencia," 151–70.

49. John C. Inscoe and Gordon B. McKinney, *The Heart of Confederate Appalachia: Western North Carolina in the Civil War* (Chapel Hill: University of North Carolina Press, 2000), 110 (first quotation), 125 (second quotation), 137 (third quotation), but see generally chap. 5. See also Wayne K. Durrill, *War of Another Kind: A Southern Community in the Great Rebellion* (New York: Oxford University Press, 1990), 166–85; and Paludan, *Victims*, for Shelton Laurel.

50. Ash, *When the Yankees Came*, 50–56, 63–67; Grimsley, *Hard Hand of War*, 111–19; Daniel E. Sutherland, "Abraham Lincoln, John Pope, and the Origins of Total War," *Journal of Military History* 56 (October 1992): 567–86; Kenneth W. Noe, "Exterminating Savages: The Union Army and Mountain Guerrillas in Southern West Virginia, 1861–1862," in Noe and Wilson, eds., *Civil War in Appalachia*, 104–30. In a broader context, Weigley, *The Age of Battles*, 500, stresses that guerrilla warfare inevitably leads to "breaking almost all the rules usually limiting the violence of war."

51. Adjutant General's Office, *General Orders Affecting the Volunteer Force, 1863* (Washington, DC, 1864), 64–87, esp. 77–78; *Official Records*, ser. 3, vol. 2: 301–9 (quotation on 304); Burris M. Carahan, "Lincoln, Lieber and the Laws of War: The Origins and Limits of the Principle of Military Necessity," *American Journal of International Law* 92 (April 1998): 213–31; Paludan, *Victims*, 87–88; Fellman, *Inside War*, 81–97; Sutherland, "Abraham Lincoln, John Pope, and the Origins of Total War," 584–85.

52. *Official Records*, ser. 1, vol. 13: 726–27, 769–70, and ser. 1, vol. 15: 519–20; Crist et al., eds., *Papers of Jefferson Davis* 8: 310 (Davis quotations), and 9: 110–11, 229–30; "Proceedings of First Confederate Congress," 284 (last quotation).

53. Sutherland, "Guerrillas," 144; Louis Fusz diary, August 4, 1864, Missouri Historical Society, St. Louis (first quotation); Frank G. Ruffin to Thomas Ruffin, December 2, 1863, in J. G. de Roulhac Hamilton, ed., *The Papers of Thomas Ruffin* (4 vols., Raleigh, NC., 1920), vol. 3: 348 (second quotation).

54. Charles Royster, *The Destructive War: William Tecumseh Sherman, Stonewall Jackson, and the Americans* (New York: Knopf, 1991), 107–9; Michael Fellman, *Citizen Sherman: A Life of William Tecumseh Sherman* (New York: Random House, 1995), 139–48; John F. Marszalek, *Sherman: A Soldier's Passion for Order* (New York: Free Press, 1993), 194–96, 246–50; Roy Morris Jr., *Sheridan: The Life and Wars of General Phil Sheridan* (New York: Crown, 1992), 205–9, 229–31; Michael G. Mahon, *The Shenandoah Valley, 1861–1865: The Destruction of the Granary of the Confederacy* (Mechanicsburg, PA: Stackpole Books, 1999), 110–12, 114–17, 126–27; James M. McPherson, "From Limited to Total War, 1861–1865," in McPherson, *Drawn with the Sword: Reflections on the American Civil War* (New York: Oxford University Press, 1996), 66–86; *Official Records*, ser. 1, vol. 17, pt. 1: 144–45, and pt. 2: 261–62, 272–74, 279–81.

55. Ramage, *Gray Ghost*, 134–36; "Proceedings of First Confederate Congress," 191, 253; "Proceedings of First Confederate Congress: Second Session in Part," *Southern Historical Society Papers* 46, new ser., no. 8 (January 1928): 4–8, 48, 184; Frank E. Vandiver, ed., "Proceedings of the First Confederate Congress: Fourth Session, 7 December 1863–18 February 1864," *Southern Historical Society Papers* 50, new ser., no. 12 (October 1953): 401, 427–28, 440, 450; *Official Records*, ser. 1, vol. 33: 1081–83 (first and second quotation on 1081; third quotation on 1082), 1107, 1124, 1252 (fourth quotation); *Official Records*, ser. 4, vol. 3: 194.

56. Kerby, "Why the Confederacy Lost," 332–35; Dunbar Rowland, ed., *Jefferson Davis, Constitutionalist: His Letters, Papers and Speeches* (10 vols., Jackson, MS, 1923), vol. 6: 530 (quotation); An-

thony James Joes, *America and Guerrilla Warfare* (Lexington: University Press of Kentucky, 2000), 69–70, 97–101; William B. Feis, "Jefferson Davis and the 'Guerrilla Option': A Reexamination," in Mark Grimsley and Brooks D. Simpson, eds., *The Collapse of the Confederacy* (Lincoln: University of Nebraska Press, 2001), 104–28; Jay Winik, *April 1865: The Month That Saved America* (New York: Harper Collins Publishers, 2001), 146–64; William C. Davis, *An Honorable Defeat: The Last Days of the Confederate Government* (New York: Harcourt, 2001), 80–83; *Official Records*, ser. 1, vol. 47, pt. 3: 821–34. For Lee's thoughts on the futility of a post-Appomattox guerrilla campaign see Gary W. Gallagher, ed., *Fighting for the Confederacy: The Personal Recollections of General Edward Porter Alexander* (Chapel Hill: University of North Carolina Press, 1989), 530–33; and Fellman, *Making of Robert E. Lee*, 223–27.

57. Fellman, *Inside War*, 112.

PART II

LEADERSHIP
xxxxxxx IN THE xxxxxxx
CONFEDERACY

JEFFERSON DAVIS AND STEPHEN D. LEE

XXXXXXXXXXXXXXXXXXXXXXXXXXXXXXXXXXXXXXXXXXXXXXX

HERMAN HATTAWAY

Jefferson Davis and Stephen Dill Lee were a generation apart in age. Davis was a native Mississippian, and Lee was from South Carolina. But the Civil War brought them together, and events resulted in Lee's move to Mississippi, where he met and married a pretty lass, and he made that state his home turf forever after. After the war Lee served in the Mississippi State legislature and thereafter was the first president of Mississippi State University. Davis and Lee surely had something of a mutual admiration society. Davis's death in 1889 was the catalyst for the forming of the United Confederate Veterans, in which Lee played an important role from the beginning, becoming the second national commander-in-chief, a post he retained until his death in 1908.

Davis became nationally famous as a result of his exploits in the Mexican War. Lee doubtless knew of them at the time. Their first official interaction came in 1854 when Lee graduated from the United States Military Academy at West Point and Davis, by then the U.S. secretary of war, signed Lee's commission as a second lieutenant. Then in 1857 Davis co-signed, with President Franklin Pierce, the commission promoting Lee to a first lieutenant of artillery.

Two months after South Carolina left the Union, Lee resigned from the U.S. army. Upon returning home Lee at once reported to Gov. Francis Pickens, who made him a captain in the state's Regular Artillery Service. In Charleston, Lee and other professional soldiers assumed various duties, relieving cadets of the Citadel and numerous other volunteers. When P. G. T. Beauregard took command of the forces at Charleston, Lee became one of the Creole's personal aides. Following the Fort Sumter episode, Lee went to Virginia to assume command of an active artillery battalion of the recently formed Confederate army.

The next twelve months constituted a critical period in Stephen D. Lee's military career. In that year, Lee grew enormously as a commander. The period was the high point of his on-the-job military education. Distinguished from the mass of other junior officers, Lee became the "can-do" commander: his guns were always operative, his men moved well, frequently under great difficulty, and he infused professionalism into his subordinates. Lee often had to work with new men—some of his units were green—but he never had raw troops because he never let them remain raw even for a single day. As Jefferson Davis said, "Stephen D. Lee was one of the best all-round soldiers which the war produced."

Lee developed the talent of being able to win admiration, confidence, and cooperation. His men always liked him and served well under his leadership. With Lee as a commander, any organization turned into a better outfit. Going about his job methodically and quietly, often unobtrusively, Lee made a remarkable contribution to the Confederate war effort—and Jefferson Davis was keenly aware of this almost from the start.

As a military trainer S. D. Lee was different from other trainers. He was better, more thorough, and always active. Some officers did little or nothing when they should have been training. Lee showed initiative, even in the absence of orders. But he never displayed much dashing élan. Much of what he did was low key though always in tune. His men secured ammunition. They located on high advantageous ground. As a unit they never became incapacitated. As a result Lee's record of achievements, and those of his men, showed quite impressively throughout the summer and early fall of 1861 in Virginia. And Lee got promoted, from captain through every rank to full colonel.

XXXXX

General Ulysses S. Grant began his assault down the Mississippi River in 1861, and by mid-1862 the situation in and around Vicksburg was growing hazardous. President Davis knew that it was very important, if at all possible, to defend Vicksburg and the Confederacy's control of at least a segment of the Mississippi River. So in October 1862 Davis began to push Robert E. Lee to name some colonel in the Army of Northern Virginia to be promoted to brigadier general and sent to Vicksburg for on-the-spot supervision of the city's defense. Stephen D. Lee was the man selected. In a speech Davis both warmly identified with and praised "his people" and sang the praises of recently elevated Lieutenant General John C. Pemberton, the Philadelphian who had chosen the southern side, and Stephen D. Lee, the twenty-nine-year-old West Pointer and newly made brigadier general.

In the speech Davis focused for a time specifically on Lee: "For the defense of Vicksburg, I selected one, of whom it is but faint praise to say he has no superior. He was sent to Virginia at the beginning of the war, with a little battery of three guns. With these he fought the Yankee gunboats, drove them off, and stripped them of their terrors. He was promoted for distinguished services on various fields. He was finally made a colonel of cavalry, and I have reason to believe that, at the last great conflict on the field of Manassas, he served to turn the tide of battle and consummate the victory."

We might briefly here probe the question: was Stephen D. Lee "kicked upstairs?" Frequently when Robert E. Lee desired to be rid of a particular officer, he would suggest to Confederate officials that the man could be more useful to the Confederate cause if stationed elsewhere. R. E. Lee wrote to President Davis, saying, "I feel that I am much weakened by the loss" of S. D. Lee, and although Davis replied, "if you require Lee, he will be sent back to you," R. E. Lee did not exercise that option. But about a year later, R. E. Lee needed a new division commander and wrote to Davis, "I think it probable that some meritorious officers . . . on duty in Gen. Johnston's Department may be without a command. If Gen. Stephen D. Lee is in this situation I would recommend that he be ordered to this army to take charge of Wilcox's brigade in case the latter's promotion." But as things were turning out, just two days after R. E. Lee penned his request, S. D. Lee himself was promoted to major general.

Meanwhile in Mississippi, Lee served quite well, most notably winning a decisive victory over invading troops under William T. Sherman at the end of December 1862 in the Battle of Chickasaw Bayou. Throughout the rest of the ultimately doomed Confederate defense of Vicksburg, Lee performed splendidly. Often under fire, Lee on occasions carried standards and personally rallied faltering troops. He consistently demonstrated that he was brave, soundly competent, energetic, and resourceful. Most important, he was rugged, hardworking, and popular with his troops. One newspaper observer wrote that "Lee never seemed to suffer, yet he shared the hardships of his command in every way He carried neither tent nor camp equipage—only such baggage as he could tie behind the saddle." On campaigns Lee shared the fighting men's frugal meals and meager shelter.

After the fall of Vicksburg on July 4, 1863, S. D. Lee was for a short time a prisoner of war. Soon exchanged, he was promoted to major general and placed in command of all the cavalry in Mississippi. As usual, Lee's methods rapidly had an effect. On September 17, 1863, William T. Sherman wrote to H. W. Halleck that "this class of men must all be killed or employed by us before we can hope for peace. . . . I have two brigades of these fellows to my front . . . Stephen D. Lee in command of the whole. . . . Am inclined to think when the resources of their country are exhausted we must employ them. They are the best cavalry in the world." Unfortunately for the South, they were not able to squelch the northern forces in Mississippi.

On May 5, 1864, S. D. Lee began acting in temporary command of Leonidas Polk's department, and on May 9 took over in his own right. Polk remained with Lee at Demopolis, Alabama. Lee expressed apprehension over the planned arrangement, saying that he preferred a field assignment. Polk preferred to keep Lee near him and telegraphed President Davis, suggesting that Lee accompany him to Georgia. "To be deprived of General Lee's services in the campaign before us," Polk reasoned, "would be a serious loss to the service," but Davis replied, among other things, that Lee's presence in central Mississippi [as things then stood] seemed necessary.

Things proceeded reasonably well for the Confederates in Mississippi, until the unfortunate failure in the Battle of Tupelo, May 14, 1864. Lee believed that Nathan B. Forrest was much to blame for the outcome but opted not to blame him either publicly or in official records because Forrest was much too valuable to the Confederate cause. Lee, however, had little time to reflect on Tupelo. He was soon promoted to lieutenant general and sent to the Confederate Army of Tennessee, to take command of John B. Hood's old corps, as Hood was moved up into command of the army.

Subsequently, as corps commander, Lee outperformed his peers but showed some weakness in independent operations. Potentially, with seasoning, he could have been an excellent corps commander, but he needed experience and growth. Intrinsically he had the prerequisites to be a great division commander, and ironically this was one of the few assignments that he never sampled. As things turned out he became Hood's best subordinate—and he did well in crucial instances. During the next five months Lee showed that he could serve creditably even in a task for which he had insufficient tactical experience. "It did not take us long to realize that he was a man of unusual ability," his new adjutant general wrote, "and we rejoiced in the good fortune that had sent us so able a commander."

As events unfolded, however, things went badly for the Confederates. Atlanta fell to the Federals on September 2, 1864. Sherman then moved to cut Hood's railroad line of communications to the south. Perceiving this, Hood devised a scheme: S. D. Lee's corps would move straight to Ezra Church on the Lick Skillet Road, take possession of that and a critical nearby junction, and entrench, thereby holding the Federals facing him.

The Confederate scheme went awry before it really got started. Lee hastened westward and found the Federals already emplaced behind logs and rails along the very line he had hoped to occupy. Lee elected to attack. The line that Lee thought "would yield before a vigorous attack" stretched along a wooded ridge overlooking an open slope. Lee hurried so much that he failed at coordinated action. Each division went forward separately, and the corps never fought as a team. The battle went on for hours. Many officers stood bravely, trying to encourage their troops. A lieutenant remembered that "Lee looked like the god of war. I can see his face now, positively radiant. . . . I expected to see him fall every moment." But all this activity proved fruitless. The spirited battle amounted to nothing but a poor showing for the Confederates, and a loss of over five thousand dead. President Davis was so shocked when he heard about the losses that he urged Hood to avoid any further frontal attacks. Soon thereafter, on September 25 and 26, Davis visited the army and discussed possibilities: what operation could the army now undertake?

Sherman meanwhile disengaged near Atlanta and commenced his famous "March to the sea," reaching and taking Savannah, Georgia, just before Christmas. The Confederates elected not to pursue, but instead opted to try thrusting into Tennessee. On September 29 Lee's corps crossed the Chattahoochee River and pushed into Alabama, fighting skirmishes at Resaca on October 12 and at Snake Creek Gap on October 15. Picking up supplies along the way, they reached Gadsden on October 21, pushed on, and forced a crossing of the Tennessee River at Florence on the night of October 29. Easily brushing aside a small Federal garrison, they occupied the town and remained there for the next three weeks.

The delay proved costly because it dulled the shock effect of Hood's bold plan, but even the aggressive Lee admitted that it was required for assembling "necessary clothing, ammunitions, and provisions." The opposing armies that clashed in Tennessee ultimately were mismatched by a better than two-to-one advantage in favor of the North. The three corps of the Confederate Army of Tennessee began marching on November 19.

After they finally got started, the southerners managed to move with remarkable speed, considering the unfavorable weather and the poor condition of the roads. Lee's corps marched ten miles the first day and within a week neared Columbia. The army moved along in a cold rain, which soon turned into snow and sleet. Where the ground did not freeze, it became a quagmire.

Hood's men made contact with the Federal forces at Columbia on November 27. The two armies drew up in line of battle and lay opposite each other throughout the day. They fired artillery barrages and exchanged small arms fire, but neither side made any charges. Lee personally directed some of the cannonading and inspired the men to be brave and steadfast. One admiring observer recalled: "I have seen General Lee under fire probably fifty times. I have stood in his presence when the earth fairly trembled, and every living thing was in danger of immediate death, but no one never [sic] saw him display the slightest emotion nor lose his dignified bearing."

The Federal commander chose not to fight the Confederates south of Columbia. During the night the Federals crossed to a new position on the northern side of the Duck River. The two armies continued to fire at each other with artillery and skirmish fire, but that was the only combat for the time being.

Hood meanwhile determined to divide his forces, leaving Lee with two divisions at Columbia, hoping to fool the Federal commander into thinking that the rest of the Confederate army still remained there too, while in fact Hood with the rest of the army would try a turning movement to reach the Federal rear at Spring Hill.

The movement, which commenced on the night of November 28, began sluggishly. Hood tried to cross the Duck River on pontoon bridges about three miles above Columbia, but the Confederate infantry did not even begin to get across until daybreak on November 29. On that day the Federal commander held his entire army opposite Columbia until nearly noon, and then he began to withdraw slowly to the north.

Meanwhile, earlier in the day, Lee not only fired at the Federal forces across the Duck River; he also attempted to force a pontoon crossing. A strong federal force resisted Lee's advance until about 2:30 a.m. then left his front. "Pursuit was made as rapidly as was prudent in the nighttime," Lee declared. He got his advance columns into Spring Hill by 9:00 a.m. There Lee learned the horrible news: Hood had not attacked and allowed the bulk of the federal forces to slip safely past toward Franklin.

Utterly disgusted, Lee later wrote that "the enemy almost in a panic passed all night along the pike. . . . Our troops were in a bivouac not eight hundred yards from the pike, seeing and hearing it all. . . . A simple advance of one division a few hundred yards would have secured the pike." Some blue-clads actually straggled into the Confederate camps "to light their pipes and were captured," Lee asserted. "Someone . . . should be made responsible for the egregious blunder, mistake, or disobedience." But never did Lee publicly accuse any specific person of the blame. In 1903 he wrote, "I do not think the record sifted down will place blame on either General Hood or [his assistant] General Cheatham, who have borne the blame these many years."

The city of Franklin, located in a bend of the Harpeth River, had been surrounded by lines of entrenchments which touched the shore both above and below the main area of settlement. These lines were fortified and now occupied by 22,000 Federal troops. Lee reached the scene about 4:00 p.m. and went ahead of his corps to report to Hood.

Lee was to advance his corps, in support of what would be the main attack, led by Hood. As soon as the Federals became aware of the beginning of Lee's advance, they opened up artillery fire all along the line. But the Confederate main attack fizzled, and soon the Federal commander evacuated Franklin. Sufficient blue-clad units remained on the battlefield to exchange skirmish fire with the Confederates until about 3:00 a.m. but then the last of the northern troops moved safely into Nashville, twenty-five miles northward.

Hood's army had suffered nearly three times the number of casualties as had the enemy and could not now pursue because of exhaustion and disorganization. The Federals had lost 2,326 in killed, wounded, or missing; the Confederates suffered 6,252 casualties, including 5 generals killed, 1 captured, and 6 more wounded. Lee's corps suffered the least by far, losing 587 men. Lee suggested that the battle was the most costly of the entire war, considering the short time of engagement. Lee proclaimed that the charge made by one of his divisions was "the most gallant feat of arms which I witnessed during the war." Lee never said that he thought Hood should have attempted the battle here, but Lee did assert later that the field had been "ill chosen."

Lee did what he could to restore morale, especially in the division that had made the main charge. On the same day, in the afternoon of December 1, the Confederate Army of Tennessee began marching toward Nashville, this time with Lee's corps in the lead. For the next two weeks both armies methodically went about strengthening their emplacements. The Confederate line stretched about five miles long, with Lee's corps in the center, covering the Franklin Pike and extending nearly to the Granny White Pike. Lee thought the move essentially a pursuit, driving against whatever Federal stragglers remained on the road. But the next real fight would be in the trenches surrounding Nashville. For the next two weeks the opposing armies went about strengthening their emplacements.

The armies fired occasional discharges of artillery at each other, but for the rest of the first half of December the southern troops suffered mostly from the elements and the lack of adequate supplies.

By the evening of December 14 the Federal commander felt ready to make a move. Hood foolishly had sent Forrest's cavalry on an independent operation against a Federal garrison of 8,000 men at Murfreesboro. Thus the bluecoats could attack the Confederates while the southerners lacked their combat eyes and their most effective flank protection. The assault was ordered for early the next day.

A dense fog in the morning concealed the northern troop movements. Hood at first miscalculated the direction of the main attack. As the day neared its close, the Federals penetrated and drove the Confederates to their front southward about two miles before halting the fighting at nightfall. The Confederate flank was now crushed. Of course the Confederates knew that assault would be renewed in the morning. Lee wrote that "night was all that prevented [the men of his corps] being cut off entirely." The Unionists opened their assault on December 16, beginning at about 9:00 a.m. They started with a two-hour artillery bombardment.

"The troops of my entire line were in fine spirits," Lee reported, "and confident of success, so much so that the men could scarcely be prevented from leaving their trenches to follow the enemy." At one point some of them did leave the trenches. A large number of Negro troops assaulted Lee's lines. Judging from the remarks made by some of Lee's men, the Confederates apparently fought even more ferociously against black troops. When one brigade of colored soldiers made a valiant assault and were halted by the fire of Lee's men, several southerners leapt out of their defensive works and captured the enemy battle flags. When Lee noticed how elated his men were over capturing it, he had those around him give three cheers and directed that the cheers be passed down the lines to encourage the Confederates on the left.

Time after time, Lee's men threw back assaults. Their morale soared, and Lee spurred on. He stayed openly with them while the battle raged. But along other portions of the Confederate line the defense was not nearly so strong as at Lee's position. On the extreme left, the Federals charged successfully over the Confederate entrenchments. The Federals managed to slip around to Lee's rear, and gradually his corps gave way. The Confederates began to pull back, "in some disorder," Lee admitted, but he soon rallied them, and they "presented a good front to the enemy," rendering enough stiff resistance to prevent a rout.

Heavy rain began to fall and slowed both pursuers and retreaters. It was imperative that Lee's men hold long enough to allow the Army of Tennessee to get at least some distance from the Federals. A private on Lee's staff recalled Lee's actions throughout the afternoon: "His example was inspiring. I recall his words. . . . They seemed to come from his very soul, as if his heart were breaking. On appeal was: 'Rally, men, rally! For God's sake rally! This is the place for brave men to die.'"

Unfortunately the Confederate army ultimately was crushed, and Lee's men were all that saved it from complete destruction. Lee deserved great credit for his contribution. He was somewhat modest in his accounts of the day, but one of his staff members penned a fitting tribute: "Gen. Lee says his troops were soon rallied. Yes indeed, they were. But who rallied them? On this point Gen. Lee is silent with his accustomed modesty. He caused them to present a good front to the enemy. Let justice be done. . . . There is not a living man who can deny that Gen. Stephen D. Lee rallied these troops, and to him belongs the credit of saving Hood's army." Even the modest Lee allowed himself to write that the holding action had been "all that saved Hood's army at this critical moment."

At least two important Confederate generals later agreed that President Jefferson Davis should have been exonerated in regard to Hood's thrust into Tennessee. Lee wrote to W. T. Walthall on July 20, 1878, that he "never believed that Davis inaugurated Hood's Tennessee campaign." And William Nelson Pendleton asserted in his memoirs, "The President was, I learn, as much amazed as everybody else at that strange manouvre of Hood's, and shocked to find that he had left Georgia at Sherman's mercy."

As for S. D. Lee personally, the Battle of Nashville began to end at 1:00 p.m.

when he received a wound from a shell fragment. It shot off his spur and passed through his heel, shattering a few small bones. One of his aides begged him to go to the rear, but he refused, continuing to direct his men, in what proved to be the last successful moments of the battle for the Confederates, saving the Southern Army from complete devastation.

The defeated Confederate Army of Tennessee limped into a position of relative safety at Tupelo, Mississippi. Lee got only as far as Florence, Alabama, where he was hospitalized for several days. Then Lee, under instruction, met with General P. G. T. Beauregard to try to explain what all had happened in Tennessee. After that, Lee went on leave, traveling to Columbus, Mississippi, where he joined the girl who soon became his bride. She was Regina Lilly Harrison, the granddaughter of Thomas G. Blewett, perhaps the wealthiest man in Columbus. Miss Regina, usually called Lilly, was a remarkable young woman. Newspaperman E. A. Pollard remembered her as "a lady known and admired for her intellectual accomplishments as well as for her large portion of beauty, wit, and amiability to her sex." In 1860 she was described by the New York *Herald*: "In the combination of intellect and beauty Mississippi undoubtedly comes first and at the head of this sovereign State's representatives stands Miss H——n of Columbia. Her exquisitely chiselled features, soul flashing eyes, fine taste in dress, and calm and confident self-possession at all times and on all occasions, mark something more than the mere transient beauty." Before and during the war she collected friendly letters from an impressive array of notable figures. These included Jefferson Davis, William J. Hardee, Leonidas Polk, and the famous filibuster—the "gray eyed man of destiny," William Walker.

She had been collecting newspaper clippings about S. D. Lee for quite a time, and it was in May 1864 that she accepted his marriage proposal. They planned a wedding for February 8, 1865. One of her disappointed suitors wrote to her: "I commission you to convey my congratulations to Gen Lee. . . . I have sometimes heard him called a pet of fortune—but never until now, have realized how favored a child he is of that usually fickle dame." He continued: "You are much stronger than most of your sex. I have sometimes thought you talk and write with the mind of a man, and the heart of a woman."

The wedding was a very elaborate affair, performed by the Right Rev. W. M. Green, the Episcopal Bishop of Mississippi. Lee had been a Baptist, but now he had denominational affiliation also in common with Jefferson Davis. Lee remained with his wife for only a short time before he began thinking of a return to the combat zones. While in Columbus, he established a reputation of being "in social life a modest unassuming unpretentatios [sic] gentleman." But he received mail from his comrades which turned his thoughts away from society, entertainment, or rest. One letter indicated that "the corps misses you very much." And another remarkable note came from a fellow officer who also was recuperating from a wound: "I am all this time, the subject of surveillance by the Surgeon who advise delay etc. till the weather becomes less rigorous etc. But I am tired—tired to death of looking out of my door daily, yea almost every hour of the day, and seeing Tom who is 'pretty well,' well enough in fact to be with regiment if he 'could get the food there, suitable to his stomach.'"

Meanwhile there was some problem with respect to Lee's rank: the Confederate Congress at first refused to confirm his original appointment to lieutenant general. President Davis resubmitted the appointment and made no mention of the proposed date of rank. The original promotion was dated June 23, 1864; and when the Senate finally acted, on May 18, 1865, the original date stood, so Lee remained the twentieth ranking Confederate general.

Soon Lee itched to get back into active duty. His corps fought very well without him in the Battle of Bentonville, March 19–21, 1865. It was overall a spirit Lee had infused into it. "No one who witnessed the inspiring sight can ever forget the charge of S. D. Lee's corps," one observer remembered. Lee then did join the unit and marched with them through Chester, South Carolina. Mrs. Mary Chesnut noticed how forlorn the men looked. She wrote in her diary: "To-day Stephen D. Lee's corps marched though. The camp songs of the men were a heartbreak, so sad and so stirring. I sat down as women have done before and wept. There they go, the gay and gallant few; the last gathering of the flower of Southern manhood." Most of them probably realized that the Civil War was almost over."

At last, on April 19, General Joseph E. Johnston announced to the army that he had agreed to a cessation of hostilities while he negotiated with William T. Sherman, and on April 26 he formerly surrendered. For the second time Lee became a prisoner of war, and, as before, he was quickly paroled. Major S. A. Jonas, Lee's chief engineer, rather touchingly and pathetically testified to the feeling that many men had, when he presented Lee with a Confederate bill on which he had written:

Representing nothing on God's earth now
And naught in the water below it,
As a pledge of a nation that's dead and gone,
Keep it, dear friend, and show it.

As the popular Confederate General John B. Gordon said, S. D. Lee was "a brilliant campaigner . . . one of the most effective commanders on the Confederate side," and he showed flashes of creativity throughout his career. In retrospect, his best performance was at Chickasaw Bayou, but he won credit at every turn: level headedness at Sumter, initiative and tenacity in Virginia, self-aided good fortune at Second Manassas, capability of functioning effectively against insuperable odds at Antietam, and executive qualities on many occasions as a general. In brigade command before Vicksburg, he stood out, having no peer; with the Mississippi cavalry division, he accomplished a difficult mission utilizing painfully limited resources, as he also did on a larger scale in departmental command; in the Army of Tennessee, he quickly became the best of its corps commanders.

What then were S. D. Lee's limitations? Modesty and inflexibility were his worst characteristics. One might justifiably add his lack of sparkling brilliance; but apparently, his stern professionalism controlled his flair. Then too, for all his good luck, his opportunities for building a big reputation were scant. Lee himself did not exaggerate his achievements. As newspaperman E. A. Pollard observed, Lee was "shy and reserved except with those he knows well, [and] it is only in such company that he does himself justice." Lee never allowed reporters to travel with him, and he gave few wartime interviews.

During the years that followed, as Lee became variously a planter, insurance executive, politician, educator, and patron and benefactor of the study and writing of history, he continued to show the same degree of competence. His administrative ability, tenacity, attention to detail, and almost uncanny luck enabled him to master a wide variety of situations, as he made a notable mark in the New South, helping and improving the region, while providing his family with an easier, richer, fuller life.

XXXXX

At the end of the Civil War, and subsequently, life was not so satisfying for Jefferson Davis. He was captured fleeing with what was left of his government, and subsequently imprisoned for two years, at Fort Monroe, Virginia. For a time he was kept in irons. He suffered dreadfully from his various physical maladies and came dangerously near death on several occasions. But he did not want to die; indeed, he much desired that he be brought to trial, where he believed he would exonerate both himself and the Cause. In his book, *The Rise and Fall of the Confederate Government,* he described his captivity: "Bitter tears have been shed by the gentile [sic], and stern reproaches have been made by the magnanimous, on account of the needless torture to which I was subjected, and heavy fetters riveted upon me, while in a stone casemate and surrounded by a strong guard; but all these were less excruciating than the mental agony my captors were able to inflict. It was long before I was permitted to hear from my wife and children, and this, and things like this, was what added to savage cruelty."

Davis lived until 1889, and both he and his wife published long, exculpatory memoirs, which did not do well when initially published and are disappointing now for their scanty personal revelations and lack of analysis. The historian William C. Davis observed that "typical of the man, it was no memoir at all, but an apologia, a defense of himself, a prosecution of his enemies—Union and Confederate—and a justification for the South in seceding and for the Confederacy in seeking independence." Davis never changed his mind on the ideology that underpinned the Confederacy. "What he did not want to admit," W. C. Davis asserts, he simply wrote out of his history. Inconvenient facts he ignored, and embarrassing incidents he expunged. His failures were really those of others; his only mistakes had been putting faith in subordinates who let him down."

Perhaps many southerners were as deluded as Jefferson Davis. "Even in defeat," the historian George Rable wrote, "many Confederates could imagine a different outcome. As one psychological study has noted, 'People can enjoy the experience of wishful thinking as long as they are willing to pay the price of painful disappointment when reality does not unfold as expected.'" Rable concludes that "to say . . . Confederate morale collapsed in the spring of 1865 is to tell at best a partial truth because rationalizing and making excuses had almost become like a narcotic, dangerous and addictive but also attractive." In observing the immediate postwar South, Rable has suggested that "this air of unreality would unfortunately suffuse Southern thought for the next several decades and beyond, casting a long shadow over those who experienced a crushing defeat without either acknowledging it or reckoning with its causes."

To his relative Mary Stamps, whom he called "Molly," Davis once confided a new sadness over "this tone to which I see a proud, honorable people reduced." Once, after a visit to Davis's home in Memphis, the rector of St. Lazarus Episcopal Church, Dr. John Thomas Wheat, said to Robert Ransom: "If that man were a member of the Romish Church he would be canonized as a saint, and his sufferings . . . should forever enshrine him in our hearts as vicarious sacrifice."

During the postwar period, and even after his death, Davis's public image underwent various transformations. William C. Hesseltine contrasted Davis with Robert E. Lee: the former looked backward at the idealized South, as he persisted in remembering it; the latter was prominent among those former Confederate leaders who looked ahead at a new and ultimately better South. As Thomas L. Connelly pointed out, in the late nineteenth century, when R. E. Lee came to be revered virtually as a Christ-like figure, someone had to be blamed for Confederate defeat, and who better than the erstwhile failure of a president? In a clever spoof of the Civil War Centennial, Connelly listed a number of factors vital to "Confederatesmanship": high among them was that one had "to hate Jefferson Davis." Nevertheless, Davis had many admirers in numerous quarters since the Civil War ended. Indeed, he still does to this day.

Davis said in an 1882 speech, "Our cause was just, so sacred, that had I known all that was come to pass, had I known what was to be inflicted upon me, all that my country was to suffer, all that our posterity was to endure, I would do it all over again." He retired in 1877 to "Beauvoir," an estate near Biloxi, Mississippi, given to him by his benefactor, Sarah Dorsey, who like so many people, saw Davis as "the embodiment of our Cause."

XXXXX

Stephen D. Lee's only child, a son, was born on March 1, 1867. The baby was named Blewett Harrison Lee—receiving the surnames of his mother's father and her maternal grandfather. Aside from a happy home life and financial help from his wife's grandfather, another factor helped Lee to enjoy peace of mind. Like many other military men, he was resigned to having lost the war. But, while willing to obey, Lee certainly was not happy about the process, especially after it became more harsh. "The reign of the provincial governors and military officers," he asserted "was very odious." Lee believed that blacks asserted much unwarranted power during Reconstruction and that the blame chiefly rested with the carpetbaggers.

With such feelings about Reconstruction, it is interesting that Lee never became contemptuous of President Ulysses Grant. In fact, Lee also spoke highly of Grant. He respected Grant and deferred to his military victory. Lee's son recalled that "during the whole of the reconstruction period . . . the burden of the defeated South was made more tolerable by the steady kindness and the understanding, one might almost say the sympathy, of General Grant."

Lee also kept aloof from the quarreling that raged occasionally among many former Confederates. Thus he never joined with the many southerners who castigated Jefferson Davis, blaming him for the South's defeat. "I have always been of the impression," Lee declared, "that no other Southern man could have held the Confederacy together as long as did Mr. Davis." In later life Lee remained a warm friend, a staunch supporter, and frequent correspondent of the ex-president.

Interestingly, unlike typical Davis sympathizers, S. D. Lee also consistently honored and respected Robert E. Lee. He was not as close to R. E. Lee as he was to Davis, but he did correspond occasionally with R. E. Lee and always lashed out at any critics of the Virginian. As S. D. Lee aged, he developed a personal philosophy that blended the "lost cause" reverence exhibited by many of Davis's other followers and the "progressive New South with emphasis upon modern education" that R. E. Lee preached.

Although Stephen Lee took part in some extra-legal activities designed to "enforce the peace" during Reconstruction, he did not join the Ku Klux Klan. Apparently, however, he did not strongly disapprove of the organization. His son recalled in a 1927 speech that "as a child I have been by my father led to his plantation gate so that I might see the long procession of the Ku Klux riding past, mysterious, silent, and white."

By the 1870s S. D. Lee had come to aspire to secure some sort of position in the field of education. Jefferson Davis, probably at S. D. Lee's request, recommended Lee for the vacant position of president at the University of Alabama. Not getting that, but while being a state senator, S. D. Lee maneuvered to become head of the planned Mississippi A&M College, which the legislature established during his term in office. Not, however, until 1880 was the school opened and the president selected. By then a considerable amount of popular sentiment had developed in favor of S. D. Lee for the post.

He began his career as an educator with an open mind and a willingness to learn, but most important, with determination to be successful. During the spring of 1880 he and his wife toured colleges in Michigan and Iowa, gathering ideas and suggestions. He recruited a number of the first Mississippi A&M faculty from these northern schools.

In his inaugural address, Lee spoke of industrial education as a necessity. Stressing the monetary value of an education, he indicated that a great many people earned their living in agriculture. But, he continued, the farming class lived at a disadvantage when contrasted with other workers. Therefore the farmers and mechanics had a right to have a college especially dedicated to training them to be better in their callings. He predicted that the South was on the verge of a great industrial development, and he enjoined all those present to recognize and take advantage of it. A reporter on the scene described the speech as "eminently practical" and well received by the crowd.

Many persons interested in the college argued about whether Lee had a plan to develop the institution. Unquestionably he did have a plan, indeed many plans, and he found it necessary occasionally to change them as situations developed. He had, by his middle age, greatly intensified his capacity for flexible response. Always pragmatic, he more clearly realized that desired goals often can be approached from several different directions. But regardless of the plan, he certainly had a clear purpose. It was to make the college an excellent agricultural school and then, if possible, a mechanical school—but never anything but practical. Lee certainly thought out every step that he took, and probably discussed each with his remarkably bright wife. A famous joke among campus wags was: "General Lee runs the college, and Mrs. Lee runs Gen. Lee."

XXXXX

Lee was active in the United Confederate Veterans from its founding. And one of the most ardent and sustained of his efforts in the UCV was to venerate the memory of Jefferson Davis, who died the same year as its founding, 1889. It took a rather long time to settle all the details concerning Davis's final burial, but at last, in 1893, he literally had a second funeral. The body was removed from the Metairie, Louisiana, cemetery, and after lying in state at the New Orleans Confederate Memorial Hall, was transported by train to Richmond, Virginia. At the numerous stops in important cities, and all along the way, hundreds of thousands of people turned out to pay homage. Lee took part in the ceremonies in both New Orleans and Richmond.

Lee became a leading force in efforts to help Mrs. Davis financially and to erect a suitable memorial to Jefferson Davis, but he achieved relatively little in tangible aid for the widow. In 1892 the UCV passed a resolution pensioning Mrs. Davis for life, but then failed to provide the funds. In 1897 the veterans officially endorsed Mrs. Davis's book, *Jefferson Davis, Ex-President of the Confederate States of America; a Memoir by His Wife,* and Lee sent out printed circulars urgings its purchase. He had more luck with a monument project. In 1894 the Confederate National Memorial Association was formed and announced that it hoped to raise $200,000 for a monument to Davis. The project succeeded, and the cornerstone was laid in 1896 during the annual UCV reunion. Lee, because of his vigorous and significant support for the effort, was given the honor of delivering the principal address.

As commander-in-chief of the UCV, Lee symbolically became the greatest living Confederate hero (during the last four years of his life). He lived up to the image magnificently. "I wonder sometimes," he said in his inaugural address, "whether . . . the cause we loved will seem lost as it once seemed to us. It may be that in the province of God and in the development of humanity these fearful sacrifices were necessary for the highest good of this nation and of the World." "Truly in the human experience," he proclaimed, "without the shedding of blood, there is no redemption. . . . [T]he shed blood has brought blessing, honor, glory, power, and incorruptable treasures." The greatest loss of the South, he went on, was not in the burned houses, wasted fields, and ravaged cities, but in the men that the South lost. Yet, "my comrades," what "a comfort to know that the South had such men to lose. . . . What a magnificent race of men! What a splendid type of humanity! What courage! What grandeur of spirit! What patriotism! What self-sacrifice! It was sublime."

XXXXX

Lee's two most significant contributions of material for other people's books were in 1868 for George Denison, an English student of cavalry, and, beginning in 1878, for James F. H. Claiborne, author of a massive and broad-scoped history of Mississippi.

It is interesting that so many of Lee's subjective statements bear upon operations that he participated in with John Bell Hood. No doubt Lee believed he had received inadequate credit for his wartime exploits, and perhaps he harbored some jealousy for not having received command of the Army of Tennessee himself. One thing is certain: Hood said nothing detrimental about Lee in his *Advance and Retreat*. It is hard to see what prompted Lee's apprehension, though he did construe certain questionable implications in some of Hood's public statements. Lee wrote to Claiborne that Hood "had best be careful in theorizing, not to reflect on me. . . . I have fairly put him on his guard, and he had best not make a mistake." One wonders what Lee would have done. Of course nothing ever became necessary because Hood never intended to criticize Lee. Nevertheless, despite Lee's final satisfaction on this point, he never particularly liked Hood's book and gave it an unfavorable review.

More pleasant by far were Lee's historical dealings with Jefferson Davis. In 1873 Lee wrote Davis asking for advice on what to do with a body of official war papers that he had retained, "hoping some depository would be indicated for them where they would be useful." Davis suggested a place for the papers and at the same time asked Lee for reminiscences to help with writing his own memoirs. The exchange began a lengthy correspondence between Lee and Davis and Davis's literary helper, William T. Walthall. Lee visited Davis to talk over the project and later provided Walthall with a considerable amount of material.

XXXXX

In all that he did Lee never ceased to display the qualities of a military man. Well prepared and always competent, he approached any task with the managerial skills of a general. In war he rose rapidly to a lofty rank at a young age, an accomplishment exceeded by only a few of the better commanders in all of history, such as Alexander the Great, Lafayette, and Napoleon. Lee's credit sprang not from transcending the system and leaving it permanently altered but from his complete mastery of it.

This same mastery propelled Lee into the New South, and for forty years after Appomattox he gave unstinting loyalty and service to the United States at the same time that he helped to organize and lead the United Confederate Veterans and engage in many activities aimed at upbuilding the Southland. Lee strove to keep his oath of allegiance taken after the war; for "what I swore I meant," he emphasized, "and it was no empty mockery." Nevertheless, no other statement sums up Lee's sentiments better than one he made in 1900, proclaiming that "the New South is the work of the Confederate soldier, as the Old South was the work of his father. The Confederate soldier loves both." Stephen D. Lee died in 1908, and in his last years he genuinely favored reconciliation between the northern and southern people.

NOTE

The material and direct quotations are based upon my previous works. See *General Stephen D. Lee* (Jackson: University Press of Mississippi, 1976), and *Jefferson Davis, Confederate President* (Lawrence: University Press of Kansas, 2002), co-authored with Richard E. Beringer. Used by permission of the University Press of Mississippi and the University Press of Kansas.

EVALUATING JEFFERSON DAVIS
AS PRESIDENT OF THE CONFEDERACY

XXXXXXXXXXXXXXXXXXXXXXXXXXXXXXXXXXXXXXXX

PAUL D. ESCOTT

E valuating the losers in history can be a complicated process. For example, consider the situation of a man named Edward John Smith. One day he probably received congratulations and was told that he was going to make history, for it was his good fortune to take command of the newest, fastest, grandest, and most advanced ocean liner of his day. The world has remembered Smith, but as the captain of the Titanic—the principal figure in a great disaster. In fairness, this was roughly the situation of Jefferson Davis, though he performed far better as president of the Confederacy than Edward John Smith did as captain of the Titanic. Smith was negligent and took unnecessary risks, whereas Davis ran great risks from necessity. Still, the course of each man ended in a disaster that has fixed his reputation. An iceberg sank the Titanic; the problems faced by the Confederacy proved, like an iceberg, to be much larger than secessionists could see and more dangerous than they ever imagined.

To assess Jefferson Davis fairly, one should first consider the dimensions of the challenge he faced. Davis took the helm of an untried nation in a situation rife with major disadvantages. Lists of these disadvantages normally begin with the North's superiority in almost every objective measure of strength and resources. In human terms, the Confederacy was severely outnumbered. It could call on only nine million inhabitants in the eleven states that joined fully in the war effort, whereas the North had a population exceeding twenty million. Although southern loyalties in two additional border states, Kentucky and Missouri, motivated approximately 90,000 men to fight for the Confederacy, far more men from those states—200,000—fought for the Union army. Close to four million of the Confederates, or 40 percent, were African Americans, 96 percent of whom were slaves suffering under and resenting their exploitation. Southern leaders often claimed that their slave population would maintain the home-front economy while white men fought. Yet from the beginning of the contest, state leaders worried about preserving "good order" on the plantations, and soon slavery proved to be, as General Patrick Cleburne put it, "our most vulnerable point . . . an insidious weakness," instead of a strength.[1]

In economic terms, the North possessed three times as much wealth as the South, nearly two-and-a-half times as much railroad mileage, and twenty-five times as much naval tonnage. The value of its factory output exceeded the South's by a factor of ten. The states remaining in the Union produced fifteen times as much iron as the Confederacy, thirty-eight times as much coal, and thirty-two times as many firearms. Factories to produce textiles were concentrated in the North, in a ratio of fourteen to one. Another vitally important resource was draft animals, needed by the thousands to pull the supply wagons and artillery for a nineteenth-century army. Fully one-third of all the South's draft animals were in the border states and thus were lost to the Confederate war effort. The Union's advantage in this respect mounted to nearly two to one.[2]

Davis also led a new nation whose sense of nationalism was undeveloped and whose reflexive devotion to states' rights suggested how unprepared the culture was for a massive war. Four key states in the upper South had held back from joining the new nation until war forced them to choose a side. "Furthermore," as historian David M. Potter has pointed out, "secession was not basically desired even by a majority in the lower South." Its advocates there triumphed through skillful use of "emergency psychology," the strategy of "unilateral action by individual states," and "the firmness with which they refused to submit the question of secession to popular referenda." Many of the most enthusiastic secessionists were states' rights ideologues, devoted to their state and suspicious of any national government. Robert Barnwell Rhett spoke inaccurately, yet expressed a common viewpoint, when his Charleston *Mercury* trumpeted that "the new Government . . . leaves the States untouched in their Sovereignty, and commits to the Confederate Government only a few simple objects, and a few simple powers to enforce them."[3]

The South was a rural, agrarian society rather than an industrializing power. Towns were small, and only 7 percent of the South's population lived in a town or city. Even in eastern Virginia a person could ride "for hours and hours . . . through the unlimited, continual, all-shadowing, all-embracing forest" and "see never two dwellings of mankind within sight of each other." In such a rural society institutions were weak, and citizens were accustomed to small governments, low taxes, and a strongly local orientation to events. The leaders of the new Confederate nation belonged to a class of proud, aggressive, and quarrelsome aristocrats who dominated all branches of government and possessed fifteen times the wealth of non-slaveholders. These proud slave-owners regularly put their interests first while preaching a myth of social equality. The subsistence farmers who heard the myth, for their part, could be equally assertive in defense of their independence and honor. Their stubbornness and sense of honor could incite resistance and strengthen endurance, but it also could spur refusals to cooperate and defiance of law or social conventions. Clearly this slaveholding society was not ideally suited to embark upon a war that would require enormous industrial output, huge expenditures, a strong central government, and a high level of cooperation among whites and between the races.[4]

Moreover, Confederates plunged into the war with a shocking misperception of what lay ahead. They resorted to arms to avoid change, which they feared would come from the so-called Black Republicans. Instead, they found that the war itself brought enormous, unexpected, and unwelcome change. Militarily, Jefferson Davis was one of the few who feared a "long and bloody" conflict. He foresaw destruction "the like of which men have not seen."[5] But most spirited young men and many older, but not wiser, heads were confident of a quick and decisive victory. When the fighting began, the Charleston *Mercury* promptly declared that southern troops were "far superior" to northern soldiers, and the Richmond *Examiner* predicted that "victory would be certain, and chance become certainty." Thomas R. R. Cobb, normally a sober Georgia lawyer and politician, proclaimed First Manassas "one of the decisive battles of the world." He and others could not imagine the bloodshed and destruction that lay ahead. Many Confederate leaders began the war deluded by what Mary Boykin Chesnut called "a fool's paradise of conceit."[6]

Such unrealistic and unfounded enthusiasm handicapped Confederate policymaking from the very beginning. As Davis dealt with Congress, he had reason to lament that "the people" were "incredulous of a long war." Davis urged long-term enlistments in the army, for three years or the duration of the war, but Congress balked. The lawmakers thought six months would be adequate, and the best that the administration could gain for its initial policy was a twelve-months' period of service. Overconfidence reinforced blatant self-interest among the legislators to damage fiscal policy as well. When Davis's pick as secretary of the treasury, Christopher G. Memminger, urged a reliance on taxation to fund the conflict, the enormously wealthy men in Congress refused to levy meaningful taxes. State lawmakers, who were supposed to collect a small direct tax, added to the damage. Instead of collecting the tax, they borrowed money or printed state notes to meet their obligation. This was the origin of the Confederacy's runaway inflation and crippling financial weakness.[7]

The South's greatest strategic advantage was also a potentially fatal vulnerability. The new nation comprised a vast territory to subdue and conquer. Carl von Clausewitz, a renowned Prussian military theorist of the nineteenth century, emphasized in his treatise, *On War*, that any army invading a large country faced severe dangers. Its lines of communication, wrote Clausewitz, could become "overstretched. This is especially true when the war is conducted in an impoverished, thinly populated and possibly hostile country." Supply lines would be "always and everywhere exposed to attacks by an insurgent population." "[I]n truly national wars with a population in arms," the invader is menaced on all sides, and the flames of resistance "will spread like a brush fire, until they reach the area on which the enemy is based, threatening his lines of communication and his very existence." Thus, the size of the Confederacy appeared to be a great advantage. As George Wythe Randolph, one of Jefferson Davis's secretaries of war, wrote, "There is no instance in history of a people as numerous as we are inhabiting a country so extensive as ours being subjected if true to themselves."[8]

But the Confederacy was not able to suffer invasion and then strike with a truly national resistance. Localism and what Jefferson Davis later called "the absence of any national character in our confederation" nullified the potential advantage of geographical extent. The costs to the Confederacy of suffering invasion anywhere were too high. True to his West Point training, Davis wanted to conduct the war "guided simply by military principles." Repeatedly he explained that "the idea of retaining in each State its own troops for its own defense" was a "fatal error." But Davis's arguments, however cogent, were in vain. Confederates wanted the government "to defend every assailed place," and every state and locality demanded priority and an effective defense against Federal threats. For example, as soon as Federal invasion seemed likely, officials from South

Carolina, North Carolina, and Arkansas clamored for reinforcements and for the return of their state troops, and their demands were merely the first of many to reach Richmond. The "absolute necessity of consulting public opinion" rather than "military principles" frustrated Davis, who once told his attorney general that "if such was to be the course of the States . . . we had better make terms as soon as we could."[9]

More importantly, popular support crumbled as soon as territory was lost. As William Cooper has written, "time and again political and military authorities both told Davis that loyalty depended upon defense." In general, Confederates did not rise up to attack and cripple an overextended invader. Instead, any Federal invasion or threat brought disabling internal consequences to the Confederacy. Davis found himself dealing with "dissatisfaction, distress, desertions of soldiers, [and] opposition of State Govts." so severe that they threatened to change "'apathy' into collapse." To abandon or give up territory was to lose not just supplies and troops, but the morale that would sustain the war effort. Local officials forecast "dire results" if troops left their area, for Confederates "wanted concrete evidence that the government in Richmond was determined to defend their region." Localism was so strong and national loyalty so weak that before the war was over commanders in the Trans-Mississippi acknowledged that they could not get their soldiers to cross the river and fight in the east.[10]

Another challenge was the necessity of creating and staffing a government from scratch. This task is rarely mentioned, but it was both essential and far from trivial. The Davis administration accomplished a remarkable feat in organizing a Confederate government and putting it in working order within a short period of time. Fortunately, southerners envisioned a structure that was similar in form and function to the U.S. government of which they had been a part; without that consensus their task would have been overwhelming. Nevertheless, it was an enormous and difficult job to create branches and bureaus *de novo* and under immense time pressure. That this was accomplished and that the government functioned normally were achievements for which Jefferson Davis deserves some credit.

This brief summary of problems suggests the enormity of the challenges Davis faced. In assessing his performance as president, it is also necessary to take into account the natural human bias in favor of history's victors. The Confederacy lost the war, and the Union prevailed. Therefore it is natural to assume that Abraham Lincoln was a superior leader to Jefferson Davis. Moreover, the

Confederacy fought to protect slavery and white supremacy, whereas the Union eventually came to fight against slavery as a means to preserve the Union. Thus, morally, Davis and the Confederacy placed themselves on the wrong side of history's judgment, while Lincoln and the Union advanced human liberty. Without in any way defending the Confederacy's goals, this essay contends that a more narrowly focused assessment of presidential performance would discount history's bias toward the victors and take into account the moral shortcomings of the North as well as of the South.

Despite everything, Davis's government succeeded in making the war a close contest. Until the fall of Atlanta on September 2, 1864, the outcome of the Civil War remained very much in doubt. To that point, more than three years into the conflict, Lincoln had not been a particularly popular president, and during the summer of 1864 discontent over his leadership reached a peak. In fact, Abraham Lincoln himself wrote on August 23, 1864, that "it seems exceedingly probable that this Administration will not be re-elected." Everywhere the political tide was running heavily against him. His closest advisers warned of imminent defeat in one major state after another. Despairing, he sought pledges from his Cabinet to help him salvage the Union before a Democratic successor could make a separate peace.[11] Had Sherman not achieved a breakthrough in the West, Lincoln probably would not have won re-election, and as a consequence his historical reputation would today be far less exalted.

It is worth remembering, too, that Lincoln's timeless reputation as the Great Emancipator is partially a product of the celebratory strain that runs so strongly in our culture's view of U.S. history. Americans are not devotees of a hard-headed, factual, realistic approach to their national story. Instead, most take pleasure in a pervasive belief, deeply rooted in the political and popular culture, in American superiority and exceptionalism. One can trace this attitude all the way back to the Puritans' aspiration to erect a "city on a hill." Over time it gained a stronger foothold as millions of immigrants braved danger and insecurity to seek—and often find—a better life. Generations of political leaders then embellished the idea of national exceptionalism through soaring rhetoric, such as Woodrow Wilson's assertion that the United States gave the world "a new human experiment . . . a new start in civilization . . . life from the old centres of living, surely, but cleansed of defilement." Lincoln's role in freeing the slaves places him at the center of this celebration of American virtue. In fact, he has become "the deity of American civil religion," in the words of James McPherson, a symbol of all that is noble and virtuous in the American people. Even though the iconic view of Lincoln, reinforced by patriotic emotions, has overemphasized his progressiveness on matters of race, he enjoys a "semi-divine status . . . in American history." Jefferson Davis's reputation, by contrast, has been shaped by a realistic, and therefore more negative, approach.[12]

In light of that fact, it is appropriate to begin an assessment of Davis with the negative. Beyond question, the Confederacy's president was far from perfect (just as Abraham Lincoln was not perfect). Jefferson Davis had personality defects that damaged his relationship with generals and politicians. He made some bad decisions in appointments, particularly in the area of military support and commands, and was too respectful of departmental commanders. Moreover, he failed, in my judgment, to meet a crucial part of the vast challenge that confronted him and his society.

In regard to his personality, it is well known that Davis satisfied the qualifications for membership in his class of proud, touchy southern aristocrats. He could be rigid, haughty, and overly convinced of his own virtues. Even his wife said that he was "abnormally sensitive to disapprobation" and sometimes adopted "a repellent manner." This chief executive was incapable of deploying political charm in the manner of Franklin Roosevelt, Ronald Reagan, or Bill Clinton. Occasionally he angered or offended congressmen and state officials. J. B. Jones, the diarist who worked in the War Department, once recorded his surprise at seeing Davis "in earnest conversation with several members of Congress, standing in the street." Why? Because this rigid and formal man did not often "descend from his office to his mode of conference." It is undeniable, too, that there were frequent resignations from his cabinet, in which a total of fourteen men occupied the six positions at some time during the war. James Seddon, one of those who served the longest, described Davis as "the most difficult man to get along with he had ever seen." If pushed too far, Davis readily became cold, correct, and defensive, justifying himself and lecturing others on their duty.[13]

But I do not believe, as William Cooper wrongly supposed, that Davis's personality flaws (though real) became more pronounced during his presidency. Rather, the Confederacy's chief executive actually improved on his prewar performance. As President Davis worked hard "just to let people alone who snap at me." He often displayed great patience under provocation, and he was more constructive and less petty than many of his political foes, who suffered from the widespread disease of planter culture that James Henry Hammond aptly called "Big Man Me-ism." Surely Senator Herschel Johnson of Georgia had this at least partially in mind when he said of Davis, "I know of no man among us, from the ranks of the extreme Sesessionists [*sic*], who would have conducted affairs half so well." Similarly, James Chesnut Jr. reacted negatively in March of 1865 when a group of dinner companions took turns lambasting Jefferson Davis. Chesnut admitted to his wife that he had "lost [his] temper." Curtly he told these critics that Davis "was a gentleman and a patriot, with more brains than the assembled company."[14]

But reining in a touchy personality did not ensure wise decision-making, and Davis made some serious errors. Generations of commentators have been correct to assail his excessive loyalty to some bad generals. Among these the most notable examples were Abraham Myers, Lucius Northrop, and Braxton Bragg. The first two performed badly in equipping and supplying the southern army, and Northrop made his challenges worse by bringing to the job "petti-ness," bureaucratic rigidity, and "the personality of a malicious old man." Yet Davis was reluctant to make changes and delayed far too long in replacing these two appointees. One of the few arguments in favor of Braxton Bragg was, per-haps, that he was from North Carolina, which felt itself ignored and under-represented in the higher councils of the Confederacy. But Bragg was not a strong field commander, and he alienated virtually all the officers who served under him. Davis's worst and most inexcusable performance as a manager of people, certainly, related to Bragg as commander of the Army of Tennessee. Bragg's army was so plagued by dissension that Davis felt it necessary to make a personal visit and convene a meeting with all the leading officers. There, in the presence of General Bragg, he encouraged the other generals to speak out frankly and give him their assessment of Bragg. To a man the subordinate gener-als unanimously urged their commander's removal. Then, astonishingly, Davis chose to keep Bragg in charge. His decision defied common sense, and before long Bragg himself recognized that he had to give up his post.[15]

In two other well-known conflicts with military commanders—P. G. T. Beauregard and Joseph Johnston—there was egotistical behavior on both sides. Davis shares some of the blame for these troubled relationships, but there is much on the record to defend the Confederate president. Beauregard certainly had excessive self-regard and a devotion to grand but impractical strategies. The strategic ideas that he repeatedly urged on the administration—and used to inflate his popularity with congressmen—were unrealistic and unworkable. Beauregard was inordinately attentive to career politics. The fact that at one point fifty-nine congressmen signed a petition urging that he receive a high command is no mark of distinction. Moreover, his ego in the weeks after First Manassas inflicted the first wound on his working relationship with Jefferson Davis. After insisting on the evening of the battle that pursuit of the Federal army was impossible, Beauregard soon was portraying himself as the victory's hero and criticizing Davis for not seizing Washington, D.C.[16] Nevertheless, despite numerous personality conflicts, the Confederate president found ways to use Beauregard profitably throughout the war. In the case of Joseph Johnston, Davis dealt with another general who enjoyed an unjustifiably positive reputation among many of his contemporaries. Johnston was the over-cautious McClellan of the Confederacy, a general who failed to act boldly either to defend Vicksburg or to stop Sherman's advance into Georgia. His record did not justify the esteem that he enjoyed in various circles. But Davis was painfully aware of Johnston's defects—it was strong political support for the general and a scarcity of alternatives that forced Davis to give him too many important responsibilities.

Davis should be faulted for his use of a military departmental system, in which designated generals had wide latitude to direct affairs in their geographical departments. During the first year and half of the war, this system worked well, but thereafter it became a source of weakness for the Confederacy. The problem was that Davis failed to intervene and force generals to take action required by the overall needs of the nation. As commander-in-chief, Davis immersed himself in many minor details but on large issues proved too respectful of his departmental commanders. They did not cooperate with each other as Davis hoped they would and as he often urged them to do. In a final analysis, however, it was his responsibility, not theirs, to determine that one department needed the assistance of troops from another, and bolder action on his part might have increased the Confederacy's chance of success.[17]

At the level of grand strategy, Steven Woodworth has contended that the harmonious collaboration of Davis and Robert E. Lee, ironically, deprived Confederate strategy of coherence. Lee doubted the staying power of Confederate morale and believed that a decisive victory was needed sooner rather than later, whereas Davis felt the Confederacy was too weak to dominate on the battlefield and therefore sought to gain independence by outlasting the foe. The two men's strategic assumptions differed, and their cooperation produced decisions that were not wholly consistent with either approach. Woodworth's insight demands respect, but a defense of Davis on this score is reasonable. As Clausewitz has written, "The defensive form of war is not a simple shield, but a shield made up of well-directed blows." Lee, more than any other southern general, proved adept at delivering those blows, and Davis was not wrong to give considerable freedom to his most talented commander. If Lee had always performed well and not made some serious errors, his success might have led to a different political result, even within the "offensive-defense" that Davis favored.[18]

Ultimately success on the battlefield depended upon strength on the home front, and that is the area of Davis's greatest failure. In dealing with the common people of the Confederacy—the non-slaveholding families who had to supply most of the Confederacy's soldiers—Davis was ultimately a prisoner of his class and of his class perspective. This author continues to believe, after more than thirty years of study and sincere efforts to view the question afresh, that Bell Wiley's judgment, penned in 1943, is correct. Wiley wrote that the failure to aid non-slaveholding soldiers' families, either by providing food or by "exempt[ing] from conscription" the men "upon whose labor the livelihood of wives and small children was vitally dependent" was one "of the greatest mistakes of the Confederate government."[19] Hunger on the home front was a tremendous problem for the Confederacy. Sober and responsible observers saw "dreadful" "suffering among the poor" and feared "actual starvation" as early as 1862.[20] Local and state governments made unprecedented but unsuccessful efforts to provide aid to a quarter or a third or more of their populations. When the central government failed effectively to aid poor soldiers' families, men left the army in steadily increasing numbers to care for their loved ones, thus depriving the Confederacy of essential military forces.

Davis himself showed some awareness of the inequities in sacrifice by rich and poor, and he emphasized to Congress that discriminations "between different classes of our citizens are always to be deprecated." But he did not take the kind of bold, energetic steps to alleviate suffering among yeoman families that characterized his action in other policy areas. His failure to act may have been due, in part, to concentration on military matters. But Davis also seemed not to appreciate the depth of suffering among the yeomen or recognize poor soldiers' culturally justified determination to aid their families. As a popular Mississippi politician he had never had to worry too much about non-slaveholders' support, and as president he continued to live a life of material comfort, complete with elegant dining. Moreover, he operated within a political universe composed of wealthy men whose class perspective was far more narrow and self-interested than his. They often saw the government's interference with their autonomy and privileges as a more serious problem than widespread hunger and suffering on the home front. Even granting that the pressing needs of the military claimed most of Davis's attention, there was a failure on his part—and that of the Confederate elite generally—to grasp the seriousness of the common people's plight.[21]

On the other hand, there are strikingly significant positives in Davis's record as well. Any assessment of Jefferson Davis as president of the Confederacy has to credit him with innovation, flexibility, and a willingness to take political risks that far exceeded Abraham Lincoln's. Davis's administration transformed the South economically, politically, and even to a considerable extent ideologically and culturally. Davis shaped an ambitious legislative agenda and dominated the Confederate Congress in a way that Lincoln never approached in the North. The policies of his administration took the Confederacy in unexpected, radically new and different directions. Facing extreme crisis, Davis rightly judged, with intellectual incisiveness, that old verities and shibboleths had to be discarded in favor of essential new measures. His administration made the Confederacy a "revolutionary experience," in Emory Thomas's accurate phrase.[22]

In a political culture devoted to states' rights and small, limited government, he built a powerful central administration larger, in relation to population, than that of the United States. In an agrarian economy whose political leaders slandered industrialism, he encouraged the development of industries that supplied the army's needs for ordnance and increased productive capacity in many other areas. In a rural landscape, his administration's initiatives caused cities to grow explosively. On a populace of independent white citizens unused to any restrictions on their freedom, he imposed a wide variety of governmental controls. In a slave society he even advocated the arming and freeing of slaves and managed to gain the support of a considerable portion of the electorate for this heretical proposal.[23]

Davis's administration was responsible for conscription—the first compulsory draft in U.S. history, controversial both in principle and because it applied to men finishing their term of enlistment (or "contract" with the government, as many southerners saw it). His administration also was responsible for the tax-in-kind, which swept up one-tenth of farmers' crops in order to feed the troops. Through the army, the Davis administration "impressed," or seized, many types of property needed for military operations. This system was universally unpopular but always necessary and far heavier in its impact than taxes. In Georgia, for example, the value of commodities seized by the army was three times greater than Confederate taxes, almost nine times greater than the tax-in-kind, and three times greater than the combined total of state and local taxes. Davis's government aided and encouraged new industries, guaranteed their profits, and used the law of conscription to assign and maintain their workforce. So extensive was government direction of the wartime economy that an earlier generation of scholars dubbed it "state socialism." Before the war was over, the Confederacy requisitioned by law one-half the cargo space on ocean-going ships, so that it could export and import in a manner that served the nation's needs.[24]

Many of these measures involved legal or military compulsion. Jefferson Davis sought and obtained three suspensions of the writ of habeas corpus— fewer than he requested but a significant number nevertheless. Not only were many citizens arrested under this authority, but generals in the field imposed unauthorized, extra-legal military arrests on many others, so that the Confederacy's restrictions on civil liberties rivaled those of Lincoln's government. In addition to the efforts of the Conscription Bureau and the provost marshals, regular units of the army occasionally conducted dragnets through the countryside to round up deserters. (North Carolina had three such expeditions within one year.) The efforts to maintain military discipline, control dissent, and manage transportation led to a passport system that by 1863 had become nearly ubiquitous. A British visitor traveling from Mississippi through Alabama to Tennessee found that soldiers demanded his papers "continually, and on the railroad every person's passport was rigidly examined." Armed guards controlled railroad cars inside and out, and sentries patrolled many "public highway[s]," especially around Richmond, where senators and representatives complained that they had to go "to the Provost Marshal's office and ge[t] a pass like a free [N]egro."[25]

With every one of these measures Jefferson Davis took great political risks, and in attacking the fundamental institution of the slave South's economic and social system he exposed himself to the public's ire beyond any risk considered by Abraham Lincoln. Criticism of Davis's initiatives was loud, impassioned, and persistent. Some Confederates, especially those planters who had championed secession to avoid change, felt that their whole movement and the South's core values were betrayed. Confederate Senator Williamson S. Oldham of Texas was one among many who blamed Davis's strong and innovative policies for the South's defeat. The people, he believed, had gone to war "for the vindication of the sovereignty of the states, the liberties of the people, and for the preservation of constitutional guarantees." Instead, under the wartime regime "absolute despotic power" was conferred "upon the executive and the military." The unexpected changes brought by the Richmond administration were too great a shock to the "habits of the people on whom they were to operate."[26]

Like many other planter politicians, steeped in states' rights theory, Oldham denounced conscription as a fundamental mistake made worse by its system of exemptions. The problem, in his judgment, was not the exemption for overseers, which discriminated against non-slaveholders, but the basic infringement of a state's right "to control the domestic interests and individual pursuits of the people." Suspension of the right of habeas corpus he condemned as "clearly unconstitutional," even though in approving suspension of the writ Congress had exercised one of its enumerated powers. Impressment constituted another abuse of central authority. In the eyes of a man like Oldham, Jefferson Davis perverted the Confederate venture. Once "the states were subordinated, governors played the part of orderlies to Generals, the constitutional tribunals and the laws . . . were practically suspended" in favor of military provost marshals, and the central government lost the "moral support" of the people. "[T]he original object of the war" was "lost sight of," lamented Oldham, and the Confederacy "became, as perfect a military despotism, as ever existed upon the face of the earth."[27]

Other members of the slaveholding elite agreed with Oldham. Governor Joseph E. Brown of Georgia persistently attacked Davis's leadership. Conscription, Brown declared on numerous occasions, was "subversive of [Georgia's] sovereignty." It made war on "all the principles for the support of which Georgia entered into this revolution." He assailed Davis for departing from Jeffersonian verities about limited government and adopting Hamiltonian principles. When Davis turned Brown's arguments aside, the governor charged that conscription "strikes down" state "sovereignty at a single blow." Nothing previously done by the government of the United States, he cried, had ever "struck a blow at constitutional liberty, so fell." To Linton Stephens of Georgia and to the *Charleston Mercury* "the essence of Conscription is the right . . . to coerce sovereign States" and "the very embodiment of Lincolnism." Vice-President Alexander Stephens joined in these denunciations, declaiming publicly that Jefferson Davis had seized "extraordinary and . . . dangerous power." Through conscription Davis had put "all the population of the country between those ages [seventeen and fifty] under military law." Through suspension of the writ of habeas corpus he had gained the power "to order the arrest and imprisonment of any man, woman, or child in the Confederacy" on a "bare oath." "Could dictatorial power be more complete?" asked Stephens. "The most ill-timed, delusive, and dangerous words that can be uttered," he charged, "are can you not trust the President?"[28] Such impassioned attacks represented the confusion and sense of betrayal of a class that had led its society into an unexpectedly demanding and punitive war.

But substantial numbers of other Confederates proved more in need of government aid, less devoted to states' rights ideology, and more receptive to Jefferson Davis's vision of a strong government that could respond to emergencies and win independence. Many common citizens in Virginia declared "with one Voice . . . that the Government has taken a step in the right direction in seizing" grain from a "Mammoth distillery" when people were going hungry. An upland South Carolina newspaper likewise called for a general crackdown on distilling and prayed, "God grant it may be done." Other suffering residents beseeched the government to impose price controls, stifle inflation, or punish speculators. "WELL DONE! WELL DONE!" was the response of a Georgia newspaper to word that the War Department had impressed commodities from speculators. Similarly, a Spartanburg, South Carolina, editor urged impressment agents to take food from "all those who have locked up their corn cribs and smoke houses against their friends and neighbors." Harsh military rule seemed welcome to many if it "shall relieve us from the intolerable oppression" of "monopoly and extortion," high prices and hunger.[29] In a time of crisis, some southern whites longed for an effective government that could aid them, and others agreed with Jefferson Davis that change was acceptable if it led to independence.

No changes were more radical than those Davis proposed for slavery. First, his administration progressively took charge of large portions of the South's slave labor force, in order to support and aid military operations. Tens of thousands of bondsmen worked as laborers or served the War Department as "butchers, bakers, cattle drivers, teamsters, boatmen, millers, and packers," among other duties. Then, in the last six months of the war, Davis campaigned (especially through Robert E. Lee) for the arming and freeing of the South's slaves. To emancipate the slaves was, of course, the antithesis of the Confederacy's original purpose. This proposal caused Howell Cobb to exclaim, "If slaves will make good soldiers our whole theory of slavery is wrong." One prominent senator denounced such "insane proposals" as "wild schemes and confessions of despair." Another asked in outrage, "What did we go to war for, if not to protect our property?" while the Richmond *Examiner* denounced the idea as "totally inconsistent with our political aim and with our social as well as political system." Davis had adopted "the whole theory of the abolitionist." In one of its calmer moments, the Charleston *Mercury* branded Davis's "extraordinary suggestion" as "inconsistent, unsound and suicidal." Others continued to insist that "the African . . . is at his best estate as the slave of the enlightened white man," or that "slavery is the best possible condition for the slave himself." Moreover, said one Confederate congressman, if emancipation were to create a country in which even some slaves were free, "Who would consent to live in it?" These statements represent only a small sample drawn from a chorus of often apoplectic outrage.[30]

The fervid determination of so many southerners to hold on to slavery was especially striking in view of Davis's limited plans for emancipation. On the one hand, Davis insisted that slaves could make good soldiers, and he maintained that they and their families deserved freedom and the right to live in the South as a reward for military service. Through Robert E. Lee, the administration argued for a gradual and general emancipation encompassing all the South's slaves. But on the other hand, the Davis administration made it clear that nothing like equality was being considered. In a letter describing the government's plans, Secretary of State Judah Benjamin explained that "ultimate emancipation" through state action would occur after "an intermediate stage of serfage or peonage." Certain reforms, such as "legal protection for the marital and parental relations" would improve the image of the Confederacy while southerners continued to "vindicat[e] our faith in the doctrine that the negro is an inferior race and unfitted for social or political equality with the white man." This firm commitment to white supremacy and rigid racial discrimination seemed to mollify none of the administration's opponents. When Congress finally, reluctantly, and by a margin of one vote passed a bill that would allow the arming of slaves, the measure said nothing about freedom. In fact, it specifically stated, "That nothing in this act shall be construed to authorize a change in the relation which the said slaves shall bear toward their owners." Only individual slaveholders and the states in which they lived could choose to change that "relation."[31]

The determination of Davis and his administration to establish serfdom for freedmen and deny "social or political equality," had their plan succeeded, does not diminish the political boldness of his action in comparison to Lincoln. In terms of political risk, the Union's chief executive never took an action that was as daring, controversial, or unpopular as Davis's proposal. Nor was Davis's view of the future status of African Americans as grossly deficient compared to Lincoln's as most people today would assume. For in his policy statements the Great Emancipator had repeatedly encouraged "apprenticeship" or "temporary arrangements" for the freedmen. These "arrangements" were meant to benefit the whites more than their former slaves. For, as Lincoln explained to General John McClernand, with apprenticeship and financial aid from the Federal government, the slaveholders "may be nearly as well off . . . as if the present trouble had not occurred." Beyond any shadow of doubt, Lincoln deserves credit for advancing the cause, prospects, and substantial reality of emancipation before his death. Yet it is often forgotten that, even though Lincoln wanted to see slavery end, to the time of his death he continued to advocate a method for ratification of the Thirteenth Amendment that would cast doubt on its success. This was a part of his consistent efforts—sustained until the time of his death—to conciliate white southerners in order to gain their participation in the process of reunion.[32]

In closing, it is important to recognize that Jefferson Davis had a major impact on U.S. history in two important areas that generally have not been emphasized. First, greater recognition needs to be taken of the extent to which Davis militarized the South during the war, compelling southerners to continue their battle for independence in accord with his determination and strong will. This fact has been overlooked, in large measure because after 1865 southerners found it inappropriate and damaging to their myth of the Lost Cause. In the postwar cultural battle to establish the meaning of the Civil War, southern propaganda created an image of a united and gallant southern people fighting for constitutional liberty rather than slavery. That image was fiction. Southern whites were not, in fact, united, and, of course, their political leaders had promoted secession in order to defend slavery. Davis's strong government contradicted the myth, yet the supposedly united Confederacy would never have survived to 1865 without Jefferson Davis. Although many individual Confederate soldiers proved tenacious and bold, Confederate society was quite disunited and, increasingly, despairing and resistant to authority under the pressures of battlefield reverses and home-front suffering. Because Jefferson Davis was determined to gain independence and opposed to negotiating for any concessions short of independence, the Confederacy kept fighting. Davis knew that he had to adopt strong measures to compel his citizens to fight on, if he wanted to have a chance of success. Because he did so, the war lasted four years, even as southern ranks thinned. Because he was so resolute and demanding of his nation, during several weeks in 1864 it seemed that northern will might falter first, leading to the election of George McClellan and very possibly the Confederacy's negotiated independence.

Second, Jefferson Davis deserves much of the blame for deepening and magnifying the intersectional hatred that came out of the war. The carnage of four bloody years would have produced much bitterness in any event, but Davis did all he could to stir up such feelings and use them in support of the Confederacy's aims. As early as 1862 he charged the U.S. army with disregard of "the usages of civilization and the dictates of humanity." He condemned Lincoln's final Emancipation Proclamation as an effort to "incite servile insurrection" and stimulate slaves to "a general assassination of their masters." Lincoln, he said, was responsible for "the most execrable measure recorded in the history of guilty man." More generally, he accused the Union army of "every crime conceivable," including the burning of "defenceless towns" and the "pillag[ing]" of people's homes by a "brutal soldiery." "Hyenas," he said, were preferable to Yankees. A northern victory would bring "subjugation, slavery, and . . . utter ruin." After condemning the "wickedness of the North," he asked the Mississippi legislature if its members were willing to "be the slaves of the most depraved and intolerant and tyrannical and hated people upon earth?" Other choice epithets included calling northerners "the offscourings of the earth." As the Confederacy's prospects darkened, so did Davis's rhetoric, as he attempted to nerve southerners for stronger resistance. The enemy's "malignant rage," he charged, would result in "nothing less than the extermination of yourselves, your wives, and children." No one, perhaps, did more to encourage sectional enmity and divisive stereotypes that would last to our day.[33]

This is the mixed legacy of Jefferson Davis's leadership in the Confederacy—a leadership that accomplished political and social change on an almost unimaginable scale, yet leadership in dedication to an immoral goal, carried out with long-lasting and destructive effects.

NOTES

1. Richard N. Current, ed. in chief, *Encyclopedia of the Confederacy* (4 vols., New York: Simon & Schuster, 1993), vol. 3: 1233; Cleburne quoted in Robert F. Durden, *The Gray and the Black: The Confederate Debate on Emancipation* (Baton Rouge: Louisiana State University Press, 1972), 56.

2. Geoffrey Barraclough, ed., *The Times Atlas of World History* (Maplewood, NJ: Hammond, Inc., 1978, 1979), 223; William W. Freehling, *The South vs. the South: How Anti-Confederate Southerners Shaped the Course of the Civil War* (New York: Oxford University Press, 2001), 18–19, 61–63.

3. David M. Potter, *Lincoln and His Party in the Secession Crisis* (New Haven, CT: Yale University Press, 1942), 208; Charleston *Mercury*, September 19, 1861.

4. Frederick Law Olmsted, *The Slave States*, ed. Harvey Wish (New York: G. P. Putnam's Sons, 1959), 73; Roger L. Ransom, *Conflict and Compromise: The Political Economy of Slavery, Emancipation, and the American Civil War* (New York: Cambridge University Press, 1989), 61, 62, 29, 139; Roger L. Ransom, *The Confederate States of America: What Might Have Been* (New York: W. W. Norton and Co., 2005), 38–39, 41, 48, 49; Ralph W. Wooster, *The People in Power: Courthouse and Statehouse in the Lower South, 1850–1860* (Knoxville: University of Tennessee Press, 1969), 41; Ralph A. Wooster, *Planters, Politicians, and Plain Folk: Courthouse and Statehouse in the Upper South, 1850–1860* (Knoxville: University of Tennessee Press, 1975), 39–40; Ralph A. Wooster, *The Secession Conventions of the South* (Princeton, NJ: Princeton University Press, 1962), 260–61.

5. Dunbar Rowland, ed., *Jefferson Davis: Constitutionalist: His Letters, Papers, and Speeches* (10 vols., Jackson, MS: Little & Ives Co., 1923), vol. 5: 21, 32; Jefferson Davis, *Rise and Fall of the Confederate Government* (New York: D. Appleton and Co., 1881), vol. 1: 230.

6. Charleston *Mercury*, June 2, 1861; Richmond *Examiner* quoted in Steven E. Woodworth, *Davis and Lee at War* (Lawrence: University Press of Kansas, 1995), 6; E. Merton Coulter, *The Confederate States of America, 1861–1865* (Baton Rouge: Louisiana State University Press, 1950), 345.

7. Jefferson Davis to Congress, February 25, 1862, in Rowland, ed., *Jefferson Davis: Constitutionalist* 5: 205; William J. Cooper Jr., *Jefferson Davis and the Civil War Era* (Baton Rouge: Louisiana State University Press, 2009), 37; Emory M. Thomas, *The Confederate Nation: 1861–1865* (New York: Harper Torchbooks, 1979), 137; Tax History Museum, "Confederate War Financing," www.tax.org/Museum/1861–1865.htm.

8. Carl von Clausewitz, *On War*, ed. and trans. Michael Howard and Peter Paret (Princeton, NJ: Princeton University Press, 1976), 346, 340, 347, 469, 350, 481. Randolph quoted in Richard E. Beringer, Herman Hattaway, Archer Jones, and William N. Still, Jr., *The Elements of Confederate Defeat: Nationalism, War Aims, and Religion* (Athens: University of Georgia Press, 1988), 13.

9. William J. Cooper Jr., editor, *Jefferson Davis: The Essential Writings* (New York: Modern Library, 2003), 422, 420; Rowland, ed., *Jefferson Davis: Constitutionalist* 5: 462; Thomas Bragg Diary, Southern Historical Collection, University of North Carolina at Chapel Hill, p. 115.

10. Cooper, *Jefferson Davis and the Civil War Era*, 45, 63; Cooper, *Jefferson Davis: The Essential Writings*, 420; Robert L. Kerby, *Kirby Smith's Confederacy: The Trans-Mississippi South, 1863–1865* (New York: Columbia University Press, 1972), 87–95, 328–29; Paul D. Escott, *Military Necessity: Civil-Military Relations in the Confederacy* (Westport, CT: Praeger Security International, 2006), 103–14.

11. Abraham Lincoln, *Collected Works*, ed. Roy P. Basler (New Brunswick, NJ: Rutgers University Press, 1953–55), vol. 7: 514

12. Woodrow Wilson, *The New Freedom: A Call for the Emancipation of the Generous Energies of a People*, introd. and notes by William E. Leuchtenburg (Englewood Cliffs, NJ: Prentice-Hall, 1961), 161, 162, 169; James M. McPherson, "Liberating Lincoln," *New York Review of Books*, April 21, 1994, 7; Adam Gopnik, "Angels and Ages: Lincoln's Language and Its Legacy," *New Yorker*, May 28, 2007, 32.

13. Paul D. Escott, *After Secession: Jefferson Davis and the Failure of Confederate Nationalism* (Baton Rouge: Louisiana State University Press, 1978), 261–65.

14. Cooper, *Jefferson Davis and the Civil War Era*, 5, 15–16; Escott, *After Secession*, 264; Thomas, *The Confederate Nation*, 140; Herschel V. Johnson to A. H. Stephens, September 28, 1864, in Bell I. Wiley Papers, Special Collections, Woodruff Library, Emory University; Mary Boykin Chesnut, *Diary from Dixie*, ed. Ben Ames Williams (Boston: Houghton Mifflin Co., 1961), 497. The deaths of two of his children, in 1862 and 1864, undoubtedly compounded Davis's difficulties.

15. Current, ed., *Encyclopedia of the Confederacy* 3: 1158; Steven E. Woodworth, *Jefferson Davis and his Generals* (Lawrence: University Press of Kansas, 1990), 241–42. Woodworth's account is more sympathetic to Davis than most, including this author's.

16. Escott, *Military Necessity*, 52, 42–3, 19–21.

17. This paragraph represents the author's judgment. In general, the departmental system is discussed in many of the works mentioned above and in Thomas L. Connelly and Archer Jones, *The Politics of Command: Factions and Ideas in Confederate Strategy* (Baton Rouge: Louisiana State University Press, 1973).

The question of Jefferson Davis's performance as a military leader is much debated, but here, too, a natural bias against the loser in a great war skews many assessments. It is often said, for example, that Davis was addicted to micromanagement and interfered with the work of his generals in the field. In comparison, Lincoln is sometimes praised for his military acumen and his development of a sound strategic understanding of the war. Yet, a fair-minded analysis would alter this assessment in a number of ways. It would reveal that the behavior of both presidents toward their generals changed over the course of the conflict. In the early months of the war both tended to make specific, even politely intrusive, suggestions to their commanders. As the conflict wore on, however, this type of communication with the generals diminished. Certainly one would have to judge that Jefferson Davis gave a great deal of latitude and support to Robert E. Lee. The Confederate president's patience in dealing with Joseph Johnston also was so great as to be excessive. In 1864, especially, Johnston seemed to be a general who was determined to avoid risks; convinced of his weakness, Johnston focused on avoiding defeat and became a man who would not fight. That Davis put up with him so long, despite a well-founded lack of confidence in the general, proves that he had learned to respect the daily challenges and responsibilities of commanders in the field. Davis did give much attention to minor military matters, but these often involved his energetic efforts to arrange and encourage support for those who were involved in crucial operations. The time he spent on these issues did not damage the military effort so much as it took his attention away from pressing social and political problems. This author takes the position that the most valid criticism of Davis's military performance lies in his failure to interfere when interference was needed. The evidence on this point is overwhelming with regard to his prolonged and misguided support of Braxton Bragg, Abraham Myers, and Lucius Northrop. As argued above, the departmental system ceased to be an asset to the Confederacy after a year or so, a major reason being that Davis declined to overrule various commanders. On a number of occasions he needed to insist that they ignore the immediate needs in their region so that troops could be transferred elsewhere, in support of the Confederacy's overall military interests.

18. Woodworth, *Davis and Lee at War*, 331; Clausewitz, *On War*, 358, 357, 370.

19. Bell Irvain Wiley, *The Plain People of the Confederacy* (Baton Rouge: Louisiana State University Press, 1943), 69.

20. Quoted in Paul D. Escott, *Many Excellent People: Power and Privilege in North Carolina, 1850–1900* (Chapel Hill: University of North Carolina Press, 1985), 54. See also Paul D. Escott,

"'The Cry of the Sufferers': The Problem of Poverty in the Confederacy," *Civil War History* 23, no. 3 (September 1977): 228–40, and "Poverty and Governmental Aid to the Poor in Confederate North Carolina," *North Carolina Historical Review* 61, no. 4 (October 1984): 462–80.

21. Message to Congress, January 12, 1863, in James D. Richardson, comp., *A Compilation of the Messages and Papers of the Confederacy* (2 vols., Nashville, TN: United States Publishing Co., 1905), vol. 1: 295; Chesnut, *Diary from Dixie*, 367.

22. Emory M. Thomas, *The Confederacy as a Revolutionary Experience* (Englewood Cliffs, NJ: Prentice-Hall, Inc., 1971).

23. See Escott, *After Secession*, chapter 3 and passim. See also Escott, *Military Necessity*.

24. Ibid. For particulars on tax-in-kind, see Escott, *Military Necessity*, 76, which draws on the fine work of Peter Wallenstein.

25. Escott, *Military Necessity*, 84; Arthur James Lyon Fremantle, *Three Months in the Southern States: April, June, 1863* (Mobile, AL: S. H. Goetzel, 1864), in Documenting the American South Project, University of North Carolina at Chapel Hill, docsouth.unc.edu/imls/fremantle/menu.html, 66, 70; Mark E. Neely Jr., *Southern Rights: Political Prisoners and the Myth of Confederate Constitutionalism* (Charlottesville: University of Virginia Press, 1999), 2–3.

26. Clayton E. Jewett, ed., *Rise and Fall of the Confederacy: The Memoir of Senator Williamson S. Oldham, CSA* (Columbia: University of Missouri Press, 2006), 105–6, 108, 102.

27. Ibid., 112, 113. 119, 134.

28. Joseph E. Brown to Jefferson Davis, Mary 8, 1862, in Allen D. Candler, ed., *The Confederate Records of the State of Georgia* (6 vols., Atlanta: Chas. P. Byrd, 1910), vol. 3: 213–14; Brown to Davis, October 18, 1862, Candler, ed., *The Confederate Records of the State of Georgia* 3: 299, 301–2; Charleston *Mercury*, December 10, 1862, 1; "The Great Speech of Hon. A. H. Stephens, Delivered Before the Georgia Legislature, On Wednesday night, March 16, 1864, to Which is Added Extracts prom [sic] Gov. Brown's Message to the Georgia Legislature," Electronic Edition, Academic Affairs Library, University of North Carolina at Chapel Hill, in Documenting the American South Project, docsouth.unc.edu/imls/stephens/stephens.html.

29. Escott, *After Secession*, 138–39.

30. Paul D. Escott, *"What Shall We Do with the Negro?": Lincoln, White Racism, and Civil War America* (Charlottesville: University of Virginia Press, 2009) 184, 189; Escott, *Military Necessity*, 131–32.

31. Robert F. Durden, *The Gray and the Black: The Confederate Debate on Emancipation* (Baton Rouge: Louisiana State University Press, 1972), 206–7, 208–9; Judah Benjamin to Fred A. Porcher, December 21, 1864, in U.S. War Department, *The War of the Rebellion: A Compilation of the Official Records of the Union and Confederate Armies* (129 vols., Washington, DC: Government Printing Office, 1880–1901), ser. 4, vol. 3: 959–80; Durden, *The Gray and the Black*, 203.

32. Escott, *"What Shall We Do with the Negro?"* 96–97, 100, 138–40.

33. Quoted in Escott, *After Secession*, 183, 186, 191–92, 219.

EDMUND KIRBY SMITH'S EARLY LEADERSHIP IN THE TRANS-MISSISSIPPI

XXXXXXXXXXXXXXXXXXXXXXXXXXXXXXXXXXXXXXXXXX

JUDITH F. GENTRY

The leadership of Lt. Gen. Edmund Kirby Smith as commander of the Trans-Mississippi Department began in the midst of a Union advance from New Orleans northward through southwestern Louisiana, a large presence of Union troops along the Mississippi River in northeastern Louisiana, an anticipated Union effort to advance in the Arkansas River Valley, and threatened attacks at several places along the coast of Texas. Lt. Gen. Ulysses S. Grant's efforts to capture Vicksburg were entering a new phase. The Trans-Mississippi Department was already essentially cut off from troop reinforcements or resupply from across the Mississippi River. Support for the Confederacy among the people of Arkansas was rapidly declining. And large numbers of Confederate soldiers had no weapons while others had only a variety of shoulder arms brought with them from home.

This essay will consider four aspects of Kirby Smith's leadership during his first six months—the summer and fall of 1863: his efforts to carry out his instructions from Richmond; his relations with state political leaders; the strategy of concentration in space he implemented in an effort to repulse Maj. Gen. Nathaniel P. Banks; and his decisions related to supply issues, including his response to the first major crisis in the Mexican border trade.

Kirby Smith began almost immediately to carry out his instructions from President Jefferson Davis and Secretary of State James Seddon. At the same time, he began to organize a system of bureaus and agencies designed to enable the army to become self-sufficient through manufacture of military necessities not available on the market in the department combined with importation of

126

supplies needed to keep the army capable of fighting the enemy. His instructions included gaining and maintaining the support of state civil officers for the military defense of the department, providing as much assistance as possible to the Confederate forces at Vicksburg and Port Hudson on the lower Mississippi River, and making the Trans-Mississippi Department self-sufficient in supplies.

When Union troops began to move northward from the area just west of New Orleans, he organized and took action to implement a strategy of concentration to face the Federal troops advancing northward in Louisiana but was unable to prevent the advance of Union forces from the north deeper into northwestern Arkansas and eventually into the Arkansas River Valley. As he tried to concentrate forces from Arkansas and Texas in the upper Red River Valley in Louisiana, his actions weakened the defense and undercut civilian morale in those two states. Kirby Smith, however, learned important lessons for the future defense of the department. His strategy for supply self-sufficiency was to expand the manufacturing projects begun by the War Department and district commanders before he arrived and to move many of them from areas threatened by invasion—Arkansas and southwest and central Louisiana—to safety in northeast Texas and northwest Louisiana. By June, he added a second strategy to impress cotton needed to pay for military imports. Together, the manufacturing and importing programs were sufficient to keep the troops in the field throughout the war, but only at a barely minimal level. He was less successful in providing meaningful help to Vicksburg and Port Hudson. The small number of available Confederate troops in western Louisiana, broken levees flooding northeast Louisiana opposite Vicksburg, Kirby Smith's focus on the Union advance from near New Orleans in April and May 1863, bad intelligence, and Union gunboat patrols on the Mississippi River, combined with Grant's excellent leadership and focus on Vicksburg as well as vastly superior numbers of troops, made the TMD effort in late May, June, and the first days in July 1863 to render aid to Confederate forces at Vicksburg and Port Hudson of little consequence to the outcome. During his first six months in command, he was successful in conciliating civilian officials and gaining their support for his policies, even to the extent of supporting the impressment of cotton to use to continue the importation of military necessities.

XXXXX

Historians, like his contemporaries, have differed on Kirby Smith's actions and policies.

Joseph H. Parks's 1954 biography included the first published scholarly consideration of Edmund Kirby Smith's military leadership in the Trans-Mississippi Department. His description of the department when Kirby Smith arrived in early March 1863 emphasizes the lack of Confederate gunboats, a "greatly inferior force on land," and three Confederate armies operating independently of each other. Kirby Smith's "most pressing problem [was] securing adequate military supplies, particularly arms," and that required acquiring cotton. Parks quotes approvingly the later assessment of the new head of the Cotton Bureau that the impressment of cotton along the Rio Grande by Kirby Smith in the summer of 1863 was necessary but was riddled with favoritism. Parks also describes the agreement reached at the meeting of Trans-Mississippi governors and justices, cautioning Kirby Smith to stay within the law when exercising the "extraordinary powers" authorized by Secretary of War Seddon, yet encouraging him to buy or impress all the cotton in the department as a way to import needed supplies, force the speculators out of the cotton trade, and perhaps decrease the depreciation of the currency. Parks largely avoids making judgments or generalizations about Kirby Smith's leadership.[1]

The best description and discussion of the events related to impressment of cotton at Brownsville in the summer of 1863 is in Fredericka Ann Meiners's 1972 dissertation. She describes in detail the reluctance of both Major General John Magruder and Kirby Smith to take responsibility for ordering impressment of cotton to pay for shipments from England of cargoes including rifles and ammunition, noting that Kirby Smith finally did so and thus bore the brunt of public anger that erupted as the policy was enforced. Meiners details some of the obstacles to a successful impressment program and the decision of General Hamilton P. Bee to replace the failed impressment effort with an offer to those whose cotton had been stopped. Bee would release 80 percent of their cotton if the owners would lend immediately 20 percent to the government. She concludes that, given the restrictions that Richmond authorities placed on military efforts to control the border trade, Bee's loan was the only way to preserve Confederate credit in Europe. Her dissertation topic was Bee during the Civil War, so she does not discuss the impact of this series of events on Kirby Smith as a military leader.[2]

Robert Kerby's 1973 study of Kirby Smith's Confederacy remains the most important book on the topic, ranging widely on economic, political, and military aspects of the struggle of Confederates west of the Mississippi River to maintain (or regain) control during the last two years of the war. Edmund Kirby Smith stands at the center of that story. Kerby adheres heroically to his goal to produce a balanced narrative of events. His overall judgment of Kirby Smith— never stated, but implied—is that Kirby Smith was competent, with the possible exception of direct command of troops in the field in Arkansas during the Red River campaign. Occasionally, he reveals a little more: Kirby Smith's judgment that the 1863 Impressment Act "seemed" to authorize the impressment of cotton to pay for supplies was, Kerby writes, "more liberal" than any opinion in Richmond. Kerby concludes that the summer 1863 governor's conference at Marshall, Texas, which agreed to broad extraordinary powers apparently conferred on Kirby Smith by Seddon, "had no legal standing," and that the conference's refusal to allow Kirby Smith to issue bonds should be interpreted as withdrawal of the conference's clearly stated approval for buying or impressing the entire cotton crop west of the Mississippi. Kerby indicates that questions remain as to the extent of the civil authority possessed by Kirby Smith and concludes that he "never did manage to unwind" the "tangled snarl" of the "cotton business." In his summary, Kerby notes that Arkansas, Louisiana, and Missouri's officials went along with Kirby Smith on states' rights, and Texas also did so after August 1864.[3]

Recently, two books have considered major elements of Kirby Smith's record as commander of the Trans-Mississippi Department. Jewett's 2002 book on nation building in Confederate Texas argues that, during the Civil War, Texas created a political and economic "identity separate from that of other Southern states." Most visible in the Texas legislature, the foundation of the emerging Texas "national identity" was "to promote [and protect] the economic security of the citizenry." Kirby Smith's efforts to mobilize the resources of the Trans-Mississippi to prevent Union military forces from taking possession of Arkansas, Louisiana, and Texas are central to the story. Jewett argues that Kirby Smith "assumed the function of both the president and the cabinet," that the Richmond authorities took no action to control Kirby Smith, and that "the governor's conference [at Marshall] was not legally binding." Also, "the Trans-Mississippi Department often operated in contradiction to established law," since the "Confederate Congress ruled [in September 1862] that the states' legal system took precedence over military authorities." The Confederate Congress failed, however, to "adequately" protect "private property and free trade." Even before Kirby Smith arrived, commissary and then quartermaster officers impressed private property for the use of the army without paying for the goods. Kirby Smith carried the attack on private property and free trade to the extreme by creating the Cotton Bureau in an effort to completely control the cotton trade. Most state politicians and citizens objected vociferously to Kirby Smith's illegal actions, and this contributed to the development of a separate Texan nation.[4]

The second recent relevant book, Jeffrey F. Prushankin's *A Crisis in Command,* is a study of the relationship between Kirby Smith and Richard Taylor as commander and subordinate officer in the Trans-Mississippi Department for the last two years of the war. Most of the book is about the last year, but Prushankin devotes two-and-a-half chapters to the first six months after Kirby Smith took command. Prushankin describes Kirby Smith as an able administrator whose department "bureaucracy [was] the single most important factor in keeping Confederate hope alive west of the Mississippi River" but focuses on Kirby Smith's role in the department as military strategist leading the effort to defeat enemy troops. He argues that Kirby Smith devoted inappropriate resources to attempts to recover the large part of Arkansas that was occupied by the enemy because he "felt beholden" to Arkansas politicians for getting him appointed to command of the department, because he sought glory as the liberator of Arkansas and perhaps Missouri, and because he realized he would have to share with Taylor the glory of any victories in south Louisiana. Instead, Kirby Smith should have provided Taylor with those resources in support of a campaign to liberate New Orleans. Prushankin asserts that Kirby Smith "[failed] to follow [Jefferson Davis's and Seddon's] explicit instructions regarding protection of the lower Mississippi [River]." Also, Kirby Smith "refused to accept responsibility for the strategic failures in the Trans-Mississippi Department." His constant redeployment of troops seemed impulsive and his orders to fall back ill-conceived." His preference for "the 'strength of the defensive' . . . often led to sluggish or ill-timed concentration that made his strategy ineffective." Since Kirby Smith could not concentrate his forces to defend against the superior numbers of the enemy and at the same time defend the territory of all three states, Prushankin concludes that he should have chosen one strategy and been straightforward with his subordinates and the politicians in each state. Throughout the discussion, Prushankin generally characterizes Kirby Smith as "autocratic," "manipulative," "duplicitous," "less than forthright," and "politically expedient." In addition, he states that Kirby Smith occasionally "misrepresented messages" and "played the innocent."[5]

✕✕✕✕✕

For the first two years of the war, the Confederate government saw the Trans-Mississippi primarily as a source of troops and of supplies for use east of the Mississippi River. Repeatedly, the secretary of war transferred troops raised in Louisiana, Texas, and Arkansas to serve in the Eastern Theater and in Tennessee. Within the Trans Mississippi, he transferred troops from Texas into Arkansas. And then in 1862, virtually all troops in Arkansas and Louisiana were ordered to northern Mississippi as a part of a grand concentration of troops at Corinth, Mississippi, for the Shiloh campaign. The troops and the arms they carried never returned to the Trans-Mississippi. The secretary of war responded in 1862 to pleas from governors, congressional delegations, and leading citizens by sending no troops but only officers—Maj. Gen. Thomas C. Hindman (May 1862) and Lt. Gen. Theophilis Holmes (August 1862) to Arkansas, Maj. Gen. Richard Taylor (August 1862) to Louisiana, Maj. Gen. John Bankhead Magruder (December 1862) to Texas, and Lt. Gen. Edmund Kirby Smith (March 1863) to command the new Trans-Mississippi Department. The secretary of war also moved a division within the Trans-Mississippi (from Texas to Arkansas) in fall of 1862, which later came to be called Walker's Division. Several of the officers were sent primarily because they were well known and popular in their state. Each was to lift the spirits of the general population, undercut growing disaffection, and raise a new army of volunteers, using the conscript law when necessary. Enforcing conscription was very unpopular, however, and contributed to continuing low civilian morale, and it removed workers from the productive economy.

In Arkansas, Confederate leaders began to create companies of partisans to operate independently, or in support of regular units. By late 1862, Arkansas, Texas and Louisiana district commanders and governors were no longer willing to keep sending troops eastward across the Mississippi. When the Richmond authorities sent Maj. Gen. Sterling Price to Arkansas in early April 1863, where it was hoped he would, when the time was right, raise a volunteer force to retake Missouri, he was ordered to take his troops across the Mississippi River with him into Arkansas. Unfortunately, it proved impractical to cross a large force, so Price and his staff were all that reached the TMD.[6]

When Kirby Smith arrived in early March 1863, on paper Arkansas had 17,000 troops, Louisiana had 15,000, and Texas had 12,000, totaling 44,000 troops. The numbers ready for duty usually were variously estimated as: Arkansas 8,500–11,000, Louisiana 6,000–9,000, and Texas 6,000, for a total of 20,500–26,000 effectives. In September 1863, Kirby Smith estimated total effective troops as 32,000–33,000. Large numbers of recruits and even veteran soldiers were unarmed or poorly armed: in Arkansas, 2,000 had no arms and 5,000 were poorly armed; in Texas, 6,000 recruits had no arms and the other 6,000 were poorly armed. They faced Banks's invasion force of 16,000, Maj. Gen. Ulysses S. Grant's force of 40,000 in northeastern Louisiana, and the 37,000 troops under Maj. Gen. Samuel R. Curtis, which operated without opposition in much of northwestern Arkansas and threatened the Arkansas River Valley. Of 16,000 stand of arms that Chief of Ordnance Josiah Gorgas marked in mid-1862 for transport to the TMD, most were delayed because they were in need of repairs, and 5,000 were captured. At most, 11,000 had made it across the Mississippi before the fall of Vicksburg. About 7,000 of these reached Little Rock on 14 November 1862; 20 percent were Enfield rifles, and most of the rest were reliable smoothbore muskets. In late 1862 and early 1863, Secretary of War James Seddon and Gorgas arranged several shipments of arms to the TMD. Lt. Gen. John C. Pemberton, commander of the troops at Vicksburg, commandeered the three heavy cannon that reached the river. A shipment of 25,000 shoulder arms plus a large amount of ammunition crossed the river at Natchez into Louisiana just before the surrender of Vicksburg, but Union soldiers captured about 7,000 of the weapons and considerable ammunition from the rear guard of the wagon train on the western side of the river. Ordnance officers found the other 18,000 to be useless, most being flintlock muskets and the rest in disrepair. Another shipment of 25,000 rifles (with accoutrements) that reached Vicksburg had not been crossed into Louisiana when Vicksburg surrendered. The record regarding successful importation of small arms for the army via the Rio Grande was mixed. The *Sir William Peel* unloaded 10,000 rifles before departing from the Rio Grande in July 1863. A French warship blockading Matamoros captured the *Caroline Goodyear* with its cargo of 10,000–12,000 rifles for the Confederacy. In the late summer of 1863, 4,200 out of the shipment of 10,000 were landed near Brownsville, Texas, before a Union blockader captured the *Love Bird*.[7]

Importation was absolutely essential to the survival of the Trans-Mississippi

Department. The productive capability of the department was insufficient to meet the needs of the army for arms, ammunition, gunpowder, leather goods, shoes, blankets, paper, and many other items essential for a modern army. In the TMD, the state and Confederate governments in 1862 preferred not to take the risks of running the blockade. The neutral border with Mexico along the Rio Grande provided a route for importing necessary goods without those risks. Goods—even munitions of war—could be carried to Mexican ports in neutral vessels and then could be transported across the Rio Grande into Texas. The trade depended upon payment for the goods in cotton.[8]

Early in the war, the army relied on local contractors—Texan or Mexican—to bring supplies to the interior, and to take payment in Confederate money, which they then invested in cotton. Soon, however, contractors began demanding payment in cotton, and army quartermasters began using appropriations for army stores to buy cotton to pay for the stores. The Richmond authorities tried to centralize such activities during the fall of 1862. In November, Major Simeon Hart arrived in Texas with exclusive authority to buy cotton in the state to exchange for imported supplies. During the next six months, Hart imported large quantities of needed goods on credit extended by Mexican merchants, who were aware of his exclusive authority and were willing to wait for payment until he had completed his cotton-buying arrangements. Hart's contracts provided for payment in cotton on the border, and he immediately began buying cotton. He soon learned that, in central and western Texas, competition for cotton to be used in the border trade, combined with the depreciation of Confederate Treasury notes, had resulted in high prices. To stretch his funds for purchasing, he bought most of his cotton in northern and eastern Texas, where there was little competition at that time, and arranged for its transportation to the border. The transport of this cotton over the long distances to the border proved to be excruciatingly slow.[9]

By the time Kirby Smith reached the TMD, depreciation of the currency had exhausted the department's funds for purchasing. Paymasters ran out of money in 1862, and no soldiers in the TMD received pay in the last two years of the war. Quartermasters ran out of currency with which to purchase food, forage, cloth, clothing, or leather goods, including shoes. In late summer 1862, after a conference at Marshall, Texas, the four Trans-Mississippi governors requested that "a branch of the Confederate treasury [be established west of the Mississippi River] with power to issue money." District ordnance officers had exhausted the local market for arms and ammunition and were already at work seeking ways to produce in the department or import across the Rio Grande rifles, gunpowder, percussion caps, machinery for manufacturing ordnance, and other ordnance stores. The letter from the four governors also requested that a Trans-Mississippi Department be established and 20,000–30,000 stand of small arms be sent. In the meantime, Hindman, and later Holmes, organized and operated in Arkansas lead mines, chemical laboratories and factories at Arkadelphia and then at Camden; a foundry and machine shop could produce cannon ball and shells. Hindman also supported efforts to make percussion caps, powder, many quartermaster goods, and medicines. The Texas State Military Board created a cap and cartridge factory and tried less successfully to produce cannon and small arms. New Iberia, on the Bayou Teche, and the surrounding area in southwestern Louisiana became a center of manufacturing for the military—an arsenal, gunpowder mills, and cartridge factories; slaughterhouse and meatpacking industry; and wagon-making shops. Most important in the area were the salt mines that supplied the Trans-Mississippi and parts of the Confederacy east of the river. In central Louisiana, at Alexandria, another slaughterhouse and tannery operation produced leather goods, including shoes. Yet, the production capabilities of these enterprises were insufficient to meet the needs of the Confederate armies west of the Mississippi.[10]

In August 1862, the War Department authorized quartermasters throughout the Confederacy to impress food and forage for immediate use if necessary and in November 1862 to impress wagons if necessary. Resentment of farmers and others whose property was impressed, with only a receipt promising payment in the future at a price well below its market value, was beginning to emerge before Kirby Smith's arrival in the Trans-Mississippi. The War Department also responded to TMD supply needs in late 1862 and early 1863 by sending not only Hart to bring order to the cotton trade but also Capt. Isaac Read to head a branch of the Nitre and Mining Bureau in Arkansas, Maj. Thornton A. Washington to set up a clothing factory and tannery at San Antonio, and Maj. Gen. Benjamin Huger, supported by Maj. Thomas Rhett, as chief of TMD ordnance and artillery. The new Nitre and Mining Bureau, charged to produce raw materials for the manufacture of ammunition, assisted contractors operating in the Ozarks by getting their workers exempted from conscription; soon the bureau began to work new mines and factories with detailed soldiers and slaves. Ordnance officers developed arsenals at Little Rock and San Antonio. The War Department also purchased in Europe rifles and other ordnance stores and shipped them to the Rio Grande. Cabinet officers scrambled to try to figure out how to send funds to the TMD. The increasing gunboat traffic on the Mississippi River, however, presented such obstacles to crossing funds that none crossed in 1863.[11]

xxxxx

When Kirby Smith arrived in the Trans-Mississippi, he carried instructions from both the secretary of war and President Jefferson Davis. He also brought his West Point training and experience acquired in the Mexican War and in Virginia and Tennessee during the Civil War. He understood that his role as commander of a department required that he bring order and cohesion to the military forces in the department. Until his arrival, each of the three armies operated as independent commands. Kirby Smith made no early personnel changes. He planned to allow each of the three district commanders—Holmes in Arkansas, Taylor in Louisiana, and Magruder in Texas—to devise and implement strategies to defend his district and retake lost territory if possible. He would only take the field when a concentration of forces across district lines was necessary. As it turned out, his first six months were characterized by the almost constant need to concentrate TMD forces to oppose enemy offensive operations in the department. He found profound disorganization and lack of order at the headquarters, and he moved immediately to remedy that situation.[12]

On the day Kirby Smith assumed command of the Trans-Mississippi Department, Union soldiers who were digging a canal in eastern Louisiana opposite Vicksburg accidentally destroyed the nearby levees, thus inadvertently flooding the Ouachita River Valley and much of the area between Monroe and the Mississippi River. Soon, persistent heavy rains in the Bayou Macon area and then planned breaking of some levees near Lake Providence, designed to make a navigable pathway through northeastern Louisiana, added to the flooding. Kirby Smith considered operations in that area to be impracticable until the waters receded. He continued to consider the flood waters too high for offensive operations until about 20 May.[13]

Kirby Smith also took action immediately to carry his instructions into effect. In response to Seddon's request of 9 February 1863, Kirby Smith left Alexandria, Louisiana, for Little Rock, Arkansas, only three days after taking command of the department on 7 March. Reports of disorder, demoralization, opposition to conscription, desertions, "bands of lawless desperados," and organized peace societies widespread in the Ozarks and parts of southwestern Arkansas in 1862 had raised concerns in Richmond. Kirby Smith found matters had already improved since the unpopular Gen. Hindman had been transferred out of Arkansas and the popular Price had been directed to proceed to Little Rock to lead Arkansas forces. Kirby Smith also credited Holmes for suppressing the Unionist clubs and enticing absentees to return to their units. Yet much of northern Arkansas was a no man's land, the Arkansas River Valley was in danger, and there were too few troops to effectively defend Arkansas (many of whom were poorly supplied with weapons and equipment). In addition, many Unionist Club members formed small groups and continued armed resistance to Confederate authority. In late January, Davis had directed Holmes to advance into Missouri "once Arkansas was secure." By late February, Davis postponed indefinitely the invasion of Missouri, but the news had not reached Holmes by the time of Kirby Smith's visit. Adhering to Seddon's directive to go directly to Little Rock after reporting to Alexandria, a distance of 124 miles by steamboat plus 213 overland, consumed approximately five weeks of Kirby Smith's valuable time. In response to Holmes's description of the president's directive, Kirby Smith authorized a large cavalry raid from northern Arkansas into Missouri, which did considerable property damage but found few Missouri volunteers and concluded with a hasty retreat through swamps, leaving behind many weapons and mounts. In addition to conferring with military and civil officials at Little Rock, Kirby Smith appears to have used the trip partly as a way to learn about the upper Red River Valley in Louisiana and about the southernmost parts of Arkansas, a sizeable part of his new command.[14]

Richmond authorities had also instructed Kirby Smith (in late February or early March) that the highest priority, after going to Arkansas, was to do all that was possible to assist Pemberton in the defense of the "lower Mississippi River." If possible without endangering his department, he should cross troops and supplies to Pemberton at Vicksburg, operate against Grant's supply lines in northeast Louisiana, and disrupt from the river banks Union supply and troop-transport vessels on the river above Vicksburg. Additional instructions in May and June included trying to use cannon on the river banks to sink troop transports and supply vessels on the Mississippi River, destroying all subsistence and forage on abandoned plantations and those being operated by Federal lessees, and burning cotton exposed to the enemy.[15]

Kirby Smith also, however, had the responsibility of every department commander to organize a defense of his department. On 5 April, as Banks was increasing the number of his troops at Brashear City and Kirby Smith was on the road back from Little Rock, Kirby Smith heard a rumor that Magruder was putting together an expedition to Arizona. Kirby Smith withheld approval for any such plan and explained that it was important to keep the troops near to areas where an attack was likely. He was nearing Alexandria on his return from Arkansas when Banks made his move across Berwick Bay to begin his first Teche campaign on 12 April. When Kirby Smith reached Alexandria a few days later, he learned that, although Taylor's force of 4,000–5,000 won the Battle of Bisland, he had been out-flanked and nearly enveloped. His forces were in a rapid retreat up the Bayou Teche. In the two weeks beginning 14 April, Kirby Smith issued a flurry of orders and appeals designed to produce a grand concentration in space at Natchitoches on the upper Red River, drawing forces nearly 300 miles from the west and almost 200 miles from the north, distances mainly to be traveled by overland marches. Historian Archer Jones describes a strategic concentration as bringing military forces together temporarily to engage the enemy in battle at a place of your choosing. It is especially used by the army that is inferior in numbers in an attempt to temporarily have superior numbers, or at least less inferior numbers, during the battle. In the Civil War, use of the telegraph and railroad connections generally enabled rapid concentrations over long distances. Perhaps Kirby Smith thought he could make a grand concentration work because, when commanding the Department of East Tennessee, he grew accustomed to repeatedly rapidly shifting troops 180 miles first in one direction and then in another by railroad. In the spring of 1863 in the Trans-Mississippi, he hoped to bring together about 10,000 infantry and cavalry against Banks's advancing force of about 15,000. On 18 April, he believed the attack on Vicksburg and Port Hudson had "been abandoned" and the main Union objective was the "conquest" of Louisiana. He feared that Maj. Gen. John McClernand's force in the Bayou Macon area of northeast Louisiana, estimated at 15,000 at that time, would join Banks's force to achieve that objective.[16]

To prepare to prevent this conquest, Kirby Smith took the following actions. He directed Holmes to send Walker's Division from Pine Bluff, Arkansas, to Monroe, Louisiana, via Camden, Arkansas; he later modified the destination to the Red River. (This transfer apparently was at first to comply with President Davis's instruction to Kirby Smith to order Walker's Division to Louisiana to put pressure on Union troops opposite Vicksburg.) Kirby Smith directed a brigade and two regiments from the District of East Texas and all "disposable" troops from the area of Galveston to move to Niblett's Bluff, Texas, at the Sabine River on the main road between Opelousas, Louisiana, and Houston. A little later, he recommended that the District of East Texas form the people into "minute-man companies." Holmes would need to exercise his judgment regarding any Union advances that might occur toward southern Arkansas. Kirby Smith even requested Pemberton (at Vicksburg) to send troops to help defend against the conquest of Louisiana. His staff would remove all stores and records from Alexandria to Shreveport, where TMD headquarters would be re-established.[17]

Banks's two-week stay at Alexandria gave Kirby Smith hope that Walker and perhaps Texan cavalry units could reach the Shreveport area before Banks reached that city or Jefferson, Texas, an important commercial town that could be reached via the Red River. He directed the Texas troops at Niblett's Bluff to head north to Nacogdoches, Texas, which was considerably closer to both of these potential enemy objectives and redirected Walker to Shreveport. When Banks moved toward Baton Rouge in mid-May, Kirby Smith at first interpreted the movement as preliminary to an attempt to occupy west Louisiana via the Red River.[18]

Kirby Smith's concentration in the spring of 1863 ran into serious difficulties. It took nine days for his directive to reach Walker. Walker's Division then found that persistent heavy rains produced mud and local flooding that prevented it from using the Camden route to Monroe, slowed it considerably, used up its supplies, and wore out its men. When he reached Monroe, he could not travel to Natchitoches or Shreveport without resupply. He thus he did not reach the concentration point in time. Walker finally reached the Red River on 24 May, thirty-two days after he received the order. Major's cavalry brigade arrived at Alexandria from Texas ten days too late but operated on Banks's flank as he retreated. The three units Kirby Smith ordered from east Texas to concentrate at Niblett's Bluff had no weapons. Although Magruder concentrated 5,000 troops at Niblett's Bluff, he dragged his feet about crossing any infantrymen out of Texas. Since the Union troops at Vicksburg and Port Hudson had not been ordered elsewhere, Pemberton could send no troops. The presence of Walker's Division at Monroe left Arkansas in danger, and the forces sent from Texas weakened coastal defenses. On the positive side, the large amount of stores and the headquarters at Alexandria were efficiently evacuated to Shreveport. Six cavalry regiments (Major's and the Old Sibley brigades totaling 3,000 cavalry-men) arrived late at the Red River. In addition, Kirby Smith could use the newly arrived troops in the effort to help Confederate forces at Vicksburg and Port Hudson, and he had learned some important lessons.[19]

He realized that infantry from Arkansas or Texas were unlikely to reach a point of concentration in the upper Red River Valley in time but believed Texas cavalry units could probably arrive in time. He began to realize that Arkansas could not help the others because of distance, terrain, road quality, and its own immediate defense needs, and it was unlikely that the others could help Arkansas. (Later, as Confederate Arkansas contracted into a small area in extreme southwestern Arkansas, he apparently revisited that issue.) He began to understand that, in addition to the major problems connected with the concentration of troops in time to be effective, the size of the department and sparseness of troops made it very difficult to defend every point where the enemy might attack. He became increasingly aware that concentrating TMD troops at one place opened vulnerabilities at all other places and created serious morale problems among troops and civilians. But he did not completely abandon the strategy of concentrating troops to confront an invading army.[20]

In early June 1863, Kirby Smith believed Banks would soon attempt to invade Texas through Louisiana or Arkansas. He requested Magruder to concentrate available troops at the Sabine River and directed Taylor to send two mounted regiments to the northeast Texas frontier "as soon as he can spare them." He ordered Walker to Alexandria, where his forces could recuperate from the unhealthy climate opposite Vicksburg and be ready to respond to a threat from the south or farther up the Red River. By 12 July, however, Kirby Smith no longer expected a Banks summer campaign in Louisiana.[21]

Having learned from his spring effort to concentrate troops in the upper Red River Valley, Kirby Smith directed Holmes to establish "forage and subsistence depots . . . through the barren country between Texas and the Red River and between Camden and Natchitoches," for the use of Arkansas forces, in case they had to fall back to the Red River, or for the use of forces concentrating in response to another invasion via the Red River. In early September, Union forces became active near Little Rock, Arkansas, in southern Louisiana, and on the coast of Texas at the Sabine River. When Union troops maneuvered around Little Rock in early September, Holmes had only 9,000 effective troops to confront a Union force of 20,000. Kirby Smith responded to Holmes's pleas for help by ordering Magruder to send all available troops to Arkansas. Magruder grumbled but started 5,000 men marching toward southwestern Arkansas. Arkansas forces abandoned Little Rock to the Federal force on 10 September. The Texas forces were by then in northeastern Texas en route to Arkansas. Magruder recalled them to defend the coast. Lt. Richard W. Dowling's small force at the mouth of the Sabine River had repelled a Union naval assault on 8 September, and Magruder prepared for a second attempt. Also in early September, Banks sent 20,000 troops under Maj. Gen. William B. Franklin to Brashear City west of the Mississippi in southern Louisiana. Kirby Smith asked each governor to form a home guard, in case the enemy succeeded and civilians would need to defend their neighborhoods. Based on intelligence that Banks planned to move Union troops westward along the coast of western Louisiana, in mid-September Kirby Smith directed Taylor's force (by then 4,200 men) to operate on the Union northern flank and, if necessary, cross into Texas to join with Magruder against the enemy along the Sabine. He directed Magruder to concentrate all disposable Confederate forces at Niblett's Bluff. Kirby Smith then awaited a clear commitment by Banks's force. He expected Banks to advance up the Red River and prepared for a concentration of TMD troops in the upper Red River valley. When summer ended, Banks's second invasion of Louisiana along the Bayou Teche was about to begin.[22]

In summary, in early September 1863, Kirby Smith was faced with Union attacks from three directions. He clearly believed Banks's army was the most dangerous threat. In late August, he apparently did not consider the threat to the Texas coast from the Union navy a priority, and the distance and quality of roads made successful reinforcement of Little Rock a long shot. By mid-September, he prepared to use Taylor's force to impede or delay any movement overland to Texas across southwest Louisiana by harassing the flank of Banks's much larger army. If that failed to prevent an invasion of Texas, Taylor and Magruder would join forces—concentrate—to oppose Banks's army in southeast Texas. Walker stood ready at Alexandria to join with Taylor if Banks's army moved northward in Louisiana.

XXXXX

Although Kirby Smith continued to believe until about 20 May that the area between Monroe, Louisiana, and the Mississippi River was too wet from the flood to support offensive operations, Grant ordered McClernand's Corps on 29 March to move along the levees and bayou banks through the flooded area from Milliken's Bend to New Carthage, the latter actually surrounded by water. By 15 April, when Kirby Smith was arranging to concentrate troops against Banks's forces, Grant made an unexpected decision. Realizing the "one narrow, almost impassable, road between Milliken's Bend and New Carthage" was too small to feed his entire army, which was by then well below Milliken's Bend, he largely abandoned his supply line along the west bank of the river and ordered rations to be delivered to his forces at Hard Times, Louisiana, by steamboats running past Vicksburg. By 3 May, the bulk of Grant's forces had crossed the Mississippi River into Mississippi below Vicksburg, and by 21 May they had a new supply line in place via the Yazoo River above Vicksburg. Grant's total reliance on the supply line through northeast Louisiana made his forces vulnerable from 29 March to about the third week in April 1863—only about three weeks—as he moved his troops southward to Hard Times. Kirby Smith was, for most of that time, on the road returning from his conference with the governor of Arkansas. As late as the first week of June, commanders of Confederate forces on both sides of the Mississippi river—Kirby Smith and Lt. Gen. General Joseph E. Johnston—were unaware of that Grant had abandoned his supply line through northeast Louisiana. Kirby Smith knew by mid-April that McClernand was moving in the Bayou Macon area but interpreted his movements as preparation for an attack on Taylor's army. From mid-April to mid-May, Kirby Smith's focus was on Taylor's rapid retreat up the Bayou Teche with Banks's army close behind.[23]

Three events in the fourth week of May caused a change of Kirby Smith's focus to Vicksburg. When he learned in late May that Banks had crossed the Mississippi to join the investment of Port Hudson, he realized that Louisiana was free of the invading army. He turned his attention to his instructions to assist in the defense of the lower Mississippi River. As soon as Banks began moving his troops eastward, Kirby Smith allowed Taylor to re-occupy the Teche valley and operate in the LaFourche area opposite Port Hudson, which Taylor believed would draw off some of Banks's forces from the Port Hudson siege. But Kirby Smith would not attach Walker's Division to Taylor's command for a campaign to liberate New Orleans. He directed Taylor to attempt to destroy enemy transports and supply vessels and disrupt commercial trade on the Mississippi between Port Hudson and New Orleans. At about that same time, Kirby Smith concluded that the flooded area in northeast Louisiana was dry enough for offensive operations. Four days later, when Walker's Division arrived at the Red River, Kirby Smith took action. He returned one brigade of Walker's Division to Holmes, to participate in the defense of Confederate-held parts of Arkansas and reassure the governor of Arkansas that the state had not been forgotten. He ordered Taylor to leave his troops in south Louisiana and take temporary command of the other three brigades of Walker's Division and several cavalry units recently arrived from Texas for action in northeast Louisiana. Taylor was to move the division by steamers up the Tensas to attempt "a *coup de main* upon [Grant's] communications" (supply line) and to move supplies across the river "into Vicksburg."[24]

Taylor divided his temporary command into three parts for simultaneous attacks on Millikin's Bend and Young's Point on the Mississippi River and the Lake Providence area on 6 June. Faulty intelligence from local cavalry greatly underestimated the numbers of enemy troops in the area; local cavalry also engaged a small group of the enemy, which eliminated the element of surprise. The mid-morning attack at Milliken's Bend succeeded in forcing the Union force to retreat to the levee and imposed heavy casualties, but the Confederates withdrew when several gunboats arrived and began firing grape and canister, devastating anti-personnel ordnance, into the area. The other two columns made no significant contact with Union forces because of a tiring night march through "thickets and briars," a bridge that was out, heat exhaustion, the inexperienced Confederate soldiers' tendency to withdraw as soon as enemy gunboats arrived, and a three-day delay in the cavalry attack at Lake Providence. Kirby Smith explained in his report to Richmond that he had taken action before Vicksburg was invested and "as soon as the water level at Bayou Macon allowed." By mid-June, Kirby Smith reported that "all of the disposable force of the Department has been thrown to the relief of Port Hudson and Vicksburg and is operating on the Mississippi to that end." Taylor's force was operating since late May in the LaFourche area and along the Mississippi River banks in an effort to attack enemy transports and gunboats on the river below and above Donaldsonville, to cross supplies for Port Hudson, and perhaps to draw enemy troops away from the investment of Port Hudson. Taylor re-joined his troops by mid-June.[25]

Walker's command continued to operate in northeastern Louisiana opposite Vicksburg, to try to disrupt enemy non-existent supply lines and get supplies across into Vicksburg. Holmes was considering an attempt to retake Helena,

Arkansas, to help relieve the pressure on Vicksburg. These efforts drew criticism from Richard Taylor, who believed he could enter New Orleans and wreak sufficient havoc to cause Banks to divert at least part of his forces then besieging Port Hudson if he could have Walker's Division attached for that purpose. Nevertheless, operating in the LaFourche region without Walker's Division, Taylor succeeded in raiding areas within sixteen miles of New Orleans, capturing large numbers of Union soldiers and large amounts of army supplies. Kirby Smith approached Walker about possibly moving his division across the Mississippi to reinforce Pemberton, but Walker explained in convincing detail why it was not feasible. The enemy could easily "crush any small force that would attempt to pass into the narrow strip leading to Vicksburg." Kirby Smith deferred to his judgment. Walker's Division slowly succumbed in large numbers to diseases endemic to low-lying areas of northeast Louisiana, with only 42 percent of the original number that entered the area fit for duty when they left.[26]

This early June campaign in northeast Louisiana opposite Vicksburg had only a minor impact on the forces Grant had left as an occupying force along the river bank in northeast Louisiana. There was, by then, no supply line through the area, and Grant had no intention to maintain a line of retreat through northeastern Louisiana. Gunboat traffic on the Mississippi prevented moving troops across the Mississippi and made crossing supplies very risky. Union forces freed the slaves they encountered in northeastern Louisiana near the river and continued the process of supporting plantations near the river where former slaves worked for wages.[27] Taylor's operations opposite New Orleans and upriver from there tempted Banks but did not produce any troop transfers away from the siege. Union forces occupying parts of Louisiana near the river heavily outnumbered Confederate forces in Arkansas and Louisiana, and Grant and Banks kept their focus on their main goal—Vicksburg.

Kirby Smith's decision to use available TMD troops in mid-April to attempt to stop Banks's army near Natchitoches instead of sending them to operate opposite Vicksburg may have been primarily based upon the flooded condition of the area, a factor that is seldom taken into consideration. Or, perhaps Kirby Smith perceived that preventing the potential conquest of Louisiana by Banks in early 1863 was more important than the minimal effect the small military force at his command could have had on the effort to hold Vicksburg. Grant's supply line functioned for only about three weeks, Confederate intelligence about Union forces in northeastern Louisiana was never good, and Grant had made other arrangements for supplying his troops long before Kirby Smith could have been able to move his troops into position to attack the supply line. Historians, like most Confederate leaders, have perhaps overestimated the significance of that short-lived opportunity to cut Grant's supply line.

Ten days after the surrender of Vicksburg, Seddon sent Kirby Smith four additional instructions: Try to make the TMD self sustaining. Try to "conciliate the governors" to the new situation in the TMD and gain their support for military efforts to defend the department. Use cavalry and field artillery battalions to try to prevent the enemy from using the Mississippi River for commercial purposes. Work to keep good relations with the Indians. Twenty days after that letter, Seddon urged him to "break up" cotton plantations in eastern Louisiana being operated under Federal auspices. Kirby Smith had already seen the need to accomplish four of the directives. For instance, he had already put Walker's division to work in the Lake Providence area, operating when possible against Federal commercial and supply and troop transport vessels on the river and destroying equipment and stores on plantations near the river. Taylor was doing the same in the LaFourche area. In addition, he was aware that any concentration of troops in one state in the TMD generally elicited concerns (and sometimes complaints) from the governors of the other states, and complaints about conscription were common. Kirby Smith corresponded regularly with each state governor and visited state capitals from time to time, assuring each that he was committed to defending the entire territory of each state and trying to resolve occasional disputes. In mid-July, he called for a conference of governors and justices to consider the intensified isolation from the rest of the Confederacy. And, from the beginning, supply issues were important to him.[28]

XXXXX

Kirby Smith understood the role of a commanding officer to include significant time and attention to issues related to supply and logistics. He found in the Trans-Mississippi chaos in the purchase and distribution of commissary, quartermaster. and ordnance supplies. There was no departmental system at all. He almost immediately created bureaus to systematize the process of supplying the troops. He completed by June the stringing of telegraph wires connecting Shreveport, Monroe, and Little Rock and had begun the process of extending the lines to Alexandria, Louisiana, and to the existing Texas telegraph line. Reliable and honest officers with skills and experience in purchasing, transporting, managing factories and mines, dealing in international trade, and other aspects of logistics were important to success. He built on the work that district commanders had begun. From the beginning, noting the vulnerability to attack of manufacturing centers in southwestern Louisiana and eastern Arkansas, he shifted the machinery and stores from those locations, centralizing manufacturing at Shreveport, Louisiana, and Marshall and Tyler, Texas. Thus, northeast Texas and northwest Louisiana became the center of an industrial complex, including a foundry to produce cannon, cannon balls, and shells; arsenals and shops to produce rifles; and slaughterhouses to produce rations and provide raw materials for the production of shoes, harnesses, and other leather goods. Shoe factories were developed in five cities in the TMD. Also, mining and nitre production moved to central Texas, and San Antonio continued to be a major center for the Rio Grande trade and the production of rifles, percussion caps, and cartridges. Home production of clothing, milling of grains, and wagon production and repair remained scattered throughout the populated areas.[29]

Kirby Smith rapidly grasped the import of the currency problem. The few treasury drafts that had successfully crossed the Mississippi from the east were for such large amounts that "it [was] impossible to cash . . . them." In early June, he ordered that currency paid into TMD depositories no longer be cancelled, and in August he directed that "notes be overstamp[ed] and reissue[d]." He used them to purchase necessities. He reported this action to Richmond each time and repeatedly requested the establishment of a branch treasury office in the TMD. The governors of the Trans-Mississippi states had made the same request in mid-summer 1862. No such office was established until February 1864. In August 1863, the secretary of the treasury was planning to send currency to the TMD "via Havana and Matamoras," and the secretary of war was devising plans to send funds safely across the Mississippi River. In October, President Davis assured Kirby Smith that safe arrangements had been made. In the meantime, Kirby Smith kept on. He reported whenever he took action regarding the currency, repeating his request for a treasury agency, and no order to cease came from Richmond.[30]

Other than the lack of funds, his most pressing supply problem was the lack of high-quality rifles and other ordnance in sufficient numbers to arm all of the troops. He reorganized and supported a competent and energetic ordnance bureau, which by the fall of 1863 was manufacturing rifles at the rate of 800 per week. He relied on the capable and experienced General Hamilton P. Bee, commander of the sub-district that included the Rio Grande area, to obtain the shiploads of Enfield rifles sent by Seddon that began arriving off the mouth of the Rio Grande in late May 1863. Unfortunately, due to the unavailability of sufficient cotton at Brownsville, the failure of some shipments to meet ordnance bureau standards, the interference of French naval vessels, and aggressive action by Union blockaders, no more than half of the arriving rifles were acquired. Nevertheless, the 14,000 rifles that were acquired on the Rio Grande during Kirby Smith's first six months were an important addition to the effectiveness of the department's military forces. Arrangements were made to get sufficient amounts of gunpowder from Mexican producers.[31]

The foundation of an efficient and secure supply system was laid in this first six months, and government production facilities operated throughout the last two years of the war to produce and repair weapons, produce ammunition, and produce clothing, shoes, harnesses, and ammunition boxes badly needed by the soldiers of the TMD. The army had enough to continue to fight. It was, however, a relative trickle of necessities compared to the need.

XXXXX

Wagon trains hauling government-owned imported goods from the Rio Grande to San Antonio and Alleyton (near Houston) were as important as the government-owned manufacturing facilities in northeast Texas and at Shreveport in keeping the TMD armies minimally supplied. In Texas, as elsewhere in the Confederacy by late 1862, the ability to import needed supplies depended on the ability to pay for them in cotton. In late May of 1863, an emergency developed when three ships bearing goods ordered by Confederate officials arrived off the coast of Texas, and the government found itself with little or no cotton available with which to pay for the cargoes. If the cotton was not obtained, not only would the needed goods be lost, but the credit of the Confederacy would be compromised. After some hesitation, Kirby Smith initiated a policy of impressment as the means of obtaining the needed cotton. Impressment—seizure of cotton by the Confederate army from persons unwilling to sell it at schedule prices—failed as a method of supplying the cotton needed in the emergency. The threat of impressment, however, produced a willingness on the part of cotton merchants to comply with a forced loan of cotton to the army. This loan, and certain other developments, produced sufficient cotton to obtain the needed supplies and protect the credit of the government. Moreover, the emergency and the difficulties surrounding the impressment demonstrated clearly to army officials in Texas that an entire reorganization of the cotton trade would be necessary if the army was to meet its commitments. In response, the Cotton Bureau evolved as an instrument to obtain cotton without impressment; central to the Cotton Bureau's bargaining power was a threat—the threat of returning to an impressment policy if the bureau should fail.[32]

Simeon Hart encountered insurmountable difficulties acquiring cotton and moving it to the Rio Grande. His principal problems were the non-arrival of his funds from Richmond and the competition from private individuals for the cotton of Texas and the transport with which to move it to the Rio Grande. In the summer of 1863, Hart's cotton was just beginning to arrive along the border, and his creditors who had already delivered him goods were clamoring for payment.[33]

The army in the TMD thus was teetering on the edge of financial crisis when the arrival of the three cargoes requiring large amounts of cotton in payment created an immediate emergency. The *Sea Queen* arrived in late May 1863, carrying goods bought under a contract between the Confederate secretary of war and Bellots des Menieres, a French firm recently established to trade with the Confederacy. The firm had important friends in Richmond and in Paris, and it was deemed essential to the survival of the Confederacy's European credit to meet the requirements of the contract. The *Sea Queen* required 2,000 bales of cotton immediately. The second to arrive was the *Sir William Peel*, under a contract between the Mexican firm of Attrill and Lacoste and several Confederate supply officers in Texas. The *Sir William Peel* needed 4,200 bales of cotton. The third cargo arrived in August per the *Gladiator* under a contract between Nelson Clements, a Confederate with good contacts in London business circles, and Hart. It included 10,000 Enfield rifles and other goods and demanded a large quantity of cotton in payment. The army had no cotton in Brownsville or nearby with which to pay for these cargoes. Hart refused to allow his small arrivals to be diverted to pay for these cargoes, insisting that the cotton he had purchased must be paid to the Mexican firms that had delivered goods in advance of payment and had already waited months for payment. The representatives of the cargoes on board the ships refused to land their goods without payment and threatened to carry the needed goods away to other markets.[34]

Under similar circumstances, in emergencies, the Confederate army—like many other armies before it—had resorted to the impressment of supplies. By custom, armies in desperate need for supplies in order to stay in the field might impress the private property of people. They generally paid lower prices than the owners of the property demanded, and they often gave only promises to pay in the future. The Confederate army had found it necessary to resort to impressment in certain emergencies even in the first year of the war. In March of 1863 Congress recognized the necessity of impressment, authorized it, and developed regulations in an effort to control the practice.[35]

When people thought of impressment, they generally thought of food and forage. The Impressment Act authorized specifically the impressment of these items, plus slaves; it did not mention cotton or transportation. It did, however, in its broadest statement authorize the impressment of anything the army required and could not acquire by other means. A debate, never resolved, developed over whether the army might impress cotton to exchange for goods it required. Richmond authorities were divided on the issue. Secretary of Treasury Christopher J. Memminger and Jefferson Davis said the act did not cover cotton to be used as currency. Secretary of War Seddon urged Kirby Smith to find a better way to achieve the goal and impress cotton only as a last resort. Kirby Smith later consulted William Pitt Ballinger, a respected Galveston lawyer and patriotic Confederate, who concluded that the army in the TMD could not survive without the impressment of cotton to pay for imports. After an initial experiment in impressment itself in the summer of 1863, the TMD relied on the threat of impressment for the next year and a half as the effective force behind the Cotton Bureau.[36]

Five men loom large in the short history of the impressment of cotton in Texas. Kirby Smith, commanding the Confederate armies west of the Mississippi River, eventually assumed primary responsibility for the impressment; Magruder, commanding the Confederates in Texas, supervised the impressment of cotton; Brig. Gen. Hamilton Prioleau Bee, commanding at Brownsville, and his quartermaster Maj. Charles Russell implemented the impressment order in the Rio Grande Valley and negotiated with the three firms for their cargoes; and Lt. Col. A. G. Dickinson, commanding the post at San Antonio, carried the order into effect in the area surrounding that city.

In response to the crisis, General Bee asked Magruder for permission to impress cotton. Magruder passed the request on to Kirby Smith. At that time,

Kirby Smith was implementing Seddon's directive to assist in the defense of Vicksburg and Port Hudson, by sending Gen. Taylor and Walker's division into northeastern Louisiana. He told Magruder to use his judgment and mentioned the general authorization in the Impressment Act, which authorized officers in the field to make impressments when necessary. Kirby Smith apparently hoped to comply strictly with the wording "in the field." Magruder issued orders in the first week in June to impress cotton but a few days later got cold feet and re-scinded it. Magruder was unwilling to take the responsibility for impressing pri-vate property that would not immediately be consumed by the army in the field. Kirby Smith tried one more time, by giving Magruder the authority to impress cotton when he thought it necessary, without asking for headquarters' approval. Magruder would not make the decision nor act on the broad authorization; he insisted on a direct order to impress cotton to use to pay for supplies. On 27 June, a week before the surrender of Vicksburg, Kirby Smith issued a direct order to impress enough cotton near the Rio Grande border to fill the ships and outlined certain groups whose cotton was to be exempt. The cotton in the Rio Grande area was en route to Mexico from cotton-producing areas farther north. Kirby Smith and the officers who acted in May acted under what they believed to be a military emergency. They believed that the needed supplies could only be acquired by paying cotton for them. They acted under the broad authority in the introductory clause of the Impressment Act.[37] Some cotton was impressed in early June 1863, but Magruder rescinded the order and directed that it be released to the owners. No cotton was impressed from mid-June until the third week in July, as the *Sea Queen* and other vessels with cargoes for the army waited.

When Bee, and later Dickinson, received Kirby Smith's order in mid-July to impress cotton, each sent out agents to detain all cotton in the areas under their control. Army officers took possession of all cotton in the district—on wagons, in warehouses, at dockside. Bee and Dickinson then listened to the claims of owners that their cotton should be exempted. If Bee or Dickinson decided that a particular lot of cotton was subject to impressment, he issued a statement that the cotton had been impressed and that the army would pay for it in Con-federate money. The price was determined by a schedule published by army headquarters and was lower than the market price. If Bee or Dickinson decided that the cotton was exempt, he issued a pass so the cotton could be exported.[38]

The impressment process was initiated against a large number of bales of cotton. Bee stopped about 11,000 bales, and Dickinson stopped perhaps 8,000.

Bee, however, discovered that impressment would produce only a small number of bales, and Dickinson's harvest of impressed cotton similarly dwindled. In the end, Bee released all, and Dickinson released most, of the bales they had stopped.[39] Thus, the actual impressment of cotton failed to supply the cotton required in the summer of 1863. Why?

Central to the explanation was the policy of exemptions which restricted whose cotton could be impressed. Kirby Smith exempted the cotton of planters and of government contractors who had goods ready for delivery on the Rio Grande. In addition, he exempted the general railroad agent, who was engaged in the transportation of cotton to pay for supplies needed to keep the railroads running. He also directed that cotton belonging to those importing machinery and other goods for the general welfare be exempted when possible. Furthermore, if possible, impressment was to be confined to the border area until after the August state elections.[40]

Kirby Smith's order reflected the conviction, widespread in Texas, that speculators and unscrupulous government contractors were making too much money from the cotton trade, and that the government was deriving too little benefit. Thus, the speculators and government contractors should bear the brunt of the impressment policy. Among these traders, only those government contractors with goods ready for delivery should be exempt. On the other hand, planters, known to be strong supporters of the war effort, were suffering during the war, and they wielded considerable influence. Their cotton should be exempt. The general southern and western reverence for the producer of agricultural goods was shared by Kirby Smith. And he also shared the general lack of awareness of the contribution of the "middle men" who transported and marketed agricultural commodities.

Hastily drawn, Kirby Smith's order required the impressment of cotton owned by the state of Texas, the cotton of small farmers and town dwellers who were exporting it to import necessities for the community, and the cotton of government contractors who had been provided as payment in advance and had not yet transported their goods to the Confederacy. As his subordinates attempted to carry the order into effect, they exempted the cotton of some of these groups in an attempt to be equitable. Magruder, for instance, exempted county associations which were attempting to supply the needs of soldiers' families through the cotton trade; he was not overruled. Kirby Smith himself modified his order and exempted state-owned cotton when he encountered resistance from state authorities. Dickinson exempted cotton being exported by government contractors who had delivered goods, arguing that equity demanded that these men be allowed to export the cotton they had received in payment for goods already delivered. Bee contended that justice required that the old debts (those contracted by Hart, for instance) be paid as soon as, if not before, new debts were paid. He therefore freed from impressment the cotton of government contractors who were creditors of the government. Bee's exemption was overruled, but Dickinson's apparently remained in force.[41]

When he became aware of the small amount of cotton being obtained, Magruder interpreted the impressment order more stringently. Both Bee and Dickinson acted on the assumption that the teamsters who had hauled the cotton and expected payment in cotton would be exempt from impressment. These teamsters had transported the cotton hundreds of miles, across areas with no roads and little grass for their animals. Their charges for freight amounted to one-half or more of the cotton transported. Magruder eventually ruled that this cotton was not exempt. Magruder also tightened the rule regarding the cotton of planters. He directed that planters be allowed to export only enough cotton to meet the needs of their families and slaves; any additional amount was to be treated as speculative.[42]

In practice, certain persons obtained exemptions through influence at headquarters. The cotton exporting firm, Vance and Brothers of San Antonio, for instance obtained an exemption for its cotton, and as news of this favoritism spread in the city, resentment at impressment increased. Certain government contractors without goods waiting on the Rio Grande also obtained exemptions from the headquarters of either Magruder or Kirby Smith, frustrating Bee and Dickinson, who were trying to enforce the order equitably.[43]

Equally as important as a confused exemption policy were the problems that developed in connection with the impressment of the cotton of foreigners. Most large government contractors and speculators in the cotton trade were Mexican nationals. Therefore, much of the cotton impressed belonged to foreigners. They argued—and the British consul at Matamoros supported their interpretation of international law—that the confiscation of the property of foreigners was contrary to international law. They argued that, if cotton illegally seized from foreigners was used to pay for imported goods and then exported, the original owners could bring suit to regain possession of the cotton. Anticipating difficulties in retaining title to cotton impressed from foreigners, the agents for the cargos of the *Sea Queen* and *Gladiator* refused to accept cotton impressed from foreigners in payment for the goods they were ready to deliver.[44]

Bee discovered that more than a third of the cotton he had impressed was subject to serious legal entanglement because it was owned by foreigners. Magruder ordered Bee to hold this cotton until the matter was decided at head-quarters. Magruder believed that international law supported impressment of the property of foreigners as well as citizens. Nevertheless, Magruder's instruc-tions to Dickinson in late July exempted the cotton of foreigners. Dickinson discovered that virtually all of the cotton he stopped for impressment proved to be exempt under one or another category.[45]

Impressment proved to be accompanied by additional grave difficulties. It angered important people favorable to the war effort, especially if enforced in the interior. When the policy was pursued only in the politically less important border region, it produced insufficient cotton, much of which was threatened by lawsuits when exported. Moreover, the exemption of large categories of cot-ton owners (but not others equally deserving) and the haphazard individual exemptions granted to persons with influence at headquarters produced serious inequities.

Although little cotton was actually acquired through impressment in the summer of 1863, Confederate officials did procure sufficient cotton to exchange for the needed supplies. The contractual obligations in connection with the cargoes were met, and no loss of credit took place. The threat of impressment produced, in the short run, a willingness on the part of exporters to submit to a forced loan and, in the long run, the bargaining power by which the Cotton Bureau obtained one-half of the cotton of Texas.

Facing the prospect of the departure of the vessels laden with needed sup-plies, and aware of the potential damage to the European credit of the Con-federacy, on 21 July, Bee devised—and Russell implemented—a program that obtained for the government sizable quantities of cotton. Bee called together all of the important merchants in the trade, to explain the great need of the govern-ment and his authority to impress all of their cotton during the emergency. He offered, however, an alternative to which they agreed. He would forgo impress-ment if they would consent to a loan to the government of 20 percent of all the cotton that crossed the Rio Grande—with no exceptions. Since their cot-ton was being detained until some arrangement could be made, the merchants agreed. From late July until November, Bee required a loan to the government of 20 percent of all cotton exported. This forced loan produced 1,000 bales of cotton by 2 August, and Russell anticipated that at least 2,500 bales would be acquired very quickly. Bee promised to replace the cotton with government-owned cotton in the interior and to pay either 10 percent in addition for the inconvenience or to transport the cotton to the border for the exporters. The 20 percent loan thus probably produced 2,500 bales of cotton, which were used to obtain the cargoes waiting off the coast.[46]

Fortunately for Bee, the large amount of cotton originally demanded was not eventually required, and the demand for immediate payment for the entire cargoes was rescinded. The *Sea Queen* and the *Sir William Peel* delivered their cargoes before cotton was delivered. Then, tiring of the delay, the *Sea Queen* took on a cargo of privately exported cotton and sailed, relying on Bee's promise that the cotton owed would be available on her return.[47]

Shrewd action and careful attention to the details of the contracts on the part of Russell reduced the amount of cotton owed. He believed that only the cargo of the *Sir William Peel* was worth having. He secured it by supplying cotton to pay for the portion worth $200,000 for which cotton had been pledged, and arranging to pay for the remainder of the cargo in Confederate money at San Antonio, as the contract provided. This included the ten thousand rifles. Russell rejected part of the *Gladiator* cargo, which was of poor quality and did not meet the specifications of the contract, and required the owners to reduce many of the charges on the goods. As a result, the amount owed was significantly reduced.

Russell took particular care with the *Sea Queen* cargo because it came as the result of a contract the secretary of war had signed and involved the credit of the government at the very highest levels. The *Sea Queen* cargo was, however, of poor quality, and many of the goods were not in great demand. In addition, Russell and Bee believed *Bellots des Menieres* was not a responsible business establishment, and the various owners of its cargo were engaged in disputes. Adhering to the letter of the contract, Russell rejected much of the merchandise that did not meet inspection. He also argued that the owners had broken the contract by refusing to accept impressed cotton. Thus he succeeded in reducing the debt owed on the account of this vessel from $500,000 to $56,000. Because Russell had succeeded in reducing the debt, and because the 20 percent loan produced cotton, needed goods were acquired and the European credit of the government survived.[48]

This crisis on the border in the late spring and summer of 1863 made Kirby Smith more aware of the severity of his supply problem, and of the need to regularize the acquisition of cotton. In August 1863, he created an army bureau to obtain control of the cotton crop of the department for the government. This Cotton Bureau inaugurated a massive program to obtain cotton for the government and established an extensive system of agents to carry its policy into effect. The Cotton Bureau owed much to the experience gained in these matters during the summer crisis, and the influence can be seen in four areas.

First, the threat of impressment was at the heart of the ability of the Cotton Bureau to acquire cotton. If a planter sold half of his cotton to the government, the government exempted his other half from impressment. It was the threat of impressment and not impressment itself that was used. Problems associated with the refusal of creditors to receive impressed cotton were thus avoided. In August 1863, Kirby Smith issued and immediately rescinded an order impressing all of the cotton of Texas. The threat of re-imposition of the order remained.

Second, the Cotton Bureau recognized the claims of those who had received cotton inside the department in payment for government supplies to be equal to those awaiting payment. Cotton received in payment for supplies was exempt from impressment. This was deemed essential to the credit of the government.

Third, the Cotton Bureau operated throughout the Trans-Mississippi Department. The border region had proved incapable of providing sufficient cotton even to meet a short-term emergency. Kirby Smith thus ended his effort to avoid totally the political repercussions of a policy of impressments. He hoped to avoid at least part of the repercussions by using only the threat of impressments and exempting half of the cotton.

Fourth, all holders of cotton (except state governments) were equally affected under the Cotton Bureau's program. Planters, small farmers, townsmen, merchants, societies aiding soldiers' families, speculators, and government contractors who had not yet delivered goods—all were required to sell half of their cotton to the Cotton Bureau.[49] The Cotton Bureau developed problems of its own and was no panacea for the problem of regulating the cotton trade and supplying the army of the Trans-Mississippi Department. However, the Cotton Bureau did not repeat the mistakes of the summer of 1863.

The events of the summer of 1863, then, are central to the history of government involvement in the cotton trade in Texas and to the history of the supply operations of the army in Texas. Impressment proved to be an unworkable solution to the problem of obtaining cotton for government purposes. Even in the emergency of the summer of 1863, impressment did not produce the needed cotton. But the threat of impressment allowed the government to obtain cotton that summer. This, and careful attention to the provisions of the contracts, enabled the army to procure needed supplies and preserve the Confederacy's European credit. Kirby Smith put to good use the experience gained in this crisis summer when he created the Cotton Bureau by an order on 3 August 1863. The Cotton Bureau was established to prevent such crises in the future. Confederate credit abroad survived this crisis. Mexican creditors on the border watched the arrival of Hart's cotton slowly and hoped to be paid in the order of their earlier deliveries.

The TMD had acquired the valuable portions of the ships' cargoes and thus improved its supply situation. Kirby Smith, however, experienced several more crises in the border trade later in the war.

XXXXX

Kirby Smith's original instructions urged him to consult with the governors, and he had regularly done so. After the fall of Vicksburg and Port Hudson, the president wrote to Kirby Smith that he had heard that there was talk in Texas of secession from the Confederacy; he emphasized the need to conciliate the governors and gain their support for continuing the Confederate war effort and making the TMD self-sustaining. He strongly urged Kirby Smith to call a conference of governors. Two weeks later, Secretary of War Seddon urged Kirby Smith to consult state governors and other "leading citizens" in an effort "to secure their efficient cooperation with your plans." Seddon also wrote Kirby Smith that the isolation of the TMD would require Kirby Smith to exercise "extraordinary" military and civil authority. The day before Davis and Seddon wrote to him, Kirby Smith, responding to the loss of the Mississippi River, perceiving the need to work with state leaders in the unprecedented situation, and cognizant of the need to become self-sufficient in supplies, issued a call to the governors and supreme court justices to meet at Marshall, Texas, in mid-August 1863. For months, it had not been possible to move significant amounts of troops or supplies in either direction, and correspondence with Richmond always involved long delays. The loss of Vicksburg and Port Hudson made these existing problems more visible. The meeting took place on 15 August, six weeks after

Vicksburg fell. On 3 August, Seddon began to backpedal about the extent of civil authority that should be extended to Kirby Smith, but Seddon's reservations did not reach Kirby Smith until late September at the earliest.[50]

Kirby Smith hoped to win at the conference the support of the state leaders for the policies he had put in place to enable the army to defend the TMD. Governor Francis R. Lubbock of Texas, Governor Thomas O. Moore of Louisiana, Governor Thomas C. Reynolds of Missouri, a representative of Governor Harris Flanagin of Arkansas, Governor-elect Pendleton Murrah of Texas, and "several . . . judges and senators . . . from the four states" attended. In late June 1863, Kirby Smith had taken responsibility for the impressment of cotton near the Rio Grande to be used to pay for imports. In early August he created the Cotton Bureau.[51] He believed these actions were absolutely necessary to arm and otherwise supply the troops of the department. He interpreted the Impressment Act of 1863 to allow the military to impress anything that was absolutely necessary to keep the armies in the field.

If one accepted the existence of an on-going emergency with regard to army supplies needed in excess of what could be procured or manufactured in the TMD and that the army could not wait until it was totally out of weapons, ammunition, lead, or other necessities to acquire the cotton necessary to pay for importations, Kirby Smith did not need state approval nor Davis's and Seddon's expanded authority for the Cotton Bureau. The Impressment Act was sufficient. The support of governors was prudent and practical. The authority granted by Davis and Seddon was welcome.

Apparently, the governors were keenly aware of the dangers facing their states—the dire military situation in southern Arkansas; the activity of General Banks on the Gulf Coast of Texas; the surrenders at Vicksburg and Port Hudson; the Union soldiers raiding into the parts of Louisiana near the Mississippi River; the likelihood that Banks would invade again along the Bayou Teche; and the paucity of arms, supplies, and funds—for the governors and other leaders approved much of what Kirby Smith put before them.[52] The letter from the Secretary of War undoubtedly carried great weight. Kirby Smith's leadership skills may also have been at work.

Among other less controversial issues, the state officials discussed the extent of Kirby Smith's authority as well as issues related to the currency and the cotton trade. The sub-committee on the extent of his authority recommended and the conference approved a statement that "Smith was only at liberty to exercise those executive powers which came within the constitutional and legal purview that came within the Confederate Executive, and which, in addition, were 'absolutely necessary' for the defense of the department. Smith's authority was to extend only to the details of administration, and was not to include the power to decide or amend policy." Seddon could not have conveyed "authority which belongs to the states."[53]

After unanimously approving the report on the limits of his authority, the sub-committee on the currency and the cotton trade nevertheless recommended to the conference that Kirby Smith buy or impress the entire cotton crop of the department (excepting whatever portion he might consider appropriate), to be used to become the basis for an issue of Confederate bonds (which would take the excess of treasury notes out of circulation, thus reducing inflation) and to purchase needed supplies. It also recommended "the recirculation of the currency paid into government treasuries." The conference voted to delete the part about issuing bonds, but approved the rest of the recommendation. Thus, Kirby Smith received the support of the highest officials of the states of the Trans-Mississippi Department (or their representatives) for implementation of his Cotton Bureau program and as the representative of the executive branch of the Confederacy authorized to do what was "'absolutely necessary' for the defense of the department" so long as it did not infringe on the rights of the states.[54] Apparently, these officials in mid-August 1863 perceived the imminent danger to their states to be sufficient to require their citizens to sacrifice their property rights in cotton for the common good. The fact that Kirby Smith's actual program in Texas regarding cotton required the sacrifice to the cause of only half of their cotton may have made it a bit more palatable.

"The future of the Trans-Mississippi States . . . must depend in no small degree upon the co-operation of the Governors of the States," wrote Secretary of War Seddon in mid-July 1863. In Arkansas, all three candidates for governor in 1863 were pro-Confederacy, and only one states' rights candidate for the legislature was elected. The winning candidate for governor of Texas in the early August elections, Pendleton Murrah, ran against an opponent of Kirby Smith; Governor-elect Murrah did not complain about military policies, and when he became governor in November, his first complaints focused on the impressment of slaves and conscription. Texas voters returned to the legislature three pro-Confederate candidates and elected three new states' rights legislators.[55]

In the spring and summer of 1863, despite complaints by state governors about conscription, moving soldiers out of Arkansas and Texas to confront Banks and operate in support of Vicksburg and Port Hudson, and moving the arsenal and foundry machinery out of Arkansas, Kirby Smith retained the respect and support of the governors of Louisiana, Texas and Arkansas. A respected scholar of the state government of Texas during the Civil War has written that Governor "Lubbock was well satisfied with the results of the second Marshall conference." A respected scholar of the state government of Arkansas has written that Governor Flanagin, although relatively inactive, "generally . . . supported the military authorities." In early October 1863, President Davis wrote to Kirby Smith: "I have been gratified to perceive the evidence of the harmonious and cordial relations existing between yourself and the Governors of the Trans-Mississippi states." Davis indicated in early 1864 that Governors Moore and Allen assured him that Kirby Smith was "a confident, faithful and acceptable Commander." At the end of summer 1863, there was no sign that Governor-elect Murrah would eventually object vociferously to the implementation of Cotton Bureau cotton acquisition. He took office in November at about the time that the Texas Cotton Office began implementing its policy. Although from about February through July 1864, Murrah's new program of buying cotton in competition with the Cotton Bureau's Texas Cotton Office brought Cotton Bureau acquisitions in Texas almost to a stop, in July Kirby Smith convinced Murrah to stop buying cotton so that the army could be supplied.[56]

Kirby Smith also gained and retained the confidence of President Davis and Secretary of State Seddon. Seddon praised Kirby Smith and Holmes as commanders in a letter to Governor Flanagin of Arkansas in mid-July 1863, defended Kirby Smith's strategy, and urged the governors to cooperate with him. Also in mid-July, Seddon recommended that it was best to arrange things so Kirby Smith seldom would need to consult Richmond. In late July, Davis wrote Lt. Gen. Robert E. Lee about the complexities of Kirby Smith's role: The Trans-Mississippi Department "will require the use of extraordinary powers by the Commander, but how far this must extend without involving opposition is difficult to forsee." In late August, commenting on Kirby Smith's report of 28 July, Seddon wrote that his "confidence in the discretion and ability" of Kirby Smith "assures me that he shall have no difficulty in sustaining any assumption of authority which may be necessary. . . . Large discretion [should be] allowed." In mid-September, when Seddon worried about whether the second Marshall conference had agreed to extraordinary powers that the president could not confer, he nevertheless wrote that he understood the "spirit and aims" of the governor's conference and commended Kirby Smith's efforts. In an extraordinary letter written in April 1864, President Davis wrote to Governor Allen that Kirby Smith was empowered to do whatever the president could do regarding the army. "He has the authority to enforce the laws and that is the only authority I have. . . . I can do nothing, that he cannot do."[57]

XXXXX

This study has brought to the surface several issues that need further research and thought. Most criticisms of Kirby Smith by historians more appropriately should be directed at Jefferson Davis or Secretary of War James Seddon or the Confederate Congress, for during the spring and summer of 1863 in almost all instances he operated under instructions or authority deriving from the Richmond authorities. The Cotton Bureau, for instance, was a military bureau staffed by military officers. In the one instance when he clearly acted outside his authority (with regard to currency), he kept Seddon fully informed and was allowed to continue his practices. Occasionally, one or more of those authorities would counsel caution or recommend that he try to find a better way to achieve the goal, but they did not reverse the actions he took during his first six months. He remained highly respected in Richmond.

In many instances, historians' criticism of Kirby Smith was unwarranted because the historian inadvertently failed to confirm that Kirby Smith had actually received a change of instructions in time. In the TMD, those instructions might arrive three to six weeks later, or not at all.

Some who criticize Kirby Smith's strategy of giving ground when faced with a superior force until a concentration of scattered units could be effected appear to write from the perspective of frustrated subordinate officers who thought he should have sent help to them sooner or of the civil authorities and prominent civilians in the areas from which the troops were drawn. Those are important viewpoints, but they provide no answer to the question of what other strategy had a greater likelihood of success in defending the Trans-Mississippi Department.

The most recent substantive study, Prushankin's 2005 book on the Kirby Smith–Taylor relationship in the TMD, argues that the best strategy for defending the TMD was to liberate New Orleans (or at least threaten to do so).

Liberating New Orleans depended on the likelihood that the people of the city would rise to the colors and drive the occupying army out once Taylor's army appeared; similar beliefs were evident in the 1862 efforts to liberate Kentucky and Maryland, but the numbers of residents who turned out were minimal. Threatening to liberate New Orleans took the form of taking back from the Union occupiers the LaFourche Valley and concentrating a large force there in an effort to cause Banks "to divest from Port Hudson" to defend the city. Banks considered sending a detachment (not his entire force) to defend New Orleans but decided to continue his full support of Grant at Vicksburg by besieging Port Hudson. Prushankin pointed out that Kirby Smith allowed Holmes and Price to attack the Union forces at Helena, Arkansas, in an effort to draw off Union forces besieging Vicksburg, at the same time that he would not withdraw Walker's Division from its operations in northeastern Louisiana opposite Vicksburg to support Taylor's hoped-for liberation of New Orleans. The Helena attack was suggested by the secretary of war and did not require Kirby Smith to take any troops away from the Vicksburg area, whereas Kirby Smith had no knowledge that the Richmond authorities desired an attack on New Orleans, and Taylor's plans required a major transfer of troops away from the Vicksburg area. The published evidence that Taylor's force, even with Walker's Division, could safely cross the Mississippi River opposite New Orleans and run off the Union occupying army, and that the residents of New Orleans in 1863 had the wherewithal and desire and will to rise to the colors, and that Taylor's force could hold the city against the Union navy and army forces that would soon have appeared, is nonexistent. The published evidence that Banks would have abandoned his siege of Port Hudson because of a concentration of Confederate troops on the west bank opposite New Orleans is not convincing.[58]

Kirby Smith is vulnerable to criticism that he often acted on information without confirming its quality. That was often the case during the spring and summer of 1863. In addition, he almost always misinterpreted the evidence at first, resulting in incorrect initial assessments of the enemy's likely course of action, and he sometimes acted on that incorrect perception. The development of a reliable intelligence-gathering system and the ability to discern correctly the intentions of the enemy are critical to success in battlefield or campaign leadership, and (from the evidence available during his first six months in the TMD), Kirby Smith appears to have lacked those skills and characteristics present in great combat leaders.

An under-studied aspect of supply issues in the TMD is that the Richmond authorities were apparently not sufficiently aware of the extent of the lack of supplies in the TMD and the minimal capabilities in the department of producing them. They were also too confident that the system in the rest of the CSA could develop ways to solve the problems quickly. A good example is the refusal of the secretary of the treasury for almost two years to establish a branch of the treasury in the Trans-Mississippi. He argued that it would have been complicated, and he was certain that Confederate currency would reach the TMD despite the complete loss of the Mississippi River. On the positive side, the secretary of war sent highly qualified ordnance and quartermaster officers in mid- and late-1862, and finally, in early 1863, they began to send a few cannon and two large lots of rifles to cross the Mississippi and made arrangements to have rifles shipped from Europe to the Rio Grande. Very few of those rifles (and none of the cannon) made it to the TMD. In the spring and summer of 1863, though, the Richmond authorities were confident that the arrangements they had made would be successful.

For Kirby Smith, the choice at the time was to wait for the CSA system to work or for Richmond authorities to begin to realize the immensity of the crisis or to do what was necessary to keep the army in the field to defend as much of the TMD as possible, even if it involved exceeding the usual authority of a department commander. He, of course, was aware of the standard military practice of assuming the officer on the ground was more current on events and conditions than his commanding officer hundreds of miles distant. In that era of poor communication over long distances, military leaders ordinarily relied on the officer in the field to take responsibility for making decisions about the best way to carry their instructions into effect. Kirby Smith chose to take on that responsibility even before Vicksburg fell.

Often, Kirby Smith's decision-making faced a two-edged sword. Concentration of troops from Arkansas and Texas to confront the enemy in central Louisiana in the spring of 1863 raised concerns in Arkansas that Kirby Smith would abandon Arkansas entirely and raised anger in Texas because this action had left the coast open to danger. Any decline in civilian morale was undesirable, and operating in areas where disaffection prevailed was dangerous for an army. The prospect that Union military forces would take the opportunity to advance in the areas from which troops were removed appeared to be real. Kirby Smith faced an unsolvable military problem. He had at most thirty thousand troops to defend three large states that were under threat from the north in Arkansas, from the east and south in Louisiana, and along the entire Gulf Coast of Texas from an enemy with at times more than triple the number of troops, superior transportation capabilities, and the advantage of being able to choose the strategic point of encounter. He worked hard to assure the civil authorities throughout the department that he intended to defend all parts of the department and that concentrating troops where the threat was greatest was the best defense.

Impressment was another two-edged sword. By 1862 the army could not survive without impressing food for its soldiers, animals for its cavalry and wagon transport, and forage for its animals. By the spring of 1863, it could not survive without cotton to pay for the importation of ordnance and quartermaster supplies. Without the army to defend the TMD, Federal forces would be able to occupy all of Louisiana, Arkansas, and Texas. The great goal of independence would fail, the institution of slavery would be at risk, and the expected horrors of occupation would descend upon them. But, the seizure of private property without immediate compensation was hard medicine to swallow. Civilians everywhere grumbled and struggled to survive. Kirby Smith believed it was his duty to keep the army in the field. He at first attempted the impressment of all cotton from San Antonio southward but, by early August 1863, shifted to a compromise: the owners of cotton throughout Texas could keep half of their cotton if they would sell half to the army for promises to pay in the future. Nevertheless, the Texas state legislature, apparently putting the right to own property above the need to keep the army in the field, mounted an angry attack on the legality of the impressment of cotton. The pattern in the Confederate Congress was that representatives of safer areas were much more likely to oppose policies involving great sacrifice than were representatives of areas at imminent risk of being occupied. The Trans-Mississippi Department conformed to that pattern.[59]

Kirby Smith had a busy and for the most part productive first six months as commander of the Trans-Mississippi Department. He spent much of his time carrying into effect his instructions from the president and the secretary of war. His early March trip to Little Rock to consult with Arkansas state officials was in obedience to a directive from Richmond. His continued efforts to conciliate all of the governors were central to his mission. The August conference at Marshall was authorized by Davis and Seddon, as were Kirby Smith's extraordinary powers. Working to decrease disaffection, maintain civilian morale, and gain support from state officials for policies necessary to keep the army in the field was central to his mission. Kirby Smith understood the "soft" elements of power, not just the power of the law or military force.

He received his first directive to provide what help he could to Pemberton before he reached the TMD. Davis and Seddon sent many additional instructions in May through late July. Kirby Smith did not act promptly for three reasons: his instructions clearly gave the Arkansas trip priority; northeast Louisiana was flooded; and Banks outflanked Taylor in the second week in April, causing Taylor to retreat all the way to Alexandria. All of the Louisiana troops were engaged in efforts to delay Banks's advance. As Kirby Smith would write to Davis later, Banks "was pressing Taylor," and the Bayou Macon area was "too much under water to admit of operations."[60] After Banks turned east, Walker's Division arrived at the Red River, and Kirby Smith learned that the flood waters had receded, he used Taylor's personal knowledge of Louisiana and Walker's three brigades to attempt to carry out all of the instructions to help Pemberton. It was too little too late, but Taylor was needed against Banks until mid-May, and little could be accomplished until the floodwaters fell.

Kirby Smith began his efforts to provide order among commissary, quartermaster. and ordnance officers in the department because it was the duty of every commanding officer to create and maintain an effective and efficient supply system. He focused first on the manufacturing facilities for ordnance and quartermaster necessities. During June, when he was organizing the effort to provide help to Pemberton, he learned of the crisis regarding the lack of government-owned cotton on the Mexican border to pay for cargoes of quartermaster and ordnance supplies, including a large number of rifles. He relied on the experience and expertise of Bee, Russell, and Magruder. Bee and Russell performed well. Magruder, however, refused to take responsibility for impressing the cotton needed to get the cargo; Kirby Smith eventually shouldered the responsibility and took on the opprobrium of owners of cotton. He relied on the general clause of the Impressment Act that Congress had passed in March 1863. When impressments proved impractical and Bee devised a compromise that accomplished the goal without impressments, he let it stand. Kirby Smith then devised a long-term solution to the problem of obtaining enough cotton to pay for imports necessary to keep the army functioning for the rest of the war—the Cotton Bureau. The impressment of forage and food for immediate consumption, and the manufacture or importation of necessities not available for sale in the department provided the army with barely enough to survive. With the exception of actions related to the currency and possibly his interpretation of the Impressment Act, Kirby Smith was either acting under instructions from Richmond or following long-established responsibilities of military commanders.

In accordance with these well-established roles of departmental commanders, he coordinated the available departmental military forces by devising a strategy of concentration in space to confront the greatest threat. In April and May of 1863, he hoped to concentrate troops at Natchitoches, but the long distances from Galveston, Texas, and Pine Bluff, Arkansas (combined with heavy rains and mud in southern Arkansas), made it impossible to move infantry quickly to the concentration point. Only Banks's decision to shift his forces to Port Hudson removed the threat. Kirby Smith retained the strategy in the upper Red River Valley for use against two more advances by Banks—in the fall of 1863 and in the Red River campaign of spring 1864. He learned from his earlier efforts and, when Banks persisted in his advance in early 1864, Kirby Smith applied these lessons and achieved success at Mansfield, Louisiana.

Kirby Smith brought order to the chaotic Trans-Mississippi Department. His supply programs were essential to the capability of the armies to defend the TMD. He kept the support of state leaders throughout the six months under study, although trouble was brewing in the Texas legislature. He developed a strategy of concentrating troops across district lines in response to the greatest threat and learned from his failed effort in the spring of 1863 to effect a concentration over great distances. He was unable to provide any meaningful help to the Confederates at Vicksburg and Port Hudson, but given the specificity of his instructions, the paucity of troops in relation to the Union forces involved, the high water in the area opposite Vicksburg until mid-May, the Union gunboats patrolling the Mississippi River, and Banks's occupation of southwestern and central Louisiana until mid-May, having an impact on the fate of Vicksburg and Port Hudson appears to have been an impossible task.

NOTES

1. Joseph Howard Parks, *General Edmund Kirby Smith, C.S.A.*, Southern Biography Series (Baton Rouge: Louisiana State University Press, 1954), 263, 283, 294–95, 312–13, 315.

2. Fredericka Ann Meiners, "Hamilton P. Bee," PhD diss., Rice University, 1972, 91, 93–97, 99–100, 102–3, 192–93. See also James Arthur Irby, "Line of the Rio Grande: War and Trade on the Con-

federate Frontier, 1861–1865," PhD diss., University of Georgia, 1969; Ronnie C. Tyler, *Santiago Vidaurri and the Southern Confederacy* (Austin: Texas State Historical Association, 1973); and James W. Daddysman, *The Matamoros Trade: Confederate Commerce, Diplomacy, and Intrigue* (Newark: University of Delaware Press, 1984).

3. Robert Kerby, *Kirby Smith's Confederacy: The Trans-Mississippi South, 1863–1865* (New York: Columbia University Press, 1973), 141–42, 149–50, 155, 174.

4. Clayton E. Jewett, *Texas in the Confederacy: An Experiment in Nation Building* (Columbia: University of Missouri Press, 2002), 145–47, 175, 186–87, 240–41.

5. Jeffrey F. Prushankin, *A Crisis in Command: Edmund Kirby Smith, Richard Taylor, and the Army of the Trans-Mississippi* (Baton Rouge: Louisiana State University Press, 2005), 7, 22, 24, 36, 53, 57, 61–62, 185–86, 211.

6. *The Papers of Jefferson Davis*, ed. Lynda Lasswell Crist and Mary Seaton Dix (Baton Rouge: Louisiana State University Press, 1997 and 1999), vol. 9: 275; vol. 10: 604–5 (hereinafter cited as *PJD*). *The War of the Rebellion: A Compilation of the Official Records of the Union and Confederate Armies* (130 vols., Washington, DC: Government Printing Office, 1880–1901), vol. 22, pt. 2: 782 (hereinafter cited as *OR*); unless otherwise indicated, all citations are from series 1). Kerby, *Kirby Smith's Confederacy*, 18, 29–31, 35–37, 130. Carl H. Moneyhon, *The Impact of the Civil War and Reconstruction on Arkansas: Persistence in the Midst of Ruin* (Baton Rouge: Louisiana State University Press, 1994), 106, 110. Anne J. Bailey, "Henry McCulloch's Texans and the Defense of Arkansas in 1862," in *Civil War Arkansas: Beyond Battles and Leaders*, ed. Anne J. Bailey and Daniel E. Sutherland (Fayetteville: University of Arkansas Press, 2000), 21–22, 27–28. Daniel E. Sutherland, "Guerillas: The Real War in Arkansas," in *Civil War Arkansas*, ed. Bailey and Sutherland, 135–36, 138, 140–42, 145, 153. Diane Neal and Thomas W. Kremm, *The Lion of the South: General Thomas C. Hindman* (Macon, GA: Mercer University Press, 1993), 89, 93, 114–15, 117–18, 122–29, 134–35. Ralph A. Wooster, *Texas and Texans in the Civil War* (Austin, TX: Eakin Press, 1995), 33–34, 64, 71–73; 75–76. Michael B. Dougan, "Arkansas," in *The Confederate Governors*, ed. W. Buck Yearns (Athens: University of Georgia Press, 1985), 48, 51; Parks, *General Edmund Kirby Smith, C.S.A.*, 253–55.

7. *PJD* 9: 290, 373 n. 6; *OR* 22, pt. 2: 1910–11; 24, pt. 2: 683; 24, pt. 3: 694. Frank Everson Vandiver, *Ploughshares into Swords: Josiah Gorgas and Confederate Ordnance* (Austin: University of Texas Press, 1952), 73, 75, 139–40, 183, 232. Wooster, *Texas and Texans in the Civil War*, 30; Kerby, *Kirby Smith's Confederacy*, 26, 44, 98, 131. Bailey, "Henry McCulloch's Texans and the Defense of Arkansas in 1862," 22–24. Paul D. Casdorph, *Prince John Magruder: His Life and Campaigns* (New York: John Wiley and Sons, 1996), 95–96, 221, 242. Richard G. Lowe, *Walker's Texas Division, C.S.A.: Greyhounds of the Trans-Mississippi* (Baton Rouge: Louisiana State University Press, 2004), 43. Parks, *General Edmund Kirby Smith*, 257, 324. Ralph A. Wooster, "Texas," in *The Confederate Governors*, ed. Yearns, 197, 199, 202. Dougan, "Arkansas," 95–96, 98. The reported numbers of troops and how well they were armed is elusive and changing. In Arkansas, by May 1863, 12,000 were ready for duty, stragglers having been rounded up; officers reporting were often not clear about whether they were counting those on the rolls or those armed and otherwise ready for duty. The same uncertainties emerge regarding weapons captured; a Confederate source indicated 7,000 shoulder arms captured near Natchez, but a Federal source said only 321 were captured. See the discussion of the *Sir William Peel* cargo later in this essay.

8. Irby, "Line of the Rio Grande," 4, 8–9, 12–13; Daddysman, *The Matamoros Trade*, 152, 154–55; Meiners, "Hamilton P. Bee," 31, 64–65, 67–68; Tyler, *Santiago Vidaurri and the Southern Confed-*

eracy, 106–8; Wooster, *Texas and Texans in the Civil War*, 119–21; Casdorph, *Prince John Magruder*, 243; Kerby, *Kirby Smith's Confederacy*, 73, 155.

9. Irby, "Line of the Rio Grande," 92–93, 104; Meiners, "Hamilton P. Bee," 31–36, 60, 68–71, 73–74, 78–79, 93, 109; Kerby, *Kirby Smith's Confederacy*, 71, 155, 165–66, 168, 171–76; Daddysman, *The Matamoros Trade*, 107, 116–18, 121, 130–32; Tyler, *Santiago Vidaurri and the Southern Confederacy*, 108–11; Wooster, *Texas and Texans in the Civil War*, 119–21; Casdorph, *Prince John Magruder*, 225–26. 243–45.

10. *PJD* 9: 78 n. 18, 382; Frank Everson Vandiver, *Rebel Brass: The Confederate Command System* (Baton Rouge: Louisiana State University Press, 1956), 88, 91–93; Kerby, *Kirby Smith's Confederacy*, 65, 68, 70–72, 76, 143, 145–46, 171–72, 175–76; Wooster, *Texas and Texans in the Civil War*, 126; Wooster, "Texas," 202, 204; James J. Johnston, "Bullets for Johnny Reb: Confederate and Mining Bureau in Arkansas," in *Civil War Arkansas*, ed. Bailey and Sutherland, 56–57, 60, 62–64, 66, 73–74; Dougan, "Arkansas," 49; Bailey, "Henry McCulloh's Texans and the Defense of Arkansas in 1862 in Arkansas," 25; Jewett, *Texas in the Confederacy*, 149–51; Casdorph, *Prince John Magruder*, 221, 225; Parks, *General Edmund Kirby Smith*, 285–86.

11. *OR* 15: 1028–29; *PJD* 9: 69; Vandiver, *Ploughshares into Swords*, 191; Kerby, *Kirby Smith's Confederacy*, 60, 71; Johnston, "Bullets for Johnny Reb," 62, 66, 73–74.

12. *PJD* 9: 221, 223; Casdorph, *Prince John Magruder*, 239; Kerby, *Kirby Smith's Confederacy*, 39.

13. *OR* 24, pt. 3: 935–36, 997, 1070; 26; pt. 2: 41–42. John D. Winters, *The Civil War in Louisiana* (Baton Rouge: Louisiana State University Press, 1963), 178, 182. Kerby, *Kirby Smith's Confederacy*, 27.

14. *PJD* 9: 44, 75, 77 n. 12 and 13, 220–21, 223 n. 2, 277. *OR* 15: 986; 24, pt. 1: 286. Prushankin, *A Crisis in Command*, 23–25. Wooster, *Texas and Texans*, 14–16, 57, 65. Neal and Kremm, *The Lion of the South*, 114–16, 151–56. Carl H. Moneyhon, "Disloyalty and Class Consciousness in Southwestern Arkansas, 1862–1865," in *Civil War Arkansas*, ed. Bailey and Sutherland, 121, 127, 129–31. Bailey, "Henry McCulloch's Texans and the Defense of Arkansas in 1862," 27. Michael B. Dougan, *Confederate Arkansas: The People and Policies of a Frontier State in Wartime* (Tuscaloosa: University of Alabama Press, 1976), 49. Michael A. Hughes, "Wartime Gristmill Destruction in Northwest Arkansas and Military Farm Colonies," in *Civil War Arkansas*, ed. Bailey and Sutherland, 37–38. Sutherland, "Guerillas," 133. Wooster, *Texas and Texans in the Civil War*, 74, 97–100. Kerby, *Kirby Smith's Confederacy*, 12, 25, 34, 53, 126–28. Parks, *General Edmund Kirby Smith*, 256. Dougan, "Arkansas," 46, 49. The fact that Seddon requested Kirby Smith to go to Arkansas before attending to other directives, and Seddon's reconsideration of that instruction did not reach Kirby Smith before he was en route to Arkansas, significantly undermines Prushankin's argument that Kirby Smith went to Arkansas first for more personal reasons.

15. *PJD* 9: 220, 223 n. 3; *OR* 22, pt. 2: 852.

16. *OR* 15: 386–87, 1036, 1041–43, 1045–46, 1083–84; Winters, *The Civil War in Louisiana*, 222, 225–26, 229–36; Archer Jones, *Civil War Command and Strategy: The Process of Victory and Defeat* (New York: Free Press, 1992), 39, 44–45, 49–55; Thomas Lawrence Connelly, *Army of the Heartland: The Army of Tennessee, 1861–1862* (Baton Rouge: Louisiana State University Press, 1967), 188–89; Kerby, *Kirby Smith's Confederacy*, 97–100, 105–7, 109; Casdorph, *Prince John Magruder*, 242, 247; Prushankin, *A Crisis in Command*, 25.

17. *OR* 15: 384, 386–87, 1041–43, 1046, 1050–51, 1054, 1057, 1083–84; 26, pt. 2: 41–42. Prushankin, *A Crisis in Command*, 23, 28, 31. Casdorph, *Prince John Magruder*, 247. Kerby, *Kirby Smith's Confederacy*, 105–8. Meiners, "Hamilton P. Bee," 78–80.

18. *OR* 15: 386–87, 1041–42, 1045–46, 1051, 1083–84; Kerby, *Kirby Smith's Confederacy,* 109.

19. *OR* 15: 386–87, 1045, 1057–58, 1062, 1083–84; 26, pt. 1: 26; 26, pt. 2: 41–42. Kerby, *Kirby Smith's Confederacy,* 109. Lowe, *Walker's Texas Division,* 71, 73–78, 80. Prushankin, *A Crisis in Command,* 28–29. Wooster, *Texas and Texans in the Civil War,* 75–77. Casdorph, *Prince John Magruder,* 247–48. Parks, *General Edmund Kirby Smith,* 272.

20. *OR* 22, pt. 1: 25, 27; 26, pt. 2: 41–42. Prushankin, *A Crisis in Command,* 7, 23. Bailey, "Henry McCulloch's Texans and the Defense of Arkansas in 1862," 30.

21. *OR* 22, pt. 1: 26–27; 26, pt. 2: 48, 108. Prushankin, *A Crisis in Command,* 52–55. Wooster, *Texas and Texans in the Civil War,* 92. Casdorph, *Prince John Magruder,* 248. Kerby, *Kirby Smith's Confederacy,* 239–40.

22. *PJD* 9: 280, 371–72, 412–13; 372n2. *OR* 22, pt. 1: 26–27; 22, pt. 2: 1011, 1030; 26, pt. 2: 48, 108–9, 323. Wooster, *Texas and Texans in the Civil War,* 80, 87, 92–93. Lowe, *Walker's Texas Division,* 115, 129, 131. Prushankin, *A Crisis in Command,* 52–55, 57. Kerby, *Kirby Smith's Confederacy,* 240–42. Winters, *The Civil War in Louisiana,* 294, 297. Dougan, *Confederate Arkansas,* 55. Casdorph, *Prince John Magruder,* 251–56, 258. Parks, *General Edmund Kirby Smith,* 317–18, 321–25, 328, 331, 336.

23. *OR* 24, pt. 3: 846, 935–36; Winters, *The Civil War in Louisiana,* 172–73, 178–79, 182, 184–85, 188–89, 191–98; Lowe, *Walker's Texas Division,* 71, 80–82, 86–87; Jones, *Civil War Command and Strategy,* 159–62.

24. *OR* 22, pt. 1: 26–27 ; 24, pt. 3: 935–36, 997; 26, pt. 2: 41–42, 71. Lowe, *Walker's Texas Division,* 71, 73, 80–82, 111–13. Prushankin, *A Crisis in Command,* 29, 31–34, 36, 41, 47. Kerby, *Kirby Smith's Confederacy,* 109, 112–15, 128. Wooster, *Texas and Texans in the Civil War,* 76.

25. *OR* 22, pt. 1: 26–27; 24, pt. 2: 466; 24, pt. 3: 997; 26, pt. 2: 71. Lowe, *Walker's Texas Division,* 86–88, 91, 94–95, 99, 101, 112–13. Wooster, *Texas and Texans in the Civil War,* 76. Prushankin, *A Crisis in Command,* 32–36, 40–42, 45. Kerby, *Kirby Smith's Confederacy,* 33, 112–13, 121, 131. Winters, *The Civil War in Louisiana,* 198–202.

26. *PJD* 9: 223, 278n5, 280. *OR* 22, pt. 2: 852; 24, pt. 1: 228; 24, pt. 2: 466; 24, pt. 3: 999–1000, 1070; 26, pt. 2: 97. Lowe, *Walker's Texas Division,* 102, 105, 107. Prushankin, *A Crisis in Command,* 41–46, 48. Kerby, *Kirby Smith's Confederacy,* 113–15. Winters, *The Civil War in Louisiana,* 284–89.

27. Prushankin, *A Crisis in Command,* 45–46; Winters, *The Civil War in Louisiana,* 181.

28. *PJD* 9: 279. *OR* 22, pt. 2: 952; 24, pt. 2: 466; 26, pt. 2: 109. Lowe, *Walker's Texas Division,* 107. Parks, *General Edmund Kirby Smith,* 307–9, 311.

29. *PJD* 9: 172, 172n2, 221, 223n16, 230. *OR* 15, 1028–29; 26, pt. 2: 42. Vandiver, *Rebel Brass,* 83, 85, 88. Hughes, "Wartime Gristmill Destruction," in *Civil War Arkansas,* ed. Bailey and Sutherland, 31–32. Wooster, *Texas and Texans in the Civil War,* 125–26. Kerby, *Kirby Smith's Confederacy,* 65–67, 71, 73–78, 143. Jewett, *Texas in the Confederacy,* 145–47, 149–51. Prushankin, *A Crisis in Command,* 49.

30. *PJD* 9: 382; *OR* 22, pt. 2: 952, 974, 1031; Kerby, *Kirby Smith's Confederacy,* 145–46.

31. *PJD* 9: 172, 172n2; Kerby, *Kirby Smith's Confederacy,* 75. See also the discussion of the crisis on the Rio Grande later in this essay.

32. Meiners, "Hamilton P. Bee," 60, 93–109; Kerby, *Kirby Smith's Confederacy,* 171–75, 206–7, 388, 407, 409–10; James L. Nichols, *The Confederate Quartermaster in the Trans-Mississippi* (Austin: University of Texas Press, 1964), 55–58; Tyler, *Santiago Vidaurri and the Southern Confederacy,* 113–14; Parks, *General Edmund Kirby Smith,* 290–93; Casdorph, *Prince John Magruder,* 243–47.

33. Meiners, "Hamilton P. Bee," 74–78; Kerby, *Kirby Smith's Confederacy,* 155–56, 162–75, 178–87; Nichols, *The Confederate Quartermaster in the Trans-Mississippi,* 53–58; Tyler, *Santiago Vi-*

daurri and the Southern Confederacy, 98; Mike Settles, "Magruder and Cotton," unpublished paper presented at the Texas State Historical Society meeting, April 1972; William T. Windham, "The Problem of Supply in the Trans-Mississippi Confederacy," *Journal of Southern History* 27 (May 1961): 149–68; Frank Lawrence Owsley, *King Cotton Diplomacy: Foreign Relations of the Confederate States of America* (Chicago: University of Chicago Press, 1959), 117–20; Samuel Bernard Thompson, *Confederate Purchasing Operations Abroad* (Chapel Hill: University of North Carolina Press, 1935), 103–11; Parks, *General Edmund Kirby Smith*, 283–94; Walter Prescott Webb, ed., *The Handbook of Texas* (2 vols., Austin: Texas State Historical Association, 1952), vol. 1: 136, 782; Althea Wanda Shaver, "The Cotton Bureau in the Trans-Mississippi Department," unpublished 1938 transcript, Archives and Manuscripts Section, Center for American History, University of Texas at Austin.

34. James J. Bennett to Simeon Hart, 30 May 1863; J. Bankhead Magruder to W. R. Boggs, 22 and 23 June 1863; Charles Russell to E. B. Pendleton, 10 June 1863; Russell to B. Bloomfield, 11 June 1863, in *OR* 26, pt. 2: 78, 89–94. W. A. Alston to Hamilton P. Bee, 3 July 1863, in James W. Eldridge Collection, Henry E. Huntington Library and Art Gallery, San Marino, CA. D. T. Bisbie to Alton, 24 June 1863; Hart to Alston, 29 June 1863; Hart to Magruder, 6 July 1863; Russell to Magruder, 10 June 1853, in *Letters Received by the Houston Cotton Bureau*, Treasury Department Collection of Confederate Records, Record Group 365, National Archives, Washington, DC (hereinafter referred to as *Houston Letters Received*).

35. "An Act to Regulate Impressments," in *OR*, ser. 4, vol. 2: 469–71; T. H. Watts to George W. Randolph, 17 October 1862, in *OR*, ser. 4, vol. 2: 469–71; Thomas B. Alexander and Richard E. Beringer, *The Anatomy of the Confederate Congress: A Study of the Influences of Member Characteristics on Legislative Voting Behavior, 1861–1865* (Nashville, TN: Vanderbilt University Press, 1972), 139–49; Wilfred Buck Yearns, *The Confederate Congress* (Athens: University of Georgia Press, 1960), 116–25; John Christopher Schwab, *The Confederate States of America* (New Haven, CT: Yale University Press, 1913), 203–8; Owsley, *King Cotton Diplomacy*, 4, 219–28, 248, 271; Horace White, *Money and Banking* (rev. ed., Boston: Ginn and Co., 1935), 59–60; E. James Ferguson, *The Power of the Purse: A History of American Public Finance, 1776–1790* (Williamsburg, VA: University of North Carolina Press, 1961), 57–69; Jewett, *Texas in the Confederacy*, 184–85; Casdorph, *Prince John Magruder*, 245–47; Moneyhon, "Disloyalty and Class Consciousness in Southwestern Arkansas, 1862–1865,"116–17.

36. "An Act to Regulate Impressments," in *OR*, ser. 4, vol. 2: 469–71; *PJD* 9: 253; Alexander and Beringer, *The Anatomy of the Confederate Congress*, 139–41; Kerby, *Kirby Smith's Confederacy*, 172–73; John Anthony Moretta, *William Pitt Ballinger: Texas Lawyer, Southern Statesman, 1825–1888* (Austin: Texas State Historical Association, 2000), 157–59.

37. Stephen D. Yancey to Bee, 22 June and 2 July 1863; Magruder to Boggs, 18 June 1863; Edmund Kirby Smith to Magruder, 23 and 27 June 1863; S. S. Anderson to Magruder, 26 June 1863; Magruder to Anderson, 17 June 1863; E. P. Turner to A. G. Dickinson, 30 July 1863, in *OR* 26, pt. 2: 75–78, 89, 94–96, 100–101, 127–28. Turner to Bee, 26 June 1863; Magruder to Bee, 2 July 1863, in Eldridge Collection. Dickinson to Alston, 21 July 1863, in *Houston Letters Received*. Meiners, "Hamilton P. Bee," 93–95, 98; Jewett, *Texas in the Confederacy*, 178–79; Casdorph, *Prince John Magruder*, 243–45; Kerby, *Kirby Smith's Confederacy*, 172–74.

38. Bee to Turner, 16 July 1863, in *OR* 26, pt. 2: 113–14; Dickinson to Santiago Vidaurri, 23 July 1863; Dickinson to Alston, 24 July, 2 and 9 August 1863; Bee to Turner, 19 July 1863, in *Houston Letters Received*.

39. Henry B. DeHamet, Statement of Cotton Impressed, 8 August and 10 September 1863;

Lorenzo Castro, Statement, 2 August 1863; Statement, n.d.; R. W. Davis, Statement of Cotton Impressed, 29 August 1863; Bee to Turner,19 July 1863, in *Houston Letters Received*.

40. Anderson to Magruder, 26 June 1863; Kirby Smith to Magruder, 27 June 1863, in *OR* 26, pt. 2: 86, 94–96.

41. Yancey to Bee, 2 July 1863; Turner to Bee, 29 July 1863; Magruder to Bee, 4 August 1863; F. R. Lubbock to Turner, 17 August 1863; Guy M. Bryan to Magruder, 15 August 1863; Bee to Turner, 27 August 1863, in *OR*, ser. 1, vol. 26, pt. 2: 100–101, 122–25, 137–38, 172, 184–86. Dickinson to Vidaurri, 24 July 1863; Dickinson to Alston, 24 July 1863; Bee to Turner, 19 July 1863; S. L. James to C. M. Fontleroy, 18 October 1863, in *Houston Letters Received*.

42. Turner to Bee, 29 July 1863; Magruder to Bee, 4 August 1863, *OR* 26, pt. 2: 122–25, 137–38. Bee to Turner, 19 July 1863, in *Houston Letters Received*.

43. Bee to Turner, 27 August 1863, in *OR* 26, pt. 2: 184–86. Russell to Magruder, 28 August 1863; Dickinson to Alston, 17 August 1863, in *Houston Letters Received*.

44. Bee to Turner, 16 July 1863; Turner to Bee, 29 July 1863, in *OR* 26, pt. 2: 113–14, 122–25. *OR* 26, pt. 2: 437–38. Boggs to Magruder, 13 August 1863, in Eldridge Collection. Bowder and Meek to Bee, 18 July 1863; Bee to Turner, 19 July 1863, in *Houston Letters Received*.

45. Dickinson to Alston, 2 August and 9 October 1863; Castro, Statement, 2 August 1863; Statement of Passes Granted, 7 August 1863; Dickinson, Statement of Cotton Passes, 8 September 1863; Bee to Turner, 21 July 1863, in *Houston Letters Received*.

46. Turner to Bee, 29 July 1863; Bee to Turner, 10 and 27 August 1863, in *OR* 26, pt. 2: 122–25, 157–58, 184–86. J. W. Zacherie et al. to Russell, 8 November 1863, in Charles Russell file, Compiled Service Records, Record Group 109, National Archives. Bee to Turner, 21 July and 2 August 1863; Russell to Turner, 10 August 1863; Bee to Alston, 25 September 1863; Magruder Order, 6 November 1863, in *Houston Letters Received*. Meiners, "Hamilton P. Bee," 102–21; Jewett, *Texas in the Confederacy*, 178–79.

47. Bee to Turner, 10 August and 14 September 1863, in *OR* 26, pt. 2: 122–25, 157–58, 184–86, 228–29.

48. Turner to Bee, 29 July 1863; Russell to Turner, 21 August 1863; Bee to Turner, 27 August 1863, in *OR* 26, pt. 2: 122–25, 176, 184–86. Nelson Clements to Hart, 16 December 1862; John Slidell to Judah P. Benjamin, 29 January 1863, in Confederate States of America Archives, Library of Congress, Washington, DC. Russell to Magruder, 28 August 1863; Hart to Henry Attrill, 11 July 1863; Bowder and Meek to Bee, 18 July 1863; Bee to Turner, 10 August 1863; Russell to Bisbie, 12 and 14 August 1863; Russell to Thatcher, 12 August 1863; Bisbie to Magruder, 13 July 1863; Russell to Turner, 10 and 15 August 1863, in *Houston Letters Received*.

49. *OR* 26, pt. 2: 437–38; Kerby, *Kirby Smith's Confederacy*, 175–78, 206–7, 385–86, 409–10; Nichols, *The Confederate Quartermaster in the Trans-Mississippi*, 58–82; Thompson, *Confederate Purchasing Operations Abroad*, 111–18; Parks, *General Edmund Kirby Smith*, 292–301; Jewett, *Texas in the Confederacy*, 186–89, 204–5. The Confederate Congress in March 1865 agreed to audit the Cotton Bureau and require payment for receipts for impressed cotton but did not place limits on the bureau's cotton acquisition program.

50. *PJD* 9: 279, 311n18. *OR* 15: 986; 22, pt. 2: 52, 952, 1031. Jones, *Civil War Command and Strategy*, 162. Jewett, *Texas in the Confederacy*, 145–47, 174–75. Wooster, *Texas and Texans in the Civil War*, 101. Kerby, *Kirby Smith's Confederacy*, 137–42. Parks, *General Edmund Kirby Smith*, 312. Dougan, "Arkansas," 54–55. Smith's exercise of civil authority seems to have been confined to the re-issuance of

treasury notes as he awaited the appointment of a Treasury Department agent for the department and an effort to get the French ships from interfering with the delivery of Confederate shipments of arms and other supplies to Matamoros. The Cotton Bureau and his other bureaus and agencies were staffed by military officers under military orders.

51. *PJD* 9: 382; *OR* 22, pt. 2: 1003–4; Kerby, *Kirby Smith's Confederacy*, 139; Jewett, *Texas In the Confederacy*, 146; Wooster, "Texas," 206.

52. Parks, *General Edmund Kirby Smith*, 317.

53. Kerby, *Kirby Smith's Confederacy*, 139; Jewett, *Texas in the Confederacy*, 145–47; Wooster, *Texas and Texans in the Civil War*, 101; Parks, *General Edmund Kirby Smith*, 312–13.

54. Kerby, *Kirby Smith's Confederacy*, 141–42; Jewett, *Texas in the Confederacy*, 146–47; Dougan, *Confederate Arkansas*, 101; Parks, *General Edmund Kirby Smith*, 315–16.

55. *OR* 26, pt. 2: 437–38; Kerby, *Kirby Smith's Confederacy*, 150–54; Wooster, "Texas," 207–9; Wooster, *Texas and Texans in the Civil War*, 102–3; Jewett, *Texas in the Confederacy*, 186–88, 190–94.

56. *PJD* 10: 327; *OR* 22, pt. 2: 1031; Wooster, "Texas," 207–9, 211–13; Dougan, "Arkansas," 55.

57. *PJD* 9: 309, 311, 360–61; 10: 327. *OR* 22, pt. 2: 931–33.

58. Prushankin, *A Crisis in Command*, 44–48; Kerby, *Kirby Smith's Confederacy*, 130–31; Dougan, *Confederate Arkansas*, 103.

59. Alexander and Beringer, *The Anatomy of the Confederate Congress*, 133, 163, 200, 228; Jewett, *Texas in the Confederacy*, 190–94, 196–99.

60. *OR* 24, pt. 3: 1070.

PART III

DESPOTISM

xxxxxx AND xxxxxx

CONFEDERATE DEFEAT

"IRRESISTIBLE OUTBREAKS AGAINST TORIES AND TRAITORS"

XXXXXXXXXXXXXXXXXXXXXXXXXXXXXXXXXXXXXXXXXXXX

The Suppression of New England Antiwar Sentiment in 1861

MICHAEL J. CONNOLLY

I n a time of war the parameters of the freedom of press, speech, and association always face scrutiny. Some see criticism of war, its tactics, and its justification as tantamount to treason and a fatal weakening of national resolve at a time when it needs to be united and resolute. Others see such criticism as central to just and authentic self-government, where citizens and the press express a healthy skepticism toward national policies and force those in power to justify their ideas rather than blithely expect public unanimity and approval. The former fears failure by showing the enemy a divided home front; the latter fears a rubber stamp will lead to emboldened power and tyranny. These concerns become more acute during civil war, when the enemy is within, sympathizers could be working in every community, and the threat to life and property feels more immediate. Here, the pressure for a united front becomes so acute that it often spills over into mob violence and government action.

During the American Civil War, examples of northern suppression of dissent abound: the 1861 Baltimore riots and the arrest of the Baltimore city government, the arrests in the Maryland legislature, the clash between President Abraham Lincoln and Chief Justice Roger Brooke Taney in *Ex parte Merryman,* the expulsion of Indiana Senator Jesse Bright (and others) from Congress, and the arrest and deportation of Clement Vallandigham, to name the most prominent. There were also actions taken against members of the northern press and local business and political leaders critical of the war effort. Some of the most fascinating cases occurred in New England. In August and September 1861, a mob tarred and feathered a "Peace Democrat" editor in Haverhill, Massachusetts, for his editorial writings; angry crowds wrecked the presses of two other editors in Concord, New Hampshire, and Bangor, Maine; and the federal government arrested two Maine citizens for disloyalty. These episodes make an interesting study on the boundaries of freedom in civil war time, the extent to which vigilante justice as much as government policies quashed dissent, and the dilemma of northern Democrats who vehemently opposed the Lincoln administration.

Further, the Confederacy lost the Civil War in many places, not only on bloody battlefields and a divided southern home front. The northern democracy divided between War Democrats loyal to the Union and Peace Democrats (also known derisively as "Copperheads") sympathetic to the South and highly resistant to emancipation. Southern independence failed when northern Republicans held off a Democratic resurgence, particularly in 1862 (when the Democrats gained dozens of House seats, but not enough to become the majority) and in 1864 when Lincoln defeated Peace Democrat George McClellan for the presidency. The forces of peace and compromise lost to those of continued war. Legal and extra-legal action against Peace Democrats chilled northern political support for peaceful southern separation and, with northern home-front dissent held sufficiently in abeyance, forced Confederates to fight for nationhood rather than depend upon sympathetic northern politicians, opinion-makers, and voters. Government and mobs marginalized the "doughfaces."

New England appears an unlikely region for dissent against the Civil War. In the public mind, it represents the abolitionism of William Lloyd Garrison; the antebellum reform impulses of Emerson, Thoreau, and the Transcendentalists; the anti-slavery Republican politics of Charles Sumner and John Parker Hale; and an avalanche of votes for Abraham Lincoln in 1860, rather than a hotbed of "Copperheads." But a closer examination of the region reveals a complexity that deserves more attention by historians. New Hampshire and Maine had been reliably Democratic states into the mid-1850s. The region's icon, Daniel Webster, had publicly broken with reformers in his 1850 Seventh of March Address by backing compromise with the South, and the region's only president between John Quincy Adams in the 1820s and Calvin Coolidge in the 1920s was the New Hampshire conservative Democrat Franklin Pierce. In the 1860 election, Vice-President John C. Breckinridge—the "Southern Democrat," "Constitutional Democrat," or "Administration Democrat" candidate—polled more votes in Massachusetts, Maine, New Hampshire, Connecticut, and Vermont (29,246) than in Ohio, Michigan, Indiana, Illinois, Iowa, and Minnesota combined (28,640), despite those midwestern states exceeding New England by over 900,000 total votes. True, the Lincoln and Douglas candidacies held down the Breckinridge vote in Illinois, but Connecticut alone returned a higher percentage of Breckinridge votes than the slave state of Missouri. A strong minority, shrinking but vocal, dissented from New England's direction in these years. Playing important (and soon nationally infamous) roles in that dissent were Ambrose L. Kimball of Massachusetts, John B. Palmer of New Hampshire, and Marcellus Emery, Cyrus F. Sargent, and Robert Elliot of Maine.[1]

By 1860 Haverhill, Massachusetts, was a bustling factory town along the Merrimack River engaged primarily in shoe-making. Its many mills produced millions of pairs of boots and shoes every year and, through efficient river and railroad shipping connections, marketed its products around the United States, particularly in the South, where plantation owners purchased shoes for their slaves. Thirty miles north of Boston and bordering New Hampshire, Haverhill stood in the shadow of larger industrial cities upstream like Lowell and Lawrence, but what the city lacked in size it more than compensated for in political passion. Haverhill was a center of abolitionism and reform. In 1842, John Quincy Adams presented a Haverhill anti-slavery petition in the House of Representatives, and it played a central role in his battle against the infamous "gag rule." Further, the town's best-known citizen was abolitionist Quaker poet John Greenleaf Whittier, who throughout the 1850s excoriated slavery and those he believed kept the institution alive, like Daniel Webster.[2]

Amidst the clatter of industry and chatter of reform, a dissenting voice emerged that infuriated Republicans and challenged Haverhill's loyalty to a free press. In November of 1859, Ambrose L. Kimball and David P. Bodfish founded a city newspaper, the *Essex County Democrat*. The thirty-two-year-old Kimball was from an old New England family and briefly worked in the Boston Custom House, while Bodfish served as Haverhill postmaster, appointed by President James Buchanan in 1858. Both men prospered in the shoe industry and were diehard Democrats. The *Democrat*, founded when the national Democratic Party split into Stephen A. Douglas and Buchanan wings after the Dred Scott, Lecompton, and squatter sovereignty controversies, allied with the president. It dedicated itself in its inaugural issue to perpetuating "the blessings of union, harmony, and general prosperity," condemned John Brown as "a Kanzas [sic] freedom-shrieker," and printed campaign materials about Democratic guberna-torial candidate Benjamin Butler. The paper was published on Wednesdays, and Kimball assumed sole management in the spring of 1861 when Bodfish became nervous with his partner's strident editorials and severed ties. It soon became a fixture in Haverhill, "the organ of the administration wing of the democratic party," and the subject of much debate.[3]

Kimball's *Democrat* backed Vice-President John C. Breckinridge in 1860 and remained fiercely critical of Lincoln and the Republicans throughout the secession winter of 1860–61. Speaking for New Englanders skeptical of aboli-tion, the paper defended President Buchanan. "Our people are for the Union and peace. They are unwilling that expressions of hostility to the institutions of the South, should be represented as the universal convictions of the State of Massachusetts. Time will prove how far the sentiments of the people of the State, are for Union, and equal rights in all the States." The paper also vigorously supported the Crittenden Compromise and implicitly advocated John C. Cal-houn's theory of "territorial equal rights": "The establishment of the line 36/30, as proposed by Mr. Crittenden is a great concession—the South yielding to the North three-fourths of the existing territories to save the rights of one-fourth, when it is clearly evident that the South have equal rights in all. How are these concessions of the South met by those who have the power to compromise? They deny the right to property in slaves, and declare that the preservation of the Republican Party is of greater importance than the Union itself."

Republicans caused secession because equal rights in the territories were not honored. Now that the Deep South was departing the Union, Republicans claimed incredulously that they had no role in splitting the nation in two. "Se-cession, at first scoffed at and treated by the North as idle boasting, has now become solemn fact. But Republicanism stands with folded arms, motion-less, inactive, and looks with cold indifference on States severed, discordant, belligerent."[4]

To the *Democrat*'s editor, the Republicans were a one issue party—"Republicanism made slavery the alpha and omega of its creed"—and they stirred up racial fears with moralistic politics:

> Throughout the North, as if by magic, the circle at the fireside, the marts
> of business, the lecture room and pulpit set up a mighty mourning over the
> unutterable sufferings and afflictions of the poor slave. Hordes of negroes,

inundating our towns and villages, rehearsed in our churches and Sabbath schools the most pitiable stories, and many an innocent child, terrified at their black visages and rolling eyes, received untruthful impressions which will never be obliterated—Many a youth, who cast his first vote on the 6th of November last, with the conviction that he was following the dictates of his own judgment, was a victim to these seductive arts. It was to this prejudice that Republicanism appealed.

Those who opposed Republican judgments on southern life were ostracized, wrote Kimball. A southern gentleman who owned slaves became "a monster of the deepest dye" and northern Democrats (like himself) who disparaged Republican plans were branded "slavery propagandists, doughfaces, and demagogues."[5]

Kimball's words against President Abraham Lincoln's 1861 war policy led directly to his inglorious treatment later that summer. The *Democrat*, like many northern papers, viewed the April 1861 shelling of Fort Sumter as a "direful calamity" but appealed for calm and understanding, particularly for dissenters: "[W]hy excite men in an hour when reason is dethroned, to engage in a conflict which is to destroy their own blood and kindred and forever ruin a country we all so much love. Let honest difference be respected as to the cause of our condition, and those who do not feel like plunging the country into a bloody war, be protected in their opinions. The time has not come when men must be held responsible to a set of men or party for their opinions and sympathies, but to their own consciences, the Constitution and the laws." By the end of April, a bald eagle and flapping American flag graced the paper's masthead, leaving readers no doubt about the paper's allegiance. Kimball's editorials even praised Federal troops: "No one, but a coward, and an enemy to his country, will impugn the motives of those who by any sacrifice are ready and willing to stand by the Union." In mid-May, he continued to praise the early war effort and chastised the South for secession: "Whatever may have been the just claims of the South four months ago they are now less credited by all classes, simply because those demands and claims have been pressed in a manner ill-becoming calm legislation and cool judgment." By all appearances, Kimball and the *Democrat* firmly backed the northern war effort.[6]

Behind these patriotic sentiments, however, was a deep suspicion of the new president. The *Democrat* greeted Lincoln's March inaugural with cool detachment but complimented him for continuing Buchanan's wait-and-see approach to Fort Sumter: "President Lincoln, with the advice of the ablest statesmen in his Cabinet, has wisely determined not to precipitate matters, or to use the means so persistently recommended by the Republican Party before they came to power." That good word would be the last from Kimball's pen. "All is vague and uncertain," the paper puzzled in April just before Sumter, "and the future as much a mystery as the past has been blank, with the exception of parceling out places to hungry office seekers." From here, Kimball's opinion of Lincoln declined precipitously, and by early summer editorials blasted Federal war policy as ill conceived and unconstitutional. Huge armies, hefty government war contracts, the suspension of habeas corpus, and the invasion of the southern states mortified Kimball as signs of Republican despotism. "The utterance of these sentiments may call down on our head the epithets of 'Secessionist' and 'traitor,' by Abolition partizans [sic] but we can well afford to be abused for advocating the sentiments of Madison, Hamilton, Colonel Mason, and other patriots of the Revolution. By civil war we can have no Union, by compromise we may." Clearly, Kimball was already hearing criticism for his words.[7]

Yet the *Democrat* continued its broadsides and ignored the abuse. By late July 1861, Kimball's editorials hammered the government for opposing free speech and a free press, no doubt thinking that federal authorities could close down the *Democrat* at any moment. "No one can be true to himself or his country unless by every laudable means and on every occasion, he expresses the unjust policy of the powers that be, and advocates the speedy restoration of the country to its wonted prosperity, and by a method too, that shall stay the bloody strife that is now going on." The paper must have faced more ominous threats, since Kimball restated the paper's principles and fended off verbal assaults: "This is a position we have deliberately taken, and shall not be intimidated by the threats of violence or revenge, trusting only in the sacredness of our cause, the Constitution, and an overruling Providence." Indeed, the threats seemed to have emboldened Kimball, for his bitter criticisms of Lincoln and the war came to a head with the August 14, 1861, issue of the *Democrat*.[8]

Reacting to federal policy in Baltimore, where the government suspended habeas corpus and imprisoned city and state officials suspected of southern sympathies, Kimball lashed out at this "act of tyranny more atrocious than has ever before been contemplated or suggested in any section of the land where American laws exist or American men hold sway." Lincoln and the officials who followed his orders were "traitorous fanatics." Restating his June warning of military despotism, Kimball wrote: "If the usurpation of which the President has been guilty be tolerated, who can foresee the character of tyranny which the faction of which he is also the leader will yet fasten upon the people of the North. We preach no treason when we warn them to resist before it is to [*sic*] late. . . . We but vindicate the rights of the American freemen and defend the integrity of constitutional liberty when we call upon the North to repudiate the despotism which, under the plea of 'military necessity,' the President and his partisans have established." In the same issue, he sarcastically mocked "Black Republican" attempts to create northern loyalty while arresting dissenters— "woe to the unfortunate wight that undertakes to question these great and mighty statesmen, or deny the truth of their dictatorial statements." He called slavery "a blessing to blacks and a benefit directly and indirectly to the civilized world" and bemoaned the fact that Baltimore crowds recently jeered former Vice-President Breckinridge (he would flee to the Confederacy in September). "And this to preserve the Union! Alack and alas! We are confident that the head-long career of these disorganizers will soon be checked, and in this hope bury the resentment that we strongly feel against the assassins of American liberty." That would not happen, because five days later Kimball became an "unfortunate wight" at the hands of a Haverhill mob.[9]

On Monday evening, August 19, 1861, a gang of Haverhill citizens (some of whom may have been soldiers of the "Hale Guards") gathered downtown to confront Ambrose L. Kimball, the plans having been worked out at a secret meeting days before. "There was the most perfect order and system ever saw in such a tumultuous assemblage," the *Haverhill Gazette* reported. When Kimball's carriage appeared, a signal was given and the mob followed the editor back to his home. There, Kimball and two friends—the wealthy shoe manufacturer (and Douglas delegate at the 1860 Charleston Democratic Convention) George Johnson and local physician Dr. James C. Howe—turned and faced their pursuers with revolvers, but many in the mob were also armed. Kimball asked the crowd what they wanted and was commanded to "recant" his editorial opinions printed in the *Democrat*. When he refused, a "general scuffle" ensued, the crowd disarmed the three men, and although no shots were fired, Dr. Howe was "severely handled" and injured. Kimball was then taken back downtown to the Eagle House, a prosperous Haverhill inn, and again directed to "retract his position, as a condition of his release from harm, which he refused to do." The mob then forced Kimball to remove all his clothes save his underwear (which were handed to the editor's friend and fellow shoe manufacturer Broadstreet P. Woodman, who accompanied him downtown), "thoroughly besmeared [Kimball] with a coat of tar and feathers," placed him on a wooden rail, carried him to the front of the *Democrat*'s offices, and "required to give three cheers for the American flag" which he did weakly. The police, who were "promptly on the spot," did nothing to stop the ruckus, either sympathizing with the mob's actions or fearful for their own safety. He was then carried across the Merrimack River to George Johnson's home in Bradford (generations of Kimballs had lived there as well), the rail discarded and later cut up for souvenirs. Next, they dragged him back across the river to the Eagle House, where he was forced to kneel before the crowd and swear with raised hands: "I am sorry for what I have done, and I promise that I will not publish anything more against the North, and in favor of secession, as long as I live. So help me God." His humiliation complete, Kimball was "conducted to his residence, and required to give three cheers for the Union, after which the crowd dispersed." The editor and his friends spent all night cleaning him, and although Kimball returned to his office the next day, he was understandably bitter and closed the *Democrat* in October.[10]

When the Essex County district attorney announced indictments in early 1862 for involvement in the mob action, stunned city leaders called a "citizen's meeting" for February 8th to craft resolutions against any trials and continue condemnation of Kimball. The meeting's participants were an interesting cross-section of Haverhill society, replete with lawyers, businessmen, doctors, publishers, and pastors, all clamoring to be heard and none of whom had anything kind to say of the ex-editor. Even Kimball attended the meeting, showing a remarkable degree of courage, but left before the conclusion. "Mr. A. L. Kimball, who had been in the hall from the commencement of the meeting, arose from his seat, and while passing out, was greeted with hisses and outcries from a portion of the audience," related the *Haverhill Tri-Weekly Publisher*, "but the cool and deliberate manner in which he met this disagreeable and decided manifestation, by facing about, and then slowly making his way out of the hall, indicated that the strength of his nervous system was proof against any operations of that sort."[11]

After comparing Kimball's treatment to that of Loyalists during the Revolution, meeting chair and city collector Christopher Tompkins recognized Judge Henry Carter, who although claiming he was not a mob member thought the punishment fully justified. The *Democrat* was "a paper without decency, without talent, without anything to recommend it to public favor, almost without subscribers, and nothing to attract notice except its unmitigated stupidity and treason." Haverhill's loyal citizens were left little choice, said the judge—"with the insufficiency of the laws, consequent upon the weakness of all things human, there are contingencies which demand the immediate action of the people themselves. . . . [T]he loyal people feel that a case like this should be treated differently, from others of less peculiar circumstances."[12]

The meeting unanimously passed a resolution asking the district attorney not to push for trials along with a wide-ranging eleven-point petition defending the community and its actions against Kimball. In printing Breckinridge's and Vallandigham's speeches and pushing for a "'peace party,' which is known to have been a movement for the benefit of the rebels," Kimball's paper "was truly deserving of the title of a secession paper." The newspaper did violence to the community with its anti-war message and instigated a violent counter-reaction. Kimball did not heed warnings from friends to desist, his violent criticism against the war effort "tended to provoke violence in return," and he was such a loathed figure in Haverhill that virtually no one objected to his punishment. Without any recourse (Kimball should have been imprisoned for treason at Fort Warren long before August, one resolution noted), loyal citizens had no choice—"we believe that in the absence of a quick remedy by the ordinary courses of law, this instance if any, in its circumstances and its nature, justified the application of law by the hands of the people." Next, the Unitarian pastor of Haverhill's First Parish Church (later chaplain for a Massachusetts regiment), Reverend Robert Hassall, stood and read excerpts from the *Democrat,* especially regarding Lincoln's Maryland policy. A city photographer named Daniel Walton followed, comparing the mob's actions to the Boston Tea Party ("Both cases were popular and irresistible outbreaks against tories and traitors"), and city historian George Wingate Chase exclaimed at the meeting's conclusion, "Sarved [*sic*] him right!"[13]

Few realized, while making comparison to eighteenth-century Tories and Loyalists, that Kimball's grandfather was a Battle of Bunker Hill veteran. Kimball and his wife eventually left the city and moved to Iowa, where the humiliated ex-editor died of tuberculosis in November 1866. His widow and her family returned to Haverhill and by 1870 worked in the city's shoe mills.[14]

Other northern Democrats suffered like Kimball. That same month, angry soldiers and citizens destroyed the presses of Concord, New Hampshire, newspaper printer John B. Palmer. The Palmers were a Democratic family of printers. John B. Palmer's father, Brackett, was a New England merchant and Democratic newspaperman, and served as postmaster of Lake Village, New Hampshire, in the 1840s. By 1850, he settled in the state capitol of Concord, and his four sons—John, Charles, Thomas Noble, and Benjamin—followed their father's footsteps to become printers, or "practical printers" as one local historian described them. Beginning in June 1856, the month James Buchanan accepted the Democratic presidential nomination, the Palmers began publishing the *Democratic Standard* with editorial contributions by New Hampshire Congressman Edmund Burke, a former newspaperman and prominent conservative Democrat active in national politics since the 1830s. For those who could not afford the subscription price, the Palmers accepted patent medicines and offered them for sale in their offices. A Concord editor noted that "they claimed to have a large subscription list, in the South and elsewhere, but the heap of paper wet for the weekly printing was guarded with jealous care from the eye of any one who could size it up at a glance."[15]

The *Standard* endured and by 1861, much like Kimball's *Democrat*, denounced Lincoln, the war, and even blasted federal soldiers as "robbers and murderers." Palmer received threats but continued the paper's hard line. "[Palmer] had been warned earlier in the summer of the personal danger which he was incurring, but his only measure of protection was the purchase of a revolver with which he declared himself ready to meet the whole of Old Abe's 'mob,' if need be," a local history recalled. In early August, the paper printed a short limerick on the recent federal defeat at Bull Run that read in part:

> The Late Battle—Impromptu
> It frightened the Federals to see them come,
> They wheeled about and away they run;
> They Run so fast to tell the news,
> They left their knapsacks, guns, and shoes.

Days after this issue, the First New Hampshire Volunteer Regiment returned to Concord as their three-month enlistment expired and many soldiers heard about the newspaper. Several actually went to the paper's offices, demanded to see copies, and Palmer grumpily obliged. Seething at what they read, at 4 p.m. on August 8, 1861, a group of soldiers and sympathetic citizens gathered outside the *Standard's* offices and began taunting the printers, "which the Palmers indis-creetly met by brandishing arms and abusing epithets." The mob moved inside and the "plucky editor," after firing several shots, fled with his brothers and hid in the attic. Everything was destroyed (including the newspaper's shingle, hang-ing outside the door), thrown into the street, and set afire. When the Palmers emerged a short time later, they were hurried away by police and spent several nights at the State Penitentiary under "protective custody."[16]

Unlike Kimball, Palmer remained in town and stubbornly returned to the newspaper business in May 1863 by launching the *Democratic Sentinel,* which he defiantly promised would carry on the work of the late *Standard.* A broadside leaflet announced the paper was dedicated to Jeffersonian principles, an end to the war, white supremacy and opposition to any black political or social rights, and federal as opposed to "Consolidated Government." The Palmer name and the *Democratic Standard,* however, were permanently blackened in the pages of New Hampshire history. No criminal charges emerged from the August 1861 ransacking of the paper's office, but Palmer sued several townsmen for damages and was eventually awarded a small sum. He died in Concord at age seventy-eight in January 1905.[17]

The Bangor, Maine, editor Marcellus Emery witnessed his newspaper de-stroyed in that same month of August 1861. Emery, different from the self-made Kimball and the craftsman Palmer, was a college-educated man. Born in 1830 in Frankfort, Maine, he graduated from Bowdoin College in 1853—along with future U.S. Chief Justice Melville Fuller—and in 1855 worked as a private family tutor in Woodville, Mississippi (once home to Jefferson Davis), about thirty-five miles south of Natchez. Here, he lived amidst cotton plantations, slaves, and the bustling Woodville Manufacturing Company, which by the mid-1850s was oper-ated entirely by slaves and produced great amounts of cotton cloth. In 1856, he studied law in Evansville, Indiana—itself distinctly "Southern" in outlook, just over the Ohio River from Kentucky—but soon returned to Bangor as an ambi-tious young Democratic lawyer and local politician. He took an interest in news-papers, owning and editing both the *Bangor Daily Union* and *Bangor Democrat* and using them as a platform to criticize President Lincoln and the Republicans. In April 1861, the Bangor Merchant's Association banned both of Emery's papers from its reading room, and when the *Daily Union* folded in June, a rival news-paper cheered, "we trust the people of the country will take the same course to suppress the weekly publication from the same office (*The Democrat*)."[18]

Like Kimball and Palmer, Emery faced threats and was warned of danger by the owner of the building which housed his press, but the mayor refused assistance to protect the property. Emery plowed ahead nonetheless, continuing to publish his paper and actively organizing a Bangor "Breckinridge Democrat" convention for the summer of 1861 to recruit candidates. In the August 12, 1861, paper, he wrote: "The loudest advocates of the existing deplorable war, in which the country has been involved, by the Abolition Republican party, are the political demagogues, the partisan priests, and the infamous speculators, who are coining fortunes out of the calamities of their country. The first want offices; the priests are for setting the niggers free; and the speculators are for the accumulating of pelf. The poor unfortunate people—the farmers, mechanics, and workingman—are to be first taxed to death, and then enslaved, as a consequence of all this infamous business." It would be the last issue of the *Bangor Democrat*.[19]

At noon on August 12, 1861, bells from the Congregational and Episcopal churches rang signaling a fire alarm, and townspeople followed the fire engines. But it was a diversionary false alarm, and a small group of men led by a "brawny blacksmith with his sledge" entered the *Democrat's* offices and smashed the presses. Everything was thrown out the window and set on fire as an enthusiastic crowd began to gather. A nearby barber, supportive of Emery, brawled with one of the crowd, and soon they sacked his barbershop as well. "[The newspaper's] office was completely emptied in the course of half an hour, the heavy cylinder press being thrown out upon the pavement along with the rest, while bonfires were kindled in West Market Square, and the inflammable materials committed to flames," the *Bangor Daily Evening News* reported. "The large sign was also wrenched off from the building, leaving the upper portion with the head of Washington intact." Emery and his associates, who had been away for lunch, arrived at the scene, and the crowd surrounded him, yelling variously, "Hang him!" and "Give him tar and feathers!" But friends quickly whisked him away and, unlike Kimball, he escaped without harm. Within two hours, the riot was over.[20]

Emery sued for damages but was awarded only a small amount. The "Breckinridge Democrat" campaign in Maine failed completely, with the *Democrat's* destruction and voter intimidation no doubt playing some role. Only thirty-one Bangor voters supported the Peace Democrat gubernatorial candidate. Someone hung a noose and a list of suspected disloyal voters in one Bangor polling place, "with a request that such of those whose names appeared upon the paper, who came to vote, be hanged." Emery returned to publishing, restarted the *Democrat* in 1863 and made it the "democratic organ of Penobscot County," and also inaugurated the *Bangor Daily Commercial* in 1872. At war's end, he assured a crowd at his Bangor home that he loved the Union and was a loyal American. He also remained active in Democratic politics, attending both the 1864 and 1868 Democratic National Conventions as a Maine delegate. In the latter, he unsuccessfully nominated George H. Pendleton of Ohio as vice-president of the United States to run with New York Governor Horatio Seymour. Emery's name disappeared from the national scene for decades after his 1879 death, only reappearing in the 1930s when genealogical research awkwardly revealed he was an ancestor of prominent New Dealer Harry Hopkins.[21]

These three editors faced public scorn, and vigilante action temporarily silenced their presses. Two other New Englanders, both from Maine, faced official charges of disloyalty, and the government arrested both in September 1861. Cyrus Foss Sargent was born in Yarmouth, Maine, in 1814 and counted some of the oldest New England families among his ancestors: Wheelwrights, Bradburys, and Pepperells. He left New England in the early 1830s and worked at a New Orleans merchant house before heading to the cotton-growing region around El Dorado, Arkansas, in the 1840s. Here he operated as a merchant and land speculator, and he married Mary Margaret Hill, the only daughter of another Yarmouth native, Captain James Coffin Hill. Soon, most of the Sargent and Hill families lived in southern Arkansas. Cyrus F. Sargent and James C. Hill invested in Union, Drew, and Calhoun County lands between 1849 and 1855, and Sargent alone purchased acreage in Little River County as late as 1860. President James K. Polk appointed his brother, William True Sargent, to the El Dorado Public Land Office in the late 1840s, an advantageous position that no doubt aided family land speculation. Another brother, Elias Haskell Sargent, graduated from Bowdoin College in 1844 and became a school teacher and merchant in Union County. Hill's sons James Decatur Hill and Andrew Jackson Hill both settled in Arkansas, and another son, Octavius A. Hill, remained back in Maine handling family business and participating in local politics. When he fell ill in the late 1850s, Cyrus F. Sargent returned to Yarmouth but could not remain away from business. By 1860, he and his brother Elias joined with Andrew Jackson Hill and Octavius A. Hill to form a New Orleans firm called Sargent & Hill, later noted as having "ship-owning and slave-holding interests."

When Cyrus's second wife died in April 1861, both Sargents returned to Maine for good.[22]

Business in Arkansas, Louisiana, and Maine made Sargent a wealthy man by 1860; his combined estate was valued at $63,200, over $1.4 million in 2007 dollars. He also had unique experiences for a Yarmouth native, having lived and worked in the South for thirty years. Thus a Democratic anti-war convention in Portland invited him to speak, and he unsurprisingly expressed sympathy for the southern states and harshly criticized the war. Rumors spread in Yarmouth, begun by the postmaster, Otis B. Pratt, and through conversations at a local store, that Sargent & Hill intended to run supplies to the Confederacy, specifically to the Texas coast. Soon Secretary of State William H. Seward received a letter from Yarmouth Baptist preacher William C. Hoben claiming that Cyrus F. Sargent and Octavius A. Hill "are now in this town denouncing the Government and boldly avowing their sympathy for treason," and preparing to escape to New Orleans to aid the Confederacy. On September 5, 1861, federal marshals arrested both men and placed them in Portland's Fort Preble. "Direct the commander also not to respect any writ of habeas corpus which may be issued in the case," Seward wired General Winfield Scott the same day. Scott immediately wrote the fort, "Refuse to obey any writ of habeas corpus that may be served upon you in their cases," and quietly put them on a boat for Fort Lafayette in New York harbor. Apparently, Scott's cable arrived too late since the U.S. District Attorney reported both released on habeas corpus.[23]

Another letter arrived in Washington, D.C., addressed to Secretary of Interior Caleb B. Smith from Daniel L. Eaton of the Public Land Office, who had heard that Sargent & Hill "have a contract to supply two rebel regiments at New Orleans" and that the firm was building a special ship in Yarmouth for that purpose. Again, Seward ordered that Sargent and Hill be arrested and sent to Fort Lafayette. For some reason, despite Seward's command, they only detained Sargent. On September 23, 1861, while riding the Portland to Boston train, U.S. marshals jumped and handcuffed Sargent, brought him to Boston, and quickly put him on a New York City train. The next day, he was incarcerated at Fort Lafayette along with other political prisoners, and in late October shifted to Fort Warren in Boston harbor.[24]

Over the next weeks, Seward received letters and petitions on the Sargent case. Republican Congressman Charles W. Walton reported that, although not personally familiar with Sargent, many citizens of "high social position" asked that Seward closely investigate the case and release him "if not inconsistent with the public welfare." U.S. Senator William P. Fessenden twice forwarded Yarmouth petitions, from "Republicans and most zealous and ardent friends of Government" and Democrats "who I have no doubt give their warm support to the Government in it present struggle." In response, Seward asked the U.S. Attorney to examine the case, take testimony from locals, and forward his conclusions.[25]

After nearly one month of investigations, the U.S. Attorney recommended Sargent's release for lack of evidence and family distress. The accusations against Sargent were fourfold: that he had a "contract" to supply the Confederacy, that he was building a ship in Yarmouth to carry supplies to Texas, that he openly "denounced the Government and avowed sympathy with treason," and that he was about to flee to Louisiana. Hoben's and Eaton's source was Professor George Woods of Pittsburgh, a former Yarmouth resident and ship owner, who was now president of the Western University of Pennsylvania (today the University of Pittsburgh). Woods expressed shock that his conversation with Eaton had led to Sargent's arrest, but that he had "already suffered greatly from this secession party in Yarmouth and had and still have no desire further to provoke them, well knowing their tyrannical disposition." He also claimed that Yarmouth sea captain Calvin Humphrey told him that he traveled through the South with Andrew Jackson Hill, who reported Sargent & Hill as having supplied Confederate regiments. Sargent revealed these plans to the Yarmouth postmaster and others in a local store, distributed "disloyal newspapers," and tried to convince a local captain, Joseph Gooding, to run the federal blockade, Woods claimed. He even heard rumors that a Sargent-owned ship, "Sam Locke," was in Portland readying for a trip south. Eaton repeated what Woods told him, and although he had not seen Sargent in years, assured the U.S. Attorney that Sargent was an Arkansas slave trader and land owner with "malignant" views on the government and secession, and "it seemed to me not amiss to have him in keeping." While he had not personally heard Sargent criticize the government, Eaton thought it consistent with his background.[26]

The case did not impress the U.S. Attorney. The evidence of a contract to outfit Confederate regiments was third person hearsay, from rumors heard by the postmaster to Professor Woods to Eaton in the Land Office. Captain Humphrey was currently sailing for the Chincha Islands off Peru, and thus could offer no details. That Sargent wanted to build or hire a ship to run the blockade may have been true, but he never followed through. Like Humphrey, Captain Gooding was also at sea and could not help the case. Clearly Sargent "was in political sympathy with the Breckinridge branch of the Democratic party in this State," which was neither treason nor a basis for further imprisonment. In fact, when pressed, the Yarmouth postmaster admitted "he heard nothing of a treasonable nature said by Sargent or imputed to him by others."[27]

Four men submitted affidavits asking for Sargent's release—his brother and business partner Elias H. Sargent, his father-in-law Captain Sylvanus C. Blanchard, Yarmouth and Boston merchant Ammi Storer, and Storer's son Ferdinand Ingraham. But Elias Sargent swore that neither he nor his brother had knowledge of Andrew Jackson Hill supplying the Confederacy, especially since both returned to Maine the previous April and never "gave any consent to the enterprise." "Doubtless his political prejudices in favor of the movers of the great rebellion were further stimulated by his business relations with the South, and by his temporary residence there," the U.S. Attorney wrote. His initial arrest was justified because "hopes were cherished by a portion of our citizens that a political demonstration might be made at the polls which would paralyze the Administration in its efforts to subdue the rebellion and would compel it to offer some ignoble and unjust concession to the armed traitors. The loyalty of the people has disappointed all such hopes." He should be released from Fort Warren, but his "unhealthy political associations" and "Southern connections" require him taking a loyalty oath and subjected to "a period of surveillance as may not be incompatible with his liberty."[28]

Cyrus F. Sargent swore the loyalty oath and was released on November 10, 1861. He remained in Yarmouth the rest of his life as a ship owner and businessman, and in 1864 he built a ship named "Eldorado," recalling his Arkansas roots in the 1840s. He likely paid for his nephew's Harvard College education; William Mitchell Sargent, an Arkansas native and son of William True Sargent, graduated in 1869 and became a prominent Maine historian. Sargent died in Yarmouth at age seventy-six in May 1880.[29]

Finally, there is the case of Robert Elliot, much heralded because of his hometown's ironic name—Freedom, Maine. Elliot was a farmer, married with no children, likely born in rural New Portland, Maine, around 1818. He settled at Freedom in Waldo County (there were also towns named Liberty and Unity—Waldo was Emery's home county too), a small potato-growing town in steady decline like many others in nineteenth-century New England. Freedom listed over 1,000 residents in 1837, but by 1860 it declined to 849, and in 1900 only 479. Elliot emerged as a local Democratic Party leader in the 1850s. After serving several terms in the Maine legislature and on the County Council, he became one of seven members of Samuel Wells's Governor's Council in 1856, the last Democratic governor of Maine until 1879.[30]

When Maine Governor Israel Washburn Jr., one of the Republican Party's founders, called for Elliot's arrest in September 1861, he likely knew the Waldo County politician from his years in state politics. The government accused Elliot of "open and avowed sympathy" with the rebels and, much more serious, attempting to raise a town militia force for "disloyal purposes," or as Secretary Seward later described it: "he had not only conceived a purpose of treasonable co-operation in the State of Maine with insurrectionary citizens arrayed in other States for the overthrow of the Government and the Union but that he had even gone to the extreme length of getting up an unlawful armed force to operate in Maine against the lawful action of the State and of the Federal Government." Like Sargent, he was arrested twice in September 1861. The first time Elliot and former Maine Democratic Congressman Virgil D. Parris were arrested, according to Senator Fessenden, the marshals were "overtaken and outwitted" by lawyers with writs of habeas corpus. The second time, only days later, Elliot alone was taken, this time avoiding any writs, and placed first at Fort Lafayette and later Fort Warren.[31]

Pleas for Elliot's release came to President Lincoln, but Seward refused: "His associates in this treasonable enterprise have since his arrest taken an oath of allegiance to the United States. . . . [T]he representations they make that they and he were loyal to the Union at the time when they were combining in arms against it cannot be accepted at least in his behalf since it appears that he is too intelligent to misunderstand the legitimate tendencies of his criminal acts. He cannot be released." Word of Seward's opposition came to Hiram F. Elliot, a Freedom, Maine, carriage maker (likely Robert's brother), who wrote the secretary a bitter, sarcastic letter. He accused Seward of obtaining evidence "to avenge vindictive personal feelings" and that the prisoner was innocent of the charges. If he knew the evidence, Elliott could vindicate his brother, "convinced as I am that your views are too exalted to wish to retain an innocent man."[32]

By late October, Seward (though convinced the arrest was justified and that petitions claiming his innocence were unfounded) advocated his release. Apparently, Elliot wrote Seward "that the fallacy of the opinion which he entertained not long since that peace could be secured without bloodshed is now fully apparent to him." Some members of Elliot's illegal Maine militia group even enlisted in the federal army. Some Maine Republican leaders disapproved of clemency. Former congressman, abolitionist, and Free Will Baptist minister Ebenezer Knowlton wrote Seward that, as a citizen of South Montville, Maine (one town over from Freedom in Waldo County), he knew Elliot and thought his return home would rally local Confederate sympathizers: "[O]ur best men there as well as through our country, even those who are his personal friends, think it would not be safe to have him released." He felt sympathy for Elliot's family but was "a stronger friend to my country and my glorious Government."[33]

Elliot took the loyalty oath and left Fort Lafayette on November 7, 1861. He remained in Freedom but, according to one Democratic partisan, paid a further cost for his southern sympathies. In August 1863, an arsonist burned his hay barns and house. Everything was rebuilt at great cost, but in December 1866 an arsonist torched the new barn while Elliot was in Boston on business.[34]

These five men reveal similarities that provide further insight into the complexity of the New England region and the larger conflict of the period. All three editors were born within three years of each other (1827–30) and came of age in the 1840s, in the domestic battles of the Tyler and Polk administrations and in the foreign battles of the Mexican War. Sargent and Elliot (born 1814 and 1818, respectively) came of age in the partisan disputes of Jackson's presidency. Three of the five had clear formative experiences—Palmer imbibing the Democratic ideology of his father, Emery graduating from Bowdoin College (which produced several prominent nineteenth-century Democratic spokesmen like Franklin Pierce and Nathaniel Hawthorne) and tutoring in Mississippi, Sargent living in Louisiana and Arkansas for thirty years. All were New England Breckinridge Democrats and all suffered persecution for their politics. The three editors and their attackers understood their actions within the context of the American Revolution. The *Essex County Democrat* constantly accused the Lincoln administration of betraying both America's revolutionary inheritance and the Philadelphia Constitution (with its suspension of habeas corpus), aggressive handling of suspected southern sympathizers in Maryland, and creation of a northern garrison state. The mob and its defenders viewed their admittedly extreme actions as a legitimate extension of Revolutionary War precedents like the Sons of Liberty in the Stamp Act Crisis and the Boston Tea Party. Tarring and feathering remained a viable tool for citizens to use when the law failed.

All five were labeled southern sympathizers. "Sympathy" and "Sympathizer" are curious terms. In its mildest form, southern sympathizing connoted an understanding of the southern distress and anger, and a shared outrage at their current situation, that drove the South to rebellion. A more serious sympathy moved past compassion to intellectual and verbal agreement with southern reasoning, perhaps exhibited in print or the public square. Finally, at its most extreme, sympathy meant new loyalties and a willingness to assist Confederate political and military goals. This last shifted into the realm of espionage, sabotage, and treason. These five men certainly exhibited the sympathetic beliefs, in print and speech, that the South was wronged and that Republican governance deviated from American constitutional norms. Investigations showed, however, they never became spies or saboteurs.

The case of the *Essex County Democrat, Concord Democratic Standard,* and *Bangor Democrat* also brings up the curious phenomenon of vigilante justice, with a majority ironically claiming to maintain community order (all the while breaking the law) and a minority exercising their traditional liberties (all the while criticizing a government that, until recently, was guaranteeing those liberties). Phillip Paludan long ago reminded historians that "violence may be the instrument of stability as well as disorder" and that there is a "persistent vigilante tradition in America." Certainly the Haverhill mob viewed themselves as protecting soldiers, defending the government, helping fight the war, and defending the good name of a "loyal" city. They repeated those sentiments endlessly in the February 1862 Haverhill citizen's meeting—that the attack preserved public order against the corrosive words of an obnoxious newspaper editor and was merely an extension of the battlefield less than a month after First Bull Run. For Kimball, that order had already been obliterated by the Lincoln administration's unconstitutional actions, and his words exhibited a northern Democrat's real shock at the creation of a northern war machine and the recent radical departure from American legal norms. He was defending order and remained "loyal" to an American Constitution that came under attack after April 1861.[35]

There exists a fine line between dissent and treason in wartime, a line that blurs and fades even further in a civil war. Editors, public speakers, and average citizens venting their opinions test the limits of freedom in a society under duress. These five northern Democrats faced a dilemma of how to express their disagreement with government policies—if not outright hostility—in a time of national distress. Language acceptable in the vitriolic atmosphere of antebellum politics was now considered treasonable by a substantial majority of the population, sometimes punishable by law but oftentimes by vigilante action. Editorial hostility and partisan differences, like Whig bitterness during Andrew Jackson's "Bank War" or Republican enmity at James Buchanan before the war, transformed into suspicious insurrectionary activity after Fort Sumter.

In the American Civil War, anti-war sentiment expressed itself through political campaigns, economic interest, racial theories of white supremacy, and constitutional history. The chilling effect of northern vigilante action and official government policies against Peace Democrats, Confederate sympathizers, and compromise advocates meant that unlike the previous forty years of American history—when southerners could count on reliable "doughface" allies to engineer political compromises—northern friends could no longer help them. There were no more northern political solutions forthcoming.

NOTES

1. For a recent national study of the Peace Democracy, see Jennifer L. Weber, *Copperheads: The Rise and Fall of Lincoln's Opponents in the North* (New York: Oxford University Press, 2006). Although not investigated in this chapter, Connecticut Democrats were a focal point of the Northern Peace Democracy. See John E. Talmadge, "A Peace Movement in Civil War Connecticut," *New England Quarterly* 37, no. 3 (1964): 306–21; Joanna Cowden, "The Politics of Dissent: Civil War Democrats in Connecticut," *New England Quarterly* 56, no. 4 (1983): 538–54; Joanna Cowden, *"Heaven Will Frown on Such a Cause as This": Six Democrats Who Opposed Lincoln's War* (Lanham, MD: University Press of America, 2001). While Chester Alan Arthur was born in Vermont, he left as a youth and is always considered a New Yorker.

2. Gary V. Wood, *Heir to the Fathers: John Quincy Adams and the Spirit of Constitutional Government* (Lanham, MD, 2004), 210–11; On Whittier, see Roland H. Woodwell, *John Greenleaf Whittier: A Biography* (Haverhill, MA: Trustees of the John Greenleaf Whittier Homestead, 1985).

3. *Haverhill Gazette*, May 23, 1887; *Haverhill Independent*, August 9, 1884; *Essex County Democrat*, November 9, 1859; *Journal of the Executive Proceedings of the Senate of the United States of America* (Washington, DC, 1887), 324; George Wingate Chase, *The History of Haverhill, Massachusetts: From Its First Settlement, in 1640, to the Year 1860* (Haverhill, MA: The Author, 1861), 657.

4. *Essex County Democrat*, January 9, 23, and 30, 1861. On Calhoun's theory of territorial equal rights see Robert S. Russel, "Constitutional Doctrines with Regard to Slavery in Territories," *Journal of Southern History* 32, no. 4 (November 1966): 466–86. Kimball claimed that Republicans planned to enfranchise blacks, "thus dragging the Anglo-Saxon down to the base level of the African race." Kimball noted with astonishment in the April 24 issue:

5. *Essex County Democrat*, January 30, 1861.

6. Ibid., April 17 and 24, May 15, 1861. Kimball noted with astonishment in the April 24 issue: "THE CLIMAX OF INSULT—It is reported that the secessionists of Richmond placed a negro astride [sic] of the statue of Washington!" Kimball also urged readers to pray for peace.

7. Ibid., March 13, April 10, and June 3, 1861. Excerpts from Confederate Vice-President Alexander Stephens's "Cornerstone" speech in Savannah were reprinted on the *Democrat's* front page.

8. Ibid., July 24, 1861. Kimball reprinted John C. Breckinridge's July 16 Senate address, attacking the Lincoln administration's suspension of habeas corpus and restrictions on citizen's freedoms, in this issue.

9. Ibid., August 14, 1861. Kimball also criticized a rival paper, the Republican *Haverhill Tri-Weekly Publisher*: "[I]t endeavors to make amends for any lack of smartness in itself by publishing the drivel of contributors, to whom, too frequently . . . it yields its editorial columns."

10. Details on Kimball's ordeal are drawn from the *Haverhill Tri-Weekly Publisher*, August 20, 1861; *Haverhill Gazette*, August 23, 1861; *Haverhill Independent*, August 9, 1884; *Haverhill Gazette*, May 23, 1887; *Haverhill Evening Gazette*, May 27, 1896; and *Haverhill Evening Gazette*, June 23, 1917. George Johnson is listed as a Douglas delegate in the *New York Times*, February 18, 1860.

11. *Haverhill Tri-Weekly Publisher*, February 11, 1862.

12. Ibid.

13. Ibid.

14. *Haverhill Gazette*, May 23, 1887. Information on Kimball's grandfather, Edmund Kimball, is listed at www.kimballfamily.com/Tree/5/5-319.htm. Ambrose Kimball never met his grandfather, however; he died in 1813. Kimball would have found sympathizers in Iowa, which had a vocal "Copperhead" community. See David L. Lendt, *Demise of the Democracy: The Copperhead Press in Iowa, 1856–1870* (Ames: Iowa State University Press, 1973), and Hubert H. Wubben, *Civil War Iowa and the Copperhead Movement* (Ames: Iowa State University Press, 1980).

15. Lucius Manlius Boltwood, *History and genealogy of the family of Thomas Noble, of Westfield, Massachusetts: with genealogical notes of other families by the name of Noble* (Hartford, CT: Press of the Case, Lockwood & Brainard Co., 1878), 794–95; *History of Concord, New Hampshire: From the Original Grant in Seventeen Hundred and Twenty-five to the Opening of the Twentieth Century* (Concord, NH: Rumford Press, 1896), 1037; Henry McFarland, *Sixty Years in Concord and Elsewhere: Personal Recollections of Henry McFarland, 1831–1891* (Concord, NH: Rumford Press, 1899), 239–41.

16. Boltwood, *History of Concord, New Hampshire*, 1183; Samuel Merrill, *Newspaper Libel: A Handbook for the Press* (Boston: Ticknor and Co., 1888), 71–72; Stephen G. Abbott, *The First Regiment New Hampshire Volunteers in the Great Rebellion* (Keene, NH: Sentinel Printing Co., 1890), 173–75; Lex Renda, *Running on the Record: Civil War–Era Politics in New Hampshire* (Charlottesville: University Press of Virginia, 1997), 102.

17. "PROSPECTUS FOR PUBLISHING AT CONCORD, N.H., A Weekly Newspaper, to be Entitled THE DEMOCRATIC SENTINEL, Devoted to Politics, Literature and General Intelligence," May 1863; McFarland, *Sixty Years*, 244.

18. Nehemiah Cleaveland and Alpheus Spring Packard, *History of Bowdoin College: With Biographical Sketches of Its Graduates, from 1806 to 1879, Inclusive* (Boston: J. R. Osgood & Co., 1882), 679; John Hebron Moore, *The Emergence of the Cotton Kingdom in the Old Southwest: Mississippi, 1770–1860* (Baton Rouge: Louisiana State University Press, 1988), 227–29; Joseph Peter Elliott, *A History of Evansville and Vanderburgh County, Indiana* (Evansville, IN: Keller Printing Co., 1897), 150; Louis Clinton Hatch, *Maine, A History* (New York: American Historical Society, 1919), 437–38; for more on Maine politics, see Jerry R. Desmond, "Maine and the Elections of 1860," *New England Quarterly* 67, no. 3 (1994): 455–75.

19. Hatch, *Maine*, 437–38; R. H. Stanley and George O. Hall, *Eastern Maine and the Rebellion* (Bangor, ME: R. H. Stanley & Co., 1887), 86.

20. Stanley and Hall, *Eastern Maine*, 83–88; Joseph Griffin, *History of the Press in Maine* (Brunswick, ME: The Press, 1872), 137; Hatch, *Maine*, 437–38.

21. Stanley and Hall, *Eastern Maine*, 155–56; Griffin, *History*, 138–39; Cleaveland and Packard, *History of Bowdoin College*, 679; *Official Proceedings of the Democratic National Convention, Held in 1864 at Chicago* (Chicago: Times Steam Book and Job Printing House, 1864), 13; *Official Proceedings of the Democratic National Convention* (Boston: Rockwell & Rollins, 1868), 34, 68; Thomas S. Mach, *"Gentleman George" Hunt Pendleton: Party Politics and Ideological Identity in Nineteenth-century America* (Kent, OH: Kent State University Press, 2007), 131; June Hopkins, *Harry Hopkins: Sudden Hero, Brash Reformer* (New York: St. Martin's Press, 1999), 210–11.

22. Charles Edward Banks, "William Mitchell Sargent, A.M.," *Collections and Proceedings of the Maine Historical Society* (Portland, ME: The Society, 1892), ser. 2, vol. 3: 114–16; *Old Times: A Magazine Devoted to the Preservation and Publication of Documents Relating to the Early History of North Yarmouth, Maine* 6, no. 4 (October 1882): 947; John A. Marshall, *American Bastile: A History of the Illegal Arrests and Imprisonment of American Citizens in the Northern and Border States On Account of their Political Opinions During the Late Civil War* (Philadelphia: T. W. Hartley, 1881), 417; Cleaveland and Packard, *History of Bowdoin College*, 603; *The War of the Rebellion: A Compilation of the Official Records of the Union and Confederate Armies* (Washington, DC: Government Printing Office, 1880–1901), ser. 2, vol. 2: 673; for information on Sargent's land acquisitions, backwardbranch.com/ardrew/dcset8.html, www.alfordassociation.org/tafels/tafel_0124.pdf, files.usgwarchives.org/ar/calhoun/land/calhoun.txt, and files.usgwarchives.org/ar/littleriver/land/littleri.txt.

23. Bureau of the Census, *Eighth Census of the United States, Schedule I—Population, 1860*, Yarmouth, Cumberland County, Maine, M653-437, page 24, image 280; Marshall, *American Bastile*, 417; *Official Records* 2, pt. 2: 673–74.

24. *Official Records* 2, pt. 2: 674–75; Marshall, *American Bastile*, 417–18.

25. *Official Records* 2, pt. 2: 675–76.

26. Ibid., 677–80; George Thornton Fleming, *History of Pittsburgh and its Environs, from Prehistoric days to the Beginning of the American Revolution* (New York: American Historical Society, 1922), 120–21.

27. *Official Records* 2, pt. 2: 677–79.

28. Ibid., 678–79.

29. Ibid., 681; *Old Times* 5, no. 2 (April 1881): 674; Banks, "William Mitchell Sargent," 116; *Old Times* 6, no. 4 (October 1882): 947.

30. Bureau of the Census, *Eighth Census of the United States, Schedule I—Population, 1860*, Freedom, Waldo County, Maine, M653-453, page 28, image 218; John Hayward, *New England Gazetteer: Containing Descriptions of All the States, Counties and Towns in New England: Also Descriptions of the Principal Mountains, Rivers, Lakes, Capes, Bays, Harbors, Islands, and Fashionable Resorts Within that Territory, Alphabetically Arranged* (Concord, NH: I. S. Boyd and W. White, 1839); Grenville M. Donham, *Maine Register or State Year-book and Legislative Manual* (Portland, ME: J. B. Gregory, 1914), 909; *The Maine Register and State Reference Book* (Hallowell, ME: Masters, Smith & Co., 1852), 31; *The Maine Register for the Year 1855* (Portland, ME, 1855), 16; George Adams, *The Maine Register, and Business Directory* (South Berwick, ME: Edward C. Parks, 1856), 17; Joseph Williamson, *History of*

the City of Belfast in the State of Maine: From Its First Settlement in 1770 to 1875 (Portland, ME: Loring, Short, and Harmon, 1877), 856.

31. *Official Records* 2, pt. 2: 689; Marshall, *American Bastile,* 153–54.

32. *Official Records* 2, pt. 2: 689–90; Bureau of the Census, *Eighth Census of the United States, Schedule I—Population, 1860,* Freedom, Waldo County, Maine, M653-453, page 28, image 218.

33. *Official Records* 2, pt. 2: 690–92; Nathan Franklin Carter, *The Native Ministry of New Hampshire* (Concord, NH: Rumford Printing Co., 1906), 614–15.

34. *Official Records* 2, pt. 2: 692; Marshall, *American Bastile,* 154–55. There is some risk of relying too heavily upon Marshall's partisan accounts, but as Mark E. Neely Jr. notes, the book has value for "important anecdotal evidence" (*The Fate of Liberty: Abraham Lincoln and Civil Liberties* [New York: Oxford University Press, 1991], 225).

35. Phillip S. Paludan, "The American Civil War as a Crisis in Law and Order," *American Historical Review* 77, no. 4 (October 1972: 1027–28. On the role of violence and mob action, also see Paul A. Gilje. *The Road to Mobocracy: Public Disorder in New York City, 1763–1834* (Chapel Hill: University of North Carolina Press, 1987).

SENATOR WILLIAMSON S. OLDHAM AND CONFEDERATE DEFEAT

XXXXXXXXXXXXXXXXXXXXXXXXXX

CLAYTON E. JEWETT

t was pitch dark the night Confederate Senator Williamson Simpson Oldham crossed into Mississippi on his trip home to Texas at the end of the
Civil War, and he was tired. At first, Oldham wandered around almost aim-
lessly, unable to find the suggested house for his stay, and caution was at a
premium, for Union soldiers could be lurking anywhere, and as a Confederate Senator he was a prize worth taking. After searching for some time, he
finally found the house and had a quite interesting evening. Reflecting upon
his stay there, Oldham remarked that the host was very agreeable, but a slight
problem existed; he had a "bad biting dog." That dog often came into the house
and attacked strangers, and this deeply bothered Oldham. "As a general rule," he
remarked, "I have adopted it as a fact that a good man will not keep a bad biting dog. He has no more right to keep a dog in his yard, to run upon his friend,
his neighbor, or a stranger and bite him upon entering, than he has to keep an
armed maniac, who has a desire to attack every person who approaches him."[1]

That was Williamson Simpson Oldham. He was opinionated and insistent
upon expressing his beliefs even on matters that might appear trivial or mun-
dane. It would be odd to find a politician today that is firm in belief and direct
with words, but that was the nineteenth century, and a man was known for his
word; his reputation depended upon it, his honor depended upon it. When men
spoke publicly in the nineteenth century, especially politicians, they understood
the weight of their words on their personal and family life, and their place in
the community. For men like Oldham, the written word held as much significance. When Oldham wrote his memoir after the Civil War, he understood

that his reputation still was at stake, his place in the community still would be judged, and his legacy in history still hung in the balance.[2]

Williamson Simpson Oldham was born on July 19, 1813, in Franklin County, Tennessee, to Elias and Mary Burton Oldham. He studied law under Judge Nathan Green and was admitted to the Tennessee Bar in 1836. He subsequently moved to Arkansas, where he married Mary Vance McKissick on December 12, 1837, and entered politics. He won election to the Arkansas General Assembly in 1838, and the Arkansas legislature elected him associate justice of the Arkansas Supreme Court in 1844. He held that position until 1848 and eventually moved to Austin, Texas. While in Texas, Oldham married his second wife, Anne S. Kirk, served as president of the Austin Railroad Association in 1852 and worked as editor of the *State Gazette,* the voice of Texas Democrats, from 1854 to 1857. In 1859, Oldham and his third wife, Agnes Harper (married November 19, 1857), moved to Brenham, Texas. Texans knew him well despite the lack of political success. He had numerous political connections and became renowned as a defender of personal and states' rights. That reputation merited him a place at the Texas Secession Convention and subsequent election as one of the seven delegates to the Montgomery Convention and Provisional Congress of the Confederate States of America, where he served as one of Texas's representatives in the Senate, along with Louis T. Wigfall, for the duration of the Civil War.[3]

As with many politicians of the day, Oldham was guided by a distinct political ideology. He believed that all men held the natural God-given rights of life, liberty, and property. Holding steadfast to the belief in a virtuous republican society, Oldham argued that the people of each state composed a political community and that the people composed the sovereign power of self-government. Oldham's adherence to a Lockean philosophy led him to understand that government held both an internal and external function. The internal function, reserved specifically for the state, operated to establish social and domestic institutions, protect the people and their right to private property ownership, and punish crime and provide for a redress of injuries. The external function, carried out by the federal government, functioned to defend the political society as a whole against foreign enemies. This mode of thought fit squarely in line with the philosophy of John Locke, who argued that government should be limited and that men entered political societies for mutual protection and defense.[4] For Oldham, no gray area existed regarding the obligation of government. The individual state functioned to preserve the rights of citizens, and the federal government existed to protect the bodies of citizens. Furthermore, even in time of war, the external function of the federal government was not to interfere with the internal function of state government. In an 1862 speech before the Confederate Senate, Oldham remarked, "For every violation of the rights of the citizen, the State laws afford the remedy, the State courts pronounce judgment, which is executed by State executive or ministerial officers. The General Government never comes into contact with the individual, or his property, or with the local interests of a State, except in a few clearly specified and expressed instances, and then only incidentally, in carrying into effect powers granted in regard to matters in which the States have a common interest."[5] More to the point, Oldham believed "it is only upon the federative principle of our Government; a local government for individual, domestic and sectional interests—with a common government to regulate affairs of general concern, that a free representative Government can be maintained over a wide extent of territory, in which there are rival interests and pursuits."[6] Later, in his memoir, Oldham reflected, "The State Government with all its laws enacted for the protection of the person and property of the citizens, with the machinery for all their execution will remain intact."[7] These various statements reflect his belief in the separate functions of state and federal government and the appropriate relationship these bodies held with the individual. Oldham wrote these words in reference to the great calamity that befell the southern states that had united themselves under a new confederate government. Southerners believed that Abraham Lincoln and the United States government violated this separation of responsibilities and therefore seceded to form a new government.

While historians often posit that the southern states seceded to defend the institution of slavery, for Williamson Simpson Oldham, that matter ran much deeper.[8] "I had not advocated the secession of my state and accepted the war that had been forced upon us," he wrote, "simply to preserve the institution of slavery, a much higher, and more vital principle was involved in the issue, it was the sovereign right of the people of the southern states, to exercise all the powers of internal government, within their respective limits, with the power to establish alter or abolish their domestic institutions, without interference by the people of the Northern States in any manner whatever, either through their state legislatures, or the General Government."[9] While slavery certainly held a significant place for southerners in the secession crisis, it must be understood that many in the South looked beyond the peculiar institution and embraced secession based upon ideological principles and the political reality of carrying those out or having them threatened. Oldham was a man of principle and thus, while acknowledging slavery in the larger equation, ultimately it was the Lockean principle of man's relationship to government and the ultimate right to wield power over government, for power did derive from the governed, that moved him to embrace the path of secession. In the southern mind, or at least in Oldham's, the North violated that sacred compact of government and threatened to destroy individual liberty and state sovereignty.[10]

Oldham's beliefs regarding the function of state and federal government guided him through political matters, as the newborn Confederate States of America attempted to wage a full-scale war, and directed his criticism in the wake of a failed Confederacy. For this Texan and Confederate senator, many factors led to confederate defeat, but chief amongst those were government interference in the market, conscription and exemption, and the suspension of the writ of habeas corpus. As with the bad biting dog, he did not mince his words on these issues.

For Oldham, "there was one abuse that loomed above and obscured all others, and was most vicious and demoralizing, to the people, the common soldiers, and many officers of the army." That molestation was government interference in the market, especially as it pertained to cotton. At the beginning of the Civil War, the Confederate Congress passed legislation outlawing the private exportation of cotton except through the seaports of Texas and across the Rio Grande into Mexico. The carnage commenced. Military officers controlling the Rio Grande, especially at Brownsville, began their plunder of private citizens' cotton.[11]

In 1861, Brigadier General Paul O. Hebert, whom many Texans disdained, issued an order prohibiting the exportation of cotton from Texas except by those individuals who obtained a license from Brigadier General Hamilton Bee.[12] Bee, also well known in Texas, placed further restrictions upon trade. As a prerequisite for obtaining permits, he required that exporters enter into a bond to return supplies bought with a portion of the proceeds from the sale of cotton. Oldham believed that this was both impractical and illegal. When planters refused to obtain a permit and sell to the government, the military illegally impressed cotton The dereliction of Jefferson Davis and the Confederate Congress on this matter outraged Oldham. For the first two years of the war, corruption lurked at every corner, and it appeared that the venality reached the top levels of government, even to Jefferson Davis himself. Convinced of this, on April 11, 1863, Oldham submitted a Senate resolution requiring Jefferson Davis to inform the legislative branch of all communications between the executive branch, the Military Department, and the Trans-Mississippi Department regarding the cotton trade, and issued an order for the injunction of secrecy to be removed from the documents. He yearned to know exactly what was said and to whom; he worked to uncover what he believed was illegal activity by the government and its unscrupulous interference in the market.[13]

Despite such political efforts to remedy the economic situation of the Confederacy, by mid-1863 matters only became worse. On August 3, 1863, Lieutenant General Edmund Kirby Smith overstepped the boundary of authority and through illegal general orders established the Cotton Bureau of the Trans-Mississippi Department. His goal was to control the cotton trade in the western Confederacy by issuing permits. Thus, a person could not trade cotton unless they obtained an official permit. To make matters worse, Texas officials had no appetite for Confederate interference in the market and therefore issued their own plan for the trade of cotton. Under Governor Pendleton Murrah's plan, cotton vendors would sell 50 percent of their cotton to the state. The Texas government paid vendors from nine to eleven cents on the pound in the form of state bonds. Vendors would retain the remaining amount of their cotton for personal use and be allowed to transport it under the authority of the state, at their own risk and expense, with the state cotton for sale in Mexico. Thus, vendors selling to the state had the advantage of trading with Mexico under state authority and protection, they were theoretically free from impressment, and their bonds yielded approximately 8 percent annum. The Cotton Bureau could not match this deal.[14]

So, by mid-1863, Texas operated according to its own rules regarding the cotton trade, the Trans-Mississippi Department under Edmund Kirby Smith had its regulations, and the Confederate government in Richmond remained uninterested in reigning in military corruption on the border. "Bee sat at the gate of the Rio Grande and Magruder at those ports of the Gulf. What a field for corruption!!" And, Oldham referred to Edmund Kirby Smith in this matter as "wholly and utterly incompetent." Chaos ensued as the Cotton Bureau continued to issue its permits; Hamilton Bee persisted in his endeavors to monopolize the cotton trade for personal profit; Texas under Governor Murrah operated according to its own plan; and the general citizen trading in cotton remained victimized.[15]

The economic chaos repulsed Oldham. Government interference was not to exist in the marketplace as it was not the proper function of government. In a speech before the Senate on December 23, 1863, Oldham addressed the status of Confederate finances. He railed against military control of the cotton trade in Texas, arguing it was one reason for disparity between the supply and demand of currency. He made the case to his colleagues that Texas should be permitted to trade its cotton supply without interference from the Confederate government. By allowing Texans to profit from such commerce, the Confederacy would in turn benefit. Oldham was one of the few politicians to truly understand the correlation between personal interests and the greater good of the Confederacy. When the people prosper, the nation progresses. The people come first, not the nation. Oldham understood this distinct difference.[16]

During the Civil War, many leaders failed to recognize this difference, as is evident in the conflict over conscription and exemption. In March of 1862, President Jefferson Davis requested that the Confederate Congress pass legislation for a military draft. Politicians answered his call two days later by passing the act "to Provide Further for the Public Defense." This Conscription Act was approved on April 16, 1862, and required all men ages eighteen to thirty-five to be placed into Confederate service, for a period of three years or until the war ended, unless they were fortunate enough to be one of the many individuals officially exempt from military service.[17]

Oldham stood opposed to conscription. Nothing, he believed, represented more of an assault on the people than the government forcing its own citizens into the military for an unspecified amount of time. He did believe that the militia was necessary for repelling invasion and suppressing insurrections, but the thought of having a long-term standing army scared Oldham for it was an assault on the constitutional liberties of the people. "No man," wrote Oldham, "is a safe repository of power under a free constitutional government, who conceives that in time of war all constitutional restrictions, are suspended and that his powers are limited alone by his judgment, as to measures of necessity." Oldham also believed that some of those seeking to pass the conscription law held ulterior motives and desired to subjugate people after the conflict with the North ended. Whether or not this was a reality or mere suspicion is not clear. Regardless, Oldham viewed the conscription law as a direct threat to the freedom and liberty of the people.[18] What really bothered Oldham about all this was that when it came to conscription, the government and its military cronies took no notice of a man's family or of a man's crops—whether it might be planting or harvest time. Again, the people come first, above all else. For Oldham, the stench of despotism enveloped the Conscription Act, and he reminded fellow politicians, including fellow senator Louis T. Wigfall, that the European "despotisms" had resorted to the unthinkable measure of conscription, and they were about to walk that same path.[19]

Not only were the interests of the people a concern, but also those of the state. For Oldham, the Conscription Law represented a clear violation of the constitution. It forced men into service against their will. It kept men out of the state militia, threatening its very existence, which the constitution sanctioned. In late 1862, military authorities pressed both Jefferson Davis and Congress for more men, resulting in an extension of the original Conscription Act. The 1863 extension of the conscription act called all men between the ages of eighteen and forty-five into service. Prior to its final acceptance, On September 4, 1862, Oldham stood before the Senate and gave his remarks in opposition to this measure. He argued against extending the act because the Confederate army already contained enough volunteers and conscription violated state practice and state sovereignty. By conscripting men into Confederate service, men were not allowed to serve in the state militia, thus stripping the state of its time-honored and constitutionally approved defense. This does not mean that Oldham stood opposed to the proper function of the federal government to provide for the common defense. He upheld the Lockean view that the federal government was created for the purpose of protection and defense. This did not mean, though, that it had a right to abolish the constitutionally sanctioned state militia. Oldham believed that by maintaining the state militia, funded and used by the Confederate government, enough men existed to safeguard the Confederacy.[20] Oldham was not the only politician who viewed matters this way. On February 5, 1863, Texas Governor Francis Lubbock spoke before a joint session of the state legislature and made it clear that he supported the Texas Supreme Court's ruling that the Confederate conscription law was unconstitutional. Moreover, Lubbock refused to transfer men into Confederate service, especially frontier troops, unless Jefferson Davis gave him the assurance that these troops would remain in Texas to protect citizens from Indian attacks. Future Texas Governor Pendleton Murrah took an even harder line. Backed by the Texas legislature, Murrah moved to exert full control over the state militia by refusing to allow troops to leave the state, refusing to transfer troops into Confederate service, and keeping the state militia in service for an additional six months past their original term of duty.[21]

To make matters worse, not only did Confederate conscription injure the state by conflicting with the state militia, it also took the power of appointment out of the hands of local officials, especially the governor, and placed it in the hands of the executive, thus serving to lay the foundation for civil and military despotism. Oldham reminded his fellow politicians, "But little danger is to be apprehended in time of peace, but it is in time of war, when society is convulsed, that danger is to be apprehended from the graspings of military power."[22] This became evident in the increasing power of the executive. Anything that increased Davis's power magnified Oldham's fears. For Oldham, the power of appointment was significant because ultimately at stake was the issue of public virtue, the sacrifice of self-interest for the common good. By taking the power of appointment out of the hands of the governors, who would appoint men to sacrifice self-interest for the common good, it left men to be appointed by the executive and the armed forces, directed by officers that had only their career in mind—officers, Oldham remarked, that were not of the men, in the sense that they did not hail from the same county, work the same dirt, drink the same water, share the same common interests. When a society has military leaders who are not "of the people," public virtue is threatened, and public virtue rests as one of the cornerstones of republican ideology; it is what the South claimed to be fighting for in the first place. The chipping away of that cornerstone signifies the rise of civil and military despotism.[23] Worried about this, Oldham remarked before the Senate, "The citizens of the States, converted by coercion into Conscript soldiers of the Confederacy, completely manacled by the chains of military law and military subordination, may be forced by some favorite ambitious military leader, to become the destroyers of their own and their country's liberties."[24] Nothing, in Oldham's mind, "could have been introduced more palpably in violation of the constitution more destructive of the confidence of the people in Congress which passed it, and in the President who recommended and approved it." Oldham did not believe that Congress actually had the power to pass a Conscription Act, much less extend it. In his mind, Congress had absolutely no authority, no power over the citizens of the states, to coerce them into military service.[25] By doing so, citizens would potentially destroy their own liberty and freedom. Nothing could have been more horrendous for Oldham than the potential destruction of freedom and liberty, even more so at the people's own hands.

If Congress did not have such power, then certainly neither did the executive, and Oldham railed again Jefferson Davis for his support of conscription. The move to conscript men into service in 1862, and to broaden the practice in 1863 and 1864, represented the wrongdoing of Jefferson Davis, General Robert E. Lee, and the Secretaries of War George W. Randolph and James A. Seddon, all of whom constantly badgered Congress for more men. As Leonne Hudson reveals in his essay in this volume, this matter became ever more heated and complex during the war as some military commanders, especially Robert E. Lee, suggested that Congress move quickly to allow for the conscription of slaves. While verbally critical of Jefferson Davis, Oldham did temper his distaste of Davis's actions by acknowledging that military officials played a significant role in influencing the president, and thus they bore the brunt of his angry words. Nevertheless, Oldham railed against Davis and fellow politicians for giving in to the demands of the military officers, "the least qualified of all men, to devise a system of policy for the government of free people."[26]

The problem extended deeper than the top echelon of civil and military authorities. Enrolling officers, the most "arbitrary set of petty tyrants," dragged men into service, leaving them without recourse. Even Oldham, in 1863, while traveling in Texas with John A. Wilcox, faced the wrath of an enrolling officer.[27] At a hotel in Rusk, Texas, the following conversation took place between the officer (speaking first) and Oldham:

"Do you belong to the army, Sir?"

"No Sir."

"Have you any papers sir?"

"No sir."

"Then you ought to have them sir."

"No sir, I presume not. I do not need papers to travel in Texas."

"But I say sir! You do need them."

"But I say sir! I do not need them."

"Who in the h—ll are you, that you can travel through Texas without papers?"

"Who in the h—ll are you who question my right to do so?"

"I am the enrolling officer of the county sir."

"I ask your pardon sir. I did not know that you were the hostler or the bootlack of the hotel. Well sir: I am W. S. Oldham, a senator from Texas, in the Confederate Congress now on my way to Richmond to attend to my duties there."

Oldham went on to give this young man a good southern tongue lashing for his insolent rudeness. The conversation between Oldham and this anonymous officer reflected the deep problems surrounding conscription. General citizens and even the top politicians of the day found themselves harassed by military officials, further proof for Oldham that military despotism was strangling the Confederacy.[28]

While the Conscription Act represented an assault on the constitutional rights of citizens, the Exemption Law made matters even worse. In April 1862, Congress passed legislation providing for numerous exemptions, including public employees, railroad workers, ministers, teachers, and more. Congress expanded the list six months later to include tanners, salt makers, shoemakers, and more. No piece of legislation according to Oldham was more damning to the South than this, especially the clause exempting one owner or overseer for every twenty slaves. To many in the South, this exemplified class legislation at its finest. Oldham denounced the Exemption Law, not necessarily for the reason that it smacked of class legislation, but because of the disastrous effect it had on southern morale and the war effort. It gave rise to the saying that the war was "the rich man's war and the poor man's fight . . . and a most fatal saying it was."[29] While the saying might have been fatal, research suggests its reality to be a myth. Historians have shown that in many places, such as Texas, Massachusetts, and Virginia, men were not co-opted into service and that poorer individuals did not enlist nearly close to the rates that wealthier slaveholding families did.[30] While the legislation was meant to maintain social order in the South, Oldham admits that the wealthy abused the system. Oftentimes, men who owned more than twenty slaves would partition their slaves, thus allowing sons or friends also to reap the benefits of exemption. Of course, military enrolling officers played a part in the abuse by doing nothing to correct this injustice, and Oldham readily blamed them for their neglect.

The exemption law was also fundamentally flawed for it assumed a uniform Confederate identity and equivalent interests across the South, which was preposterous, and Oldham knew it. While congressional debate over the Exemption Bill took place, in secret session of course, Oldham left the Senate chamber and decided to lay down on a sofa located in the lobby. Mr. Yancey, a radical fire-eater from Alabama, came out of the Senate chamber and asked Oldham why he did not partake in shaping the bill, and Oldham answered him, "I did not conceive it any part of the duty which the State of Texas had sent me there to perform; that she had a state government, into whose hands she had confided the duty of regulating the domestic affairs of the state and the individual pursuits of the people; that I did not know, what pursuits should be fostered and what classes of persons should be exempted from military service in Virginia, South Carolina, or Alabama, and that I conceived that the senators from those states were as equally ignorant of the interests of my state upon that subject."[31] Oldham could not have been more direct about his beliefs. He was Texas's representative, sent to serve the interests of the Lone Star State. He had no intention to stand for the interests of other states or even guess their needs. He hailed from Texas, and it was Texans he spoke for. After all, his power descended from those who put him into office; he understood this, and carried out that understanding.

According to Oldham, conscription and exemption provided the foundation for civil and military despotism. The manner in which they were carried out "chilled every sentiment of patriotism and even excited their feelings and passions against the Confederate Government and its cause."[32] Oldham's views on conscription and exemption reveal his convictions that the ordinary citizen came first, that it is the state's responsibility to protect individual rights and liberties, and that the federal government has no business legislating in any manner that potentially violates this distinction. Any action that did so smacked of despotism, and Oldham would have no part of it. Walking out of the Senate chamber and lying down on a sofa might not have been the most appropriate action to take or example to set, but in his words and actions Oldham made it clear where he stood on the debate between liberty and order. He provided clear guidance for those seeking to protect individual freedom and liberty from civil and military despotism that surely should have put such arguments to bed.

After passing the Conscription and Exemption acts, both houses of Congress passed, almost unanimously, legislation granting Jefferson Davis the power to suspend the writ of habeas corpus. In short, the writ of habeas corpus compels authorities to produce the body of the prisoner and explain his detention under the law for in practical terms no person can be jailed without being charged with a crime. This right is established in Article I, Section IX, of the U.S. Constitution, which also states that the writ can only be suspended "when in cases of rebellion or invasion the public safety may require it." The writ of habeas corpus in effect assigns authority to the judiciary to review and overturn actions taken by authorities. Granting Davis the power to suspend the writ transferred power from the judiciary to the executive branch. Oldham stood fundamentally opposed to this transference, and from his recollection he was the only member of the Senate to vote against it. At first, the suspension was limited to thirty days. When the measure came up again in the next session of congress, though, Oldham spoke before the Senate of his belief in the unconstitutionality of the measure. He believed the power to suspend habeas corpus was a matter for the legislature to decide, and it was only the legislature that could determine whether there was due cause and emergency enough to do so. The bill, however, granted the president the power to suspend the writ, and Oldham railed against fellow politicians for considering such legislation for he did not believe that the legislature had a right to delegate its legislative powers to the executive branch. His belief in the supremacy of the legislature also fits squarely with Locke's arguments regarding the sacred and unalterable nature of the legislature, which Locke believed to be the supreme power in a commonwealth. Unwittingly, granting President Jefferson Davis the power to suspend the writ of habeas corpus helped set a precedent for the executive usurpation of power and civil liberties that continues to haunt this country.[33]

When the matter came up a third time at a subsequent session of Congress, many senators realized they had made a grave error passing the previous acts, violating the Constitution, and the matter was referred to the Judiciary Committee of the Senate. This committee subsequently reported on a bill that provided for the suspension of the writ of habeas corpus for "certain enumerated acts."[34] Furthermore, the bill provided that arrests for those acts could be carried out by order from the president, the secretary of war, and the general in command of the Trans-Mississippi Department, Edmund Kirby Smith. This outraged Oldham. Congress absolutely had no authority to take power away from the judicial branch and confer it upon the executive. Oldham argued that the power to arrest and imprison lay solely with the judicial branch of government, "that no man could be legally arrested except, upon information supported by oath or affirmation—that he could not be held to answer, except upon indictment or information by a grand jury, that he was entitled to an impartial and speedy public trial, by a jury of the district in which the offense was alleged to have been committed, to have counsel for his defense, to confront the witnesses against him, and to have compulsory process to secure the attendance of witnesses to testify in his defense." Thus for Oldham, even in time of war, official or not, suspending the writ of habeas corpus by any official body other than the legislature was a gross violation of the Constitution, and was not a power to be granted to or seized by the judicial or executive branches. Those in Congress, however, who argued in favor of the bill cited precedents from acts passed by the British Parliament. Those opposed argued that the powers of Congress were defined and limited, whereas the powers of Parliament were "omnipotent." Moreover, opponents argued that the Constitution stood above the powers of Congress, and that such rights were beyond the reach of the legislature, being inserted directly into the Constitution (in the Bill of Rights) to prevent government from trampling upon the rights of citizens as Parliament had done. Thus, opponents indirectly harkened back to the American Revolution and the issues that forced colonists to break away from Great Britain. They did not escape the tyranny of a king and parliament, fight for their freedom, create a new nation and government all for naught. In the end, it mattered not; the bill passed both houses of Congress.[35]

For Oldham, this whole matter appeared somewhat more complex. Oldham believed that Jefferson Davis's suspension of habeas corpus also violated state sovereignty for it indicated to state courts over what subjects it had jurisdiction. For Oldham, this disregarded the organic law of the state courts which derived their power from the state constitutions, and were not subject to suspension or annulment by the federal government.[36] His belief regarding the writ's suspension reflected his conviction regarding the internal and external function of government. What really reeked about this whole matter, though, was the disastrous effect it had on the citizens and the country. In the wake of congressional action to grant the president such power, military authorities took it as a cue to further trample upon the freedoms and liberties of the citizens. For example, on May 30, 1862, Brigadier General Paul O. Hebert declared martial law over the state of Texas and appointed for each county a provost marshal who held unlimited power. Brigadier General Earl Van Dorn declared martial law over a number of counties in Mississippi and Louisiana. General Braxton Bragg appointed a military governor for the city of Atlanta. The same scenario occurred for all of Arkansas, portions of Louisiana, Mississippi, Virginia, Tennessee, Georgia, North and South Carolina.[37] In this whole melee, the provost marshal proved the worst culprit. "In the Provost Marshal," Oldham wrote, "was the combined

Legislative, Judicial, and Executive powers. His orders were law, his decisions were the judgments, which were executed in obedience to his mandates. No Eastern Potentate ever combined in his august person more fully all the powers of absolute despotism than did these petty provost marshals, the petty tools of military usurpation. Never did an eastern despot exercise his power in a more tyrannical mode that did many of those petty upstart usurpers." With the assumption that they controlled everything, these military officers took charge of the internal trade in the country, ranging from produce to railroad transportation. "A magnificent field for gain, speculation, and rascality was cultivated," claimed Oldham. No product or item could be shipped or transported without a military pass; they took charge of every aspect of trade, and Oldham remained infuriated by it all.[38]

This brings everything full circle to Oldham's first complaint, government interference in the market. A vicious cycle existed that violated the very rights of all individuals, broke the sacred division of powers established in the U.S. Constitution, and violated the very ideology the country was founded upon and the South claimed to be abiding by. Historians have debated, for over a century, the question of Confederate defeat. For some, it was a matter of a pre-modern agricultural society suffering defeat at the hands of a modernizing industrial society. For those historians caught up in the numbers game, the North simply overwhelmed the South with more men, with some historians focusing on conscription and others on desertion. Other schools of thought point to leadership issues surrounding military commanders or juxtapose Lincoln and Davis. For Williamson Simpson Oldham, who lived during the unpleasantness, the Constitution was neglected and Congress caved to the wishes of military leaders and the president, ceasing to rule for and represent the will of the people. In a speech before the Senate, Oldham remarked, "In times of war, like those in which we live, above all others, the Constitution should be strictly observed, by those charged with the administration of government. It is then, that the sentiments of the people are most yielding and submissive to usurpations of power, under the plea of necessity." In his memoir, Oldham wrote, "We must take men as they are, and not as we would have them. If we would legislate for them as free men we must adapt our laws to their sentiment in order to command their support—if we legislate in disregard and defiance of their sentiments, they will feel, that they are treated as slaves, and will rebel against our measures."[39] That is exactly what happened, in Oldham's view, and in the final analysis, the Confederacy suffered defeat due to civil and military despotism. The leaders of the Confederacy forgot or more likely ignored the fact that their powers derived from the people, and it was the people who delegated those powers to the leaders; they were the sole source of political authority. Holding steadfast to his Lockean roots, Oldham strove to be a guiding light for the Confederacy during its time of crisis, a beacon of hope for the preservation of freedom and liberty. That hope, though, much as in recent years, was snuffed by the despotic actions of the nation's leaders—a true tragedy.

NOTES

1. Clayton E. Jewett, ed., *Rise and Fall of the Confederacy: The Memoir of Senator Williamson S. Oldham, CSA* (Columbia: University of Missouri Press, 2006), 73 (hereafter, *Oldham Memoir*). I would like to thank Brian McKnight at UVA as well as Wise and Brian Stacey from St. Edward's University for taking the time to read this and saving me from many mistakes.

2. For the role of honor in southern society, see Bertram Wyatt-Brown, *Southern Honor: Ethics and Behavior in the Old South* (New York: Oxford University Press, 1982).

3. Williamson Simpson Oldham Papers, RG 2R130, Center for American History, 152, 163; *War of the Rebellion: Official Records of the Union and Confederate Armies* (Washington, DC: Government Printing Office, 1883), vol. 53, pt. 2: 635; *Journal of the Congress of the Confederate States of America, 1861–1865* (7 vols., Washington, DC: Government Printing Office, 1905), vol. 2: 14 (hereafter, *JCCSA*); E. Fontaine, "Hon. Williamson Simpson Oldham," Oldham Papers, RG 2F164.

4. *Oldham Memoir*, 136; Jerome Huyler, *Locke in America: The Moral Philosophy of the Founding Era* (Lawrence: University Press of Kansas, 1995), 225–27.

5. W. S. Oldham, "Remarks of W. S. Oldham, of Texas, Upon the Amendment to the Exemption Bill, Proposed by Mr. Dortch, That Justices of the Peace Shall be Liable to Conscription. Made in the Senate, September, 9th, 1862," 14.

6. "Remarks of W. S. Oldham," 14.

7. *Oldham Memoir*, 137.

8. Due to the nation's racial crisis in the 1950s and 1960s, historians stressed the centrality of slavery in southern secession. Major works in this historiographical line include Steven A. Channing, *Crisis of Fear: Secession in South Carolina* (New York: Simon & Schuster, 1970); William L. Barney, *The Secession Impulse: Alabama and Mississippi in 1860* (Princeton, NJ: Princeton University Press, 1974); J. Mills Thornton III, *Politics and Power in a Slave Society: Alabama, 1800–1860* (Baton Rouge: Louisiana State University Press, 1978); and Michael P. Johnson, *Toward a Patriarchal Republic: The Secession of Georgia* (Baton Rouge: Louisiana State University Press, 1977).

9. *Oldham Memoir*, 197.

10. Ibid., 107.

11. Ibid., 225; *JCCSA* 1: 250–51, 264, 477.

12. Paul Octave Hebert (b. December 12, 1818, Iberville Parish, LA) graduated from West Point in 1840. He served in the Mexican War, was elected governor of Louisiana in 1852, and was

210

commissioned colonel of the First Louisiana Artillery in 1861. During the war, he commanded the Department of Texas and the subdistrict of North Louisiana (Ezra J. Warner, *Generals in Gray: Lives of the Confederate Commanders* [Baton Rouge: Louisiana State University Press, 1975], 131–32).

Hamilton Prioleau Bee (b. July 22, 1822, Charleston, SC) assisted in the boundary dispute between Texas and Mexico in 1839, served as secretary of the Texas Senate in 1846, fought in the Mexican War, served in the Texas legislature from 1849 to 1859, and was Speaker of the House from 1855 to 1857. He enlisted in the Confederate army and earned appointment as brigadier general in 1862, serving at Brownsville, Texas, where he controlled much of the border trade. In 1864, he fought in the Red River campaign, and in 1865 he commanded divisions under John A. Wharton and later Samuel Bell Maxey (Warner, *Generals in Gray*, 24–25). See also Fredericka Meiners, "Hamilton Prioleau Bee," M.A. thesis, Rice University, 1972, and "Hamilton P. Bee in the Red River Campaign," *Southwestern Historical Quarterly* 78 (July 1974).

13. *Oldham Memoir*, 360–62; Fredericka Meiners, "Texas Border Cotton Trade," *Civil War History* 23 (December 1977): 294; Ronnie C. Tyler, "Cotton on the Border, 1861–1865," *Southwestern Historical Quarterly* 73 (April 1970): 460–61; *JCCSA* 3: 277, 333.

14. Clayton E. Jewett, *Texas in the Confederacy: An Experiment in Nation Building* (Columbia: University of Missouri Press, 2002), 190. Pendleton Murrah served as Texas governor from 1863 to 1865.

15. *Oldham Memoir*, 236; Robert L. Kerby, *Kirby Smith's Confederacy: The Trans-Mississippi South, 1863–1865* (New York: Columbia University Press, 1972),138; Agnes Louise Lambie, "Confederate Control of Cotton in the Trans-Mississippi Department," M.A. thesis, University of Texas, 1915, 36. General Edmund Kirby Smith (b. May 16, 1824, St. Augustine, FL) attended the U.S. Military Academy, served in the Mexican War, and fought the Comanche Indians in Texas. During the Civil War, he served as General Joseph E. Johnston's chief-of-staff, was wounded at the battle of First Manassas, commanded the Department of Tennessee in 1862, and then headed the Trans-Mississippi Department in 1863.

16. Williamson Simpson Oldham, "Speech of Hon. W. S. Oldham of Texas, on the Subject of Finances," Senate, December 23, 1863.

17. George C. Rable, *The Confederate Republic: A Revolution against Politics* (Chapel Hill: University of North Carolina Press, 1994), 139–40; *JCCSA* 2: 253–54, 5: 228.

18. *Oldham Memoir*, 110–11.

19. Rable, *The Confederate Republic*, 139.

20. Oldham, Williamson S., "Speech of W. S. Oldham, of Texas, Upon the Bill to Amend the Conscript Law, Made in the Senate, September 4, 1862," 3–7; Huyler, *Locke in America*, 156.

21. Jewett, *Texas in the Confederacy*, 130–34. Francis R. Lubbock served as Texas governor from 1861 to 1863.

22. Oldham, "Speech—Conscript Law," 3–5.

23. Ibid.

24. Ibid., 7.

25. Ibid., 7.

26. *Oldham Memoir*, 138.

27. John Allen Wilcox (b. April 18, 1819, Greene County, NC), before moving to Texas, served in the Mississippi State Legislature, fought in the Mexican War, and was elected for one term to the U.S. Congress. In Texas, he was a member of the secession convention, served in the First Confederate House, and was elected to the Second House, but died before taking office. He earned

a reputation as one of Davis's firmest supporters. Ezra J. Warner and Wilfred Buck Yearns, *Biographical Register of the Confederate Congress* (Baton Rouge: Louisiana State University Press, 1975), 257–58.

28. *Oldham Memoir*, 122.

29. Ibid., 111.

30. See Michael J. Connolly, *Capitalism, Politics, and Railroads in Jacksonian America* (Columbia: University of Missouri Press, 2003); John O. Allen, "The Wealth of Antebellum Southside Virginia: Tobacco or Slaves?" Ph.D. diss., Catholic University of America, 2002; and Jewett, *Texas in the Confederacy.*

31. *Oldham Memoir*, 109–10. William Lowndes Yancey (b. August 10, 1814, in Warren County, GA) attended Williams College, read law, moved to Alabama in 1836, and served in the Alabama state legislature and U. S. Congress. Yancey was one of the radical fire-eaters, sought foreign recognition for the Confederacy, and served in the First Senate of the Confederate government before dying on July 23, 1863 (Warner and Yearns, *Biographical Register of the Confederate Congress,* 264–65).

32. *Oldham Memoir*, 112.

33. Ibid. According to the *JCCSA*, Senators Baker, Haynes, Hill, Jemison, Johnson of Georgia, Reade, Semmes, and Louis T. Wigfall of Texas also voted against the measure. The House vote was 58–20 with the following representatives voting against the bill to suspend the writ: Ashe, Atkins, Baldwin, Bell, Briders, Clopton, Dargan, Davidson, Farrow, Foote, Gaither, Garland, Hanly, Holder, Jones, Martin, Menees, Simpson, Smith of Alabama, Smith of North Carolina; *JCCSA* 3: 712, 7: 674; Huyler, *Locke in America,* 157.

34. *Oldham Memoir*, 113.

35. Ibid., 113–15.

36. Ibid., 125–26.

37. Ibid., 223.

38. Ibid., 126, 127.

39. "Remarks of W. S. Oldham," 14–15; *Oldham Memoir*, 134–35.

PART IV

RECONSTRUCTION

xxxxxxxxxxxxxxxxxxx AND THE xxxxxxxxxxxxxxxxxxx

NEW SOUTH

TRANSFORMING ORIGINAL INTENT

XXXXXXXXXXXXXXXXXXXXXXXXXXXXXXXXXXXXXXXXXXXXXXXXXXX

The U.S. Constitution in the Civil War and Reconstruction Era

DAVID E. KYVIG

T hose who in recent decades have argued that the original intent of the Constitution's framers should still be the guiding force in every instance where the judiciary is called upon to resolve a constitutional dispute would do well to devote attention to the work of Civil War historians, Jon L. Wakelyn among others. In the course of the past forty years, they have called attention to a great variety of ways in which the sectional conflict and its resolution transformed thought and practice concerning the structure and operation of the United States government. Governmental powers only loosely spelled out in the 1787 document were applied in the 1860s in distinctly new ways. Furthermore, the very terms of the Constitution were fundamentally altered by means of the transformative process specified by the framers. Such changes incorporated principles into the Constitution that in Article V the framers had directed "shall be valid to all intents and purposes, as part of this Constitution," or in other words, should be regarded as of equal weight as the original provisions and override contradictory stipulations previously adopted. If original intent possesses any validity, it ought to incorporate the belief of the framers that formal alterations to the Constitution, such as those made during the 1860s, superceded the document's earlier contrary language.

Much of the sectional conflict that preceded the Civil War resulted from the failure of the architects of the 1787 Constitution to resolve fundamental differences among the original states. In the modern era, when Constitution worship far exceeds detailed historical understanding of the founding, the compromises made to achieve reform of the basic instrument for governing the barely united states of the Confederation are often overlooked.[1] The conflicts between large and small states, as well as between states with room to expand versus those with confined borders, those with thriving seaports versus those lacking such advantages, and those dominated by entrenched elites versus those of more egalitarian character, not to mention those with economies dependent on an enslaved workforce versus those otherwise structured made agreement on a blueprint for governance difficult.

A notable degree of civility prevailed throughout the Philadelphia convention, and thereby a remarkable, if not total, unity was ultimately achieved. Less surprising is that some issues, such as slavery, were essentially postponed, and others, such as the disequilibrium among states, were dealt with in ways that would make their later resolution more difficult. The so-called great compromise that granted every state equal representation in the Senate and the amending article that perpetuated the oversized influence of small-population states in any process of constitutional alteration may have been vital to the convention's adoption of the Constitution and its subsequent state ratification, but those same agreements would prove to be obstacles to renegotiation of the issues that the framers found intractable. The requirements of supermajority consensus for constitutional change, approval by two-thirds of each house of Congress and ratification by three-fourths of the states, stood thereafter as apparently insurmountable obstacles to substantive reform.[2]

From the establishment of the Constitution until the Civil War, the structures created by the framers proved to be substantial barriers to resolving the issue of slavery. At the federal level neither the political branches of government nor the judiciary possessed the power to impose a solution. Meanwhile the states found themselves unable either to go their separate ways or to reach collective agreement. The balance initially struck in 1787 between slave and free states as well as between national and state power meant that neither could achieve the constitutional upper hand needed to impose its preferred solution. At the same time, the Constitution's provisions for expanding the union kept the fundamental disputes as matters of constant tension, a situation that by the late 1850s had reached crisis proportions.

Secession from the United States, referred to ever since the Virginia and Kentucky resolutions of 1798 as the ultimate alternative to acceptance of constitutional change, became a frequent subject of discussion in the 1850s. As tensions ratcheted ever higher, increasing numbers of southerners came to regard the Constitution as a trap into which they had innocently strayed. In an expanding union, the Article V amending process was the hinge that could suddenly snap and crush the South's distinctive culture. The North only needed the will and the power to spring the trap: the former was clearly great and growing while the latter appeared to nervous southerners to be nearly in hand. More and more, the only available escape hatch for the South appeared to be secession.[3]

When the 1860 election results were counted, it was evident that change in the constitutional blueprint was pending, one way or another. The nature and extent of the transformation soon to come was, however, not at first evident. Most attention both then and since focused on growing northern antislavery attitudes and countervailing southern beliefs. In the opinion of many southerners, withdrawal from the existing union had become necessary. It is well to keep in mind that some contrary opinion existed among southern leaders, though far less than sentiment favoring secession.[4]

Disunion was scarcely the only constitutional alternative considered at the time. Amendment of the Constitution to guarantee the status quo had numerous advocates. Between December 3, 1860, and March 4, 1861, fifty-seven distinct amendment proposals were laid before the expiring Thirty-sixth Congress.[5] With the nation teetering on the brink of collapse, some still thought disaster could be avoided by restructuring the fundamental law.

About-to-depart President James Buchanan characteristically made the first effort to mollify the South and find a compromise to prevent secession. He had little prospect of success for he was, after all, "the retiring head of the minority wing of a divided party that had been repudiated at the polls."[6] In his State of the Union message opening the second session of the lame duck Thirty-eighth Congress, Buchanan declared secession unconstitutional but nevertheless contended that no branch of the national government had the authority to block it. Only good will could repair the breech, he said, and that required a demonstration to the South that secession was unnecessary. The only realistic solution, Buchanan believed, was constitutional amendment. He offered a package of three amendments that would protect slavery in states where it existed, allow slaveholding in territories prior to establishment of a state constitution in which residents would decide the issue for themselves, and provide a strong federal fugitive-slave law. With Republicans disinclined to grant slavery official sanction, much less agree to the other measures, and the South's acceptance uncertain, his proposal was promptly rejected.[7]

Although Buchanan's proposals died quickly, hopes for a solution to the secession crisis through constitutional amendment did not. Attention centered
on amendments because bitter experience had demonstrated that compromise
arrangements expressed in legislative enactments such as the Missouri Compromise and the Compromise of 1850 could easily be upset by further legislation
or judicial decree. Only a constitutional settlement difficult or impossible to
overturn would insure stability.[8]

Congressional committees sifted through the many amendments being
offered. The effort, which seems wholly unrealistic in retrospect, may have
been so recognized at the time. Yet to those desperate to find a way of avoiding
disunion and possible war, it possessed the appeal of a tested mechanism for
obtaining an acceptable permanent resolution of the problem. Ultimately the
leading seeker of compromise, Senator John J. Crittenden of Kentucky, would
confess, "We have done absolutely nothing." However, he remained unwilling
to concede this until the final hours of the congress, after many people had
expended a great deal of effort in the search for an amendment cure.[9]

Crittenden offered a series of amendments that would have reestablished
and extended the sectional compromises of 1820 and 1850 and made their
provisions permanent. Congress would be stripped of power to alter the Constitution to abolish or interfere with slavery.[10] Less a true compromise than a
concession to reassure the South, the Crittenden plan could only succeed if a
very broad political consensus could be assembled to support it. Although Republicans rejected his proposition as 1860 ended, Senator Crittenden continued
searching for constitutional accommodation. He brought a modified plan before
the Senate and proposed that it be submitted to a national plebiscite.[11] Although
his ideas on how such a referendum would be conducted were vague, the concept accorded with traditional American constitutional theory that sovereignty
ultimately lay with the people. Following the Senate's narrow twenty-five to
twenty-three defeat of this proposal, attention shifted to the House of Representatives, where the Crittenden plan was again the most discussed approach.[12]

Meanwhile, a parallel search for constitutional solutions went on outside
Congress. The legislature of Virginia, a state very much torn between southern
and unionist loyalties, sought to follow its own example from the 1780s by calling for a conference of the states. Since it was not convened according to the
procedure outlined in Article V of the Constitution, this "Peace Conference"
was of uncertain standing. Nevertheless, twenty-one states accepted Virginia's

invitation to attend the gathering beginning February 4, 1861, at Washington's Willard Hotel, a block from the White House. However, the seven secessionist states meeting in Montgomery, Alabama, at the same time to draw up a constitution for the confederacy did not send delegates. After more than three weeks of debate, the Peace Conference produced its own solution, a set of constitutional amendments based on Crittenden's package. Submitted first to the Senate, the Peace Conference amendments were soundly defeated. They never even came to a vote in the House.[13]

As Lincoln's inauguration drew close, efforts to find a sectional compromise centered increasingly in the House of Representatives. Thomas Corwin of Ohio finally obtained agreement on a single constitutional provision to prohibit abolition of slavery where it existed at that moment. Corwin's amendment was itself to be unamendable. Submitting his measure to the House on February 27, the day the Peace Conference adjourned, Corwin thought this might be the one measure that would win over the South while not provoking Republican objections. Guaranteeing slavery where it already stood did not controvert stated Republican policy. Furthermore, the Constitution already contained a feature— its provision for equal representation of states in the Senate—unamendable without unanimous consent.[14]

The Corwin unamendable amendment came before Congress after nearly every southern senator and representative had withdrawn. News of the enactment of a Confederate constitution had already reached Washington, and all thoughts that secession talk was not to be taken seriously had evaporated. A preponderant majority of those remaining in Congress were ready to clutch at any device to avert catastrophe. The House adopted Corwin's measure by a vote of 133 to 65, and the Senate, rejecting all modifications that would need to be sent back to the House for concurrence, followed suit on March 3 by the bare-minimum constitutional majority. It was, nevertheless, an impressive consensus of two-thirds of the members of Congress still in their seats. On its very last day, the Thirty-sixth Congress threw the Article V amendment mechanism into motion in a final attempt to avoid chaos. The support for an unamendable acceptance of slavery, even among Republicans, provides a measure of how far a supermajority of the Congress was willing to go at that moment to avoid disunion. Immediately sent to the states for ratification and endorsed by Abraham Lincoln in his inaugural address, the Corwin amendment was nevertheless quickly overtaken by events.[15]

How should the futile quest for amendment on the eve of the Civil War be evaluated? Alabama fire-eater William L. Yancey, speaking to his state's secession convention, sneered at the very idea. "No guarantees—no amendments of the Constitution—no compromises patched up to secure to the North the benefits of Union yet a little longer, can reeducate that people on the slavery issue, so as to induce them, having the majority, to withhold the exercise of its power," he declared.[16] Yancey was an extremist, but in 1861 his words reflected much southern distrust of amendment gestures.

Amendment by the Article V method always posed difficulties, but with seven of the thirty-four states having seceded, the obstacles were unusually formidable. Twenty-six of the remaining twenty-seven states would have to ratify to meet the three-fourths requirement, unless the number was lowered by acknowledging secession as a legal right and an accomplished fact, something "most Republicans and many northern Democrats were fiercely unwilling to do."[17] Therefore, contrary action, or even inaction, by any two states could block amendment. However, before dismissing the amendment discussions out of hand, it ought to be remembered that Americans at the time could look back to the only comparable period of constitutional stress, the 1780s, and see all but one state (Rhode Island) agreeing on fundamental constitutional reform when it was perceived necessary to rescue their crumbling union.

In the secession crisis, amendment was an unlikely solution but not an entirely implausible one and certainly no worse a course to pursue than available alternatives. No wonder so much hope and energy was invested in this olive branch to the South. In the end, of course, amendment proved no more effective than any other strategy pursued in the futile hope of reconciliation during the last months before the war commenced. Only the Civil War itself and its decisive outcome would render constitutional reform an effective means of finally resolving the dilemmas that hamstrung the United States during its first three-quarters of a century, producing a new union on different basic principles.

Confronted by the reality of southern secession, Abraham Lincoln chose to assert the authority of the Constitution as well as interpret its broad language to extend dramatically the powers of the presidency. No shrinking Buchanan, Lincoln boldly took advantage of every opportunity to stress the authority of the federal government and that of his own office.[18] Declaring secession illegal and using the law enforcement powers granted the president in Article II of the Constitution to suppress what he characterized as unlawful actions by the southern states stood as the most decisive act of his presidency.

Lincoln's view of the Constitution as establishing an enforceable perpetual union set in motion all that would unfold. Heavily criticized but ultimately upheld by the force of arms, Lincoln's reading of constitutional sovereignty and the president's inherent authority to defend permanent national unity produced a linguistic as well as constitutional shift. Thereafter, *the United States is* would replace *the United States are* as the standard way of referring to the country.

Lincoln's assertion of implied presidential authority in the spare words of the Constitution continued throughout his presidency, most dramatically in his Emancipation Proclamation. The presence of plausible justification in the language of the Constitution overrode the need for explicit authorization, as far as Lincoln was concerned. Once again claiming that his law enforcement powers gave him the right to take action against those in rebellion, Lincoln's emancipatory initiative was essentially symbolic. At the moment he issued his proclamation, it only had effect in places engaged in rebellion. For the moment, the federal government lacked the means to enforce the proclamation, but it was a bold claim of adequate constitutional authority nevertheless. The president's edict only gained practical significance as northern troops advanced and as actual emancipation began to occur. Constitutionally speaking, of course, the measure had less consequence for slavery than the Thirteenth Amendment to follow, but in terms of expanding the dimensions of presidential authority, it was extraordinary. Other Lincolnian assertions of the power of his office to prosecute the war, such as his suspension of habeas corpus, were significant, but none of them reached the level of the Emancipation Proclamation.

Lincoln recognized that his view of implied constitutional authority did not offer a complete solution to the slavery question, since it did not address the situation of states such as Delaware, Maryland, Kentucky, and Missouri that permitted slavery but had not left the union. Nor did Lincoln's declaration surmount the 1857 ruling of the Supreme Court in *Dred Scott v. Sandford* that had upheld the constitutionality of slavery. Therefore, even before the Emancipation Proclamation took effect on January 1, 1863, President Lincoln proposed, in a December 1862 message to Congress, three constitutional amendments that would abolish slavery gradually. The first would grant states power to end slavery with compensation to owners until January 1, 1900. The second would validate the Emancipation Proclamation and free slaves who fought for the Union, again with compensation to owners who had remained loyal. The final proposal would grant Congress power to arrange colonization abroad for freed slaves. Even at this late date, Lincoln's caution regarding the property rights of loyal citizens and his social conservatism regarding the creation of a multiracial society were evident as he searched for a constitutional solution.[19]

Congress proved much bolder than Lincoln regarding constitutional reform to deal with slavery. When the Thirty-eighth Congress convened in December 1863, Ohio Representative James Ashley offered a simple and straightforward amendment "prohibiting slavery or involuntary servitude in all of the States and Territories now owned or which may be hereafter acquired by the United States."[20] While the Ashley resolution languished in the House, the Senate heatedly debated, then adopted by the necessary two-thirds majority, a similar resolution introduced by Lyman Trumball of Illinois. A month later, the larger Democratic minority in the House balked at passing Trumball's measure by the required two-thirds. Frustrated Republicans, conceding Lincoln's judgment that Congress lacked the constitutional power to eliminate slavery by statute, called for a constitutional amendment to do so in their 1864 platform.[21]

The 1864 election increased the Republican majority in Congress and manifested the mounting strength of northern antislavery sentiment. Momentum to complete the Trumbull amendment quickly accelerated. Enough Democrats were defeated to assure the Republicans a three-fourths majority in the next House, but that body would not convene for thirteen months. Continuing to resist, Democrats contended that, since it was unrelated to any provision of the existing Constitution, the proposed amendment exceeded the bounds of Article V, which they claimed only sanctioned modification of existing constitutional authority. Dismissing the argument that the amending power was limited, President Lincoln appealed to them to support immediate bipartisan action. Whether responding to his pleas or their own sense of their party's best interests, sixteen representatives, fourteen of them lame ducks, abandoned the official Democratic position to vote for the slavery abolition amendment. Eight others remained absent during the roll call. The House was thus able to approve the amendment on January 31, 1865, by the necessary two-thirds margin. The action, among other things, acknowledged bipartisan acceptance of the principle that amendments could totally transform the original Constitution. When the result was announced, the galleries cheered, outside the Capitol cannons boomed a hundred-gun salute, and on the floor of the House, Representative George Julian of Indiana noted in his diary, "Members joined in the shouting and kept it up for some minutes. Some embraced one another, others wept like children. I have felt, ever since the vote, as if I were in a new country."[22] Constitutionally speaking, Julian was right on target: the original intent of the founders as well as the fundamental rules governing the nation were being changed dramatically.

State ratification of the Thirteenth Amendment proceeded rapidly. Eighteen northern states ratified within a month. By July 1, a nineteenth northern state and four secessionist states had approved the measure. Four more southern states acted by December 6. Even though five more states, four of them northern, would add their endorsements within the next seven weeks, Secretary of State William Seward stirred controversy by immediately announcing that the antislavery amendment had been adopted by the action of twenty-seven of the thirty-six states. Seward ignored the congressional refusal days earlier to seat representatives of formerly secessionist states, declaring they had forfeited their privileges of government. How could states not competent to conduct elections and legislative affairs have authority to approve federal amendments? Seward took the position that constitutional amendment ratification was an act of the sovereign people, and chose to ignore awkward procedural details.

Of course, if the eleven secessionist states and their eight favorable votes had been removed from the equation, the Thirteenth Amendment would still have been sanctioned by nineteen of the twenty-five unquestionably legitimate state governments, again a three-fourths margin. Even though the new amendment met Article V's standard of validity by either measure, there was no way it could have achieved ratification by three-fourths of all states without the inclusion of the votes of those whose legitimacy was under challenge. Lincoln's insistence that the union remained unbroken led directly to this ratification controversy. Ultimately the view prevailed that the secretary of state and Congress possessed the power to confirm the Thirteenth Amendment's ratification.[23]

Many historians agree that, had the South simply acknowledged its defeat and demonstrated its assent to the sort of union for which the North had fought, a smooth and rapid return to a normally functioning government might well have followed the adoption of the Thirteenth Amendment. More than anything else, considerate southern treatment of the former slaves would signal its acceptance of Union victory. "Given the strong desire for 'normalcy,'" wrote a respected Civil War scholar, "it is most likely that the South could have satisfied northern opinion by ratifying the Thirteenth Amendment, repudiating secession, and acquiescing in the exercise by blacks of civil, but not political, rights."[24]

Instead, the South conceded no more than ratification of the Thirteenth Amendment. Several state legislatures did even that with obvious reluctance, and Mississippi flatly refused to do so at all. Then, rather than repudiate secession as constitutionally wrong in the first place, most states merely repealed their secession ordinances, declaring them no longer in effect. Furthermore, the recalcitrant states moved immediately to adopt legal codes severely restricting freedmen. The South was responding to the stated expectations of President Andrew Johnson, the assassinated Lincoln's successor, but much of the North was furious. Constitutional defeat, the North believed, was being snatched from the jaws of victory, notwithstanding the achievement of the Thirteenth Amendment. Johnson's refusal to require further southern reform and his insistence that the national government had no power to compel state action led frustrated northerners into protracted conflict with the president as well as to the conclusion that further explicit constitutional reconfiguration was required to preserve their triumph.[25]

Upon convening in December 1865, the Thirty-ninth Congress immediately began exploring means, including further amendment and other constitutionally valid measures, to protect the North's victory. By March an aroused Congress was ready to claim federal responsibility for guarding individual rights. Despite some hesitancy about intruding into what had traditionally been an area of state authority, both houses approved a Civil Rights Act. When Johnson sought to block the legislation, an increasingly combative Congress overrode his veto. The battle over the Civil Rights Act of 1866 led the North to recognize that the Thirteenth Amendment did not assure blacks all the protections they needed. Prohibiting slavery itself was not enough to guarantee civil freedom in the face of southern white hostility and persistent presidential obstruction.

Proposing what would become the first section of the Fourteenth Amendment, Ohio Congressman John Bingham brought forth an amendment proposal granting Congress the power to pass all laws necessary and proper to secure equal rights to all persons. Bingham disparaged claims of independent state authority in this regard, insisting "The spirit, the intent, the purpose of our Constitution is to secure equal and exact justice to all men." States had ignored, he said, the "guarantee of your Constitution [that] applies to every citizen of every State of the Union; there is not a guarantee more sacred, and none more vital in that great instrument." Therefore, he proposed explicit language to treat the privileges and immunities of all citizens as a national matter. Rather than merely give Congress authority to protect citizens' rights if it chose to do so, those rights were proclaimed as absolute. The guarantees of equal protection and due process of law in matters of life, liberty, and property would give specific meaning to American citizenship.[26] During the debate and in a later speech to Congress, Bingham stressed that his language was designed to make the Constitution's first eight amendments binding on the states.[27] Its principal architect had none of the doubts about the Fourteenth Amendment's meaning expressed by later generations.[28] His direct approach to a grant of federal authority offered, he believed, as momentous a constitutional change in respect to federalism as ending slavery itself.

Congress's Joint Committee on Reconstruction combined into one amendment Bingham's proposal, a Senate addition conferring citizenship on all persons born or naturalized in the United States, and several measures more narrowly focused on punishing the rebellious South. Designed to enlist the broadest possible coalition of support, this tactic increased the likelihood of congressional adoption and state ratification of a reconstruction amendment but departed significantly from earlier amending practice.[29] In the only previous episode of simultaneous multiple amendments, the Bill of Rights, various propositions were offered by Congress as separate amendments to be decided upon individually. Ten were adopted; two were not. Combining a number of proposals into a single measure shifted critical decision-making from the ratifiers to the initial adopters of an amendment resolution. States would confront a take-it-or-leave-it, all-or-nothing choice. This method of designing an amendment, never used again, produced the longest, most complex, and arguably most influential of all the U.S. Constitution's amendments.

The proposed Fourteenth Amendment gave Republicans a rallying point in the 1866 election, especially after President Johnson began disparaging it. The Republicans' overwhelming victory reflected a large measure of northern public support for the constitutional changes underway. Rapid ratification of the Fourteenth Amendment proceeded across the North. Except for Tennessee, most southern states initially rejected it, then faced Congress's adoption of the Military Reconstruction Act, and quickly saw that acceptance of the amendment was necessary if they were to end military occupation, regain their seats in Congress, and renew their full membership in the union.

One other explicitly sanctioned but uncommon constitutional action proved influential in the South's grudging acceptance of the Fourteenth Amendment.

Congress employed its Article II, Section IV, power of impeachment to demonstrate that the South would need to bow to its will. It adopted, over yet another Johnson veto, a Tenure in Office Act requiring Senate approval of a successor before the dismissal of any official whose appointment required Senate approval. The measure, of dubious constitutionality itself, was an obvious attempt either to stifle Johnson or lead him into committing an impeachable offense. The House, although increasingly unhappy with the president, did not at first rush to impeach him, even after the 1866 election gave the Republican Party more than three-quarters of all seats and the power to do so. Instead, when Ohio Representative James Ashley called for an impeachment investigation in December 1866, the House declined to take up his resolution. The following month a second Ashley resolution was referred to the Judiciary Committee, which reported that it did not have enough time to complete an investigation before the Thirty-ninth Congress expired but recommended that the inquiry continue. Ashley's third resolution, at the start of the Fortieth Congress in March 1867, led to a lengthy Judiciary Committee inquiry and an impeachment recommendation the following November. Even then the House heeded a minority report asserting that Johnson had not committed impeachable offenses and in December firmly rejected its committee's recommendation. Despite widespread hostility toward Johnson, most House members clearly took seriously the Constitution's specific and narrow requirements.[30]

In less than three months, however, the situation changed. Johnson at first tried to comply with the Tenure in Office Act. submitting for Senate approval the name of a replacement, General Ulysses S. Grant, as he suspended Secretary of War Edwin Stanton. When the Senate refused to concur in Stanton's dismissal, Grant departed and Stanton resumed his position. Furious and feeling betrayed by Grant, Johnson formally removed Stanton from office on February 21, 1868. Later the same day, an impeachment resolution was introduced in the House charging Johnson with "high crimes and misdemeanors" for violating the Tenure in Office Act.

The pace of the Johnson impeachment proceedings thereafter was breathtaking. The Reconstruction Committee took one day to return a recommendation of impeachment. After two days listening to speeches denouncing the president, the House voted along strict party lines—126 Republicans voting yes and 47 Democrats voting no—to impeach Johnson. Four days later, the House approved eleven articles of impeachment, nine dealing with Stanton in one way or another, one concerning Johnson's "intemperate, inflammatory, and scandalous harangues" against Congress, and a final one charging the president with repeatedly disregarding acts of Congress. Five days after that, the Senate opened its trial, a mere thirty-one days after Stanton's firing.

Much of the trial itself focused on the Stanton affair. Relatively little time was devoted to the final article of impeachment, which many then and since regarded as having the best chance of adoption. The Senate voted first on the last, most sweeping article on May 16. Thirty-five Senators, all Republicans, voted for conviction, while nineteen, all twelve Democrats as well as seven Republicans, voted no. Had a single senator in the minority switched to vote with the majority, the president would have been convicted and removed from office. The stunned majority obtained a ten-day recess, hoping to change the mind of at least one of their apostate colleagues, but to no avail. On May 26, votes on other articles produced the exact same result, after which the Senate adjourned the trial.

The outcome of the impeachment and trial of Andrew Johnson left a lasting impression of failed partisanship. All the votes in the House for impeachment and in the Senate for conviction had come from Republicans. Too often overlooked is the fact that Johnson's narrow escape was due to the abandonment of their party's majority view by seven Republican senators unconvinced that Johnson had committed an impeachable offense. A constitutional procedure was followed to the letter, and although a partisan majority was unhappy with the outcome, respect for the original intent of 1787 prevailed.

The impact of Johnson's impeachment was far more significant than his lame-duck survival as president following his Senate trial. The initiation of impeachment efforts led the recalcitrant states of the former Confederacy to realize that, whatever the outcome of Johnson's trial, the Congress would continue to insist upon southern compliance with the unambiguous requirements of the Reconstruction Act, including approval of the Fourteenth Amendment, before their representatives would be allowed to take their seats in Congress. Watching Andrew Johnson, their strongest supporter in the federal government, reduced to political impotence, most southern states moved ahead quickly to comply with the terms of military reconstruction. Southern state ratification of the proposed Fourteenth Amendment was, arguably, the greatest constitutional consequence of impeachment. The Fortieth Congress's conclusion that a specific guarantee of the freedmen's voting rights required further constitutional protection against recalcitrant southerners and uncooperative Democrats was the next important outcome, the Fifteenth Amendment that emerged as the final act of that Congress.[31]

While the constitutionally prescribed impeachment procedure played an important role in the Reconstruction process and would effectively render Congress dominant in the federal system for the rest of the nineteenth century, the three amendments adopted according to Article V were what secured the permanent constitutional transformation of the 1860s. Only amendments approved by two-thirds of each house of Congress and ratified by three-fourths of the states could give full legitimacy to the substantive alteration that had been brought about. Through means endorsed by the framers, the Constitution of 1787 had been replaced by the Constitution of the 1860s.

A critical element in the change from limited to broader construction of constitutional authority was the alteration of attitudes about amending the Constitution. Previous amendments, most of the many proposed as well as all of the twelve enacted, had been designed to construct additional curbs on federal power or further define limits and procedures already in place. Indeed the belief was widespread that amendments could only restrict, not extend the original declaration of constitutional authority. The 1860s brought a perceptible shift to amendments granting greater powers to the federal government or declaring new national policy. Furthermore, in the new environment of constitutional adequacy, amendments came to be thought of as necessary only if power to carry out a desired objective was clearly absent or if existing terms thwarted a preferred policy.

Abstract developments in constitutional thought were less immediately obvious than the practical effect of the three crucially important amendments added to the Constitution in the 1860s. The Thirteenth Amendment abolishing slavery represented a dramatic statement of social policy. It erased the 1787 Constitution's original intent to protect "the peculiar institution." Instead, it placed the federal government on the side of human rights at the expense of what had been understood to be private property rights. Of particular note, this amendment won approval less than five years after an earlier Congress, desperately seeking to mollify the South, endorsed a polar-opposite Thirteenth Amendment permanently sanctioning slavery in states where it then existed. A reversal of congressional direction has seldom been so obvious. The Fourteenth and Fifteenth amendments that soon followed the ratified antislavery Thirteenth carried forward a social as well as political and legal transformation hardly imaginable just a few years earlier. Together these three amendments established new federally enforceable standards of personal liberty and civil rights, the precise details of which were debatable but whose overall magnitude was undeniable. The epitome of Civil War change, these amendments were founded on a new constitutional philosophy. Each markedly enlarged the federal government's mandate and reduced state authority, something no earlier amendment had attempted, much less achieved.

At the same time, traditional notions of federalism did not altogether disappear. Defense of states' rights remained a concern in many quarters during the effort to devise the new constitutional provisions. Once the new amendments were in place, courts at first interpreted them in ways that preserved state power, even at the expense of the civil rights and centralized authority that their proponents thought they had advanced. Conservative Supreme Court decisions beginning in the 1870s made clear that the Civil War constitutional revolution had, at least for the moment, definite limits. When the potential implications of the amendments were not consistent with dominant political and racial beliefs, they could not by themselves immediately overturn the status quo. The Civil War amendments, adopted during a brief moment when political idealism and opportunity crested simultaneously in the aftermath of battlefield victory, would thereafter lie dormant for decades before the political climate shifted enough to allow their implementation. What is remarkable a century and a half later is not that the constitutional reforms of the 1860s in terms of federal-state relations and the legal rights of every individual finally took hold, but rather that some professed defenders of the Constitution continue to deny their transformative effect. The reality is that the framers in 1787 established a procedure for changes to the Constitution that would give properly adopted alterations equal validity to the remaining unaltered sections of the document. Ignoring that such changes were made in the amendments of the 1860s is, in itself, a violation of the Constitution's "original intent."

NOTES

1. The best study of popular understanding of the Constitution is Michael Kammen's *A Machine That Would Go of Itself: The Constitution in American Culture* (New York: Transaction, 2006).

2. A fine account of the 1787 Constitutional Convention can be found in Richard R. Beeman, *Plain, Honest Men: The Making of the American Constitution* (New York: Random House, 2009).

3. William W. Freehling, *Prelude to Civil War: The Nullification Controversy in South Carolina, 1816–1836* (New York: Harper & Row, 1966), *The Road to Disunion, Vol. 1: Secessionists at Bay, 1776–1854* (New York: Oxford University Press, 1991), and *The Road to Disunion, Volume II: Secessionists Triumphant, 1854–1861* (New York: Oxford University Press, 2007).

4. See Jon L. Wakelyn, *Southern Pamphlets on Secession, November 1860–April 1861* (Chapel Hill: University of North Carolina Press, 1996); *Southern Unionist Pamphlets and the Civil War* (Columbia: University of Missouri Press, 1999).

5. Herman V. Ames, *The Proposed Amendments to the Constitution of the United States During the First Century of its History,* part 2 of *Annual Report of the American Historical Association for the Year 1896* (Washington, DC: GPO, 1897), 194, 354–65.

6. Albert D. Kirwan, *John J. Crittenden: The Struggle for the Union* (Lexington: University of Kentucky Press, 1962), 367.

7. James Buchanan, "Fourth Annual Message," in James D. Richardson, ed., *A Compilation of the Messages and Papers of the Presidents, 1789–1897* (New York: Bureau of National Literature, 1897), vol. 7: 3167–70; Ames, *Proposed Amendments,* 194, 354–55; Harold M. Hyman, *A More Perfect Union: The Impact of the Civil War and Reconstruction on the Constitution* (New York: Knopf, 1973), 40–41.

8. For a detailed discussion of the rise of this belief, see David E. Kyvig, *Explicit and Authentic Acts: Amending the U.S. Constitution, 1776–1995* (Lawrence: University Press of Kansas, 1996), especially chapter 7.

9. Quoted in Kenneth M. Stampp, *And the War Came: The North and the Secession Crisis, 1860–1861* (Baton Rouge: Louisiana State University Press, 1950), 123.

10. Ames, *Proposed Amendments,* 357; Kirwan, *Crittenden,* 375.

11. Ames, *Proposed Amendments,* 358: Kirwan, *Crittenden,* 392.

12. Kirwan, *Crittenden,* 396–400.

13. Robert G. Gunderson, *Old Gentlemen's Convention: The Washington Peace Conference of 1861* (Madison: University of Wisconsin Press, 1961); Jesse L. Keene, *The Peace Convention of 1861* (Tuscaloosa, AL: Confederate Publishing, 1961); Ames, *Proposed Amendments,* 364.

14. A useful legislative history of the Corwin amendment can be found in R. Alton Lee, "The Corwin Amendment in the Secession Crisis," *Ohio Historical Quarterly* 70 (1961): 1–26.

15. Ames, *Proposed Amendments,* 196, 363; Kirwan, *Crittenden,* 410–21.

16. Quoted in Jesse T. Carpenter, *The South as a Conscious Minority, 1789–1861: A Study in Political Thought* (New York: New York University Press, 1930), 157.

17. Don E. Fehrenbacher, *The Dred Scott Case: Its Significance in American Law and Politics* (New York: Oxford University Press, 1978), 547–48.

18. Lincoln's constitutional thought and action are thoroughly and well examined in Harold M. Hyman, *A More Perfect Union: The Impact of the Civil War and Reconstruction on the Constitution* (New York: Knopf, 1973), and Hyman and William M. Wiecek, *Equal Justice Under Law: Constitutional Development, 1835–1875* (New York: Harper and Row, 1982).

19. Abraham Lincoln, "Annual Message to Congress, December 1, 1862," in Roy P. Basler, ed., *The Collected Works of Abraham Lincoln* (New Brunswick, NJ: Rutgers University Press, 1953), vol. 5: 527–31.

20. Ames, *Proposed Amendments,* 214.

21. Ibid., 214–17, 367–68; Earl M. Maltz, *Civil Rights, the Constitution, and Congress, 1863–1869* (Lawrence: University Press of Kansas, 1990), 14–25.

22. Quoted in James M. McPherson, *Battle Cry of Freedom: The Civil War Era* (New York: Oxford University Press, 1988), 839–40.

23. An excellent full account of the adoption of the Thirteenth Amendment can be found in Michael Vorenberg, *Final Freedom: The Civil War, the Abolition of Slavery, and the Thirteenth Amendment* (New York: Cambridge University Press, 2001).

24. Phillip S. Paludan, *A Covenant with Death: The Constitution, Law, and Equality in the Civil War Era* (Urbana: University of Illinois Press, 1975), 214.

25. Reconstruction, its constitutional aspect in particular, received a great deal of attention in the late twentieth century. Noteworthy studies include Michael Les Benedict, *A Compromise of Principle: Congressional Republicans and Reconstruction, 1863–1869* (New York: W. W. Norton, 1974); Joseph B. James, *The Ratification of the Fourteenth Amendment* (Macon, GA: Mercer University Press, 1984); Michael Kent Curtis, *No State Shall Abridge: The Fourteenth Amendment and the Bill of Rights* (Durham, NC: Duke University Press, 1986); Eric Foner, *Reconstruction: America's Unfinished Revolution, 1863–1877* (New York: Harper & Row, 1987); William E. Nelson, *The Fourteenth Amendment: From Political Principle to Judicial Doctrine* (Cambridge, MA: Harvard University Press, 1988); and Maltz, *Civil Rights, the Constitution, and Congress.*

26. *Congressional Globe*, 39th Cong., 1st sess., 157–58.

27. Maltz, *Civil Rights, the Constitution, and Congress*, 114–15.

28. Richard L. Aynes, "On Misreading John Bingham and the Fourteenth Amendment," *Yale Law Journal* 103 (1993): 57–104.

29. James, *The Ratification of the Fourteenth Amendment*, 100–102, 172; Maltz, *Civil Rights, the Constitution, and Congress*, 79–81.

30. An excellent account of the entire Johnson impeachment episode can be found in Michael Les Benedict, *The Impeachment and Trial of Andrew Johnson* (New York: W. W. Norton, 1973).

31. The complex story of the Fourteenth Amendment's ratification as well as the Fifteenth Amendment's adoption is recounted in Kyvig, *Explicit and Authentic Acts*, chapter 8.

GOLDBERGER AND GERSHWIN

XXXXXXXXXXXXXXXXXXXXXXXXXXXXXXXXXXXXXXXXXXXXX

*Two New York Jews Encounter the American South
in the Early Twentieth Century*

ALAN M. KRAUT

etween 1870 and the early 1920s, over 2.25 million Jews emigrated from Central and Eastern Europe to the United States. Most of them entered the United States through the port of New York, and the vast majority spent at least some time in New York City, the place that historian Moses Rischin dubbed "The Promised City."[1] There those displaced by poverty and/or oppression found opportunity for employment, education, and hope, if not always a land flowing with "milk and honey." In New York, many Jewish immigrants and their children tasted poverty in the city's urban industrial environment even as they strove to craft a future of plenty. Through their own struggles and those of their neighbors, they learned firsthand about the interplay of poverty, culture, and society.

Two such children of the "Promised City" were a physician, Dr. Joseph Goldberger, and a musical composer, George Gershwin. Raised and educated in the urban cauldrons of New York's Lower East Side and Brooklyn streets, respectively, Goldberger and Gershwin each achieved world renown in their respective fields. What they had in common besides their religious heritage and immigrant pasts was that each applied their understanding of poverty's constraints and the accompanying social marginalization to illuminate the American South, a region still struggling to reconcile its past with the modernity of the twentieth century. Poor southerners, like poor Jews, were in search of a "promised land."

For many Americans the South has been synonymous with mystery or enigma, difficult to completely understand and reconcile with the democratic values, egalitarian aspirations, and industrial development overtly embraced by the rest of the nation in the nineteenth and twentieth centuries. "A kind of sphinx on the American land" was how one southern historian, David Potter, characterized the states south of the Mason-Dixon line.[2] If the South was a mystery, it also at times bore the burden of historic tragedy. The punishment for the sin of slavery was conquest and military occupation, according to the great southern scholar, C. Vann Woodward.[3]

It is this sense of historic tragedy that southerners shared with other groups in the United States, defined by racial, religious, or ethnic identity. One such group was the Jews. Present in North America since 1654, Jews had played significant roles in the life of the South Atlantic region since the colonial era. Before the Civil War, Christians often encountered Sephardic or German Jewish merchants in port cities such as Savannah, Charleston, and New Orleans. Other encounters were in the small towns where Jewish peddlers, mostly German immigrants, chose to settle and open small stores. And still other encounters occurred when southerners traveled to the North on business or leisure.[4] Over ten thousand Jews fought for the Confederacy in the Civil War and one Jew, Judah P. Benjamin, served as President Jefferson Davis's attorney general, secretary of war, and secretary of state during the Confederacy's brief existence.[5]

In the decades after the Civil War, Jewish immigration to the United States increased, largely from Southern and Eastern Europe. While most Eastern European Jews headed for the factories and shops of the North, some did settle in southern towns and cities. Interestingly, the arts as much as commerce served to create ties between the regions. Journalist and humorist Harry Golden, born Herschel Goldhirsh in Mikulintsky, Ukraine, and raised in New York, the publisher of the *Carolina Israelite*, gave mid-twentieth-century northern Jews a window on what life was like for their southern cousins in a syndicated column and book.[6] Meanwhile, young, ambitious southern writers and intellectuals ventured into the canyons created by New York's skyscrapers to talk to publishers and become part of the twentieth-century literary establishment. In Manhattan's bars and coffee houses, southern writers and New York Jewish intellectuals found more common ground than they might have expected.

In his 1967 autobiography, Mississippian Willie Morris, the renowned editor of *Harper's* magazine, who had encountered so many Jews in the publishing capital of the country, recalled:

> On a fall afternoon in 1966 I sat in a bar on Third Avenue with Norman Podhoretz, Midge Decter, and Marion Magid, who were then involved in editing

Commentary. . . . For three or four hours we sat talking about the places we had come from, about home, about people from our pasts. We told stories. We talked about editing, and about the things we were writing. I felt here, as I had perceived before, a certain electricity between Eastern Jewish intellectuals and white Southerners when the mood is relaxed and the pretensions gone, a certain élan in the casual talk about great characters, about comic moods, about Waspish Easterners more "inside" than we, and even, perhaps, an affinity in the historical disasters of our ancestral pasts.[7]

Jews and black southerners were tied together by the historic memory of slavery, oppression, discrimination, and especially diaspora. However, Jews and white southerners were bound by "historical disasters" of their "ancestral pasts," as well. If the Jews had been marginalized, persecuted, and expelled from many lands, southerners in the post–Civil War era found themselves confined to the margins of an American modernity that included industrialism, urbanism, and a multi-ethnicity resulting from immigration. Even as they sought economic recovery from the devastating effects of the Civil War on the southern economy, the section that gave the nation several of its seminal political thinkers—Jefferson, Madison, Clay, and Calhoun—now seemed anchored to a states' rights ideology that Americans outside the South characterized as out of step with the centralized power of the national government and liberal democratic values of modern society. The presence of an occupying army until 1877 and the physical destruction that took decades to repair were merely visible embodiments of the South's recent "historical disaster."

Jews and southerners—black and white—had all known suffering and exclusion. Nor was Willie Morris the first white Christian southern writer to recognize that young Jewish newcomers as well as young southerners yearned to redeem modern America's promise. Thomas Wolfe in his 1934 novel, *You Can't Go Home Again,* in a chapter entitled "The Promise of America" wrote lyrically, if stereotypically, of the aspirations of the young African American who had migrated out of the South and the young white southerner, as Wolfe understood them. It was the "Negro boy" who left behind the historic "memory of cotton fields" and "slave-driver's whip" to find America's promise fulfilled in a "roped-in ring, a blaze of lights, across from him a white champion; the bell, the opening, and all around the vast sea-roaring of the crowd."[8] It was the young lad from "the clay-baked piedmont of the South, that lean and tan-faced boy" who dreamed of the "packed stands of the stadium, the bleachers, sweltering with their unshaded hordes, the faultless velvet of the diamond, unlike the clay-baked outfields down in Georgia. The mounting roar of eighty-thousand voices and Gehrig coming up to bat, the boy himself upon the pitching mound."[9] And, Wolfe wrote, the immigrant Jewish lad yearned no less to redeem the country's promise:

> [I]n the East-Side Ghetto of Manhattan . . . there in a swarming tenement, shut in his sweltering cell, breathing the sun-baked air through opened window at the fire escape, celled there away into a little semblance of privacy and solitude from all the brawling and vociferous life and argument of his family and the seething hive around him, the Jew boy sits and pores upon his book. In shirt-sleeves, bent above his table to meet the hard glare of a naked bulb, he sits with gaunt starved face converging to his huge beaked nose, the weak eyes squinting painfully through his thick-lens glasses, his greasy hair roached back in oily scrolls above the slanting cage of his painful and constricted brow. And for what? . . . Because brother, he is burning in the night. He sees the class, the lecture room, the shining apparatus of gigantic laboratories, the open field of scholarship and pure research, certain knowledge and the world distinction of an Einstein name.[10]

Amidst the anti-Semitic images of the Jew's appearance, not infrequent in Wolfe's fiction, is the author's understanding and appreciation that this Jewish lad no less than the others was fleeing the past and in search of a better future in the United States.

But if some white southern writers saw in the Jew someone else who was a victim of "historical disaster" and in search of fulfillment of America's promise, what did the Eastern European Jewish immigrants see when they turned their gaze South? If the decades well before the civil rights movement created new bonds between Jews and African American southerners even as it fractured the relationship of many northern Jews to the white Christian South, how did northern Jews perceive the South, especially Jews raised on New York's steamy streets? Did the South and the problems of southerners white and black in the early twentieth century excite the imagination of these New Yorkers? How was that expressed? Did those white southerners who dreamed of a more progressive South find unexpected allies in these unlikely visitors? The experiences of two New York Jews—one an immigrant and one the child of immigrants, one a brilliant physician who saved untold millions of lives, and one a world-famous composer who enriched the lives of millions—open two unique windows on southern life early in the last century. Dr. Joseph Goldberger and composer George Gershwin were both raised in the southern reaches of Manhattan Island, but in the course of their lives they would venture much farther south than that.

The encounter between northern Jew and white southerner could be dangerous. Take the tragic lynching of Leo Frank, for example.[11] Frank was born in Cuero, Texas, in 1884, but his family moved to Brooklyn not long after his birth. He was educated in the Brooklyn public schools and at Pratt Institute, eventually earning a degree in mechanical engineering from Cornell University in 1906. He ended up in Atlanta working as a supervisor in a pencil factory owned by his uncle, a Confederate veteran. In 1910, the slender, bookish-looking Frank married Lucille Selig, daughter of a wealthy Jewish family that made its money in industry and was important in the growing Atlanta Jewish community. Three years later, Leo Frank was accused of killing thirteen-year-old Mary Phagan, who worked in the pencil factory fitting metal tips to pencils for twelve cents an hour.

The daughter of dispossessed white sharecroppers, Phagan disappeared on Confederate Memorial Day, April 26, 1913. Her badly bruised body was found lying face down in the factory basement the next morning. Missing were her purse and $1.20. In an atmosphere charged with anti-Semitism and anti-northern sentiment stirred by a rabid press, Frank was tried, convicted, and sentenced to death. But in July 1915, Georgia Governor John M. Slaton commuted the convicted felon's death sentence to life imprisonment because he believed there had been a miscarriage of justice that would forever besmirch his state's reputation if Frank was executed.

Slaton's pardon destroyed his political career, and it did not save Frank's life. Fueled by the poisoned pen of Populist-turned-bigot Tom Watson, thousands of Georgians carrying guns, hatchets, and dynamite surrounded the governor's mansion. Jewish businessmen boarded up their windows and doors against armed mobs while almost half of the state's three thousand Jews temporarily fled. On August 16, 1915, the mob kidnapped Frank from a prison farm at Milledgeville and lynched him. Frank's name, and with it Slaton's, would not be cleared until the early 1980s, when a witness, wishing to salve his conscience, identified an African American night watchman as the killer.

Although the Leo Frank lynching sent a shiver up the spine of many Jews both north and south, it was the exception rather than the rule.[12] The very year that one New York Jew was being dragged from his cell in Milledgeville, another was paying regular visits to an asylum in that very town to battle a disease that plagued the South, killing many thousands each year. Well understood today as a niacin deficiency, pellagra was once a mystery disease that killed a hundred thousand Americans between the early twentieth century and the 1940s. The physician who learned how to cure and prevent it was a Jewish immigrant physician raised on the streets of New York, Dr. Joseph Goldberger.[13]

By the time that the surgeon general of the United States ordered Dr. Joseph Goldberger into the South to assume responsibility for the Public Health Service's pellagra study, the immigrant physician already had extensive experience with the South and even a family connection. Born in Giralt, Hungary, in 1874, the child of German-speaking Jewish immigrants, former sheepherders who arrived in the United States on the S.S. Lessing in 1883, Joseph helped in his father's Lower East Side grocery store as he was growing up. He graduated from Bellevue Hospital Medical College in 1895 and, after a brief stint in private practice, joined the United States Marine Hospital Service in 1899 (later the USMHS was renamed the U.S. Public Health Service).[14]

An early assignment in the uniformed USMHS took Goldberger to the Reedy Island Quarantine Station at Port Penn, Delaware, where he served with a southerner, Thomas Farrar Richardson, the scion of a prominent southern family. Richardson and Goldberger became fast friends. An introduction to Richardson's young cousin, Mary, began a courtship leading to nuptials in 1906. The second of ten children, Mary was born into southern wealth and prominence. Her father, Edgar Howard Farrar, was a successful and wealthy New Orleans attorney. On her mother's side Mary was related to Confederate President Jefferson Davis. Goldberger could hardly have selected a southern woman with deeper ties to the South and its tragic past.

Edgar Farrar was hardly pleased at his daughter's decision to marry a non-southerner and a non-Christian. An old adage goes that in the North they ask you what you do, but in the South they ask you who your people are. Farrar launched an investigation of the young man and the Goldberger family before giving his consent to the wedding.[15] Receiving sterling reports about both the young doctor and the Goldberger family, Edgar Farrar consented to the wedding, but he also made clear his fears, writing directly to Joseph: "But I have advised her not to accept you unless she is willing to take upon herself and her children that unfortunate and unwise prejudice which exists in the minds of the great majority of people against your race and your creed. She has been brought up in this community where such prejudice is at a minimum, but she will have to follow her husband and it is doubtful whether his life will run here."[16] However, Farrar was wrong in believing that Dr. Joseph Goldberger's life would not "run" through New Orleans or the rest of the South. Indeed, by the time of his death Dr. Joseph Goldberger would be regarded by many southerners as their scientific savior.

In 1914, Goldberger assumed leadership of a floundering federal investigation of pellagra. Known as the disease of the 4ds—dermatitis, diarrhea, dementia, and death, by the second decade of the twentieth century, the mysterious disease had also become known as the "scourge of the South." Preliminary research caused Goldberger to doubt that it was a germ disease, although many other physicians believed there to be a "pellagra germ" that must be discovered before the disease could be prevented and cured. Goldberger requested that the surgeon general ship food to two Mississippi orphanages ravaged by pellagra. Poverty diets of corn bread, syrup, fat back, and grits were replaced by a balanced diet that included milk, eggs, fresh cuts of beef, as well as fresh fruits and vegetables. Improving the diets of the children cured those stricken with the disease and prevented it in those still healthy. A similar experiment had like results at the Georgia State Asylum at Milledgeville, not far from the prison from which Leo Frank would be seized. Goldberger and his assistant, Dr. George Wheeler, manipulated the diets of two experimental groups of female pellagra patients, one white and the other African American. Both groups were fed fresh milk, eggs, meat, and vegetables. A control group continued eating the traditional corn-based diet of the southern poor. Almost half of the control group showed pellagra symptoms, while all of those fed the modified diet recovered. However, such demonstrations were hardly at the standard of double-blind experiments, and many physicians remained doubtful that pellagra was merely a dietary disorder.[17]

Goldberger now hoped to isolate a healthy group of volunteers and induce pellagra symptoms through dietary manipulation alone. Where could he find such a population of volunteers and a control group? And what could he offer them to engage the volunteers' interest in participating? Prisoners wishing pardons were one option. Before the evolution of contemporary ethical reservations about the use of prisoners as experimental subjects, medical scientists regularly turned to prison populations for medical experiments. On the morning of January 21, 1915, Dr. Joseph Goldberger met with Governor Earl Brewer of Mississippi for the first time. Dr. E. H. Galloway, secretary of the Mississippi Board of Health and a trusted friend of Brewer's, had laid the groundwork so the meeting could proceed expeditiously. In his diary Goldberger recorded that he had informed Brewer that he had received the surgeon general's "authority to go ahead with the diet test on the convict volunteers." Needed now was Brewer's participation and the promise of pardons. After a few questions about the diet, Brewer and his advisers agreed.[18] Each prisoner-participant was asked to sign a form acknowledging the circumstances of the experiment, and Goldberger urged all the men to consult their attorneys.[19]

Earl Brewer was a progressive southern governor, though less colorful than James K. Vardaman, Theodore Bilbo, James Hogg, and Huey Long. As did the others, Brewer was willing to enact reforms and take all sorts of political chances to dispel the popular image of the South as a primitive backwater where few would want to spend their lives or their investment dollars. During the first two decades of the twentieth century, southern states embraced a broad array of reforms, restricting child labor, outlawing the blacklisting of union members, setting safety standards for railroads, financing new roads, making school attendance compulsory, and adopting such democratizing devices as the initiative, referendum, and presidential primary. They were ending the county convict lease system and public hangings. They were passing state income taxes and using the revenue to build schools, tuberculosis hospitals, charity hospitals, juvenile reformatories, and junior college systems. The South was rising, and a new generation of progressive governors, such as Earl Brewer, was willing to put their faith in northerners with Jewish-sounding names who worked for the federal government, such as Dr. Joseph Goldberger, if the results yielded a healthier, more productive state.[20]

With the assistance of Mississippi's progressive Governor Brewer, then, Goldberger began a dramatic controlled experiment in which he manipulated the diets of eleven prisoner volunteers (one of the original dozen withdrew because of other health issues) at the Rankin State Prison Farm to induce pellagra. There had been no pellagra at the prison farm, where the inmates raised their own food. In November of 1915, Goldberger began his experiment. He fed the eleven participants a classic southern corn-based poverty diet of corn bread, corn meal, molasses, fat back, corn syrup, and coffee. By April, six of the eleven prisoners in the experiment showed pellagra lesions. Goldberger then demonstrated he could cure pellagra by substituting a well-balanced diet rich in animal protein.[21] Governor Brewer rewarded the prisoner volunteers with pardons. The experiment received wide acclaim and, whereas late-twentieth-century critics speculate about whether Goldberger's technique of informed consent of his subjects was sufficient, southerners at the time were primarily critical of Brewer for agreeing to reward hardened convicts with release.[22] Goldberger did not ask Brewer to challenge the prevailing practice of racial segregation by including black prisoners. Offering pardons to black offenders might well have caused even greater outrage among those who opposed the pardons.

Goldberger's prisoner experiment silenced many critics, but not all. Some remained skeptical, still committed to the hunt for a pellagra germ, and at least one hinted at allegations that Goldberger had faked his results.[23] While some criticism was the product of professional jealousy, critics with some justification noted that the Rankin experiment might only have proven that bodies weakened by poor nutrition were susceptible to the elusive pellagra germ.

How could Goldberger persuade the doubters that pellagra was not an infectious disease? Goldberger's solution was a "party." Fourteen friends and colleagues turned out for what Goldberger termed his "filth parties." Mary Goldberger insisted on joining her husband at one of them. On April 26, 1916, at Spartanburg, South Carolina, Goldberger injected five cubic centimeters of a pellagrin's blood into Mary's shoulder and into Dr. George Wheeler's shoulder. Wheeler did the shot six cubic centimeters into Goldberger. Then came the "filth" as they swabbed out the secretions from a patient's nose and applied the swabs to their own noses and throats. Flecks of pellagrins' feces were ingested in capsules, a part of the experiment in which Mary Goldberger did not take part. No one got pellagra; still some physicians remained skeptical.[24]

Between 1916 and 1919, Goldberger and his associates, including renowned statistician Edgar Sydenstricker, focused their efforts on southerners and their lifestyles. Goldberger and Sydenstricker conducted a comprehensive epidemiological study in seven cotton-mill villages in South Carolina. The late historian of medicine Dr. George Rosen dubbed them "a series of classic studies in the social epidemiology of pellagra."[25] In these mill villages, as well as among the tenant farmers and sharecroppers, there was an inverse correlation between family income and pellagra incidence. Also important were the sources of food supply and dietary habits. When mill-village families were limited to the mill store or commissary during the late winter or spring because of the absence of other food sources, this restriction plus the southern poverty diet combined to increase the likelihood of pellagra. More and more, Goldberger was convinced that pellagra was related to poverty and that the economic patterns that yielded poverty produced the disease. Making the case that how one lives can make one sick, Goldberger broke new ground by making the household the unit of analysis and tracing the habits of all its members.[26]

Gradually physicians, north and south, acknowledged that Goldberger's bold experiments had established pellagra as a nutritional deficiency rather than a germ disease. However, while some were nominating him for the Nobel Prize in medicine, others rejected the implications of Goldberger's equation of pellagra with poverty. Because diseases are social as well as biological phenomena, every disease has a politics. The politics of pellagra was directly threatening to many in the South. In the 1920s, some southern politicians were adamant in challenging Goldberger's assessment of pellagra, vociferously denying that southerners were suffering disproportionately from a dietary deficiency that was the direct result of poverty. Accepting such a diagnosis seemed tantamount to confessing to the scathing indictment of stubborn backwardness at just the moment when the South was scrambling to assert itself politically and anxious to seem economically dynamic to potential investors.

Sensitive to the poverty and suffering he witnessed, but not attuned to the broader agenda of southern politicians or skilled in public relations techniques, Goldberger was outspoken in his criticism of the southern economy. In the early 1920s, he predicted a dramatic rise in the number of pellagra cases as cotton prices plummeted. The demand to increase cotton production even as prices fell discouraged sharecropping families from diversifying their crop. Owners wanted more cotton. Even a milk cow and a small garden seemed impossible to maintain. Similarly, Goldberger criticized mill owners for paying wages too low to permit their workers to afford a balanced diet. He condemned a production system that had simply transplanted the poor from rented farm to mill floor, where the pressure of the production schedule no longer even allowed the time to tend a modest garden and the rock-bottom wages meant keeping a family milk cow or chickens an unaffordable luxury. Corn meal, fat back, syrup, and coffee—not fresh beef, eggs, milk, fruits, and vegetables—graced the poor southerner's table.[27]

In July 1921, the politics of pellagra spilled onto the front pages of newspapers around the country. A fuming South Carolina Congressman Jimmy Byrnes complained to President Warren G. Harding that statements attributed to the U.S. Public Health Service (he did not mention Goldberger by name) about a dramatic spike in pellagra mortality in the South, perhaps as many as a hundred thousand deaths, was not true and threatened to have a deleterious effect on the South's reputation and economy.[28] Byrnes growled, "We may be oversensitive, but the average American dislikes to have placed in front of his door a flag indicating the presence of plague, when . . . there exists within his home nothing to justify that characterization. And likewise, when there is no famine he dislikes to be held up as the object of charity, and compared with the 'unfortunates of other lands' for the relief of whose starvation and disease our people have so generously contributed [during and after World War I]."[29] Livid, Byrnes demanded that Harding take action against those he believed had misrepresented the situation to the president. Instead, Harding, who is often better remembered for his sexual trysts than his staunch loyalty to any but his poker partners, stood by the Public Health Service and the words of its zealous, if impolitic, epidemiologist.[30]

Byrnes was not the only angry southern politician. Other senators and congressmen leaped to the South's defense. Georgia Congressman William C. Wright proclaimed that there was no "grim and gaunt spectre of famine . . . walking abroad in the Empire State of the South." Tennessee's Senator Kenneth McKellar carried an invitation from the state's public health officer. He said that all the fearful should come see how healthy Tennesseans treated the rumor of famine. Tennessee, he said, was prepared to ship beef, pork, poultry, and mill to its poorer neighbors should they need it.[31]

Support for the PHS and Harding came from the African American community. James Weldon Johnson, Harlem Renaissance writer and a founder of the NAACP, blasted what he called "The Super-Sensitive South," a section that "offers an interesting field of investigation by both psychologists and pathologists." What especially rankled Johnson was a statement made by R. W. Hall, the statistician of the Mississippi Board of Health, who said, "Of the 2239 cases shown in the June [1921] morbidity report, fully eighty percent are among Negroes chiefly in the Delta section. "John denounced the remark as "absurd" because even if all the cases in Mississippi were "among Negroes," it would be "just as damaging to the health and safety of the State and its population. We wonder whether if smallpox was raging in Jackson [Mississippi], the statistician of the State would say, 'I can see nothing whatever in the situation to cause alarm because eighty percent of the cases are Negroes.'"[32]

A PHS-sponsored conference in Washington, D.C., in August 1921 brought together state public health officers, agricultural experts, and relief agencies to plan an aid program for those felled by pellagra. Instead of being constructive, the session degenerated into little more than an opportunity for southerners to evince their anger. Goldberger explained how the figure of potentially one hundred thousand cases of pellagra had been derived, denying that this was an estimate of deaths, as mistakenly reported by the press. However, little progress was made in convincing some southerners that pellagra was an increasing menace to the public's health as cotton prices declined.[33] Goldberger remained wildly impatient with those who refused to accept his dietary theory of pellagra and loudly condemned the South's economic system. Perhaps because he had seen poverty up close as a child on New York's Lower East Side, Goldberger could not understand how southerners could fail to change a system that caused such suffering.

As Goldberger's laboratory research progressed, events offered him ample opportunity to aid those stricken with pellagra and to criticize the South's leadership. Having learned that small amounts of brewer's yeast prevented pellagra and could also cure the disease, Goldberger and Edgar Sydenstricker responded to the needs of southerners who were menaced by pellagra when the Mississippi River overflowed its banks in 1927. During the great Mississippi Flood, Goldberger and Sydenstricker went South.[34]

In Mississippi, where Goldberger was known and celebrated because of the Rankin experiment, his impending visit made the front page of the *Jackson Daily News*. On July 25, 1927, the main headline read "DELTA IN GRIP OF NEW MENACE FROM PELLAGRA." Right beneath it was the subhead line, "Poor Diet Causes Wide Spread of Disease, Goldberger Coming."[35] The man some southerners once saw as bearing the unwelcome message that diet, not microbes, was at the root of the pellagra problem was now described by the press as the "World's renowned authority on pellagra."

Pulling no punches, the physician and the statistician later wrote of what they saw during the flood.[36] The tenant farming system and the low price of cotton in 1926 would have caused an increase in pellagra even without the flood. However, the overflow had made matters worse. The number of milk cows was decreased by drowning or sale by owners. Inadequate food for the cows meant less milk as well. Fresh meat and eggs were rare because home-owned poultry was drowned, and the supply of fresh vegetables was diminished by gardens that were flooded or not planted until late in the season. Even before the flood, impoverished tenants were existing on a 3m diet—meat, meal, and molasses. Such fare was all but guaranteed to yield a bumper crop of pellagra. In addition to sending large amounts of brewer's yeast to the South, Goldberger again lambasted the land distribution system and the unwillingness of southern politicians to admit the problem and advocate change. According to Goldberger, husband of the grandniece of the Confederacy's first family, science could not readily undo the damage of history and human greed in the South.[37]

In 1928, Goldberger fell gravely ill. Speaking in public for the last time, he reminded his listeners that medical science alone could never remedy social conditions, adding that "the problem of pellagra is in the main a problem of poverty." Near the end of his life, Goldberger was disappointed that identifying pellagra as a problem of poverty simply did not suffice to win the cooperation of southerners, those he most wanted to help. In his autobiography, popular science writer Paul De Kruif describes an interview with the sick, fragile Goldberger. As they parted company outside the red brick Hygienic Laboratory, De Kruif quotes Goldberger as saying that "Pellagra is only ignorance; pellagra is only poverty," but then adding, "You understand De Kruif, I'm no economist, I'm only a doctor."[38]

If Goldberger faced the end of his life thinking himself a failure, others did not. Dr. Joseph Goldberger died of hypernephroma, a rare form of cancer, on January 17, 1929. He was fifty-six. Goldberger's remains were cremated and his ashes sprinkled over the Potomac River as Rabbi Abram Simon of the Washington Hebrew Congregation chanted the Kaddish.[39]

Obituaries and letters of condolence poured into the Goldberger household. A special bill was passed by Congress to provide Mary Goldberger with a pension, as had been done for the widows of those who died in Cuba investigating yellow fever. Philanthropist Julius Rosenwald, who had made his fortune with Sears, Roebuck & Company, and provided so much philanthropy to the South, visited the widow and offered financial support for the children's educations.[40]

Southern newspapers, as well as those in Washington and New York, eulogized Goldberger. In Columbia, South Carolina, the announcement made the front page. In Natchez, Mississippi, the *Democrat* told readers, "Dr. Goldberger

Who Conquered Palagra [*sic*] Dead." In the state capital of Jackson, where Gold-berger had worked with orphan children and persuaded Earl Brewer to gamble with his political career, the *Daily Clarion-Ledger* said of him, "Civilization owes a debt of gratitude to this soldier of science who attacked and conquered an unknown enemy." In New Orleans, Mary's hometown, the *Times-Picayune* ran a picture of her husband and a long article.[41]

The Yiddish language press in New York mourned, as well. Always seeking news of a Jewish American hero to demonstrate the loyalty of immigrants toward their adopted home, editors embraced the Goldberger story and made his demise front-page news. *Forverts* (*Jewish Daily Forward*), the most popular of such newspapers, lauded him as a "discoverer of important remedies" and a "martyr to science."[42]

Goldberger's work continued without him. Not long afterwards, researchers identified nicotinic acid, or niacin, as the nutrient missing from pellagrins' diets. In 1937, researchers working with Conrad A. Elvehjem discovered that a deficiency of nicotinic acid (a precursor of niacin) caused black tongue in dogs, the canine equivalent of pellagra. Dr. Tom Spies used nicotinic acid to treat pellagra patients in Cincinnati and Alabama. State laws mandating the enrichment of certain foods sold in the United States with niacin, among other nutrients, has all but ended the threat of pellagra here, although there are rare outbreaks in parts of Asia and Africa.[43]

The passage of years has not diminished the respect with which southerners hold the New York Jewish immigrant who not only understood their pain but wanted desperately to relieve it through social change. In 1964, the Mississippi Department of Archives and History erected a metal sign near Whitfield Road outside Jackson, Mississippi. On it is the doctor's name, and under that the following inscription: "Dr. Joseph Goldberger found the cause and cure for pellagra near here at the Rankin Farm of the Miss. State Penitentiary. His research identified the nutritional deficiencies which cause pellagra."[44] By the 1990s the sign was rusted and pock marked by bullet holes, the product of locals needing a target for practice, no doubt. While not completely correct—Goldberger did not discover that the cause of pellagra is a niacin deficiency, nor was the Rankin experiment the conclusion of his investigation—the sign's presence speaks to a different truth, the influence that an immigrant from south of the Carpathian Mountains, raised near the southern tip of Manhattan, had on the American South and the complex feelings of affection and alienation that characterized

Goldberger's feelings toward the region. It is hardly surprising that a Jew in the diaspora, whose family wandered to America in flight from poverty and who found yet more poverty on the streets of the Lower East Side, could emerge from the tragedy of his people's history to so clearly comprehend that the suffering of poor southerners, white and black, was a legacy of poverty resulting from the "historical disasters" of southerners' "ancestral pasts."

Not many blocks from the Goldberger grocery store on Pitt Street lived another Jewish immigrant family whose son would find challenge and inspiration in the early twentieth century South. Rose Bruskin and Moshe (later Morris) Gershovitz were Russian Jews who emigrated and later met in New York, marrying in 1895. Morris had become a skilled leather worker abroad and continued that trade as the young couple began their family above a shop on the corner of Hester and Eldridge streets. Their first child, Isadore (later Ira) was born in 1896 at the Hester Street address. However, a job in Brooklyn took Morris and Rose to a tree-lined street in Brooklyn where Jacob (later George) Gershowitz (Gershwine on the birth certificate and later Gershwin) was born in 1898. Two other siblings followed, a son, Arthur, in 1900 and a daughter, Frances, in 1906. The name changes suggest the family's effort to negotiate a comfortable identity in their new country. Many newcomers feared that their names would either be difficult for the American tongue or too easily identify them as recently arrived aliens.[45]

Almost from the beginning, George Gershwin loved music. Never a scholar, the child was drawn to performance at an early age. His mother purchased an upright piano because she regarded pianos as marks of refinement in the home. From the moment workmen hauled it via pulleys through the apartment's front window, twelve-year-old George sat down and played, showing a facility beyond his brother Ira, who was the more disciplined music student.

Small, wiry and mischievous, George Gershwin had little use for school, but was early drawn into the world of popular entertainment. In the summer of 1915, while Joseph Goldberger's Rankin experiment was in progress, Gershwin got his first musical engagement in one of the Catskill Mountains resorts that comprised the "Borscht Belt," where Jewish businessmen and workers alike vacationed when they could afford it.

Young George Gershwin was getting serious about music and took formal lessons from pianist Charles Hambitzer, who had come to New York from Wisconsin. However, when Hambitzer's personal circumstances forced him to curtail teaching, Gershwin went off on his own. Resisting family efforts to make him an accountant, the practical path taken by many a Jewish lad from an immigrant family, Gershwin dropped out of high school and proclaimed himself a musician.

Gershwin's career began humbly, as a piano player at fifteen dollars per week in New York's Tin Pan Alley, the block of West Twenty-eighth Street between Fifth and Sixth avenues. In the days before the widespread availability of recorded sound, song pluggers were singer pianists who played the sheet music being sold in their shops so that potential customers could hear the tunes before they bought it to play at home. Sheet music was a crucial aspect of a music business that catered to family parlors, vaudeville shows, and musical theater alike. Those who heard a song played by a favorite performer could buy it directly from the music publisher. Publishers competed vigorously and with few scruples, though most proprietors knew little about the product they peddled. Songwriters made very meager wages but were required to churn out whatever their employers thought would sell. Whether it was songs derived from the minstrel tradition, "mammy songs," sung on stage by white performers in black face crooning a tribute to the black women who supposedly had raised them, or imitations of ragtime, or love ballads, what mattered was that customers were willing to buy. This was where George Gershwin found his entry-level position, working for Jerome H. Remick and Company.[46]

In Tin Pan Alley, so named, tradition has it, because the din of so many pianists playing so many different songs simultaneously sounded like the banging of tin pans, George met lyricists such as Irving Caesar with whom he collaborated on "Swanee," a "mammy song" made famous by Al Jolson. Meanwhile, George's brother Ira was making it through New York's famed tuition-free City College. However, Ira, too, was drawn to a career in music—as a lyricist—and soon joined his brother in the trade. Success came slowly, but on the road George Gershwin met and was influenced by those he idolized, such as composers Victor Herbert and Jerome Kern. In 1915 he met the young Fred Astaire.

Between 1915 when he wrote his first popular song, "Since I lost You," and 1923 when he wrote "Rhapsody in Blue," boldly bringing jazz rhythms into the concert hall, George Gershwin's talent exploded. He wrote song after song for show after show. Not all were major hits, but the overall effect was to make Gershwin a popular music success. He became one of the most important figures in American show business and aspired to be recognized as a classical composer as well as a writer of memorable show tunes. Gershwin composed "Concerto in F" (1925), "Preludes for Piano" (1926), "An American in Paris" (1928), "Second Rhapsody" (1931), "Cuban Overture," and *George Gershwin's Songbook*, his piano transcriptions of eighteen songs (1932), establishing him in the eyes of many as a serious composer. All echoed his commitment to jazz as the crucial ingredient in American music. He told a reporter, "There can be no question but that jazz is the first real American music. When you look into any other kind you find the influence of some other country, but not so in jazz."[47] He yearned to expand his range of creations and try a jazz opera. Could he find a story with the plot and characters that could be transformed into lyrics and music?

Gershwin's first inclination was to look to his heritage in Eastern Europe. He went so far as to sign a contract with the general manager of the Metropolitan Opera in 1929 to write an opera based on *The Dybbuk*, a play by Shloyme Zanvl Rappoport, known to most by his pen name, Szymon Ansky. Originally writing in Russian in 1914, Ansky penned a Yiddish version as well. Based on a Hasidic folktale, *The Dybbuk* told the story of a couple betrothed before their birth, Chanon and Leah. However, when Leah's father forbids the marriage because Chanon is a poor student, the groom falls away from God and dies, entering his beloved's spirit as a dybbuk, or migrant soul. Following a failed exorcism, Leah also dies so that her soul can merge with Chanon's. The play enjoyed success in English, Yiddish, and Hebrew. Gershwin was fascinated by the mysticism and the operatic possibility of all the changes in voice as the evil spirit speaks through the two young people. However, by the end of 1929, Gershwin had to abandon the project because the rights for the play's operatic adaptation had already been granted to an Italian composer, Lodovico Rocca.[48]

Gershwin's early biographer Isaac Goldberg noted that, as Gershwin worked on *The Dybbuk*, he had become "increasingly conscious of the similarity between the folk song of the Negro and of the Polish [Hasidic] pietists."[49] Gershwin considered the African American experience exciting and provocative because it was outside the American mainstream. A friend, Emily Palely, observed, "George saw blacks and Jews as being the same in relation to the rest of American society." Both were outsiders, who had migrated, willingly or unwillingly, from countries and cultures vastly different from that of the United States.[50]

Cultural critic Morris Dickstein has observed that, in the 1920s, "Ragtime, jazz, tap dancing, syncopated rhythms, blues singing—everything that could be borrowed from Negro culture—seemed more hip, less inhibited, more directly sexual, just as minor chords lifted from Jewish or Russian music seemed more soulful." Today, he observes, "this effacement and appropriation of Negro culture has its scandalous side, like the nightclubs in Harlem . . . where blacks held the stage, but couldn't join the audience." Still, Dickstein contends that many who "borrowed, adapted, and softened the black idiom genuinely loved it, and saw themselves as bringing its thrilling and unconventional energies into the mainstream." Many of those who appropriated what was black were Jewish, and their embrace of black culture, even blackface performance, was "especially intense, perhaps because, like them, it stood outside the emotional rhythms and hierarchies of white Protestant culture."[51]

In an article on Aaron Copland, Isaac Goldberg, eventually Gershwin's biographer, called the jazz of the era "musical miscegenation," the "musical amalgamation of the American Negro and the American Jew."[52] Indeed, Dickstein suggests that, rather than seeing themselves as engaged in cultural thievery, these composers and performers saw themselves as "popularizers of black rhythms." Certainly that is how Gershwin understood what he was doing.[53] "Swanee," written early in his career, was a vestige of the low form of Tin Pan Alley tune then in demand. Certainly it was out of character for the later Gershwin. Instead, Gershwin's one-act Harlem opera, *Blue Monday*, written with Buddy DeSylva for George White's *Scandals* (1922), but dropped after the first performance, was a precursor to the jazz opera produced thirteen years later, *Porgy and Bess*.[54]

As with so many other white artists and writers, Gershwin's introduction to African American artistic accomplishment, especially the writers, artists, and musicians of the Harlem Renaissance, was via the white novelist, photographer, and music critic, Carl Van Vechten. Described by one Gershwin biographer as a midwesterner and married homosexual who was primarily a "Jazz Age purveyor of urban chic," Van Vechten championed African art "to the point that he himself emerged as a central figure of the Harlem Renaissance."[55] Gershwin grew especially close to two brothers, James Weldon Johnson and J. Rosamond Johnson. Before the former became the fiery writer scolding the South's reaction to Dr. Joseph Goldberger's prediction of a rise in pellagra mortality in the early 1920s, he was his brother's partner in a songwriting team not unlike the Gershwins. Attorney James Weldon was a scholar and a lyricist; J. Rosamond was the composer. Their song "Lift Every Voice and Sing" is still regarded by many as a kind of national anthem for African Americans. After 1906, J. Rosamond pursued a musical career while James Weldon's interests veered into diplomacy, poetry, social criticism, and activism. James Weldon became a professor of literature at Fisk University. It was Gershwin's sense of the otherness of African Americans that attracted him to a novel written by a white southerner, DuBose Heyward, about the black experience in the American South. James Weldon Johnson was an avid fan of DuBose Heyward's novel *Porgy* and was present to celebrate Heyward when the book's stage adaptation was produced on Broadway. Although Gershwin was not present when Heyward was feted at Van Vecten's home in 1926 on the occasion of *Porgy*'s success, by then he had already read and appreciated the novel.[56]

George Gershwin wanted to write a jazz opera, and as with all his operetta projects, he wanted his full-length opera "to represent the life and spirit of the country." Years before he negotiated for the *Dybbuk*, Gershwin pondered the possibility of a jazz opera which would be "a Negro opera, almost a Negro 'Scheherazade.' Negro, because it is not incongruous for a Negro to live jazz. It would not be absurd on stage. The mood could change from ecstasy to lyricism plausibly because the Negro has so much of both in his nature." At first Gershwin projected something "whimsical" and thought that Carl Van Vechten could do the libretto. It "could not, I am afraid, be done at the Metropolitan [Opera]. It is a typically opéra comique venture." Gershwin envisioned this opera on Broadway. "I would like to see it put on with a Negro cast. Artists trained in the old tradition could not sing such music, but Negro singers could. It would be a sensation as well as an innovation."[57]

Gershwin's desire to do a serious opera converged with his belief in a jazz opera that could be based upon DuBose Heyward's 1925 novel, *Porgy*.[58] By chance both Gershwin and Heyward found themselves in Atlantic City in November 1927 and decided to discuss the possibility of turning *Porgy* into an opera, the kind that could be performed at the Met.

Edwin DuBose Heyward, who went by his middle name, was born in 1885 and grew up in Charleston, South Carolina. He was descended from Thomas Heyward Jr., who had signed the Declaration of Independence. Young Dubose, as he was known, was a Charleston insurance and real estate salesman, but with a deep interest in literature and writing. When he was financially able, he abandoned sales for stories. In 1922 he married Dorothy, whom he met at a writer's colony; they pursued their writing careers, supported by wages Heyward earned from teaching at a local military academy.

Heyward was fascinated by the lives of blacks in Charleston, especially those descended from the Gullah tribe, who were brought from Angola and still spoke and sang with the intonations of the Gullah dialect. Heyward's mother was an amateur folklorist and participated in a singing society that performed Gullah songs. Dubose joined her occasionally. Inspired by characters in the local African American community, Heyward published *Porgy* in 1925. In the South it was not unusual for whites to write about blacks, but usually in unflattering stereotypes that emphasized characteristics of stupidity, laziness, or lasciviousness. Heyward's biographer referred to *Porgy* as "the first major Southern novel to present blacks realistically, rather than in the stereotyped roles of happy darkies or loyal body servants."[59] Poet Langston Hughes, no stranger to play writing and a giant of the Harlem Renaissance, described Heyward as one who "saw with his white eyes, wonderful poetic qualities in the inhabitants of Catfish Row that makes them come alive."[60] It was Dorothy Heyward who adopted her husband's novel for the stage.

Heyward's novel is set in a community of southern blacks on South Carolina's Catfish Row, a fictional community that Heyward created by figuratively superimposing a tenement borrowed from the agricultural marketplace near his home onto a fictitious waterfront. The novel was inspired by a lame black beggar and seller of peanut cakes, Samuel Smalls, known in Charleston as "Goat Sammy" because he transported himself on an inverted soapbox pulled by a goat. Sammy had been held on two aggravated assault charges for attempting to shoot a woman. The dichotomy between Sammy's crushed body and his moments of towering passion fascinated Heyward. The name "Porgy" that Heyward used in the novel was originally "Porgo," after an African wooden doll in one of the Gullah stories that fascinated Heyward's mother. However, before publication the name was changed to Porgy, after a local fish and the well-known fishmongers' call, "Porgy in the Summer-time!"[61] The name may also have originated with Captain Porgy, the main character in *Woodcraft*, a popular antebellum novel written by Charleston author William Gilmore Simms.

In the novel, Porgy is a crippled beggar who befriends Bess, a starving, drunk, and gaunt young woman looking for her muscular stevedore lover, Crown. The latter has been arrested for killing a fellow gambler in a brawl occasioned by a game of craps. An octoroon cocaine peddler in fancy attire, Sporting Life, who has worked as a waiter in New York, also arrives on Catfish Row. Bess is jailed after she takes cocaine from Sporting Life. After her release, she falls ill and is cared for by Porgy until she is well. Crown accosts Bess and attempts a seduction, and when he breaks into Porgy's room at night in pursuit of Bess, Porgy kills him. When a frightened Porgy refuses to identify Crown's body, he is imprisoned for contempt of court. Porgy finally returns to Catfish Row only to learn that Bess has been abducted by a gang of stevedores. The novel ends with Porgy having been aged by the episode, losing the joy and satisfaction that he had known so briefly during his summer with Bess.

After agreeing to collaborate, Heyward and Gershwin changed the plot to accommodate the opera.[62] Among the changes was a new conclusion. At the end of the opera, Bess would leave with Sporting Life for New York and Porgy, deeply in love with her, would attempt to follow her in his goat cart, no matter how long the journey. Heyward's work even in the 1920s was not without controversy. Was Heyward a racist who regarded blacks as inherently inferior in their morals and behavior? Or had he overcome crude stereotypes to depict African Americans as human beings in all their complexity, retaining traditions from their past that were now threatened by the mass migration of blacks to cities, especially those in the North, and the stress of confronting modernity there? His biographer characterized Heyward as a man who, in the course of his life, experienced a transformation of his beliefs, "from social conservatism to a liberal, although nonrevolutionary advocacy of black rights—a man who developed a social conscience through writing . . . neither completely an apologist for the Old South nor a propagandist for the New South."[63]

Heyward still heard ties to the African homeland in the black music of the Low Country, writing, "We can still hear the Negro singing the songs of his own creation. We can see him hale, vigorous, and glad under the sun by day, and at night surrounded by wide, still fields and mood-drenched marshes. We watch him with his family, his unquestioning belief in a personal God, his spontaneous abandonment to emotion, his faith in his simple destiny."[64]

Whatever DuBose Heyward heard, George Gershwin wanted to hear it as well. After they agreed to do the opera together, Heyward kept urging Gershwin to spend time in South Carolina and to work with him closely so that they might move ahead expeditiously. In late November 1933, Gershwin wrote to Heyward that he would stop briefly in Charleston on his way to Florida: "I would like to see the town and hear some spirituals and perhaps go to a colored café or two if there are any."[65] Indicative of how unusual it was for white artists to cross the color line was a Charleston newspaper report in early December that Gershwin and Heyward "went to a negro church and listened to the singing."[66]

Early the following year, Heyward wrote to Gershwin of his own efforts to move from the stage production to the opera with greater authenticity. For Heyward, the project was becoming almost an exercise in cultural anthropology; he hoped to "cut out the concentrated negro vaudeville stuff that was in the original play and incorporated material that is authentic and pleanty [sic] 'hot' as well. I have discovered for the first time a type of secular dance that is done here that is starlight from the African phallic dance, and that is undoubtedly a complete survival. Also, I have seen that native band of harmonicas, combs, etc. It will make an extraordinary introduction to the primitive scene of passion between Crown and Bess."[67]

Finally, in the late spring of 1934, Gershwin came South for a month. His intention was to compose after absorbing the rhythms and emotion of Gullah music. Other than the resorts of Florida, Gershwin had spent little time in the South, and the prospect of doing without the comforts to which he had become accustomed likely did not excite him. Gershwin, a brash and egocentric genius, rented a beach house on Folly Island, a popular beach getaway for many South Carolinians, including Jews; there was even a Jewish delicatessen on the island.[68] Jews had lived in Charleston since 1695. By 1800, the largest Jewish community in America lived there, and the oldest synagogue in America, K.K. Beth Elohim, was founded in Charleston. Gershwin, then, was hardly the first Jew in South Carolina, even if at times he talked and behaved as if he were.

Gershwin brought with him his valet, Paul Mueller, and his cousin Henry Botkin, an artist interested in painting southern scenes. After encountering Gershwin on the beach, Abe Dumas, a local Jewish college student, was hired to help with the driving. The boys were playing stickball when, Dumas recalled, "this guy came up and was walking down the beach in a pair of cut-off pants. This was before the days of attractive Bermudas. You took old pants and took a scissor or knife and cut 'em off. And he had about a ten-day growth of beard and I said, 'Do you know the game?' He said, 'Yes, I'm from Brooklyn, New York.' I said 'Get out in the field.'" He did just that and later invited the boys to dinner at his beach home, where black servants served "a lovely dinner with wine and whatever." Later, Gershwin "entertained his guests on the piano."[69]

Writing to relatives, Henry Botkin described Folly Beach: "It is very lovely here 12 miles from Charleston—on [a] real South Sea Island covered with palms & very primitive. Sharks & porpoises & great turtles a few yards ahead of us—& Negroes & cabin plantations—alligators & all just back of us—we have been dined and wined all over and have [made] all sorts of trips to churches of the colored folk & plantations, etc."[70] When the month at the beach was over, Botkin wrote, the Gershwin party would head for the Heywards' new home in Hendersonville to work more on their opera before Gershwin and his entourage returned North.

For the local white community, Gershwin's arrival at Folly Beach was an occasion, and a reporter was assigned by the local newspaper to cover his visit. In the glamour department, Gershwin did not disappoint. The reporter described the New York visitor as "tanned, muscular, dark, wearing a light palm beach sport coat and an orange tie" and as "playing jazz as it has never been played at Folly before." Noting that the composer had "spent almost all his life in or near New York city," the reporter was quick to note Gershwin's own tongue-in-cheek observation as to the contrast to his life at Folly Beach: "I have never lived in such a back to nature place. . . . At home I get up about noon. Here I will get up every morning at 7 o'clock—well at 7:30 o'clock, anyway." In response to the reporter's question, Gershwin said that what had most impressed him the previous December when he was in Charleston was an "experience service" at the Macedonia Church where a woman stood up and sang, "Oh, Dr. Jesus—Put your hands around my waist, And give me a belly-band of faith."[71] Jokes about his urbanism aside, George Gershwin was in search of the South's soul, especially the dimension of it that resided in the breasts of black southerners.

Several weeks later, the reporter returned to find a somewhat different Gershwin. "Bare and black above the waist, an inch of hair bristling from his face, and with a pair of tattered knickers furnishing a sole connecting link with civilization, George Gershwin composer of jazz, music and jazz music, has gone native." Telling the reporter, "I have become acclimated," Gershwin then "ran a hand experimentally through a crop of dark matted hair which had not had the benefit of being combed for many, many days." He confessed, "You know it's so pleasant here that it's really a shame to work." Joking that Gershwin could play Crown, the reporter chortled, "Two weeks at Folly Beach made a different Gershwin from the sleek creator of 'Rhapsody in Blue' and Concerto in F.' . . . Naturally brown, he is now black. Naturally sturdy, he is now sturdier."[72]

Gershwin and Heyward were spending every afternoon together working. Gershwin explained, "We are attempting to have an opera that is serious and dramatic. . . . The whites will speak their lines, but the Negroes will sing throughout. I hope that the audience will get the idea. With the colored people there is always a song, see? They find something to sing about somewhere. The whites are dull and drab." Gershwin's only complaint was that local amateur composers kept bringing him their pieces to play, and he found most of them "very bad—very, very bad."[73]

DuBose Heyward later described Gershwin's encounter with black life in Charleston as "more like a homecoming than an exploration." He recalled that one night, "at a Negro meeting on a remote sea-island, George started 'shouting' with them, and eventually to their huge delight stole the show from their champion shouter.'" Gershwin later said that, after the shouting ended, an elderly man clapped him on the back and said, "By God, you sure can beat out them rhythms, boy. I'm over seventy years old and I ain't never seen no po' little white man take off and fly like you. You could be my own son."[74] After Gershwin's death, his dear friend Kay Swift met a Macedonian church member who recalled that Gershwin had "come often to sing with them and that he always spoke to them when he came."[75]

Porgy and Bess opened in Boston on September 30, 1935, with an all-black cast featuring Todd Duncan and Anne Brown in starring roles. It was a hit but, at over three hours in length, it had to be cut. The version that opened at the Alvin Theater on Broadway on October 10, 1935, was sleeker and well received, but views were mixed. Some thought it lacked correct operatic technique and was still a bit too Broadway to succeed as grand opera. Some reviews were tinged with a decidedly anti-Semitic tone. Virgil Thomson, who had collaborated with Gertrude Stein on an all-black opera, *Four Saints in Three Acts*, which at least one historian has described as "incomprehensible," wrote that Gershwin's Tin Pan Alley past ill prepared him for opera because the former was material "straight from the melting pot. At best it is a highly unsavory stirring up of Israel, Africa, and the Gaelic Isles." As for *Porgy and Bess*, Thomson wrote, "I don't like fake folklore, nor fidgety accompaniments, nor bittersweet harmony nor six-part choruses, nor gefilte fish orchestration." Although Thomson acknowledged that Gershwin was gifted, he denounced the composer as not really knowing what opera was, stating "The most authentic thing about it all is George Gershwin's sincere desire to write an opera, a real opera that somebody might remember."[76] Gershwin foolishly answered his critics in *The New York Times*, writing "I am not ashamed of writing songs at any time so long as they are good songs." and compared his work to Verdi's *Carmen*, which also had "song hits."[77]

However, another of Thomson's criticisms struck a deeper chord. Thomson observed that "Folklore subjects recounted by an outsider are only valid as long as the folk in question is unable to speak for itself, which is certainly not true of the American Negro in 1935."[78] Duke Ellington also thought Gershwin did not do justice to the black musical idiom, though he later claimed that the many negative views of Gershwin attributed to him were misquotations by an interviewer. It is clear that, much as he liked the score, he did not regard it as distinctly African American in character.[79] Another journalist entered the fray, observing that neither Ellington nor William Grant, an African American composer, "could have written anything like 'Porgy and Bess,' however, because they are too close to the life pictured in that opera. It took a cosmopolitan Jew to give it perspective. It requires a forceful sophisticated representative of the same race to make jazz song writing meet high brow composers on their own terms." To this journalist for the Los Angeles Times, Gershwin had done "the natural thing in expressing the exiled and persecuted two races in music. Only in America could it be realized. 'Porgy and Bess' is genuine American opera, when viewed from that standpoint. It is a true combination of Hollywood and Harlem."[80] More recently, the African American cultural critic Stanley Crouch rejected African American criticisms of Gershwin for "stealing" from blacks as falling flat on its "lewdy duty," attributing derogatory remarks about Gershwin to "an extremely complicated history fundamental to the tale of Negroes and Jews in show business. It is a story of alliance, animosity, success, failure, exploitation, transcending friendships and on-going shifts of attitude and economic position."[81]

The news from the box office was bad. The opera closed after 124 performances and lost about seventy thousand dollars, a great deal of money during the Great Depression. Gershwin's own share of the box office receipts was insufficient to even cover the cost of copying the score.[82]

Two years later, on July 11, 1937, George Gershwin died of a brain tumor. He was thirty-nine. His large corpus of work is considered by many as one of the most important in the history of American music. An obituary for Gershwin in the Los Angeles Examiner quoted his observations on his own music and its origins: "My people are Americans; my time is today. No composer knows what the future of music will disclose, but to be true music, it must reflect the thoughts and hopes of the people of the times."[83] Porgy and Bess has gained in recognition in the many decades since Gershwin's death to become perhaps the most beloved American opera ever written. It is performed at the Metropolitan Opera in New York and at opera houses all over the world. The composer from a New York Jewish immigrant family had found in the novel of a white southerner and the Gullah music of South Carolina a vestige of the black slave experience in America. He reminded the world of the cultural richness that was the legacy of the South's "historical disaster," a fragment of its "ancestral past" that ought to be a fixed part of American culture.

Physician Joseph Goldberger and composer George Gershwin each opened a window on southern life in the early twentieth century. Jews of immigrant heritage, raised in New York City, they were outsiders to Dixie but chose to know the South firsthand and tell others what they had learned. Each derived a view of life south of the Mason-Dixon Line that was nuanced and complex, seeing through the stereotypes to focus on individuals in their daily comings and goings.

Just as Joseph Goldberger refused to accept the existence of a pellagra germ, so he refused to accept that there was no connection between how poor southerners lived and what made them sick or killed them. The notion that Goldberger shared with Paul De Kruif that "Pellagra is only ignorance; pellagra is only poverty," was anathema to many southerners, who were defensive about how their region was perceived by the rest of the nation.[84] Science and not slavish conformity to popular misconceptions, however politically convenient they might be, gave Goldberger an advantage over those southern investigators loathe to challenge the establishment that had nurtured them and of which they were charter members. What opened Goldberger's eyes? His knowledge of poverty and displacement came firsthand. Just as internal migration had brought southern farmers to the mills and changed their diets, international migration had brought his family from the sheep-grazing fields at the base of the Carpathian Mountains to the streets of New York City. The poverty that Goldberger witnessed in the South he well recognized because of the poverty that had surrounded him growing up on the Lower East Side.

Similarly, George Gershwin did not confine himself to his Manhattan apartment when composing *Porgy and Bess*. Because Gershwin listened to African American musicians, shouting in church with the faithful, he was able to portray the lives of black southerners with a poignancy that overrode the prejudice of white audiences. His collaboration with a white southerner and identification with the oppression suffered by black southerners allowed him to turn his opera into an American classic. Gershwin's family, too, had experienced a long-distance migration, and he, too, had witnessed the poverty of the New York tenements, which he could recreate in the tenement that DuBose Heyward had envisioned on Catfish Row.

An outsider's vision has its limitations. Goldberger never appreciated the reasons or historical origins of southern politicians' unwillingness to accept that poverty born of their system of land distribution required reform. Nor did he ever fully comprehend their refusal to accept that pellagra could be banished if only they would facilitate the access of even the poorest southerners to a balanced diet. George Gershwin resisted the opinions of critics who thought that he could never fully reveal the soul of the black musical experience, that collaborating with a white author and surrounding himself with an entourage of northern and southern Jews might conceal even more than it revealed about some of the realities of African American life in the South.

In the end, though, Goldberger and Gershwin, two sojourners from what immigrants called the "promised city," each aware of the "historical disasters" of their own "ancestral pasts" found themselves well positioned not just to observe, but to comprehend and respond to the hardships and cultural complexity characteristic of the ever mysterious and elusive American South.

NOTES

1. Moses Rischin, *The Promised City: New York's Jews, 1870–1914* (Cambridge, MA: Harvard University Press, 1962).

2. David M. Potter, *The South and the Sectional Conflict* (Baton Rouge: Louisiana State University Press, 1968), 4. More recently Potter's observation has been appropriated by Peter Kolchin for the incisive published version of his Walter Lynwood Fleming Lecture, *A Sphinx on the American Land: The Nineteenth-Century South in Comparative Perspective* (Baton Rouge: Louisiana State University Press, 2003), xi.

3. These themes are explored in Woodward's *The Burden of Southern History* (Baton Rouge: Louisiana State University Press, 1960). See especially the first essay in the volume, "The Search for Southern Identity." Woodward observes that, in contrast to the rest of the nation, "The South's preoccupation was with guilt, not with innocence, with the reality of evil, not with the dream of perfection" (21).

4. The historical literature on the Jews in the South has become increasingly rich. See Marcie Ferris Cohen and Mark I. Greenberg, eds., *Jewish Roots in Southern Soil: A New History* (Hanover, NH: University Press of New England, 2006); Mark K. Bauman, *Dixie Diaspora: An Anthology of Southern Jewish History* (Tuscaloosa: University of Alabama Press, 2006); and Theodore Rosengarten and Dale Rosengarten, eds., *A Portion of the People: Three Hundred Years of Southern Jewish Life*

(Columbia: University of South Carolina Press, 2002). A splendid personal perspective is Eli N. Evans, *The Provincials: A Personal History of Jews in the South* (New York; Free Press, 1973), and his later volume of essays, *The Lonely Days Were Sundays: Reflections of a Jewish Southerner* (Oxford: University of Mississippi Press, 1994). Evans also authored a valuable biography of an eminent Confederate, *Judah P. Benjamin, the Jewish Confederate* (New York: Free Press, 1989).

5. See Evans, *Judah P. Benjamin.*

6. Harry Golden, *Our Southern Landsman* (New York: G. P. Putnam's Sons, 1974).

7. Willie Morris, *North Toward Home* (New York: Dell Publishing Co., 1967),

8. Thomas Wolfe, *You Can't Go Home Again* (New York: Harper & Row, 1934), 392.

9. Ibid., 392–93.

10. Ibid., 393. Wolfe's biographer David Donald makes clear that "Wolfe was, in fact, anti-Semitic." Donald attributes the bias to Wolfe's upbringing in Asheville, North Carolina, where "As a child he was brought up to deride and torment the few Jewish families." Wolfe denied that he was anti-Semitic, claiming that he took pains to offer a nuanced, human portrait of Jews, one that was often quite sympathetic to their suffering and oppression. And, as in the case of many whose anti-Semitism haunts their thoughts and words, Wolfe counted many Jews among his personal friends. See David Herbert Donald, *Look Homeward: A Life of Thomas Wolfe* (Boston: Little Brown and Co., 1987).

11. The first historian to give the Frank case scholarly treatment was Leonard Dinnerstein in *The Leo Frank Case* (New York: Columbia University Press, 1968). Jeffrey Melnick explored the social implications of the case in *Black-Jewish Relations on Trial: Leo Frank and Jim Conley in the New South* (Jackson: University Press of Mississippi, 2000). The most comprehensive treatment of the case since the Alonzo Mann revelation of Jim Conley's guilt is Steve Oney, *And the Dead Shall Rise: The Murder of Mary Phagan and the Lynching of Leo Frank* (New York: Random House, 2004).

12. Lynching was a punishment that not only connoted public outrage at the crime, but in the postbellum South it indicated a special repugnance and social denigration of the victim. African Americans who had somehow violated the social norms imposed upon them by the white community were the most frequent targets of lynching. See Philip Dray, *At the Hands of Persons Unknown: The Lynching of Black America* (New York: Modern Library, 2003).

13. Much of the material on Dr. Joseph Goldberger has been excerpted from Alan M. Kraut, *Goldberger's War: The Life and Work of a Public Health Crusader* (New York: Hill and Wang, 2003). An almost daily correspondence between Joseph and his wife, Mary, is located in the Joseph Goldberger Papers in the Southern Historical Collection at the Wilson Library, University of North Carolina, Chapel Hill (hereafter Goldberger Papers).

14. Kraut, *Goldberger's War,* 13–41.

15. For a detailed account of the investigation, see Kraut, *Goldberger's War,* 28–31.

16. Edgar Howard Farrar to Dr. Jos. Goldberg [sic], telegram, February 16, 1906, and Edgar Howard Farrar to Goldberger, February 16, 1906, Goldberger Papers, box 1, folder 5.

17. Goldberger reported his Milledgeville results in Joseph Goldberger, C. H. Waring, and David G. Willets, "The Prevention of Pellagra: A Test Among Institutional Inmates," *Public Health Reports* 30, no. 43 (Oct. 1915): 3120–21. Also, Kraut, *Goldberger's War,* 97–119.

18. Goldberger diary, Jan. 21, 1915, Dewitt Stetten Jr. Museum of Medical Research, National Institutes of Health Historical Office, building 31, Bethesda, MD.

19. The letter is reproduced in Kraut, *Goldberger's War,* 125.

ALAN M. KRAUT

20. For discussions of southern progressivism and social reform, see Edward I. Ayers, *The Promise of the New South: Life after Reconstruction* (New York: Oxford University Press, 1992), 413–22, and William A. Link, *The Paradox of Southern Progressivism, 1880–1930* (Chapel Hill: University of North Carolina Press, 1992).

21. Joseph Goldberger and George A. Wheeler, "The Experimental Production of Pellagra in Human Subjects By Means of Diet," *Hygienic Laboratory Bulletin* 120 (Feb. 1920): 7–115.

22. W. H. Rucker to Brewer, Sept. 16, 1915, RG 27, box 390, folder 159, Mississippi State Archives.

23. W. J. MacNeal, "The alleged Production of Pellagra by an Unbalanced Diet, " *Journal of the American Medical Association* 61 (Mar. 25, 1916): 975–77. Also, Goldberger's response, "A Reply," *Journal of the American Medical Association* 61 (Mar. 25, 1916): 977.

24. Joseph Goldberger, "The Transmissibility of Pellagra: Experimental Attempts at Transmission to the Human Subject," *Public Health Reports* 31 (Nov. 17, 1916): 3159–73.

25. George Rosen, *A History of Public Health* (New York: MD Publications, Inc., 1958), 414.

26. Goldberger's and Sydenstricker's results were published in several articles, including Joseph Goldberger, G. A. Wheeler, and Edgar Sydenstricker, "A Study of the Relation of Diet to Pellagra Incidence in Seven Textile-Mill Communities of South Carolina in 1916," *Public Health Reports* 35 (Mar. 19, 1920): 648–714; Joseph Goldberger, G. A. Wheeler, and Edgar Sydenstricker, "Pellagra Incidence in Relation to Sex, Age, Season, Occupation and 'Disabling Sickness' in Seven Cotton-Mill Villages of South Carolina during 1916," *Public Health Reports* 35 (July 9, 1920): 1650–65; and Joseph Goldberger, G. A. Wheeler, and Edgar Sydenstricker, "A Study of the Relationship of Family income and Other Economic Factors to Pellagra Incidence in Seven Cotton-Mill Villages of South Carolina in 1916," *Public Health Reports* 35 (Nov. 12, 1920): 2673–2715. See also, Kraut, *Goldberger's War*, 152–71.

27. Kraut, *Goldberger's War*, 188–91.

28. *New York Times*, July 25, 1921.

29. Byrnes to Harding, July 27, 1921, and July 30, 1921, Warren G. Harding Papers, presidential case file 712, Pellagra, folder 1, Ohio Historical Society, Columbus. Also, Kraut, *Goldberger's War*, 191–99.

30. Harding to Farrand, July 25, 1921, Harding Papers. Harding to Cumming, July 25, 1921, RG90, file 1648, box 152c, National Archives.

31. Congressional Record, 67th Cong., 1st sess. (1921), 4428, 4398, 4478, 4367.

32. *New York Age*, Aug. 6, 1921.

33. Minutes of Conference of State Health Officers of the South, Aug. 4–5, 1921, 3–10, 64–66. RG 90, file 1648, National Archives.

34. Kraut, *Goldberger's War*, 216–21.

35. *Jackson* (Mississippi) *Daily News*, July 25, 1927.

36. Joseph Goldberger and Edgar Sydenstricker, "Pellagra in the Mississippi Flood Area," *Public Health Reports* 42 (Nov. 4, 1927): 2706–25.

37. Kraut, *Goldberger's War*, 218–31.

38. Paul De Kruif, *Hunger Fighters* (New York: Harcourt Brace, 1928), 369; Paul De Kruif, *The Sweeping Wind: A Memoir* (New York: Harcourt, Brace, & World, 1962), 132.

39. Kraut, *Goldberger's War*, 239–43.

40. Ibid., 245–48.

41. (Columbia , SC) *State,* Jan. 18, 1929; Natchez *Democrat,* Jan. 18, 1929; *Daily Clarion-Ledger,* Jan. 18, 1929; (New Orleans) *Times-Picayune,* Jan. 18, 1929.

42. *Forverts,* Jan. 18, 1929.

43. Kraut, *Goldberger's War,* 257–61.

44. Ibid., 4.

45. Over the years a number of biographies have told the story of George Gershwin's rise to musical eminence from his humble origins in New York City. Several excellent studies are Isaac Goldberg, *George Gershwin: A Study in American Music* (New York: Frederick Unger Publishing Co., 1958}; Edward Jablonski, *Gershwin: A Biography* (New York: Doubleday, 1987); Deena Rosenberg, *Fascinating Rhythm: The Collaboration of George and Ira Gershwin* (New York: Dutton, 1991); Ruth Leon, *Gershwin* (London: Haus Publishing, 2004); Howard Pollack, *George Gershwin: His Life and Work* (Berkeley: University of California Press, 20006); and Walter Rimler, *George Gershwin: An Intimate Portrait* (Urbana: University of Illinois Press, 2009). Also helpful are Edward Jablonski and Lawrence D. Stewart, *The Gershwin Years: George and Ira* (New York: Doubleday, 1958); and Robert Wyatt and John Andrew Johnson, eds., *The George Gershwin Reader* (New York: Oxford University Press, 2004).

46. Ruth Leon's *Gershwin* offers an especially clear description of the Tin Pan Alley scene. Historian Stephen J. Whitfield offers a perceptive account of Jewish composers' appreciation for the popularity of southern themes in the popular music produced in Tin Pan Alley. He observes that such composers offered listeners "an entirely fanciful South, which does not mean that it was utterly false, only that it was a fabrication." See Whitfield, "Is It True What They Sing about Dixie," *Southern Cultures* 8 (Summer 2002): 9–37.

47. *Charleston News and Courier,* Dec. 4, 1933.

48. Pollack, *George Gershwin,* 461–62.

49. Goldberg, *George Gershwin,* 41.

50. Emily Paley as quoted by Pollack, *George Gershwin,* 463.

51. Morris Dickstein, *Dancing in the Dark: A Cultural History of the Great Depression* (New York: Norton, 2009), 367.

52. Quoted by Michael Rogin, "Blackface, White Noise: The Jewish Jazz Singer Finds His Voice," *Critical Inquiry* 18 (Spring 1992): 437–38.

53. As musicologist Richard Crawford observes, Gershwin envisioned *Porgy and Bess* as a folk opera treating what the composer called the characteristics of "Negro Life in America," and for which he intended to convey respect. Crawford contends that Gershwin failed to see that the definitions of "the folk" and "race" were "contested and sensitive" in the 1930s. Gershwin knew that folk tales and songs were derived from a folk community of which he was not a member. However, he was reassured that he was not misrepresenting black folk traditions because, according to Crawford, Gershwin believed that "the operatic stage speaks to humankind at large through the mimetic medium of music. As a work of art, an opera makes its own truth transcending the conventions of its subject." Gershwin therefore did not worry about being an outsider or causing offense to the African American community. See Richard Crawford, "Where Did Porgy and Bess Come From?" *Journal of Interdisciplinary History* 36 (Spring 2006): 697–734.

54. Dickstein, *Dancing in the Dark,* 367–68.

55. Pollack, *George Gershwin,* 101.

56. Ibid., 105–6.

57. Gershwin as quoted in Pollack, *George Gershwin,* 567.

58. Dubose Heyward, *Porgy* (New York: Doubleday, 1925).

59. James M. Hutchisson, *Dubose Heyward: A Charleston Gentleman and the World of Porgy and Bess* (Jackson: University Press of Mississippi, 2000), xiii.

60. Langston Hughes as quoted in John O. Killens, ed., *"Writers: Black and White," The American Negro Writer and His Roots: Selected Papers from the First Conference of Negro Writers, March, 1959* (New York: American Society of African Culture, 1960).

61. Pollack, *George Gershwin,* 570.

62. Hollis Alpert, *The Life and Times of Porgy and Bess: The Story of an American Classic* (New York: Alfred A. Knopf, 1990).

63. Hutchisson, *Dubose Heyward,* xix.

64. James M. Hutchisson, ed., *A Dubose Heyward Reader* (Athens: University of Georgia Press, 2003), 45.

65. Gershwin to Heyward, Nov. 25, 1933, box 64, folder 23, George and Ira Gershwin Papers, Library of Congress.

66. *Charleston News and Courier,* Dec. 4, 1933.

67. Heyward to Gershwin, Feb. 6, 1934, box 64, folder 24, Gershwin Papers.

68. Interview with Abe Dumas, Dec. 14, 1996. Transcript located in the Jewish Heritage Collection of the Archives of the College of Charleston.

69. Ibid.

70. Henry Botkin to Benjamin and Gertrude Botkin, July 3, 1934, box 63, folder 45, Gershwin Papers.

71. *Charleston News and Courier,* June 19, 1934.

72. Ibid., June 29, 1934.

73. Ibid.

74. Heyward and Gershwin quoted by Pollack, *George Gershwin,* 578.

75. Swift as quoted by Pollack, *George Gershwin,* 577.

76. Virgil Thomson, *A Virgil Thomson Reader* (Boston: Houghton Mifflin Co., 1981), 23–27. The essay was originally published in *Modern Music,* 1935.

77. *New York Times,* Oct. 20, 1935

78. Thomson, *Virgil Thomson Reader,* 26.

79. Edward Morrow, "Duke Ellington on Gershwin's 'Porgy,'" *New Theatre,* Dec. 1935, 5–6. Richard Mack, "Duke Ellington—in Person," *Orchestra World,* May 1936. Both are included in Mark Tucker, ed., *The Duke Ellington Reader* (New York: Oxford University Press, 1993), 114–18. An excellent discussion of reaction to *Porgy and Bess* in the African American community is Ray Allen and George P. Cunningham, "Cultural Uplift and Double-Consciousness: African American Responses to the 1935 Opera *Porgy and Bess,*" *The Musical Quarterly* 88 (2005): 342–69.

80. Isabelle Morse Jones, "Controversy Rages Over 'Porgy and Bess,'" *Los Angeles Times,* Feb. 21, 1937.

81. Stanley Crouch, "An Inspired Borrower of a Black Tradition," *New York Times,* Aug. 30, 1998.

82. Goldberg, *George Gershwin,* 332.

83. *Los Angeles Examiner,* July 12, 1937.

84. De Kruif, *The Sweeping Wind,* 132.

PART V

MEMORY
xxxxxxxxx AND THE xxxxxxxxx
AMERICAN CIVIL WAR

THE PSYCHOLOGY OF HATRED AND THE IDEOLOGY OF HONOR

XXXXXXXXXXXXXXXXXXXXXXXXXXXXXXXXXXXXXXXXXXXXXX

Current Parallels in Booth's Lincoln Conspiracies

BERTRAM WYATT-BROWN

For Americans at this hour, it is disturbing to think how easy, predictable, and tragic are the assassinations of individuals who become targets of ideological hatred, past and present. Most notably we have the case of Abraham Lincoln's murder in 1865. The story has been narrated and explored many times, but its pertinence today has become frighteningly relevant. Moreover, contemporary analogues exist between John Wilkes Booth's crimes and the climate of hatred that war and ideological rigidities engender whether they arose in the past or today. "Human beings," writes E. O. Wilson, "are strongly predisposed to respond to external threats with unreasoning hatred and to escalate their hostility sufficiently to overwhelm the source of the threat by a respectably wide margin of safety." In the United States, we have recently had news of an abortion physician slaughtered at his church in Kansas, a security guard killed at the entrance to the Holocaust Museum in Washington, women gunned down in a Pittsburgh, Pennsylvania, fitness center.[1]

In all these atrocities, a frustrated, unstable perpetrator—an anti-abortion extremist, a white supremacist, and an unbalanced man who hated all members of the opposite sex—demonized and dehumanized their victims. To these killers, the subjects of their fury represented all that was evil and threatening. Abroad, we face similarly destructive forces, especially in the Middle East. Inspired by a religious construction of hate and the ethic of honor, raging young men (and sometimes women) lay down their lives in bomb explosions. They seek to restore a lost sense of honor and empowerment and to reestablish stern and unforgiving Islamic traditions. Without exception each participant in these ideological imperatives hears only speakers and reads only pages that conform to already deeply embedded convictions. By wearing such blinders, they inoculate themselves from contrary opinions and pursue excessive means to overcome their enemies. As we shall see, John Wilkes Booth revealed psychological links with such driven souls when he fired at a sitting president. Today, Lincoln's most recent successor in that office and his legislative colleagues are greeted by large throngs. Some bear weapons at the ready. Many more entertain a tough-spoken determination to challenge administrative policies. No doubt, the Secret Service is vigilant. Yet weapons are as available today as they were when Booth brought his single-shot derringer into Lincoln's box at Ford's Theatre.

With these somber thoughts and references to current affairs in mind, we shall pursue the psychological factors that shed light on the nature of Booth's offense. First, his emotional temperament suggests how he selected his mission of vengeance against a hated foe. Second, the prevailing southern system of values to which Booth wholeheartedly subscribed will help to explain his motivations. As an actor, immersed in Shakespearean concerns with honor and revenge, Booth felt further justification in bringing the world of the stage into the contemporary political realm. Third, the climate and the activities of espionage, in which Booth was directly or indirectly involved, encouraged him to pursue his ultimate aim. Finally, we touch on the far-reaching effects that grew out of the national trauma. Rather than dwell on the assassination and the subsequent manhunt as well as the fate of the other conspirators, the purpose at hand is to apprehend Booth's personality, his theatrical model of violent action, and the milieu of conspiracies to which he dedicated himself. This analysis diverges from prior interpretations and offers a portrait of a brilliant but insecure figure whose actions at Ford's Theatre radically altered American history in a tragic way.

XXXXX

We begin with the career and character of John Wilkes Booth—his personality and ideological impulses. Booth had been born the ninth offspring in a family of ten on 10 May 1838. Adopting a Freudian approach, some writers before World War II argued that Booth's assault on the president was an act of patricide, motivated by an oedipal hatred of his father. Junius Brutus Booth was an English actor who had immigrated to the United States as a young man and sired ten children with his London-born mate. Philip Van Doren Stern, a New York editor and fiction writer, and psychiatrists Edward J. Kempf, George W. Wilson, and Francis Wilson took this position. Even the more responsible historian Stanley Kimmel, author of a family biography, followed the Freudian course. Each furnished different sources for substantiating their case. But the documentation was sometimes completely inaccurate and much of it misleading.[2]

Indeed, Junius Brutus Booth was a very complex figure. On the one hand, he had a brightly loquacious nature and a learned disposition. Unlike his youngest offspring, he was heartily opposed to violence of any kind. In 1833, during one of his many acting tours, he wrote home to request a young son, Junius, to foreswear "opossum hunting." The lad should set no "rabbit-traps, but to let the poor devils live. Cruelty," the solicitous parent lectured, "is the offspring of idleness of mind and beastly ignorance, and in children should be repressed." Moreover, the father Booth disliked slavery. Year after year he rented only one, "old Joe," a house servant and valet. Booth eventually helped to free Joe's wife and some of their children. He did hire slaves from neighboring farmers and paid the bondsmen wages.[3]

Yet, he was far from being an exemplary parent. The elder Junius was given to periodic states of derangement and frequent lapses of self-control. Alcohol, often a depressive's liquid resource, made his mental aberrations worse. Thoroughly drunk, he once fell into a theater pit, and the spectators booed him unmercifully. A present-day psychiatrist might well diagnose Junius Booth's state of mind as affective mood disorder or manic depression. He may have thought about suicide more than once. On learning that a friend had drowned himself, Booth leaped from a ship to Charleston, and onlookers had to pull him from the water.[4]

The actor came to be known as "Crazy Booth, the mad tragedian." At Natchez, Mississippi, he once had mounted a ladder and crowed "like a rooster." Helpless and embarrassed, the stage manager watched from below.[5] At his Harford County, Maryland, home, Tudor Hall, as he called it, Booth once invited neighbors to attend a funeral. (Ironically, the eight-room house was named to honor an English assassin, Henry Tudor, Earl of Richmond, who slew Richard III.) The obsequies, however, proved to be the cremating of a favorite horse, in which ceremony he asked his friends to participate. Some did, but others left in derisive amazement. Sometimes he would forget to appear for a performance and would be found wandering elsewhere in full stage regalia. His family worried whenever he wandered off into the countryside unexpectedly. Many hours later he would return to the Harford County farmhouse. But he would be unable to explain why he had gone out or where he had been. He once was discovered disoriented and naked in the street.[6]

Despite the signs of mental disorder, contemporaries thought Junius the finest actor of his day. Indeed, his madness and the emotional legacy that John Wilkes inherited help to account for their innovative and charismatic performances. Manic depressives with a gift for artistic expression are often most successful. Upon learning of Junius Booth's death at age fifty-six in 1852, Rufus Choate, the well-known politician and attorney of New England, mourned, "Then there are no more actors." Long after Booth's demise, Walt Whitman remembered him fondly: "His genius was to me one of the grandest revelations of my life, a lesson of artistic expression." Moreover, Junius Booth was an insatiable reader of the classics—Dante, Racine, Leibniz—and learned to master these authors in their own tongues, medieval Italian, French, and German respectively. He greatly relished reading the Koran, underlining passages that struck him as particularly worthy of remembering. He could converse learnedly with rabbis at synagogues and recite passages for them from the *Talmud*. His daughter Asia found these verses to be among his favorite lines: "Why then doth flesh, a bubble-glass of breath / Hunt after honor and advancement vain, / And rear a trophy for devouring death, With so great labor and long-lasting pain, / As if his days forever should remain? / Sith all that in this world is great or gay / Doth as a vapor vanish and decay."[7] The verses he chose suggest Junius Booth's intimate acquaintance with the darker aspects of his own nature.

The actor had good reason for moments of severe distress, one source of which would also affect his son acutely. It concerned the family's marital scandal. Junius Brutus Booth had married Christine Adelaide Delannoy of Brussels, and they had one child, Richard. The infant was two years old when Junius absconded with Mary Ann Holmes, a London flower seller. They left for America in 1821. Discovering at last where her husband was, Marie Delannoy Booth traveled to America in 1846 and at once made her presence unpleasantly known to all and sundry. Rumor had it that she, drunk and swearing like a sailor, walked the streets of Baltimore cursing her husband and his second family. According to one of his biographers, John Wilkes, age eight, took the humiliation to heart and "determined to reclaim the family honor, follow his family profession, and adopt the family politics." Marie obtained her divorce uncontested in 1851. On his thirteenth birthday, three weeks after Junius was once again single, John Wilkes watched the marriage ceremony of his mother Mary Ann and his father. Illegitimacy would be a hard matter for a child to deal with in that era.[8] Even though in theatrical circles co-habitations were more common than in the ranks of the respectable, scandal would have swirled freely, especially given the fame of the elder Booth. Neighborhood boys would be quite capable of unsettling John Wilkes in light of his father's embarrassment.

Far more serious was the loss of John Wilkes's father the following year, when the boy was a vulnerable fourteen-year-old. Junius had been on a months-long trip to California engagements. He brought with him Edwin who was as-signed to keep his father as sober and fairly rational as he could. Leaving Edwin behind, Booth then traveled to New Orleans on the return trip and played some weeks in the city. On the steamboat to Cincinnati, he caught a fever and un-wisely drank polluted Mississippi water. Booth expired before the boat docked at the river port. Mary Ann had to hurry there to retrieve the body.[9]

The effect of parental influence on John Wilkes was profound. His father's premature death was a blow to the son who adored him. But in addition, Junius bequeathed John Wilkes a genetic, neurological element that was to shape his entire life. It is quite possible that John Wilkes inherited, albeit to a lesser de-gree, the mood swings and compulsions of his father. Through careful study, experts in genetics have found that a descendant of a depressive, whether from a mother or father, is twice as likely to inherit the genes responsible for affective disorder than the individual without such a background. Despondency and ina-nition are common manifestations, along with rage and lack of self-control. John Wilkes lost his father when the boy was very young and profoundly attached to his parent. The psychoanalyst John Bowlby argues that anger at a parent's death can lead to a redirection of that wrath. If his analysis is plausible, Booth, it could be said, transferred his anger from a beloved and sorely missed father and directed it toward a prominent father-figure, Abraham Lincoln. Such a displace-ment is certainly unprovable. Yet John Wilkes's father was a very unpredictable character, as we shall see. As a result his sensitive son held feelings of ambiva-lence toward him—both love and exasperation. Such mixed emotions could have been a factor in Booth's contempt toward and fury against the president.[10]

Regrettably, Junius Brutus Booth had removed himself from the family in life even before his death. As a busy and sought-after actor, he was away from home much of the time. Although not always in command of his senses, he undertook long tours that deprived his wife and children from seeing much of him. At the same time, John Wilkes was very proud of his father and his many talents. As a result, his loss would have been a terrible blow and could affect his own self-esteem. Without being very conscious of it, children often blame themselves for the absence of a parent. A sense of confusion and anger emerges from such feelings. "With dangerous ease," writes E. O. Wilson, "hostility feeds on itself and ignites runaway reactions that can swiftly progress to alienation and violence."[11]

After his beloved father's demise, John Wilkes, his teenage son, was determined to emulate his acting abilities. The affection between parent and child had been very close, and fantasies of heroic daring could have filled the emotional void in a son angry and emotionally wounded by the unexpected loss. Unfortunately we have no contemporary documents by which to assess the young John Wilkes's reaction to the loss.

Fantasies of heroic daring could have further filled the emotional void in his similarly manic and wildly erratic son. Edwin, five year older, recalled that his brother used to gallop through the nearby woods, shouting madly. He would have a lance in hand, a souvenir from the Mexican War. However manic the "wild-brained boy" was, one can only guess that his dreams of heroic action might be connected to these troubling boyhood experiences. In terms of his schooling, young Booth was no scholar and had difficulty concentrating on his assignments and tests. He barely kept up with the advances of his schoolmates. Judging from hints in his sister's recollections, he could have been dyslexic. He did possess, she insisted, "a tenacious rather than an intuitive intelligence like his brothers." Yet, he went at everything, studies and games, with a high degree of "combativeness."[12]

Growing up in rural Harford County and in downtown Baltimore, where slaveholding was a general practice, Booth mingled only with other very southern-minded playmates. In his mature years, his devotion to the southern cause and to the ethic of honor became paramount. Faced with his family's disarray at times, his doting mother, who pitied her fatherless boy, and the fitfulness of an often absent father, Booth sought a source of strength and trust especially after he lost his father in death. He found it in the southern culture in which he had been reared in Maryland. Southern ethics and principles offered stability, order, rules to follow, and age-old tradition. His devotion to plantation ways and values provided him with an emotional anchor. Yet, at some level he was not as secure and self-confident as he, often arrogant and vain, presented himself to the world. No wonder, though, that he became a favorite performer throughout the slave states. There most everyone wholeheartedly believed in the justice of white mores and ideals of honorable conduct.

During the last months of the war, as Confederate fortunes eroded, desperation to fend off the shame of defeat, desire for vengeance, and sheer sadism animated Booth's daily life. From any rational viewpoint, he was scarcely oppressed by anyone. Yet, he identified with a beleaguered Confederacy as if the whites were themselves soon to be enslaved to a brutal northern juggernaut. Secessionists referred to that threat as the prospect of northern efforts to conquer and practically enslave them and set the former slaves over their lives, their women, and their livelihood. Stephen Fowler Hale, an Alabama secessionist, had ranted on the eve of war, how could honorable southerners submit to Yankee rule if it meant subjugating their families, "wives and daughters to pollution and violation to gratify the lust of half-civilized Africans"[13]

Swept up in the fervor for retaliation and white purity, Booth reflected these ideals of the southern slaveholding elite. In a statement for the Washington *Intelligencer* shortly before the assassination, the actor lamented the fall of "southern rights and institutions [i.e. slavery]."[14] Seeking to retrieve an idyllic southern past that never existed, Booth, like the modern-day extremists and bigots at home and abroad, despised modern and commercial innovations. In his time Booth feared that northern enterprises and industrial progress would gradually or abruptly obliterate age-old traditions and virtues. Those glories included, he believed, feminine deference to the male sex, the license and liberty of slaveholding, and the reign of white over the inferior black, free or slave.

We find nowadays similar attitudes in the honor systems of the Middle East. The Islamic societies in that region have an emotional similarity to the traditional foundations of the slave South—if only in an adherence to an ancient code. In the case of the religiously driven Middle Eastern militant, one can see that the stronger, successful, secular societies of the West seem oppressive and demeaning to the people of Islamic nations. Colonial occupations in the past that drove home that sense of helplessness and inferiority afford fertile ground for resentment and violence. Likewise, what whites of the Confederate states— and Booth himself—feared most was a systematic reduction of their region into a state of colonial dependency. Just as the southerners dreaded subjugation under a Yankee dictate, so too in the Middle East, desire for vindication and revenge informs the school textbooks, the media, and the minds of the ordinary Islamist. "The masses can be aroused," writes the historian John Ashley Soames Grenville, "by hatred of the 'imperial' West." Likewise, Iranian extremists warn the unwary about the evil seductions of colonial powers leading to the danger of becoming "Westoxicated."[15]

When threatened and under duress, social orders of this kind tend to become cultures of hatred. Following these themes of honor and resistance to impending catastrophe, Booth fantasized that, unless defeated, Lincoln would actually extinguish the Negro race with his false promises of freedom. Slaves needed their white masters' protective arms. "Witness their elevation in happiness and enlightenment above their race, elsewhere," he wrote. He had lived with slaves all his life and "have seen *less* harsh treatment from Master to Man than I have beheld in the north from father to son. Yet Heaven knows *no one* would be willing to do, *more* for the negro race than I could I but see a way to still better their condition. But Lincoln's policy is only preparing the way for their total annihilation."[16] Preserving the domestic institution, prohibiting racial mixing, and rescuing the South from "her threatened doom," as Booth framed it, required immediate, bold measures. For too long had the Union flag waved above scenes of blood, "spoiling her beauty and tarnishing her honor." In closing, he referred to his favorite Shakespearean character: "I answer with Brutus: 'He who loves his country better than life or gold.'"[17]

That reliance on Shakespearean reference was not disconnected from Booth's radical secessionism. Historian John Barnwell points out that the secession extremists, like Booth, proudly accepted their pre–Civil War southern critics' charge of being "Hotspurs." They were referring to the valiant, rash, and honor-obsessed character in Shakespeare's *Henry IV, Part I*. At the same time, Booth might well have chosen not Hotspur as his foremost chivalric hero but rather Prince Hal. His complex ideas of honor were more calculating, more effective than those of the Second Earl of Northumberland (1392/1393–1455). Nevertheless, there was something of a psychological affinity between the fourteenth-century Harry Percy, as the English playwright portrayed him, and the nineteenth-century Booth. In a sense, both were driven by a common obsession with honor both personal and collective. They also shared a tendency toward an almost suicidal recklessness. James Jones, one of the South Carolinian ultras, predicted, "If we fail, we have saved our honour and *lost nothing*." The alternative was too demeaning to be considered: the slavery of *"Submission."* In essence this was the meaning of honor for Hotspur—and Booth.[18]

Still more significant, however, was Booth's relationship to the figure of Brutus in *Julius Caesar*. "Of all of Shakespeare's characters, Booth once declared, "I like 'Brutus' best, excepting only Lear." As a young actor himself, George W. Wilson speculated that it was John Wilkes's identification with Brutus that prompted his neurotic fixation. "Booth's delusion that Lincoln wanted to become king," Wilson conjectured, "was probably based on his early relationship to his own father, who was a stern, domineering man and as a consequence repressed his hostility for the father and the older successful brothers as well." Once again the oedipal interpretation proves wrongheaded. Wilson mischaracterized the actor.[19]

Evidence indicates that Booth's acting was uniquely robust and could have reflected his manic character. At a time when the prevailing style was hands on hips and arm extended in sweeping gesture, "It is indecent to make a Gesture with the Left Hand alone. . . . [N]ever let either of your Hands hang down, as if lame or dead," declared an actor of the old school. It was the mode still extant from the eighteenth century.[20] Such violence was often incorporated into the main action of Renaissance and Tudor plays. Booth even expanded the level of physical encounters when the script did not call for a jump from a stage prop or the drawing of a saber. In this connection, he loved to draw a parallel between himself and Brutus, the fixated murderer of Julius Caesar, a crime done in the name of Roman Republican liberty. In his view, the idea of the justified killing of the president and the ancient Roman, needless to say, placed Lincoln among the most infamous despots of western civilization.

In a conversation with a famous French actor, Edmond Got of the Comédie Française, Booth on a trip to Paris asked what the French thought of Caesar's assassin. Got replied that they generally admired him. He added, however, "what was Brutus save an ungrateful and sinister dreamer—a sophist in his very blood? Did he not pronounce judgment on himself, and on the part he played, in that final cry of his: 'Virtue, thou art nothing but a name!'?" Booth, he recalled years later, grew very agitated and after a few moments changed the subject. Not long afterward, Got introduced him to a young and beautiful girl of his acquaintance. Booth had taken a fancy to her. Got was surprised when he next saw her. She burst out in fright. Booth, she told the French actor, was "a madman. She said that he would get up in the night and walk in his sleep and jabber with spirits." She left Paris for Nice to escape any further contact with him.[21]

Hatred often arises from not only stark impressions of injury by another party but also from a deep sense of humiliation that must be assuaged by the death of the hated. In 1860, as the storm clouds of war approached, Booth had written, "Now we have found the serpent that madens [sic] us, we should crush it in its birth." He meant the viper of abolitionism.[22] Thus, it is not far fetched to draw upon the examples of hate crimes today and the current struggle against terrorism to recapture something of the sense of desperation, truculence, and obsessiveness of Booth's state of mind. At home a rash of atrocities against ethnic and gender targets indicates the perpetrators' sense of despair against such social and political changes that have seemingly overwhelmed the old certitudes. "Hatred raises the extremist to a greatness that compensates for the ineffectuality in his world," offers political scientist Shelby Steele.[23] Words like *disgraced, shamed, demoralized, dishonored,* and *humiliated,* all of which permeated secessionist rhetoric in speeches and in print, referred to the calamity of lost self-esteem. The far less radical Senator Judah P. Benjamin of Louisiana and future promoter of the Confederate Secret Service as secretary of war, chose passionate terms on the eve of war. In December 1860 he promised the Republican opposition in the Senate that the North might be fashioning the prospect of war, servile insurrection, and atrocity into an "instrument for subjugating and enslaving us." That effort, he protested, would be in vain. The southern states would call upon all their "freemen" to protect and defend "all that is dear to man . . . and you never, never can degrade them to the level of an inferior and servile race . . . Never! Never!" Even the southern clergy adopted the same language in their sermons. The Rev. H. N. Pierce of the Episcopalian St. John's Church in Mobile declaimed that the South "cannot give up their fair land to degradation and infamy." Nor should the slave states "permit our churches, our schools . . . our temples of justice, to be swept into one common ruin."[24] Historians tend to underrate the role of hot rhetoric or outraged speech acts in the incitement to rash and truculent action. But in the mid-nineteenth century, especially in southern quarters, such modes of public address had a powerful effect.

These kinds of overwrought warnings of doom and the need for stalwart defense were the sort to stir Booth to action. As northern contemporaries believed, southern polemics far exceeded the actual causes. The historian J. Mills Thornton observes that Lincoln's elevation to commander-in-chief signified "an abomination with which the Republicans menaced the South." It was not only black freedom but white "slavery" that meant denial of southern racial hierarchy in the realm of white honor. Fear of a publicly humiliating state of subjection can set aflame all-consuming passions.[25] At the same time, the glory of self-sacrifice in a righteous cause animates the militant in a culture where honor is esteemed. In her memoir, Booth's sister Asia explained that he had killed Lincoln "so that his [that is, Booth's] name might live in history." Regarding the assassin "in a high, honorable light, a Patriot and Liberator," whites would forever rejoice, she rhapsodized, that his "single arm raised" at a "critical moment" had retrieved southern liberty.[26]

The only photograph of the second inaugural on 4 March 1865, taken by Alexander Gardner, shows John Wilkes Booth listening to Lincoln's profound address. He must have heard his deeply moving and conciliatory words: "It may seem strange that any man should dare to ask a just God's assistance in wringing their bread from the sweat of another man's face; but let us judge not that we may not be judged. The prayers of both could not be answered; that of neither has been fully."[27] Booth was present not to entertain Lucy Hale, his fiancée. Instead he sought to witness the alleged monster whose blood he intended to be that "drop" to which the president himself had referred in his speech. He later told himself, "What an excellent chance I had to kill the president."[28] His views and Lincoln's hopes opposed each other—one for democracy, the other for hierarchy.[29]

As for Booth himself, he saw no necessity in joining a Rebel unit, the surest road to glory if that was one of his aims. He had promised his mother that he would never enlist. Nonetheless, he castigated himself as a fool and "coward" at the start of the fighting. Perhaps the actor, used to the comforts of civilian life, had no yearning for the strains of interminable marching, digging trenches, struggling against cold and rain in a flimsy tent. Instead, he found a more useful enterprise by traveling to and from the slave states engaging in reconnaissance and plotting with Rebel operatives. Booth later boasted that "an uncontrollable fate" led him to confront "the most ruthless enemy the world has ever known." "Sacred duty" required that he do all in his power to locate ways to strike out against "my country's foes."[30] The ethical force behind his words was grounded in the ethic of honor.

In keeping with notions of male honorableness and social order, Booth often deplored the state of northern women. They lacked restraint in talking and

laughing with men of a lower social standing than themselves. Such shameless-
ness defiled, in his eyes, the moral principles that ladies should never abandon. Booth had no difficulty in reconciling this position with his own consort-
ing with women of doubtful virtue. Reflecting her brother's views, Asia later
denounced "the refuse of other countries" who had come these shores. They
should, she pontificated, keep a distance from their betters. Booth was, of
course, willing to appeal to northern theatergoers regardless of their status in
the social and ethnic hierarchy, but he scolded Asia and brother Edwin about
the enlistment of Irishmen in the Union armed services.[31]

In the 1850s Booth had admired the anti-immigrant Know Nothing partisans
and had attended some of their rallies in Baltimore. A decade later, he found
even more reason to disdain the Irish. "The suave hordes of ignorant foreigners, buying up citizens before they land, to swell their armies . . . Americans
will blush to remember one day when Patrick coolly tells them that *he won
their battles for them, that he fought and bled and freed the nagur.*" When his sister
retorted that Booth ought to join the Confederate army, if he felt so, he causti-
cally responded by pointing out his other ways for pressing forward the Rebel
undertaking. His "knowledge of drugs," his "profession" being his "passport,"
also his "beloved precious money" for the cause were far more valuable than
serving as an officer or even a foot soldier in the army of General Lee. Although
a poor investor, he earned in one year the present-day equivalent of a quarter-
million dollars in box-office share and acting contracts. Booth funded his band
of conspirators during their original plot to capture and then, when that idea
failed, to assassinate Lincoln. In addition, he had been saving sick fighting men
by smuggling such medications as quinine into the blockaded South.[32]

Throughout 1864 Booth's hatred of the Union president increased into
a full-blown mania. In his opinion, Lincoln aspired to become an American
Bonaparte, a tyrant who would obliterate the principles of the Constitution and
inaugurate a monarchy. Lincoln would exploit the naivety and mindlessness of
"false-hearted, unloyal foreigners who would glory in the downfall of the Republic" to achieve this purpose. Every evil means would be employed to "crush
out slavery, by robbery, rapine, slaughter and bought armies." Once, Junius, a
brother and fellow actor, and he were strolling through the evening shadows
when Junius observed him weeping tears. In halting, broken tones, Booth mur-
mured "Virginia—Virginia." Asia heard the story later and wrote that, "it was
like the wail from the heart of the Roman father over his slaughtered child. This

idealized city of his love [Richmond] had a deeper hold upon his heart than any feminine beauty." To deny that Booth was in any way effeminate, she quickly added that "this very weakness of tears was proof of the depth of his strength."[33] Yet, this loyal sister had no deeper understanding of Booth's inner life that could nail down his passionate regard for the South and its slaveholding traditions. His theatrical approach to intrigue and espionage is more comprehensible. It was as if he were converting a stage performance in a contemporary romance into a semblance of reality. Thus, John Wilkes Booth carried a heavy psychological burden. He had admired his father and had sought to achieve the greatness on stage that Junius had won, but the old man was often physically absent, and then he had died far away and all too soon. He had left behind a son painfully compensating for his inner demons of a lost self-esteem. The culmination of John Wilkes's choler and mania would result in murder, but the act was also a form of suicide, albeit in the name of an ideological cause already dead.

XXXXX

Although Booth's motives and character remain the chief factors in the assassination plot, the context of pro-southern subversion must be considered as well. The underground milieu in which Booth operated appealed to the histrionic aspect of his nature. Secessionists tried to poison the president-elect by sending ostensibly congratulatory gift packages of food to Springfield, Illinois. The suspicious mailings were quickly discovered and disposed of. Greater dangers lay closer to the District of Columbia. Owing to the efficient intelligence work of New York police and Pinkerton detectives, President-Elect Lincoln was spirited in late February through Baltimore before an assassination could occur.[34] Similar plots and threats of assassination simmered throughout the war. The government departments were riddled with southern sympathizers. Nor could longtime Washington residents be casually trusted. After Lincoln announced the Emancipation Proclamation and after he authorized African American recruitment, Confederates and proslavery elements in the other states, slave and free, reached frightening heights of indignation.[35]

Booth was tangentially involved in some other Confederate activities behind the lines which, though ingenious in planning, generally fell short in implementation. Biological terrorism was a case in point. Operating from Toronto in neutral Canada, Luke Pryor Blackburn, a Kentucky physician whose specialty was treating yellow fever, collected victims' garments during an epidemic in 1864 on the island of Bermuda. Eight trunks of allegedly contaminated apparel were readied for the destinations of Washington; Norfolk, Virginia; and New Bern, North Carolina, all occupied by federal troops.[36] Failing to receive his promised compensation, Godfrey Joseph Hyams, a disgruntled British-born operative, took his story to the American consul's office at Toronto. He hoped for immunity and greater reward from the United States.

Booth often traveled to Canada because of the number of Confederate operatives in Toronto and Montreal. A Boston Customs officer noted Booth and three Canadians were staying at the Parker House hotel where the poisoned apparel in the trunks were to be picked up on arrival from Halifax, Nov Scotia. To be sure the connection between Booth and the Blackburn scheme remains unproven and unprovable. Nonetheless, Booth was certainly well within the orbit of the plot.[37]

As his expeditions to Montreal and Richmond demonstrated, Booth had developed a wide range of reliable conspiratorial friends. Booth was probably unaware, however, of another exploit in which he would participate but not as a principal agent. As in the tragedy of 9/11, New York City, nerve center of national commerce and finance, was a symbol of villainy to its enemies. Lt. Col. Robert M. Martin, commanding the expedition, Captain Robert Cobb Kennedy, and compatriots hoped to light a fast-spreading conflagration. After his capture as a Confederate operative, Martin boasted to two fellow prison inmates that he and Booth had conferred and had drinks together in Toronto in the fall of 1864.

Thus, quite possibly Booth knew about the Rebel plot to burn down New York City. On 25 November 1864, with the explicit approval of such Confederate authorities as Secretary of War Benjamin in Richmond, the arsonists carried out their plan. They poured "Greek fire," a mixture of turpentine and phosphorus, around Barnum's Museum and in at least eleven hotels. Fires broke out at the Astor House, Belmont, LaFarge, St. Nicholas, St. James, Metropolitan, Howard, Love-Joy's, Tammany, New-England, Hanford, and others. All were bursting with thousands of guests and service personnel. Most of the buildings were situated along Broadway from Courtlandt to Twenty-fifth Street. The Confederate Secret Service agents sought revenge for "Sheridan's atrocities" in the Shenandoah, as Kennedy later put it. The saboteurs, however, erred in their haste. They neglected to open windows to feed oxygen to the fires they were setting.[38] At Barnum's, thoroughly inebriated, the party doused the stairs with their mixture. That selection was scarcely the most flammable part of the hall filled with exhibits.[39] Miraculously, no fatalities or injuries ensued anywhere in the city.

Adjacent to the Lafarge Hotel stood the Winter Garden playhouse. That very night before a packed house of two thousand ticket holders, John Wilkes Booth played Marc Anthony in Shakespeare's *Julius Caesar*. His talented elder brother Edwin took the demanding part of Brutus. Junius Booth appeared as the dignified patrician Cassius. The brothers did not share the same political views. Edwin had only recently voted for Lincoln in the 1864 election. When he got the news, John Wilkes retorted, "Lincoln will be king of America." Edwin left the room to terminate the unpleasantness. The family tacitly agreed not to speak of politics when John Wilkes was present. He avoided Edwin's house thereafter and visited only to see his mother "when political topics were not touched on," at least in Edwin's presence.[40]

On stage, though, the Booth brothers worked in full professional harmony. The first act ended with a thunderous ovation. It was a stellar performance, many said, seldom seen on the American stage. The three Booths' mother, Mary Ann, was seated with her daughter Asia in a private box. Asia was heard to gush, "Our Wilkes looks like a young god!" Delightedly Mary Ann received her sons' bows as they turned toward her at the footlights. Then, just as the curtain went up for the second act, the alarm of fire rang out. The lobby of the LaFarge was aflame. Smoke began to invade the neighboring theater. Edwin Booth calmed the audience down before panic set in. Soon afterwards, John Decker, the city fire chief, arrived and reported that the flames were being rapidly extinguished. Act Two then began again.[41]

Meanwhile, the federal authorities caught up with Captain Kennedy, who was trying to slip back from Canada on a train chugging toward Detroit. Defiantly, Kennedy waved his handcuffs about and roared to the startled passengers, "These are badges of honor! I am a Southern gentleman."[42] After a brief trial, he was hanged on March 25, 1865, at Fort Lafayette in New York harbor. Kennedy was the only arsonist to be convicted. Booth's comments on the incident were not recorded.

Most serious was the effort in which Booth plotted to kidnap the president. Thomas Nelson Conrad of the Confederate Signal Service, but later transferred to the Secret Service, was the chief figure in the plan. His idea was to seize Lincoln, unprotected, and carry him across the Potomac into Virginia. In the summertime, the president, always cavalier about his security, often traveled without sufficient escort to a cottage on the grounds of the Soldiers' Home, three miles north of the White House. General Bradley T. Johnson, originator of the scheme and in charge of clandestine operations, ordered Conrad to lead the two hundred cavalry raiders. The expedition had the endorsement of General Wade Hampton and high officials in Richmond. Conrad discovered, however, that a cavalry detachment had begun to ride alongside the president on his trip to the Solders' Home. The historian William A. Tidwell is persuasive that the actor was deeply involved. He points out that Conrad and Booth met in November at the National Hotel in Washington. No doubt they discussed the aborted kidnap effort and future plans.[43]

Conrad and Secretary of War James B. Seddon had reasoned that any such abducting of the president would bring the fighting to a halt. Bestowal of Confederate sovereignty would follow. The unanticipated appearance of a cavalry guard escorting Lincoln's carriage on the three-mile trips frustrated the plan—much to Booth's disappointment. Hijacking the president would most likely have resulted in homicide. Yet, Lincoln refused to take the issue very seriously. "I know I am in danger," he told John W. Forney, a newspaper reporter, "but I am not going to worry over threats like these." He was referring to some eighty life-threatening letters that he kept in a pigeonhole of his desk.[44]

Despite a series of disappointments, Booth continued to propose the snatching of the president. He enlisted his old schoolmates from Baltimore—Sam Arnold and Michael O'Laughlin. He told them in mid-January that Lincoln would most likely visit Ford's Theatre when Edwin Forrest, his favorite actor, would head the playbills. They were highly skeptical. Booth, however, persisted. On the spur of the moment Booth thought an opportunity had materialized when he heard that Lincoln would be at Campbell Hospital near the Solders' Home to see a performance of *Still Waters Run Deep*. The play was produced to entertain wounded veterans. Earlier that day, his informant, a fellow actor in the comedy, had merely said that the president had been invited, not that he would definitely be there. Excitedly, Booth, John Surratt (the landlady Mary Surratt's son), Sam Arnold, and Mike O'Laughlin met at Gautier's restaurant to go over their project. Booth went up to the theater and found that Lincoln was not in the audience after all. Arnold and O'Laughlin realized that Booth's schemes were impractical and even suicidal. They went back to Baltimore and broke with their old friend. O'Laughlin was in Washington, however, on the night of the assassination. Luckily, he had witnesses who testified at his later trial that he had spent the entire evening drinking at Lichau House.[45]

In early 1865 another scheme, organized out of Richmond, nearly carried equally grave consequences. Again with Jefferson Davis's explicit approval, Sergeant Thomas F. Harney, an expert in the Torpedo Bureau, headed for Washington with a powerful explosive to demolish the White House. Accompanying him were 150 irregular cavalrymen in John Singleton Mosby's command, who worked behind Union lines.[46] Luckily, on 11 April 1865, Harney and three others fell into federal hands not far from the city and were sent to the Old Capitol prison.

Booth's anger at the outcome of this event and the impending Confederate defeat reached a fever pitch. On the evening of the same day when Harney's effort had failed, Booth listened to Lincoln's words before a large, cheering crowd on the grounds in front of the White House. The president stood on a small balcony. Louisiana had just abolished slavery but offered the freemen nothing further. "It is unsatisfactory to some that the elective franchise," the president said, "is not given to the colored man." As for himself he favored limited black suffrage, confined to Union veterans and those who were literate. "Concede," Lincoln continued, "that the new government of Louisiana is only to what it should be as the egg to the fowl; we shall sooner have the fowl by hatching the egg than by smashing it."[47]

In the midst of the hundreds of happy listeners, Booth stood there with two fellow conspirators: David Herold and Lewis Powell, a Floridian who had earlier served in the Confederate forces. He whispered to Powell that he should kill the president then and there. Aware that they would be immediately seized, Powell sensibly refused. Booth retorted, "That means nigger citizenship." He turned to Herold, "Now, by God, I'll put him through." As the crowd dispersed, Booth mumbled, "That is the last speech he will ever make."[48] Desperate to act before all hope of Rebel victory had vanished, Booth and company abandoned the kidnapping idea and planned to strike down not just Lincoln but also Vice-President Andrew Johnson and Secretary of State William H. Seward—all simultaneously. Such a decapitation of successive chiefs would have deposited Lafayette Sabine Foster, an obscure senator pro tem from Connecticut, in the president's chair.[49]

It is very probable that Booth orchestrated his own plans but had the tacit if not explicit approval of Judah P. Benjamin, the last secretary of war in Richmond. During his postwar imprisonment, Davis contemptuously dismissed accusations of collusion. Nevertheless, Benjamin, Davis's confidante, was conversant with all aspects of Confederate espionage and shared much information with his chief. Confederate agents had long been highly active. They used all the means of communication available: coded messages; apparently unlimited cash for bribes, weapons, and travel; prearranged signals, and other subterfuges. The network stretched from Canadian cities to safe houses along a route to the Maryland-Virginia border. (Ironically, the Rebel lines of communication paralleled the antebellum Underground Railroad by which fugitive slaves reached Canadian safety.)[50]

Fortunately, Booth's colleagues were neither as competent nor as properly equipped as he. While the actor was occupied at John Ford's Theatre, Powell slashed his way to Seward's bedside at his house near Lafayette Square. The wounds to Seward's chest and throat nearly finished his life. A pistol instead of knife would have been more effective, but Powell's gun would not fire. Meantime, George (sometimes Andrew) Atzerodt was supposed to dispatch Andrew Johnson at the Kirkwood Hotel. Unnerved by the hazards of his task, though, Atzerodt drank his opportunities away, and then fled. Booth should have known his associates better. As one historian remarks, "If Wilkes Booth thought of himself as a modern Brutus, striking to free his nation from an ambitious despot, he must have closed his eyes hard to Atzerodt."[51]

Booth's well-known success warrants only brief recounting. Resigned to fate, Lincoln had often remarked that, if someone sought to end his life, they would find the means. As it happened, Booth met no impediment to the president's box for that evening's performance of the comedy *Our American Cousin*. He moved comfortably through the crowds and crossed under the stage, eluding close observation. With the muzzle of his derringer only two feet from the president's head, Booth fired. Seated next to his fiancée, Major Henry R. Rathbone, a young member of the presidential staff, quickly tried to grab Booth, who dropped the pistol but pulled out a knife. He cut Rathbone's arm just as the officer forced him toward the balcony. As he tumbled from the box, Booth snagged his left-foot spur on some patriotic bunting and fractured a bone in his leg upon hitting the stage twelve feet below. With hands upraised, the actor faced the stupefied theater-goers and shouted, "Sic semper tyrannis!" Quickly Booth limped past the lone, benumbed actor then before the lights and staggered outside.[52] In the meantime, a physician in the orchestra hastened up to the president's box. He ascertained at once that the bullet had penetrated Lincoln's left ear and rested behind the right eye. The president could not move, and his breath was ominously shallow. The rescue party then carried him to the lodging of Henry Safford, a tailor, who lived across from the theater on Tenth Street. The president's life came to a close at 7:22 a.m. on 15 April, nine hours after the assault.

During the period when the shock of the assassination was still bursting forth, Booth was seeking safety in flight. After leaving the stage, he limped to the rear of the theater, went through the backstage door, and mounted a horse awaiting him. Joining David Herold, another operative, Booth headed for southern Maryland. Sympathizers, he assumed, would marvel at his pluck and aid his flight. Indeed, Dr. Samuel A. Mudd set the bone and hid the pair in his Bryantown house overnight. Later, the physician maintained that Booth was barely a chance acquaintance. The horseman simply required Hippocratic ministrations after taking a fall. Striving to reach Virginia and safety, the pair then fled southward. In a diary the fugitive grieved that he was pursued "like a dog." What a "degenerate people" his unmanly fellow Americans were. They had dubbed him "a common cutthroat." He moaned, "I am here in despair. And why? For doing what Brutus was honored for." His only crime was to slay a "greater tyrant" than any out of the past. Unlike other assassins of rulers, "I hoped for no gain. . . . I struck for my country and that alone. . . . God cannot pardon me if I have done wrong. Yet I cannot see any wrong except in serving a degenerate people." He admitted that he had "brought misery upon my family, and am sure there is no pardon in the Heaven." Like the arsonist Kennedy, Booth thought himself a gentleman of unimpeachable reputation. If allowed to return to Washington, his station, dignity, and uprightness would be universally acclaimed. Once in the public eye, the former matinee idol pledged, "I will clear my name which I feel I can do."[53] For ideologues like Booth, reputation for valor is always uppermost. Recently, Maulvi Saif-ur-Rehman, an Al Qaeda leader in the mountains of eastern Afghanistan, proclaimed, "We prefer death than living a shameful life." The same code of honor and dread of shame that animated Booth appears in many instances of terroristic warfare.[54]

With federal troops swarming everywhere, the fugitives were traced to Garrett's Farm just south of Port Royal, Virginia. On the night of 26 April, Union cavalrymen surrounded Garrett's barn. The troopers set it ablaze. Shaking abjectly, Herold surrendered, but, gun in hand, Booth refused. Before he could fire, Sergeant Boston Corbett shot him in the neck. Booth fell paralyzed. His final words were: "Tell my Mother I die for my country. I did what I thought was best."[55] He was then only twenty-six years old. Perhaps it was just as well. Had he lived, he might have earned in the South the reward of martyrdom that John Brown had won in the northern states when executed at Charlestown, Virginia, with all the panoply and the rituals customary for such dramatic occasions.[56]

XXXXX

The long-term effect of Lincoln's assassination was profound. Gone was the leader who had patiently guided Union victory, deftly steered the Congress and nation through successive crises, and established black freedom. As Drew Faust in *This Republic of Suffering* noted, "Lincoln's death was at once each soldier's death and all soldiers' deaths." As she observes, "the parallels between Lincoln and Christ were powerful and unavoidable," given that he died in Holy Week. Implying a connection between Lincoln and the Good Shepherd, a northern clergyman preached to his congregation, "The Shepherd of the People! that old name that the best rulers ever craved. . . . He fed us faithfully and truly. He fed us with counsel when we were in doubt, with inspiration when we sometimes faltered, with caution when we would be rash, with calm, clear, trustful cheerfulness through many an hour when our hearts were dark." Another parallel linked Booth and the sinfulness of theater-going. The Rev. E. J. Goodspeed warned his congregation in the Second Baptist church of Chicago that Lincoln had chosen most unwisely to attend a play on Good Friday—or at any time. Theaters were houses of "perdition" where "men are trained for villainy or nurtured in vice." After all, he reminded the worshipers, Booth himself learned his nefarious role in the world of immoral players. "Familiar with tragedies where the dagger and poison played important parts, intoxicated by a vain ambition which the theater fosters, he was ripe for any crime which might be suggested."[57]

For the most part, northern clergy dwelt less on Booth's treasonable crime and more on Lincoln as a martyr in a great and God-ordained cause. Bishop Matthew Simpson declared, "the nation had come to see that God had prepared him through life for the ordeal that lay ahead and that 'by the hand of God' he has been 'especially singled out to guide our nation in these troublesome times.'" The Episcopalian Wilbur Fisk, a veteran from Vermont, asked a question that was on many minds: how could a just God permit so abominable an act to happen? "We must quote in view of this event," he reasoned, the explanation that Lincoln himself had rendered in his Second Inaugural Address: "the judgments of the Lord are true and righteous altogether." It was then simply another punishment for its sins that the nation had to undergo.[58]

The Booth family was perhaps as mystified as the general public about the roots of Booth's act of so tragic a magnitude. Of course, he had spent his early years, as his sister Asia argued, in the company and culture of white southerners, many of his acquaintances being as devoted to slavery and secession as he. Still, the war was nearly over, and the act would not restore slavery nor the old southern way of life with it. The Booth family felt acutely the shame and humiliation that their brother had caused them and all Union loyalists. In a memoir about her father, Asia Clarke had not sought to defend her brother but rather charge him with staining the family honor. It was written close to the event itself and reflected the general grief that was to dissipate with a matter of a few years. Asia wrote, "We of all families, secure in domestic love and retirement, are stricken desolate! The name we would have enwreathed with laurels is dishonored by a *son*,—his well beloved—his bright boy Absalom!"[59] In another memoir, she wrote, "I could not believe him safe or beyond danger at any time, knowing his Southern principles. . . . I knew now that my hero was a spy, a blockade-runner, a rebel! I set the terrible words before my eyes, and knew that each one meant death. I knew that he was today what he had been from childhood, an ardent lover of the South and her policy, an upholder of Southern principles. . . . I knew that if he had twenty lives they would be sacrificed for that cause."[60] Yet, in later years she began to excuse and even glorify her brother and his murderous intent.

The national mourning and sense of grave loss that the northern clergymen adumbrated was not soon to revive in a new and more positive form. Instead, at the White House, Andrew Johnson of Tennessee prided himself on being a war Democrat, not a Republican. His political talents were limited, his intellectual horizon narrow, his racism and his devotion to the old doctrines of states' rights unshakeable. Those freed by the war had every reason to grieve that the "Great Emancipator" had been killed. A nation still shackled to the ancient but flourishing prejudices of race and class distinctions gradually lost interest in the principles for which so many had died. The former slaves soon found themselves once more ruled under new constrictions by former masters and mistresses despite the hopes for equity that they and the abolitionists had anticipated. The Reconstruction state governments under congressional mandates could do little to make working conditions for the freedmen better. The Union public gradually relinquished commitments to the forsaken. Northern voters grew ever more weary of crippled Republican efforts to create a two-party, biracial southern political system. Lincoln could not have solved all the problems of the postwar years. Yet, the loss of the great Union leader was John Wilkes Booth's legacy for his fellow white supremacists. A century would pass before the egalitarian dream that Lincoln espoused would begin to possess some reality.

NOTES

1. Wilson, *On Human Nature,* quoted in Kay Redfield Jamison, *Night Falls Fast: On Understanding Suicide* (New York: Knopf, 1996), 178. Dr. George Tiller was killed on 31 May 2009 as he was passing out service programs at the Reformation Lutheran Church in Wichita, Kansas. The deed was not sponsored by the anti-abortion organizations, but the pro-life ideology was promulgated widely in conservative circles with fearfully menacing and mounting indignation. See "Bill O'Reilly Encourages Dr. Tiller's Assassination," www.prosebeforehos.com/video-of-the-day/06/01/bill-oreilly-encourages-dr-tillers-assassination/; "Dr. George Tiller Assassinated," commentsfromleftfield.com/2009/05/breaking-dr-george-tiller-assassinated; Joe Stumpe and Monica Davey, "Abortion Doctor Shot to Death in Kansas Church," *New York Times,* 31 May 2009. One journalist on the left declares that in "the hysterical voices of those like Rush Limbaugh, fear and paranoia continue to reign as evidenced in this assassination." Michelle Kraus, "Domestic Terrorism Strikes in the Assassination of Dr. George Tiller," *Huffington Post,* 31 May 2009; "Randall Terry on the George Tiller assassination," www.youtube.com/watch?v=08C9O_4BbcA, argues that Tiller "reaped what he sowed." Terry scoffed at the Obama administration for urging that there be no more demonizing of those favoring women's choice, but, Terry insists, what is more demonic than the mass murdering of unborn souls? "James von Brunn, 88, a white supremacist and Holocaust denier, describes the assault with apparent pride on his Web site, the source of fulmination against Jews and races other than his own." Devlin Barrett and Calvin Woodward, "Holocaust Museum Shooter Von Brunn Is Elderly White Supremacist," *Huffington Post,* 10 June 2009; Greg Mitchell, "What White Supremacists Are Saying Today About Holocaust Museum Gunman," *Huffington Post,* 10 June 2009; "Police: Gym Shooter 'Had a Lot of Hatred' for Women," CNN.Com/Crime, 5 August 2009; Jeremy Boren and Michael Hasch, "'Senseless' LA Fitness Killings Summon Call to Faith," *Tribune-Review Service,* 8 August 2009.

2. Stanley Preston Kimmel, *The Mad Booths of Maryland* (1940; New York: Bobbs Merrill, 1969); Philip Van Doren Stern, *The Man Who Killed Lincoln: The Story of John Wilkes Booth and His Part in the Assassination* (1942; Cleveland, OH: World Publishing,1965), esp. 95–97; George W. Wilson, "John Wilkes Booth: Father Murderer," *American Imago* 1 (1940): 49–60; Francis Wilson, *John Wilkes Booth. Fact and Fiction of Lincoln's Assassination* (Boston: Houghton Mifflin Co., 1929). Wilson, however, had collected recollections from Booth's contemporary friends.

3. Asia Booth Clarke, *The Elder and the Younger Booth* (Boston: Houghton Mifflin, 1881), 70;

286

see also Izola Forrester, *This One Mad Act: The Unknown Story of John Wilkes Booth and His Family* (Boston: Hale, Cushman & Flint, 1937), 138–48.

4. Clarke, *The Elder and the Younger Booth,* 89, 93–94; Gene Smith, *American Gothic: The Story of America's Legendary Theatrical Family—Junius, Edwin, and John Wilkes Booth* (New York: Simon & Schuster, 1992), 17, 82.

5. Quoted in Thomas Goodrich, *The Darkest Dawn: Lincoln, Booth, and the Great American Tragedy* (2005; Bloomington: Indiana University Press, 2007), 35.

6. Clarke, *The Elder and the Younger Booth,* 110, 114.

7. Choate quoted in Lloyd Lewis, *The Assassination of Abraham Lincoln: History and Myth* (Lincoln: University of Nebraska Press, 1944), 132; Whitman quoted in Michel Kauffman, *American Brutus: John Wilkes Booth and the Lincoln Conspiracies* (New York: Random House, 2004), 83; Clarke, *The Elder and the Younger Booth,* 114.

8. Smith, *American Gothic,* 22–25; Lewis, *The Assassination of Abraham Lincoln,* 136.

9. Kauffman, *American Brutus,* 89; Smith, *American Gothic,* 55.

10. See John Bowlby, *Attachment and Loss: Sadness and Depression* (New York: Basic Books, 1980), 28–29, 141, 214–28; E. F. Coccaro et al., "Heritability of Aggression and Irritability: A Twin Study of the Buss-Durkee Aggression Scale in Adult Male Subjects," *Biological Psychiatry* 41 (1997): 273–84; James C. Coyne, ed., *Essential Papers on Depression* (New York: New York University Press, 1985), 1–22, 424; Kay Redfield Jamison, *Touched with Fire: Manic-Depressive Illness and the Artistic Temperament* (New York: Free Press, 1993), 149–90. The range of first-degree relatives of depressives with bipolar symptoms is, according to one study, 5.8 percent to 7.8 percent, much higher than the proportion in the general population. See L. Rifkin and H. Gurling, "Genetic Aspects of Affective Disorders," in R. Horton and C. Katona, eds., *Biological Aspects of Affective Disorders* (London: Academic Press, 1991), 305–34. See also R. C. Bland, "Epidemiology of Affective Disorders: A Review," *Canadian Journal of Psychiatry* 42 (May 1997): 367–77, and M. Webb, "The Years of Silence Are Past: My Father's Life With Bipolar Disorder," *American Journal of Psychiatry* 160 (December 2003): 2257; Douglas F. Levinson, "The Genetics of Depression: A Review," *Biological Psychiatry* 60 (15 July 2006): 84–92.

11. Wilson, *On Human Nature,* quoted in Jamison, *Night Falls Fast,* 177.

12. Asia Booth Clarke and Eleanor Farjeon, *The Unlocked Book: A Memoir of John Wilkes Booth by his Sister Asia Booth Clarke* (New York: G. P. Putnam's Sons, 1938), 44, 45; Lewis, *The Assassination of Abraham Lincoln,* 141, 144.

13. See, for instance, Sami Alrabaa, "Culture of Hatred," www.amislam.com/hatred.htm; William Ian Miller, *Humiliation and Other Essays on Honor, Social Discomfort, and Violence* (Ithaca, NY: Cornell University Press, 1993), 84; Leon Würmser, *The Mask of Shame* (Baltimore, MD: Johns Hopkins University Press, 1981); Sami Alrabaa, "To Defeat Terrorism, First Uproot the Hate Culture," *World Tribune,* 21 July 2009, www.worldtribune.com/worldtribune/WTARC/2007/ss_terror_06_12.asp. Hale quoted in Charles B. Dew, *Apostles of Disunion: Southern Secession Commissioners and the Causes of the Civil War* (Charlottesville: University Press of Virginia, 2001), 56. On southern honor, see Bertram Wyatt-Brown, *Southern Honor: Ethics and Behavior in the Old South* (1982; New York: Oxford University Press, 2005).

14. John Wilkes Booth, "To the Editors of the *National Intelligencer,* Washington, D.C. 14 April 1865," in John Rhodehamel and Louise Taper, eds., *"Right or Wrong, God Judge Me": The Writings of John Wilkes Booth* (Urbana: University of Illinois Press, 1997), 148–50.

15. John Ashley Soames Grenville, *A History of the World from the 20th to the 21st Century* (Cambridge, MA: Harvard University Press, 2005), 903; Emmanuel Sivan, "The Holy War Tradition in Islam," *Orbis* 42 (Spring 1998): 190.

16. John Rhodehamel and Louise Taper, eds., *"Right or Wrong, God Judge Me": The Writings of John Wilkes Booth* (Urbana: University of Illinois Press, 1997), 125.

17. Rhodehamel and Taper, eds., *"Right or Wrong, God Judge Me,"* 147.

18. John Barnwell, *Love of Order: South Carolina's First Secession Crisis* (Chapel Hill: University of North Carolina Press, 1982), 188; see also David S. Reynolds, *Walt Whitman's America: A Cultural Biography* (New York: Knopf, 1995), 158.

19. See William Hanchett, *The Lincoln Murder Conspiracies* (1983; Urbana: University of Illinois Press, 1986), 149, who notes the fallacies in the earlier biographies.

20. See www.baroquegestures.com/. See also Anke te Heesen, *The World in a Box: The Story of an Eighteenth-Century Picture Encyclopedia* (Chicago: University of Chicago Press, 2002), 108–10.

21. Got is quoted in translation in George S. Bryan, *The Great American Myth* (New York: Carrick & Evans, 1940), 379–80.

22. Terry Afford, ed., *John Wilkes Booth: Sister's Memoir by Asia Booth Clarke* (1874; Jackson: University Press of Mississippi, 1999), 57, 88. See also Michael E. Woods, "Rethinking the Emotions of Disunion: Jealousy and the Politics of Southern Secession," unpublished paper presented at the St. George Tucker Society, 3 August 2009, Augusta Ga.; Jeffrey Rogers Hummel, *Emancipating Slaves, Enslaving Free Men: A History of the American Civil War* (Chicago: Open Court, 1996); Mills Thornton III, *Politics and Power in a Slave Society: Alabama, 1800–1860* (Baton Rouge: Louisiana State University Press, 1978), 413, 414.

23. Bob Herbert, "Women at Risk," *New York Times,* 7 August 2009; Franz Alexander, "Remarks about the Relation of Inferiority Feelings to Guilt Feelings," *International Journal of Psycho-Analysis* 19 (1938): 41–49. "Muslims are forbidden from imitating the ways of life of other people. The psychology of imitation suggests that it springs from a sense of inferiority and its net result is the cultivation of a defeatist mentality." The Pakistani Sunni theologian Abul Ala Maududiayyid Abul A'la Maududi is cited in the article in *Encyclopedia of the Middle East* about his biography and thought. See also Lawrence Howard, *Terrorism: Roots, Impact, Responses* (Westport, CT: Greenwood Publishing Group, Inc., 1992). and Shelby Steele, "The Middle East: White Guilt and Radical Islam," *Hoover Digest* 4 (2006).

24. Judah P. Benjamin, "The Right of Secession," in Jon L. Wakelyn, ed., *Southern Pamphlets on Secession, November 1860–April 1861* (Chapel Hill: University of North Carolina Press, 1996), 114; Pierce quoted in Mitchell Snay, *Gospel of Disunion: Religion and Separatism, in the Antebellum South* (New York: Cambridge University Press, 1993), 171.

25. J. Mills Thornton III, *Politics and Power in a Slave Society: Alabama, 1800–1860* (Baton Rouge: Louisiana State University Press, 1978), 413, 414.

26. Clarke and Farjeon, *The Unlocked Book,* 157–58.

27. Quoted in Roy P. Basler, ed., *The Collected Works of Abraham Lincoln* (9 vols., New Brunswick, NJ: Rutgers University Press, 1953), vol. 8: 404.

28. Lincoln balcony speech, quoted in Orville Vernon Burton, ed., *The Essential Lincoln: Speeches and Correspondence* (New York: Hill and Wang, 2009), 175. Booth quoted in Jay Winik, *April 1865: The Month that Saved America* (New York: HarperCollins, 2001), 345.

29. See Orville Vernon Burton *The Age of Lincoln* (New York: Hill & Wang, 2007).

30. Booth to Mary Ann Holmes Booth, November 1864, in Rhodehamel and Taper, eds., *"Right or Wrong, God Judge Me,"* 130.

31. Anthony S. Pitch, *"They Have Killed Papa Dead!" The Road to Abraham Lincoln's Murder, and the Rage for Vengeance* (Hanover, NH: Steerforth Press, 2008), 42, citing Henry Clay Ford Statement, 20 April 1865, M599, 5: 459–88. Ford was the treasurer at Ford's Theatre.

32. Clarke and Farjeon, *The Unlocked Book*, 115.

33. Ibid., 64, 116–15, 119–20, 124–25. Booth was particularly attached to the state of Virginia. See Clarke and Farjeon, *The Unlocked Book*, 119–20.

34. Pitch, *"They Have Killed Papa Dead,"* 1–26.

35. Hanchett, *The Lincoln Murder Conspiracies*, 9–10; Charles P. Stone, "Washington on the Eve of the War" (1883), in Philip Van Doren Stern, *Secret Missions of the Civil War* (New York: Bonanza Books, 1959), 51.

36. Nancy Disher Baird, *Luke Pryor Blackburn: Physician, Governor, Reformer* (Lexington: University Press of Kentucky, 1979); Charles Higham, *Murdering Mr. Lincoln* (Beverly Hills, CA: 2004), 58; Edward Steers Jr., *Blood on the Moon: The Assassination of Abraham Lincoln* (Lexington: University of Kentucky Press, 2001), 46–54.

37. William A. Tidwell with James O. Hall and David Winfred Gaddy, *Come Retribution: The Confederate Secret Service and the Assassination of Lincoln* (Jackson: University of Mississippi Press, 1988), 262–63.

38. Higham, *Murdering Mr. Lincoln*, 152; Tidwell et al., *Come Retribution*, 334–36.

39. P. T. Barnum's letter to the editor, *New York Times*, 27 November 1864.

40. Francis Wilson, *John Wilkes Booth: Fact and Fiction of Lincoln's Assassination* (Boston: Houghton Mifflin, 1929), 45; Clarke, *The Elder and the Younger Booth*, 159; Richard Lockridge, *Darling of Misfortune: Edwin Booth 1833–1893* (Chicago: Century Co., 1932), 139; *New York Times*, 27 November 1864.

41. Stanley Kimmel, *The Mad Booths of Maryland* (Indianapolis: Bobbs Merrill, 1940), 191–92; Bryan, *The Great American Myth*, 101.

42. Nat Brandt, *The Man Who Tried to Burn New York* (Syracuse, NY: Syracuse University Press, 1986), 151, 223.

43. Steers, *Blood on the Moon*, 26; Tidwell et al., *Come Retribution*, 234–37.

44. David Herbert Donald, *Lincoln* (New York: Simon & Schuster, 1995), 550.

45. Elizabeth Steger Trindal, *Mary Surratt: An American Tragedy* (Gretna, LA: Pelican Press, 1996), 105–7; Kauffman, *American Brutus*, 162–63; "Testimony Concerning Michael O'Laughlin," www.surratt.org/documents/Bplact10.pdf; "Michael O'Laughlin, 1840–1867," www.law.umkc.edu/faculty/projects/ftrials/lincolnconspiracy/olaughlin.html.

46. Hanchett, *The Lincoln Murder Conspiracies*, 30–31; Steers, *Blood on the Moon*, 90–91; H. Donald Winkler, *Lincoln and Booth: More Light on the Conspiracy* (Nashville, TN: Cumberland House, 2003), 62.

47. Quoted in Roy P. Basler, ed., *The Collected Works of Abraham Lincoln* (9 vols., New Brunswick, NJ: Rutgers University Press, 1953), vol. 8: 404.

48. Hanchett, *The Lincoln Murder Conspiracies*, 37.

49. Tidwell et al., *Come Retribution*, 422.

50. Ibid., 403 passim; Hanchett, *The Lincoln Murder Conspiracies*, 72–90.

51. Lockridge, *Darling of Misfortune*, 139.

52. There are so many narratives of Booth's near escape, not already cited, that only a few should be noted here: Jay Winik, *April 1865: The Month That Saved America* (New York: HarperCollins, 2001); Elizabeth D. Leonard, *Lincoln's Avengers: Justice, Revenge, and Reunion after the Civil War* (New York: W. W. Norton, 2004); and James L. Swanson, *Manhunt: The 12-Day Chase for Lincoln's Killer* (New York: HarperCollins, 2006).

53. Entry for 21 April 1865, diary, in Rhodehamel and Taper, eds., *"Right or Wrong, God Judge Me,"* 154–55.

54. Quoted in *USA Today*, 1 March 2001, A2. Jonathan Rauch writes in the *National Journal* that in the West honor has lost its ancient meanings, thanks to Christianity and the ideals of rationality in the Enlightenment. In Arab countries, however, "one's standing in the community is of paramount importance. What Easterners call 'saving face' is a real force in the Middle East." Saddam Hussein lied about holding WMDs because, if his weakness had been exposed, he would have been shamed and perhaps killed. Preserving reputation is paramount in such cultures. Donald Sensing, "Honor/Shame, the Middle East and the American Left," WindsofChange.net, 19 October 2006.

55. Smith, *American Gothic,* 213.

56. Booth himself had posed as a militia officer in full uniform to attend John Brown's hanging back in December 1859. Booth had admired Brown's self-possession as he mounted the gallows steps. In 1864, Booth told his sister that Lincoln was "walking in the footsteps of old John Brown, but no more fit to stand with that rugged hero—Great God! No." No less ideologically driven than Brown himself, Booth anointed him as "a man inspired, the grandest character of the century!" Clarke and Farjeon, *The Unlocked Book,* 124; Kaufman, *American Brutus,* 105–6.

57. David B. Chesebrough, *No Sorrow like Our Sorrow: Northern Protestant Ministers and the Assassination of Lincoln* (Kent, OH: Kent State University Press, 1994), 34, 79. See also Drew Gilpin Faust, *This Republic of Suffering: Death and the American Civil War* (New York: Knopf, 2008), 156.

58. Richard J. Carwardine, *Lincoln* (Harlow, Essex: Pearson Education, Ltd., 2003), 309; Fisk quoted in Steven E. Woodworth, *While God Is Marching On: The Religious World of Civil War Soldiers* (Lawrence: University Press of Kansas, 2001), 267.

59. Asia Booth Clarke, *Booth Memorials: Passages, Incidents, and Anecdotes in the Life of Junius Brutus Booth* (New York: Carleton, Publisher, 1866), vii.

60. Asia Booth Clarke, *John Wilkes Booth: A Sister's Memoir* (Jackson: University of Mississippi Press, 1996), 83.

FIELD OF MIGHTY MEMORY

XXXXXXXXXXXXXXXXXXXXXXXXXXXXXXXXXXXXXXXXXXXXX

Gettysburg and the Americanization of the Civil War

KENNETH NIVISON

O n November 18, 1863, a train carrying President Lincoln and his entourage entered the town of Gettysburg, Pennsylvania. On the following
day, the dignitaries were scheduled to assemble atop a gentle ridge just
outside the town center to dedicate a cemetery to those who had fallen
there the previous July. What happened on November 19 is by now quite
familiar to Americans. But on the evening prior to the dedication, hours before
Edward Everett's Pericles-inspired funeral oration and Lincoln's brief yet enduring words, a small informal gathering that greeted the party upon its arrival listened to William Seward, the secretary of state, as he delivered his own address.

Seward began by noting that he was pleased to finally be heard in a place "so
near to the border of Maryland." Doubtless those gathered knew exactly what
he meant. Though Adams County voted for Abraham Lincoln in the presidential contest of 1860, the area had long been a Democratic Party stronghold, and
despite Pennsylvania's generally solid opposition to slavery, citizens in the area
were decidedly lukewarm on the prospect of freeing slaves elsewhere.[1] Now,
with the war in full swing, Seward could be "thankful that you are willing to
hear me at last." For his entire political career, he saw that "slavery was opening
before this people a graveyard that was to be filled with brothers falling in mutual political combat."[2] While absolutely certain in his belief that slavery was the
direct cause of the war, Seward nonetheless expressed lamentation, rather than
contempt, for those who fought on the Confederate side. "Tomorrow," he said,
"we shall feel that we are not enemies, but that we are friends and brothers, that
this Union is a reality, and we shall mourn together for the evil wrought by this

rebellion. We are now near the graves of the misguided, whom we have consigned to their last resting place, with pity for their errors, and with the same heart full of grief with which we mourn over a brother by whose hand, raised in defence of his government, that misguided brother perished."[3] With these words, Seward set a tone that later generations of political leaders and memorialists would adopt and adapt for their own purposes, one that would ultimately blur the distinction between Union and Confederate military service and one driven by the desire to preserve and enhance a nation that Seward believed was "the purest, the best, the wisest, and the happiest in the world."[4]

In many ways, Seward's words that evening were the beginning of the long and powerful process of constructing a national narrative of the Civil War through a remembrance of Gettysburg, one that catapulted the battle to mythic heights while simultaneously serving the desire of white middle-class Americans to forge national unity and economic prosperity in the postbellum era. This process necessitated elevating both Union and Confederate military service as two brands of the same valor, while also requiring a kind of historical disenfranchisement for black Americans, whose cause and triumph was marginalized in an attempt to reconcile North and South, particularly following the divisive era of Reconstruction.

Several factors combined to create a climate suitable to such remembering. On the national level, the Gilded Age and Progressive Era were marked by the rise of a new brand of nativism resulting from increased immigration and the opening of the Spanish-American War, both of which emphasized America's Christian and Anglo-Saxon heritage as the source of national cohesion. Moreover, increasing levels of segregation, notably the landmark *Plessy v. Ferguson* Supreme Court case, legitimized efforts to downplay or omit altogether the story of race in the re-telling of the Civil War. Perhaps as important, the rise of leisure activities and the emergence of a lucrative tourism industry in the age of Victorian sentimentality gave new life to historic sites like battlefields and other places of Americana. Disunity and grim reminders of the racism of a bygone era would not have sold as well as a narrative of heroism, inspiration, and happy endings; it also might have been an uncomfortable reminder of a similar brand of racism in the present.[5]

More specifically, several key factors rendered Gettysburg perfect for those seeking to purge race from the story and elevate Confederate and Union service as two versions of the same virtue. Its location meant that the Confederate presence in Gettysburg represented, as Edward Everett noted, an "invasion" of the Union, and the town's proximity to New York, Philadelphia, and Richmond meant that battle would capture the imaginations of those cities' reading publics in a special way, thus planting the seeds for the notion of Gettysburg's profound importance in the earliest days after the battle. Moreover, the timing of the battle—leading up to the Fourth of July—combined with the easily discernable nature of each day's battle surely contributed to its allure as a historical event. The battle was classical in its military geography and tactical orientation, and, as a result, it lent itself to an almost Homeric retelling of acts of heroism, bravery, and leadership.

Equally as critical, though, was the fact that no black soldiers played a role in the three days of combat at Gettysburg. This permitted those who shaped Gettysburg's story to ignore slavery and race as a part of the conflict as they reconstructed the place and its memory for its middle-class consumer public. The absence of black participation in the battle and the remembrance helped fuel what was perhaps the most important explanation of why and how Gettysburg became such an icon of selective remembrance: its conclusion was consistent with those of epic battles from antiquity, battles that well-educated Victorian Americans had come to revere. In the end, the Gettysburg myth was created as a unique moment of American greatness: a Union victory with Confederate valor. In the telling and re-telling of the events, the efforts of both Union and Confederate soldiers were thus gradually Americanized; combatants were hailed for their common honor, bravery, and manliness, while the distinct causes for which they fought escaped the narrative and, in large measure, the national memory. Transcending both the Union and the Confederacy, this mythic narrative made possible the kind of "tomorrow" of which William Seward spoke.

The analysis that follows owes much to the growing number of historians who have examined the creation of national consciousness through the construction of historical memory. In particular, David Blight's landmark book, *Race and Reunion*, shapes the parameters of the argument below. Discussing the period from Appomattox to the First World War, Blight demonstrates how Civil War memory emerged as the product of a struggle among three different versions of the war: the reconciliationist vision, beginning even as the war ground to a halt; the white supremacist vision, which spawned a homogeneous, whites-only interpretation that also included violence toward blacks; and the emancipationist vision, guarded by abolitionists and freed blacks, which sought to retain the war's focus on the wrong of slavery as an essential component (a process made difficult amid the chaos and radicalism of Reconstruction). According to Blight, the reconciliationist vision, which embraced at least the less violent aspects of the white supremacist vision, emerged as dominant over the emancipationist vision as the decades passed. "The sectional reunion after so horrible a civil war," he argues, "was a political triumph by the late nineteenth century, but it could not have been achieved without the resubjugation of many of those people whom the war had freed from centuries of bondage." He calls this process a "tragedy lingering on the margins and infesting the heart of American history from Appomattox to World War I."[6]

According to Blight, Union and Confederate veterans played a key role in this process of reconstructing national memory. While joint reunions took time to develop—gaining distance from the war experience was essential in creating a reunion narrative—they ultimately fostered what Blight calls "bonds of fraternalism and mutual glory" among participants.[7] By the 1880s, veterans, politicians, newspaper editors, and social commentators routinely emphasized shared sacrifice for national growth over the sectional division, most notably that of slavery, that were the locus for the conflict. Cause, in other words, was downplayed, except insofar as all involved in creating this dominant vision embraced its racialized characteristic—the whiteness that was central to the "Lost Cause" ideology. As Blight notes, "In the half century after the war, as the sections reconciled, by and large, the races divided."[8] The process of reunion, of creating a new nationalism, required Americans to overcome not just the Confederacy, but the Union as well, to leave behind them the very real struggles that divided them in the antebellum and war years. From this perspective, the true victors of the Civil War were white, industrious, "virtuous" Americans, regardless of whether they wore blue or gray on the battlefields.

This dominant narrative took time to develop and was the result of several key stages of remembrance and mythmaking. This process began with the addresses of November 18 and 19, 1863, which planted the seeds for the later development of the reconciliationist version of the Battle of Gettysburg at the expense of the causes for which each side in the conflict fought. The process grew and matured at the hands of several individuals, most importantly in the hands of a landscape artist, who saw remembrance both as economic opportunity as well as a chance to create a sense of immortality among combatants. This narrative crystallized as the nineteenth century gave way to the twentieth, when prominent citizens and politicians used the battle to celebrate what they saw as the greatness of national reunification.

While he clearly would not have appreciated the removal of race and slavery as a central issue in the conflict that marked the decades of forging memory following Reconstruction, William Seward's remarks at Gettysburg nonetheless provided the beginnings of a kind of reconciliation narrative that facilitated precisely that kind of "whitewashing" of the war. Rather than denigrating Confederate service, Seward referred sympathetically to the "graves of the misguided," and mourned with a "heart full of grief" over the "pity of their error." In this way, the Confederate soldier was, at least partially, exonerated for his mistake. Left unsaid that night was where Seward thought the blame ought to rest. Hinting at a possible target, Seward argued that the war's conclusion must witness the "establishment of the principle of democratic government," namely, the principle that those rightfully elected to power ought to be permitted to govern. To strike against this principle meant the embrace of "universal, cheerless, and hopeless anarchy."[9]

The following day, Edward Everett drove that point home more clearly and more forcefully, leaving no doubt as to where the blame for the war ought to lie. Portraying the Union effort as "one of self-defence, waged for the right of self-government," he argued that the conflict "is in reality a war originally levied by ambitious men in the cotton-growing States."[10] The soldiers fighting for the Confederacy were, as Seward had noted the previous evening, misguided souls; the real blame for the war, Everett contended, rested with Confederate politicians, leaders of men who put personal gain ahead of public good. Labeling Confederate political action as a "crime" and as "treason," Everett dismissed the southern argument that theirs was a just rebellion against an unjust government as a "cloak of sophistry" designed to diminish the power of the U.S. Constitution as the supreme law of the land.[11]

By the time Abraham Lincoln rose to speak, Everett had set the table clearly enough: this rebellion was the result of greed, and every American ought to bear this fact in mind when assessing the course and conclusion of the war. Viewed in this context, then, Lincoln's words were stark not just because they were comparatively so brief, but also because they eschewed any effort to lay blame or to dispute causes. Instead, he focused on work to be done, on a "new birth of freedom." Like Seward and Everett, Lincoln provided an opening for healing by choosing not to denigrate Confederate military service. In so doing, they set a tone for remembrance at Gettysburg, starting a process that would become as powerful as the battle itself. Lincoln's concern that the world must remember the "last full measure of devotion" that was sacrificed at Gettysburg was allayed only partly. The people would remember deliberately and selectively, choosing to build upon the conciliatory nature of these remarks while shunning the cause of ending slavery to which Lincoln had committed the Union. While a litany of characters followed Seward, Everett, and Lincoln onto the stage to shape the battle's interpretation, a few mythmakers who emerged at critical junctures of the process of remembrance are worthy of particular mention for their efforts at Americanizing the battle and, by extension, the war.

Perhaps the unlikeliest yet most consequential of these characters was John Badger Bachelder. A landscape artist hailing from New Hampshire, Bachelder served for a time as a professor at the Military and Scientific Institute in Reading, Pennsylvania. Though he did not serve in either army during the war, Bachelder became the de facto official historian of the Battle of Gettysburg by the early 1870s. His fascination with the event and its location was driven by his singular desire to find the one "great battle" of the war—every epic war had such a battle, he believed—as well as his dogged determination in extracting as much information as possible from those who fought or witnessed it. Initially intent on producing a definitive visual portrait of the battle, he soon realized the location's cachet as a destination for visitors. As a result, the focus of his work broadened to encompass an effort to catapult Gettysburg into a grand interactive vacation destination for postwar Victorian Americans. In large measure, the Gettysburg story began its ascent as a full-fledged American myth at the hands of John Bachelder.[12]

To his credit, Bachelder labored hard and long to create his story. He traveled with the Army of the Potomac in 1862–63 in search of the great battle that might become a subject of his painting. When he arrived in Gettysburg only days after the fighting, he decided his search had ended. From these earliest moments to his death in 1894, sculpting the story of Gettysburg for the consuming public was the principle work of his life. Throughout the winter of 1863–64, he gathered information from Union soldiers who fought in the battle. Determined to produce a definitive map of the battle, complete with markings of important conflicts, troop locations, and lines of battles, he produced a detailed print of Gettysburg that secured the imprimatur of most of the Union's commanding generals, including General Meade.[13]

In the years that followed the conflict, Bachelder sought as much information from as many sources as possible in an attempt to create the definitive guidebook for Gettysburg tourists. Indeed, the guidebook became the ultimate expression of his labor. So consuming was this project that he ultimately left the painting of the grand portrait that inaugurated his quest at Gettysburg to another artist that he hired specifically for that purpose. The book revealed his desire for a thorough and compelling account of Gettysburg. His account, he states, was the result of "interviews with thousands of Confederate officers and soldiers," as well as interviews with "officers of every regiment and battery of the Army of the Potomac." In addition, he claimed to have made multiple visits to the battlefield with forty-six different commanding generals of the battle in an attempt to pinpoint troop locations and movements.[14]

Bachelder's *Gettysburg: What to See and How to See It*, published in 1873, was in every sense a detailed and comprehensive touring guide. The guide offered extensive information on lodging and entertainment opportunities in Gettysburg as well as information on surrounding attractions. Bachelder also provided an overview of the origins of the town and boasted of nearby "healing water, said to possess wonderful virtues, to which the feeble, the sick, and the weary resort for strength and rest."[15] The central focus of the book, though, was clearly the battlefield, and in his portrayal of the place Bachelder spared no creative impulse. He devised two key visual devices to aid tourists in their visit. The first was a "compass-face guide," which consisted of the location of key areas of the battlefield around the rim of a compass. The second, and clearly more intricate, was what he called an "isometrical plan" of the entire battle area, which depicted in three dimensions both the topography of Gettysburg and the locations of particular armies and their officers who were engaged in the battle. The plan laid the area out into squares that were lettered on the side and numbered on the top for ease of reference.[16]

The battlefield of Gettysburg, however, was but a stage for Bachelder. The ultimate goal was to place visitors upon that stage, to walk them through the events and movements of July 1–3, 1863, as though they were witnessing it firsthand. Thus, Bachelder's account of the battle, while one of the earliest and most detailed, serves primarily to create a sense of drama, to create for the visitor not a static viewing but an experiential integration into the landscape. Woven into his account of the battle's details are instructions to the visitor—to look a particular way, or to wander a short distance, or to take in a certain vista, and imagine this or that regiment traversing this or that plot of land. For example, of the first day of battle, he writes, "General Buford was watching with deep anxiety from the cupola (where we are supposed to stand, D-12), the advance of the Confederate lines."[17] With his written account, compass key, and isometrical plan, Bachelder sought nothing less than to put the visitor in the thick of the event itself. Yet, there was a limit to this experiential tourism; in describing the action on the second day of battle, Bachelder provided a small bit of the hand-to-hand combat, but then cut himself short: "Why repeat the sickening details. This is not intended as a history of the battle."[18] Bachelder intended his visitors to immerse themselves in the greatness of the conflict, and in the surrounding beauty as well; but creating a positive experience meant carefully avoiding the bloodiness and gore that was a defining characteristic of the place in early July 1863.

Although Bachelder's 1873 account relied more heavily on details provided by Union troops than Confederate troops, and as such clearly identified the Union cause as just and righteous, it nonetheless treated Confederate service with respect. Bachelder desired Gettysburg to become a destination for both Union and Confederate veterans and sympathizers; as such, his account asks visitors to recall a military virtue common to soldiers on both sides of the conflict. Initially he faced a bit of resistance on the part of some veterans to travel to Gettysburg or to provide their accounts. Robert E. Lee likely spoke for many veterans in the immediate aftermath of the war when he declined an invitation to participate in a memorial at Gettysburg, telling the Battlefield Memorial Association that it was best "not to keep open the sores of war, but to follow the examples of those nations who endeavoured to obliterate the marks of civil strife and to commit to oblivion the feelings it engendered."[19] Yet, with the passage of time, and with the success of Bachelder's efforts, Confederate and Union veterans offered increasingly more information. As they witnessed the remaking of history, they wanted to be sure that their own account was included and that their actions and the actions of their men received proper attention. The challenge, of course, was sifting fact from pseudo-fact, and reconciling accounts that were often conflicting. More than one veteran commented that the haze of the years, as well as the fog of war, likely wreaked havoc with his memory.[20]

As the outpouring of testimonials fed the growing sentiment that Gettysburg was the decisive battle of the war, and the recording of certain elements of the story elicited yet more details from a wider range of witness and veterans, the battlefield itself was marked and reshaped to coincide with particular accounts of the conflict. Here too, John Badger Bachelder was a key player. Along with the Gettysburg Battlefield Memorial Association, Bachelder worked to dot the landscape with all manner of markers so as to fix the myth's key elements upon the field permanently. And as his efforts vaulted Gettysburg to the preeminent place among Civil War battlefields, nearly every regiment of every army that fought there sought to commemorate its presence and contribution in a material way. The result has been the installation of over thirteen hundred individual markers on the battlefield, ranging from the simplest stone "spot" makers to cast iron signs for individual regiments to the mammoth Pennsylvania monument at the center of the field of battle.

Perhaps not surprisingly, Bachelder's desire for a tourist-friendly landscape, combined with conflicting accounts from veterans and witnesses, led to some reshaping of the landscape that was not entirely accurate. The best example of this is the erection of the "High Water Mark of the Rebellion" monument. According the Bachelder, the prominence of the spot came about during a conversation he had with Colonel Walter Harrison, who was inspector general under General George Pickett. Surveying the landscape with Bachelder, Harrison noted the importance of a small grove of trees in orienting the famed Confederate assault on the third day of battle. Referring to the trees as a "copse," Bachelder posited that the site represented the high water mark of the rebellion. From that point forward, Bachelder became a personal watchman for the spot. Choosing the word "copse" to describe the trees all but guaranteed the site's uniqueness. Reflecting a desire to commemorate what he saw as the height of Confederate strength and the beginning of the restoration of the Union, he convinced the Battlefield Association to empower him to erect a monument commensurate with the subject. The resulting monument consisted of a bronze book with the names of Union army units that met Pickett's Charge on July 3, 1863, and it ballooned in size to occupy over eight hundred square feet. Modern historical scholarship has discounted the notion that this particular episode represented any kind of "high water mark" for the Confederacy, and historians have also argued persuasively that the bulk of the charge was aimed well to the south of the grove of trees, thereby discounting the importance of the "copse" to the Confederate assault.[21] Despite such work, the monument still stands, and the general public continues to regard the assault as the apex of Confederate strength.

In the end, the High Water Mark of the Rebellion monument—rare in that it signifies an interpretation of the battle rather than a unit, leader, or factual event—is as much a memorial to the man who put it there as it is to the moment he sought to make permanent. Bachelder wanted yet another mythic hook for the eager tourist to latch onto as part of the Gettysburg experience, and the High Water Mark monument was perhaps his ultimate achievement in this regard. In his desire to create out of Gettysburg a destination for tourists, however, Bachelder was hardly alone. Instead, he was perhaps the most aggressive and most dogged member of a growing movement: the effort to commercialize Gettysburg.

The nearly limitless variety of battle-themed books, clothing, weaponry, food, entertainment, and general kitsch that confronts the twenty-first-century visitor to Gettysburg is anything but a contemporary phenomenon. As historian Jim Weeks has demonstrated, Gettysburg the place and the townspeople, from the very moment of the battle's end, participated in a kind of paradox: the memory of the battle itself was used to commemorate all that was great about the republican values for which the war was believed to have been fought, while this message was simultaneously communicated in an almost crassly materialistic and opportunistic manner that exposed the republican memory as myth. In this the citizens of Gettysburg were often portrayed as moneygrubbers, ghouls looking to profit from the carnage of the battlefield and its legacy. Moreover, the postwar reputation of Gettysburg residents as uncouth flowed neatly with wartime reports (in both instances from New York newspapers) that Pennsylvanians in general were at best lukewarm supporters of the Union, and likely harbored a substantial pro-Confederate population. Weeks pinpoints the crux of the paradox: "Gettysburg faced a problem whose solution was denied by circumstances. Successive civic and business organizations over the years promoted tourism and spectacles, which attracted media attention. The media repeated embarrassing old stories about the town or else linked old stories to excesses in the tourist business. Townspeople tried to refute the charges through the press or by other means." This they did to no avail. Noting the irony, Weeks says, "Although Gettysburg in the late nineteenth-century served as a tangible link to America's republican past, it pushed Americans to adopt a consumer ethic through its packaging of commercial leisure."[22]

To be sure, there was no shortage of crass opportunism at Gettysburg by the end of the nineteenth century. Perhaps the most outrageous example of this trend was the creation of Round Top Park. In addition to the growing number of rail and trolley lines that crisscrossed the battlefield, the Gettysburg & Harrisburg Railroad Company created Round Top Park at the southern end of the battlefield, promising entertainment to go along with the historical tour. Round Top Park "featured refreshments, souvenir and photography stands, pavilions for dancing, a shooting gallery, a casino, and flying horses."[23] Here we witness a scene well beyond that which John Bachelder could have imagined as he began his quest in 1863; indeed, such commercial excess seems to have turned Bachelder's formula for Gettysburg on its head. Whereas Bachelder believed that the historical value of the place could yield popular and commercial benefit, by the end of the century Gettysburg had become a place where the popular and commercial value reaped a historical benefit.

With so much money on the line, it became even more imperative that the mythic narrative of national unity and prosperity, fueled by the great deeds of great men north and south, continued to dominate the remembrance of the battle. Gettysburg, much like the country, would not abide the loss of potential economic gain that might result from division in the postwar remembrances. There was money in feeling good about the conflict. Feeling good meant finding common ground, and finding common ground meant the sanitization of the horrors of war as well as the re-subjugation of race. Slavery, and black Americans generally, were shunned from official events of remembrance at Gettysburg. This is not to say that African Americans were not present at Gettysburg, however. Gettysburg in the Gilded Age afforded blacks the opportunity to travel from cities like Baltimore to partake in the jovial atmosphere of the site, to engage in the kind of play that, according the Jim Weeks, permitted working-class blacks with the opportunity to "escape the city and break the behavioral boundaries that black elites hoped to restrain."[24] The carnival-like atmosphere of Gettysburg and the conditions of the working-class black presence there only served to underscore the systematic effort of re-subjugation at work both at Gettysburg and across the nation. As David Blight notes, discussing the fiftieth-anniversary celebration in 1913, "Jim Crow, only half-hidden, stalked the dirt paths of the veterans' tent city at Gettysburg. He delivered supplies, cleaned latrines, and may even have played the tunes at the nation's feast of national memory. Jim Crow stalked the streets and backroads of the larger nation as well, and he had recently arrived with a new mandate in the bureaucracies of the federal government. The Civil War had become the nation's inheritance of glory, Reconstruction the legacy of folly, and the race problem a matter of efficient schemes of segregation."[25]

The work of Bachelder and others who crafted an almost carnival-like atmosphere at Gettysburg elevated the site to such heights that veterans could not afford to ignore it. By the late 1870s, it was clear that Gettysburg was THE place where the stories of the battle, and thus the war, were to be told and retold. If a particular leader or regiment wanted its place to be secure in the historical narrative, it needed to present itself at the battle's many reunions. And here we see the critical nexus between the veterans and the mythic narrative of which Blight spoke. The commercial impetus had, by the 1880s, required a careful forgetting (a process that would take on new importance and become more pronounced with the advent of the Spanish-American War and the greater desire for national unity). As veterans issued increasing numbers of remembrances, both at Gettysburg and from afar, they were thus compelled to emphasize common bravery north and south, while elevating their own contributions as particularly critical to creating a strong nation. To do otherwise—to raise the specter of slavery or to cast Confederates as treasonous—would likely have been seen as disrespectful or perhaps even un-American.

A look at one of those prominent veterans and his public memory of the conflict helps explain the ebb of the emancipationist view and the rise to permanence of the reconciliationist view. By now, the wartime exploits of Joshua Lawrence Chamberlain are fairly well known to students of the American Civil War. Awarded the Medal of Honor for his actions on Little Round Top on the second day of battle at Gettysburg, Chamberlain spent a good deal of his postwar years, particularly after serving as governor of Maine and president of Bowdoin College, to the telling and re-telling his stories of the war, especially his story of Gettysburg. Prodded to publish his accounts in the decades that followed the war, Chamberlain often demurred. He preferred to deliver his papers in person, and in many different locations (thus securing repeat speaking fees for each of his talks), and he did not "like to 'cut the heart of it' by publication beforehand."[26] Occasionally, though, Chamberlain permitted his thoughts to be reprinted and circulated for wider consumption. This was particularly true in the later years of his life, when his ability to travel was limited due to poor health. A comparison of two of those writings offers a window into the shifting emphasis in the memory of Gettysburg.

In 1889, Chamberlain attended the ceremony dedicating the Maine monuments at Gettysburg. Asked to provide his recollections of the event, Chamberlain used the setting to offer a dissertation on the political legitimacy of the states' rights doctrine as the alleged central cause of the Confederate rebellion. According to Chamberlain, the cause of the conflict "was, on the face of it, a question of government."[27] The Confederacy, he argued, claimed "a boastful pretense that each State held in its hands the death warrant of the Nation"; that any given state could, of its own accord, "set up its own little sovereignty" and thus "destroy the body and soul of the Great People."[28] Such a position was, from Chamberlain's perspective, self-defeating folly. He dismissed the moniker "The War between the States" as a label resulting from "a false assumption that our Union is but a compact of States." On the contrary, he said, the Union "was the country of the South as well as of the North. The men who sought to dismember it, belonged to it."[29] And that belonging, from Chamberlain's perspective, bound the states together in an identity that could not be severed, even by a bloody and exhausting war. The cause and legitimacy of the Union, he concluded, had been vindicated by the outcome of the war.

In keeping with the trend established as early as November 18, 1863, Chamberlain eschewed any criticism of Confederate military service, laying the blame for the war instead on the shoulders of political leaders of the southern states. "The leaders," he stated, "in that false step knew how to take advantage of instincts deeply planted in every American heart." These leaders were guilty of "perverting" this noble American instinct, and the soldiers themselves were "misled by fictions; mistaught as to fact and doctrine by their masters of political history and public law."[30] For these misled Confederate soldiers, Chamberlain had only pity and respect. "No one of us," he stated, "would disregard the manly qualities and earnest motives among those who permitted themselves to strike at the life of the Union we held so vital and so dear, and thus made themselves our foes. Truly has it been said that the best of virtues may be enlisted in the worst of causes."[31] In this address, then, Chamberlain clearly chose to focus on the "cause" of the war; but he did so in a precise, almost forensic way. Notably, he largely avoided the issue of slavery, making only an oblique reference to the conflict as part of a national "deliverance from evil."[32] This fact is curious, insofar as Chamberlain himself was strongly committed to the abolition of slavery, a man whose college education included participating in parlor discussions of *Uncle Tom's Cabin* with the book's author, Harriet Beecher Stowe. Slavery's omission here, combined with the blame of Confederate political leaders and the recognition of bravery on the part of Confederate military personnel, placed Chamberlain's address squarely in line with the prevailing sentiments of the day.

Yet, as time passed, even the practice of laying blame at the doorstep of Confederate politicians faded from the narrative. Veterans like Chamberlain instead dwelled in the details of the battle, striving to ensure that their versions of the story were preserved in the annals of history. For Chamberlain, this task took on a particular hue. As the former rhetoric professor neared the end of his own life, he began to tell his war stories with a literary flourish clearly influenced by the likes of Homer and Thucydides. As much as anyone, Joshua Chamberlain labored to cast the Civil War, and Gettysburg particularly, as an American Iliad. Several addresses and writings that appeared in the first decade of the twentieth century suggest this trend, but the effort reached its crescendo in his 1913 essay on the Battle of Gettysburg for *Hearst's Magazine*. One of many essays that appeared in the popular press as the nation neared the fiftieth anniversary of the Battle of Gettysburg in July of 1913, Chamberlain's "Through Blood and Fire at Gettysburg" focused not on cause or blame, but rather on the radical self-sacrifice that appeared to be in wide supply at Little Round Top on July 2, 1863. Loaded with vivid imagery (and in this way in stark contrast to Chamberlain's own after-action report following the battle in 1863), the essay again casts Confederate military service in a flattering light. Of the "formidable Fifteenth Alabama," the regiment under the command of William C. Oates that several times sought to drive the Twentieth Maine from Little Round Top, Chamberlain says that "these were manly men, whom we would befriend, and by no means kill, if they came our way in peace and good will."[33] As the decades passed, these men did indeed befriend each other in times of peace, forging a kind of kinship that rendered an open discussion about the very real conflicts between the Union and the Confederacy almost impossible.

Absent again in this account is any discussion of slavery—the cause to which Abraham Lincoln committed the Union army with the Emancipation Proclamation, the cause that spurred Chamberlain into service in the Union army in 1862. With age, and with the advent of a new nationalism in the political culture, Chamberlain found himself in the position of facilitating the reconciliationist vision of the Civil War. This can be seen perhaps most clearly in an address he gave in New York in 1907, recalling his legendary role in the surrender at Appomattox. Defending the sense of mutual admiration that emerged among Union and Confederate soldiers, Chamberlain pleaded with his audience not to blame him and his comrades "for not blaming them more. . . . We could not look into those brave, bronzed faces, and those battered flags we had met on so many fields where glorious manhood lent a glory to the earth that bore it, and think of personal hate and mean revenge. Whoever had misled these men, we had not. We had led them back, home."[34]

Chamberlain would not be present at Gettysburg for that grand fiftieth anniversary—dubbed the "Peace Jubilee"—in June of 1913. He played an important role in coordinating the efforts to transport hundreds of Maine veterans to the event, but his poor health, aggravated by a trip to Gettysburg in May of that year to attend a planning meeting, prevented him from traveling to the anniversary celebration.[35] Though he was not present, the tone of the event clearly bore the stamp of reconciliation that he and countless other veterans and memorialists had sought to forge as the nineteenth century gave way to the twentieth. The event's most prominent speaker, President Woodrow Wilson, went further than anyone in trumpeting the narrative of reconciliation as a source of national strength. A Virginia-born Democrat elected with a mere 42 percent of the vote, it is perhaps not surprising that Wilson sidestepped the touchier issues of slavery and Confederate leadership in his remarks at the celebration. Indeed, he focused his attention on a different past, not the past that was the battle or the war generally, but the fifty years since the end of the war. He described the process of reunion "wholesome," he declared "the quarrel forgotten—except that we shall not forget the splendid valor, the manly devotion" of those who fought the battle. Referring to the "tragic, epic things" that were the "costs to make a nation," Wilson used the event to call for yet more national pride and vigilance, for "action never ceases."[36] If Wilson had any thoughts about the causes of the war or about the triumph of freeing the slaves, he chose not to share them that day.

As Wilson's tone clearly indicates, the Peace Jubilee was conceived and executed as an exercise in the celebration of national reunion and national strength. It was not meant to rehash old conflicts or the causes of the war, but to celebrate the valor and manhood that was forged in its cauldron. As David Blight points out, the event "was about forging unifying myths and making remembering safe." But in order to do so, the event became "a Jim Crow reunion," where "white supremacy might be said to have been the silent, invisible master of ceremonies."[37] Blight notes that "the veterans, as well as the gazing crowds, had come to commemorate a glorious fight; and in the end, everyone was right, no one was wrong, and something so transforming as the Civil War had been rendered a mutual victory of the Blue and the Gray by what Virginia Governor Mann called the 'splendid moment of reconciliation.'"[38]

By the time Franklin Delano Roosevelt delivered his Gettysburg Address at the seventy-fifth anniversary of the battle, in 1938, this mythic, racially pure narrative of common bravery and sacrifice that yielded a strong, unified nation was as unmovable as the granite and bronze that had come to define the battlefield's landscape. But whereas Wilson's pivot away from the causes of the war and toward an appreciation of reconciliation as a means of building a stronger nation spoke in only vague terms, Roosevelt clearly offered a goal to which that common national heritage, north and south, ought to labor. Like many who came before him, Roosevelt did not distinguish between Union and Confederate, instead honoring them equally, "not asking under which flag they fought then—thankful that they stand together under one flag now." Such unity, he argued, was essential to America's success as it faced a profound challenge. "It is another conflict, a conflict as fundamental as Lincoln's," he stated, "fought not with glint of steel, but with appeals to reason and justice on a thousand fronts—seeing to save for our common country opportunity and security for citizens in a free society."[39] Swiftly and cleanly, Franklin Roosevelt invoked the mythic narrative of reconciliation as a central strength of his New Deal policies.

Roosevelt dedicated the Peace Monument at a critical juncture both in the history of the United States and in the post-Gettysburg era. Following the Seventy-fifth Jubilee, fewer and fewer Civil War veterans were available to give memorial talks, publish firsthand accounts, or organize and lead reunions, and as such the fuel to the fire of places like Gettysburg slowly ebbed. Moreover, the public appetite, already changing because of the cultural impact of the Great Depression, would soon shift its focus to a new, global, and arguably more epic war than the Civil War. A grand centennial celebration of the Civil War in the early 1960s struggled to gain traction, due in no small measure to the narrative of unity and strength, which planners exhumed from the Gilded Age and Progressive Era, running smack into the realities of the civil rights movement in the late 1950s and early 1960s.[40] Centennial commissioners effectively asked Americans to embrace a kind of national cognitive dissonance, to see no contradiction in the omission of slavery from a memorial celebration of the Civil War while watching the fruits of a hundred years' worth of racial discrimination and violence, itself the result of such careful forgetting in the decades after the Civil War, unfold before their eyes, on their televisions, in their homes.

The lackluster Civil War Centennial notwithstanding, the long and often difficult process of wresting a narrative of national unity, common bravery, and fraternal glory from the bitterness of the era of the Civil War generally, and of Gettysburg in particular, has largely been effective. Though debates over the right to fly or display a Confederate flag flare up from time to time, the American public appears to have arrived at a place where it accepts the mythic narrative without much fuss. Union and Confederate military leadership and service are similarly revered and subsequently Americanized, a process made possible only by suspending from the public memory the fact that soldiers on either side during the war risked their lives for fundamentally different notions of freedom.

The last several decades have witnessed a flowering of public attention to the Civil War. Gettysburg in particular has benefited from this increased focus. From Michael Shaara's landmark novel *The Killer Angels*, to Ken Burns's monumental series *The Civil War* in 1990, to the film version of Shaara's novel, *Gettysburg*, in 1992, and to the hundreds of other representations of the Civil War on television, in the movies, and in print, the American public has had no shortage of opportunities to enter into the Civil War. Yet the vast majority of these productions have only served to solidify the basic framework sketched out by the first generation of memorialists. (Ed Zwick's award-winning film *Glory* is an obvious exception to this trend, but one that tends to prove the rule.) Americans now flock to the sites of the Civil War, and none receives as many visitors as Gettysburg. These millions of Americans, who doubtless would agree that slavery was and is immoral and that secession was and is treasonous, nonetheless find themselves inspired by the actions of all of the war's combatants, regardless of the political cause for which each army fought. In so doing, they choose the path of careful forgetting and selective celebration. They perpetuate the process of separating race and slavery from the actions of the armies that bloodied each other from 1861 to 1865, thereby Americanizing the Civil War.

NOTES

1. For a detailed analysis of Pennsylvania electoral politics in this period, see William Gienapp, *The Origins of the Republican Party, 1852–1856* (New York: Oxford University Press, 1987).

2. *Address of Hon. Edward Everett, at the Consecration of the National Cemetery at Gettysburg, 19th November, 1863* (Boston: Little, Brown, and Co., 1864), 20.

3. Ibid., 21.

4. Ibid.

5. For a discussion of race and ethnicity in this period, see John Higham, *Strangers in the Land: Patterns of American Nativism, 1860–1925* (Piscataway, NJ: Rutgers University Press, 1955);

Gail Bederman, *Manliness & Civilization: A Cultural History of Gender and Race in the United States, 1880–1917* (Chicago: University of Chicago Press, 1995); Gary Gerstle, *American Crucible: Race and Nation in the Twentieth Century* (Princeton, NJ: Princeton University Press, 2001).

6. David W. Blight, *Race and Reunion: The Civil War in American Memory* (Cambridge, MA: Harvard University Press 2007), 3.

7. Ibid.

8. Ibid., 4.

9. *Address of Hon. Edward Everett*, 21.

10. Ibid., 38.

11. Ibid., 68–69.

12. Thomas A Desjardin, *These Honored Dead: How the Story of Gettysburg Shaped American Memory* (Cambridge, MA: Da Capo Press, 2003), 83–107; Blight, *Race and Reunion*, 187–89.

13. Ibid., 85.

14. Bachelder, *Gettysburg: What to See, and How to See It* (Boston: John B. Bachelder, 1873), 20; Desjardin, *These Honored Dead*, 92.

15. Bachelder, *Gettysburg*, 4.

16. Ibid., 14–15.

17. Ibid, 24

18. Ibid., 43

19. Quoted in Blight, *Race and Reunion*, 149

20. Blight, *Race and Reunion*,188.

21. Desjardin, *These Honored Dead*, 95–102.

22. Jim Weeks, "'A Disgrace that Can Never Be Washed Out': Gettysburg and the Lingering Stigma of 1863," in William Blair and William Pencak, eds., *Making and Remaking Pennsylvania's Civil War* (University Park: Pennsylvania State University Press, 2001), 189–209 (quotations on 205, 208).

23. Jim Weeks, *Gettysburg: Memory, Market, and American Shrine* (Princeton, NJ: Princeton University Press, 2003), 76.

24. Jim Weeks, "A Different View of Gettysburg: Play, Memory, and Race at the Civil War's Greatest Shrine," *Civil War History* 50, no. 2 (June 2004): 175–91.

25. Blight, *Race and Reunion*, 387.

26. Joshua L. Chamberlain to Frank A. Garnsey, Brunswick, Maine, January 18, 1899, Joshua L. Chamberlain Collection, M27, George J. Mitchell Department of Special Collections & Archives, Bowdoin College.

27. "General Chamberlain's Address at the Dedication of the Maine Monuments," October 3, 1889, in *Maine at Gettysburg: Report of the Executive Committee* (Portland, ME: Lakeside Press, 1898), 547.

28. Ibid., 547–48.

29. Ibid., 548–49.

30. Ibid., 550.

31. Ibid., 549.

32. Ibid., 546.

33. Gen. Joshua L. Chamberlain, "Through Blood and Fire at Gettysburg," *Hearst's Magazine* 23 (June 1913): 905, 908.

34. Gen. Joshua L. Chamberlain, "Appomattox," paper read before New York Commander Loyal Legion of the United States, October 7, 1903, 20.

35. John J. Pullen, *Joshua Lawrence Chamberlain: A Hero's Life and Legacy* (Mechanicsburg, PA: Stackpole Books, 1999), 160–66.

36. Woodrow Wilson, Address at the Fiftieth Anniversary of the Battle of Gettysburg, July 4, 1913, John T. Woolley and Gerhard Peters, *The American Presidency Project* (online), Santa Barbara: University of California (hosted), Gerhard Peters (database), www.presidency.ucsb.edu/ws/?pid=65370.

37. Blight, *Race and Reunion*, 9

38. Ibid., 386.

39. Franklin Delano Roosevelt, Address at the Dedication of the Peace Monument, Seventy-Fifth Anniversary of the Civil War, July 4, 1913, Woolley and Peters, *The American Presidency Project,* www.presidency.ucsb.edu/ws/?pid=15669.

40. Robert J. Cook, *Troubled Commemoration: The American Civil War Centennial, 1961–1965* (Baton Rouge: Louisiana State University Press, 2007).

OF HEALTH AND HISTORY

XXXXXXXXXXXXXXXXXXXXXXXXXXXXXXXXXX

The Museum of the Confederacy

EMORY M. THOMAS

S urely I visited the Confederate Museum on some school field trip while I was growing up in Richmond. Two scrapbooks from my days at Ginter Park Elementary School contain photographs of the Confederate White House, but I cannot recall going to the place until I was conducting research for my doctoral dissertation at age twenty-five. Whenever I did begin my visits to the Museum of the Confederacy, I was impressed.

The Museum of the Confederacy contains what one staff member describes matter-of-factly as "the largest and most comprehensive Confederate collection in America." Visitors may see Jefferson Davis's White House almost exactly as Davis himself saw it. A very high percentage of the furnishings now in the house were there in the 1860s.

Other museums have swords and saddles and uniforms; this one has the sword, saddle, uniform, and more that belonged to Robert E. Lee. Other museums have flags. This museum has the flag that draped the casket of Stonewall Jackson, as well as more regimental flags than I want to count. This museum has artifacts of Jefferson Davis with labels handwritten by his wife, Varina Howell Davis. This museum is to the Confederate States of America what Wimbledon is to tennis, what Wall Street is to money, or what Hollywood is to film.

To get there, visitors usually exit an interstate highway and plunge into the depths of downtown Richmond, Virginia. The White House of the Confederacy and the L-shaped museum building that flanks the mansion seem to cower beneath glass and masonry towers that compose the Medical College of Virginia (of Virginia Commonwealth University) Hospital.

The place seems very much out of place amid the emergency rooms, ambulances, and attendant bustle of a large, urban medical center. But the museum has to be there because the Confederate White House was there when the medical college and its hospital occupied two smaller buildings two blocks away. It is appropriate for the museum to be there, too, because it is the Confederate mecca, and pilgrimages are supposed to be arduous.

Step one in the journey is the parking deck that cascades eight levels down the face of the ridge overlooking the valley of Shockoe Creek. This edifice serves both the Medical College Hospital and the Museum of the Confederacy. On my visits to the museum I play a game—Ponder the Parkers or Guess the Goal—attempting to figure out whether my fellow parkers are bound for the museum or the hospital as they walk to the elevators or stairs to ascend again to the level of Clay Street.

I would have bet many dollars that the very pregnant woman and her solicitous male companion were en route to a delivery room—until I saw them soon after, staring at the paintings of Conrad Wise Chapman in the museum. By definition tourists are in a new place for the first time; they often seem lost and confused. Hospital visitors seem equally lost and confused in the labyrinths which house modern medicine. Only back on the street do people sort themselves by entering a long tunnel into the hospital or by strolling past the anchor of the CSS Virginia (formerly USS Merrimack) to the museum.

What follows is a series of stories, impressions, and "fun" facts gleaned from my visits to the Museum of the Confederacy. This is disparate stuff, the accumulation of over forty years filtered through my contorted mind. It may seem more like a kaleidoscope than a composition. But I do adhere to a rough chronology, and I shall try to draw dissonant elements into some coherent whole in the end.

My first memory of the MOC was my journey to the bowels of the White House in search of materials for my history of Richmond as Confederate capital. In that antique time, the Confederate White House held the treasures of the museum crammed into display cases throughout the mansion. The library was in the basement, and generations of historians visited the facility to do research in its rich collections of manuscript, archival, and photographic materials. There is a story (which I believe) that the eminent scholar Bell Wiley, while working in the museum library one warm day, took off his sports jacket and hung it neatly on the back of his chair. A short time later India Thomas, who served as house regent from 1939 to 1962 and thus had charge of the museum, asked Wiley to put his coat back on. She had thought about the matter, she said, and she just did not think it proper for a man to address these "sacred relics" (or words to that effect) in his shirt sleeves.

By the time I began doing research in the MOC library, Eleanor S. Brocken-brough was assistant house regent and librarian. Eleanor knew the various collections intimately and was a wonderful, lively, and thoughtful person as well. I best recall working in the library with her during the summer of 1968. The Democratic Nominating Convention was taking place in Chicago at the time, and each of the three of us who happened to be working in the library favored a different candidate. Judy Gentry from the University of Southwestern Louisiana had supported Robert Kennedy and followed many of his supporters into the camp of George McGovern after Kennedy's assassination. I wanted Eugene McCarthy to get the nomination, and Eleanor clung to "the happy warrior," Hubert Humphrey. Each day we discussed the events of the previous evening at the convention and spoke the language of liberal hope, all the while rummaging through the detritus in the estate of a nation dead for more than a century.

Eleanor sometimes speculated aloud about what "the people upstairs" would think of the liberal heresy we were spouting in the basement library. Our smug chuckles revealed what we assumed about "the people upstairs." We believed they were, most of them, some species of reactionary, unreconstructed crazies come to worship at the Confederate shrine, or in a word—Republicans.

I have reflected upon this incident while people-watching in the museum since 1968. "The people upstairs" have multiplied, and, contrary to our assumptions in 1968, visitors more recently seem to defy generalization. To this place come "all sorts and conditions" of people—in white gloves and heels, tank-tops and flip-flops, coats and ties, shorts and T-shirts, incredible combinations of stripes and plaids, "WOBs" (wear only black), young, old, men, women, people babbling in their pabulum at age six months and at age ninety-six. A composite photograph of the clientele could also serve as a poster for the promotion of cultural diversity. House regents used to report the number of "Northern and Foreign Visitors." Later they listed "Northern, Western, and Foreign Visitors." Invariably the number of people who came from "enemy country" or "neutrals" was only slightly less than half of the total number of visitors (e.g., 5,316 of 11,149 in 1939, and 6,760 of 14,383 in 1949).

In a sense Abraham Lincoln established the precedent. Soon after Federal troops occupied Richmond in 1865, Lincoln came to the fallen capital, and he visited the Confederate White House. Maybe Lincoln was trying to put himself in his rival's place and to look at the world from his enemy's perspective. Perhaps the same inclination persists among non-southern visitors to the museum.

After Abraham Lincoln left the Confederate White House in 1865, his army continued to use the mansion as a headquarters in Richmond until Virginia fulfilled the terms of Reconstruction and resumed her place in the Union in 1870. The City of Richmond, which had purchased the property and rented it to the Confederate government, reclaimed the house, then sold its furnishings at auction, and used the building as a public school for the next twenty years. In 1890 Richmond's city fathers decided to demolish the house and construct a larger school building in its place.

At this juncture some women in Richmond formed the Confederate Memorial Literary Society, held a huge bazaar, and raised enough money (thirty thousand dollars) to buy the property. They were able to repair considerable wear and tear in the mansion and preserve it as a museum. From the beginning the Confederate Memorial Literary Society dedicated itself to collecting and preserving the records and relics of the southern nation "for the use of said Society and the Public." The museum opened officially on February 22, 1896, the thirty-fourth anniversary of Jefferson Davis's inauguration as permanent president and the birthday of George Washington.

The women of the society collected a fascinating variety of materials for the museum. In 1892 one veteran donated "two tablespoons of coffee (ration for 12 men), the last issued to mess #1, Co. E., 4th Va. Cavalry." In 1899 Varina Howell Davis, widow of the former president, sent boxes of Davis family items, each of which she carefully labeled herself. In 1912 Gaillard Hunt of the Manuscripts Division at the Library of Congress was able to locate the Great Seal of the Confederacy, which he offered to acquire and give to the museum in exchange for "a selected part of its historical manuscripts." Susie B. Harrison, house regent at the time, wrote Hunt that his offer had her "floating on pink clouds." She promised to "give you a reception and crown you King of Kings waving Confederate Flags and Singing Dixie." As it happened, a group of southerners bought the seal in 1913, gave it to the museum, and spared Hunt his reception and crown.

The museum survived. And the women of the Confederate Memorial Literary Society continued to own the property and control the institution. Female house regents Isabel Maury, 1896–1912; Susan B. Harrison, 1912–39; and India

Thomas, 1939–62, had direct charge of the museum and its collections until 1963, when the society hired a man to run the place.

By the mid-1960s the society and the museum faced a challenge every bit as severe as that of 1890, when the city threatened to tear down the White House. To say that the museum had to "expand or die" might be too melodramatic; "expand or wither" is more accurate.

For a long time, really from 1896 when the ladies of the Confederate Memorial Literary Society saved the White House and installed in the mansion relics of the Confederacy, the museum existed essentially as a shrine. Curating the collections consisted of dusting the display cases periodically and collecting admission fees. However, by the latter half of the twentieth century, museums in general and the Museum of the Confederacy in particular required more than caring for secular cathedrals. The MOC had to engage in "public history"—offer analysis, enlightenment, and understanding to folks beyond the "true believers" who had worshipped at the White House in time past. The leaders of the Confederate Memorial Literary Society realized that they needed to construct a museum building for the artifacts they possessed and to refurbish the White House as a "house museum." To do these tasks they knew that they would have to raise lots of money.

The crisis peaked in 1965 at a meeting of the society's Building Committee and the Advisory Council, a long-moribund committee of prominent Richmond men who had become alarmed at the society's fund-raising and expansion plans. For two hours the participants harangued. Minutes of the meeting include statements like: "Confusion on this subject seemed unending"; "this began a heated discussion"; and one participant's threat that he "would hesitate to give fifty cents to such a fund-raising campaign." The museum director repeatedly attempted to remind participants that "now is the time for action." But the minutes conclude with the chilling statement, "The conversation continued along these lines without reaching either a solution or a conclusion." And in the wake of the confrontation, a number of influential members of the Advisory Council resigned in protest.

I have no idea precisely how the officers of the Confederate Memorial Literary Society resolved this crisis. Resolution took time, however. In 1970, more than five years after the Advisory Council impasse, public relations consultants advised the society to make peace with the alienated men. Hold a dinner for the dissidents; elect men as officers in the society; indeed create a male majority on the Executive Committee. Only then, the consultants counseled, might fund-raising go forward. Officers of the society did make overtures to some of those who had become disaffected. The museum did launch a fund-raising drive to construct the current museum building. The society enlarged its purpose and committed the museum to communicating, interpreting, and educating, in addition to collecting and preserving. But the Confederate Memorial Literary Society did not then admit men as trustees or officers of the organization. And after twenty years and three male directors, in 1983 the society's trustees elected Elizabeth Scott Lux executive director.

Only after Betsy Lux presided over the reopening of the White House of the Confederacy, which hosted about as many guests during one festive week as visited the museum during several years while I was growing up in Richmond, and imported New York Times food critic Craig Claiborne to oversee preparation of the breakfast following a "Summer Dress Gala" black-tie dance—only then did the women who led the Confederate Memorial Literary Society reconsider the wisdom of electing males to the board of the society. Finally, in 1991, having demonstrated that they could not only survive but thrive without men, the board elected male members.

I detect more than a modicum of irony in all this. At the same time that at least some of the members of the board of the Confederate Memorial Literary Society were probably assaulting gender barriers ("glass ceilings") in their private lives, within this separate sphere they possessed a gynarchy. They chose to share power—from a position of strength.

Of course irony to the point of paradox is and has been important in more than one aspect of the life of the museum. Consider the White House of the Confederacy. Designed by architect Robert Mills in 1818, the neoclassical mansion first belonged to Dr. John Brockenbrough. When the Confederacy came to Richmond, the house was the property of Lewis D. Crenshaw, a wealthy flour miller in the city. This executive mansion of a de facto nation of farmers and planters, self-styled agrarian aristocrats, was in fact the home of an urban, industrial capitalist.

While it was the White House, the building was antique and modern at once. It dripped with gilt and fringe. Furniture was ornate and massive. Gasoliers (as opposed to chandeliers) lit rooms adorned with rich colors, intricate carvings and moldings, brocades, and sculptures. The interior of the mansion was absolutely up to date during the 1860s, and it flaunted the luxury, comfort, and indulgence of the industrial era. But the Davises represented landed wealth and in other contexts scorned (as George Fitzhugh did) "these vulgar parvenus . . . these worshipers of mammon." For all its mid-nineteenth-century modern appointments, though, the White House spoke also to a distant past. Its neoclassic design may have been an accident of birth—its construction in 1818. But the classical influence persisted in the place, and Greek Revival style complemented it elsewhere in the South. The White House spoke and speaks to a tension between past and present, a tension which I believe to be universal, but which the Davises must have felt more acutely than most people.

Material objects, the "things" that are the heart and soul of any museum, can have transcendent values. The objects that adorn the White House help the visitor understand the folks who lived there. Likewise, the "things" in the museum offer insights into the people associated with these artifacts. It becomes important to focus upon the human dimension in material objects. And I constantly ask the question, "So what?"

Once I had the opportunity to visit the storage area for artifacts not then on exhibit. There, among the other "things," I saw the above-ground remains of Major General Dorsey Pender. The young (age twenty-nine) North Carolinian had marched his division into Pennsylvania in June 1863. From Fayetteville, Pennsylvania, Pender wrote his wife Fanny: "This is a most magnificent country to look at, but the most miserable people. I have yet to see a nice looking lady. They are coarse and dirty, and the number of dirty looking children is perfectly astonishing. . . . Their dwelling houses are large and comfortable looking from the outside—have not been inside—but such coarse louts that live in them. I really did not believe that there was so much difference between our ladies and their females. I have seen no ladies." Five days later on July 2, 1863, a fragment of an artillery shell struck Pender's upper thigh. He seemed to be disabled; but not in much danger. Then on July 18 Pender suffered a hemorrhage, endured the amputation of his leg, and suddenly died.

Howard Hendricks was then curator of collections, the principal "thing" person for the museum. Howard had charge of Dorsey Pender's last uniform. We went to some gray metal cabinets with wide flat drawers and put on cotton gloves. Howard pulled Pender's drawer from the cabinet and placed it on a long table. Pender's gray military jacket and pants were "laid out" in the long drawer. Here seemed to be "forensic history." It was not at all hard to imagine a morgue and a corpse; Patricia Cornwell visits the Civil War.

The uniform jacket still had sweat stains from July 1863 and dirt from southern Pennsylvania. Howard gently set the jacket aside, removed some tissue paper, and exposed Pender's pants. Very high on the left leg, about even with the fly, was the jagged hole, somewhere between the size of a golf ball and a tennis ball, made by a shell fragment. Above and below the hole was the cut the surgeon made to examine the wound. Blood stains dotted the fabric on either side of the fly. There were moth holes, too, and Howard explained that the moths favored cloth stained with blood for the protein it contained. "When I look at this uniform," Howard said, "Dorsey Pender was a real person, and the war was grim." Then we returned Dorsey Pender to his cabinet and removed our gloves.

Robert Penn Warren has written that southerners possess an "instinctive fear that the massiveness of experience, the concreteness of life will be violated: the fear of abstraction." Dorsey Pender could never more be simply a name in an order of battle.

However, much as I appreciate artifacts, I do instinctively gravitate to the Eleanor Brockenbrough Library when I visit the museum. I do so because the books and manuscripts are there and because Guy Swanson who once worked there was my friend. One of Guy's special chores was questions and correspondence, and I loved to read his "bizarre file." Someone in Minnesota wrote to announce that he or she had embarked upon a "personal study of the Civil War." The person was interested in "letters, documents, maps, etc," and merely wanted Guy to "send me some of these items." Would that it were that simple. Someone in North Carolina sent a copy-machine copy of a five-hundred-Confederate-dollar note to "Confederate States, State of Richmond, Richmond 1," and invoking the advice of her lawyer demanded five hundred dollars, presumably in United States currency. Guy referred that one to the president of the Virginia Numismatic Association, who pronounced the copy worthless and pointed out, "Even if your bill were genuine, its redemption is prohibited by Section 4 of the 14th Amendment to the U.S. Constitution, a fact that your lawyer should have known." A prison inmate in Virginia wrote to ask for another copy of a map Guy had sent in response to a previous request. The man explained: "Last week one of the other inmates tried to make a homosexual pass at me, when I refused he assaulted me. I'm okay except for a scar which I now have on my face that I didn't have before where he kicked me, but in the process of my property being gathered by the guards to be brought to me in isolation after I returned from the hospital, my map turned up missing." Some folks have more trouble conducting research than museum visitors.

During the summer of 1988 Guy Swanson encountered at least one criminal who was not in prison. I happened to be working in the library one afternoon when another patron arrived and expressed an interest in examining "cartes de visite" from the collections. By coincidence I happened to know that on the previous day the Virginia Historical Society had lost a carte de visite. I told Guy about the suspected theft *sotto voce*, and soon thereafter photograph librarian Cory Hudgins slipped Guy a note saying that she believed she had seen the man steal something and that she had taken a telephone call from VHS warning her about this person.

Guy was professionally courteous about the matter. He told the patron that another institution in the city had suffered a loss of late, and therefore he must insist upon a thorough search. As he shuffled through the man's papers and files in his briefcase, he found a carte de visite of Jefferson Davis. On the back of the document Guy saw "Jeff Davis" written in a style resembling that of the Confederate president. He also saw "Kentucky Collection" in handwriting unmistakably that of Eleanor Brockenbrough.

"Kentucky Collection!" Guy said, and he threw the carte de visite down on the table. Then Guy said some more things—things like: "Leave now, and never come back!" "You are not welcome here!" "We don't appreciate thieves!"

The man slunk away, protesting, but quite weakly. Research libraries are seldom scenes of such high drama. Most librarians I know have risen above the zeal to have all the books in order on the shelves and nothing ever used or checked out. But librarians are extremely intolerant of thieves, and Guy was a hero among his colleagues and counterparts for several weeks.

The attempted theft made a loud statement that many people consider the "stuff" from the period of the American Civil War valuable, and a few are willing to try to steal a piece of history either for themselves or to sell to others. Most of us, however, are content to purchase our pieces of history from the Haversack, the museum's gift shop. In doing so we display rather good taste. The Haversack helps by refusing to stock offensive goods like license plates that advise, "Put Your Heart in Dixie, Or Get Your Ass Out." Indeed books have ever been the bestsellers in the shop. To the degree that people are what they buy, that retail reveals, and shopping sorts, the museum has a discerning set of patrons.

But the Haversack, during the two decades just past, has not had nearly enough patrons, tasteful or otherwise. From the halcyon days associated with the completion of the restoration of the White House of the Confederacy in 1988, the Museum of the Confederacy thrived. Attendance at the museum and White House peaked in 1991, in association with the exhibit "Before Freedom Came," which chronicled the experience of African Americans before and during the Civil War. Then the MOC began to experience what became an increasingly precipitous decline—in attendance, integrity, and financial well-being.

At just about the time that the Museum of the Confederacy was reopening the White House and emerging as a modern museum, several unfortunate factors coalesced. Together these events, actions, and attitudes provoked a crisis every bit as severe as the planned demolition of the White House in 1890 or the transit from shrine to museum in the 1960s and 1970s. This most recent crisis began during the 1990s while the Museum of the Confederacy was still celebrating itself and its success as a "modern" museum. At issue have been essentially three factors—location, legacy, and race.

The Museum of the Confederacy is where it is because the White House is there, and together these buildings compose a three-fourths-acre parcel of real estate. But surrounding this parcel is the Medical College of Virginia, that teaching-hospital complex that was a couple of blocks away when Jefferson Davis lived in White House. Now the Medical College of Virginia Commonwealth University and its hospitals are massive and very nearby.

To get some sense of this situation, imagine a half-pint container common in school lunch rooms for milk or filled with whipping cream in the dairy case of a supermarket. Imagine also two sticks of butter or margarine arranged in an L pattern and placed near the milk/cream container. These items represent the White House and the museum. Then conjure family-sized cereal boxes—Cheerios, Shredded Wheat, Honey Bunches of Oats, whatever—arranged on three sides around the milk/cream and butter. (You MAY try this at home.)

Hospitals, in the contemporary sense of specialized places for treatment, care, and repair of ill or injured people, appeared in the United States in large measure as a result of the American Civil War. In Richmond, Virginia, as elsewhere, disease is a growth industry. Hospitals in the present and recent past come with chain-link fences, huge construction cranes, and "hard-hat" areas alongside emergency rooms. For the Museum of the Confederacy, the Medical

College of Virginia is a problem. Construction debris and detours compound the intimidation of would-be visitors attempting to find the museum and then find some place to park their cars.

Imagine a tour bus driver/guide trying to decide what to do with his or her vehicle and forty septuagenarians in an alien place with two ambulances bearing down, sirens screaming. Location has been a problem.

In recent years the museum and the White House have attracted about 45,000 to 46,000 visitors per year (down from about 92,000 in the early 1990s), and this estimate includes off-site presentations by members of the staff. But location is not the only reason for declining visitation.

Face it. The Museum of the Confederacy exists to remember an attempt at violent overthrow of the United States of America as the nation existed in 1861. "If this be treason," to invoke Patrick Henry, "let us make the most of it." I can imagine a circumstance in which the museum might remind Americans that "Patriotism is the last refuge of a scoundrel." But the Confederate States of America was by the standards of the nineteenth century absolutely un-American. And many people in the United States at this moment, obsessed with the states of war which the nation endures and inspired by the Patriot Act, look upon the Confederacy as treason on a massive scale. This institution is, of course, the Museum OF the Confederacy, not the Museum FOR the Confederacy. But rebellion is less than chic in these early years of the twenty-first century.

And during the waning years of the twentieth century, the Museum of the Confederacy seemed to embrace a conservative/reactionary ideological stance. One example of such activity involved what became known as the "re-enactor community." Lots of re-enactors are nice people; some of my best friends have been re-enactors. In the course of acting out their informed imagination of the past, these people can expand their experiences temporally and thus confront the present with the added prospective of having "lived' in the past. This is pretty healthy.

But some of these folks are much less than healthy. Some of them attempt to use the past, in this case the Confederate past, to render authentic some right-wing political cause. "There's still a misconception that the war was waged for the preservation of slavery," the commander of the Military Order of the Stars and Bars said once upon a time, adding, "If Jefferson Davis were here today, he'd probably be a Republican." Such statements are at least ahistorical and sound to me like sickness.

Is it possible that some of these people have abandoned the present and are attempting to live in the past? "Some of the people become what they are portraying. Re-enacting for most of us isn't a hobby. It's a way of life," says one pseudo-soldier. That is an appalling statement. It does not merely sound sick; it is sick. We can do many things with the past, but we cannot live in it.

During a crucial period in the life of the museum, the leadership fired a director deemed "soft" on Yankees and certainly seemed to crawl into bed with the neo-Confederates. The long-term results proved disastrous for the institution. Perhaps the "Peer Review" report commissioned by new leadership in 2006 says it best: "The word 'Confederacy' at the heart of the MOC name and public perception carries enormous, intransigent, and negative intellectual and emotional baggage." The sad fact is that some members of the Museum of the Confederacy leadership consciously packed those bags.

Closely linked to legacy among the museum's problems is race. The museum suffers from the simplistic equation—Confederacy equals slavery, and slavery equals evil—quantities equal to the same quantity are equal to each other. Therefore, the Confederacy (and any institution that bears the name) is evil. I believe that this is over simple in the extreme. Logic like this makes all Americans alive after March 2003 guilty of torture and sadism on the scale of Abu Ghraib. And even though "tu quoque" (you also) is a logical inconsistency, it is worth noting that the vast majority of Western Civilization during the nineteenth century was racist in the extreme.

The Confederacy had a lot to do with slavery and even more to do with race. Factor slavery out of the sectional equation during the nineteenth century, and the Confederacy would not have existed; the American Civil War would not have happened.

But this does not mean that African Americans have no stake in the MOC. Recent scholarship about the African American experience in slavery portrays a people in brutal adversity who not only endured but prevailed as individuals, community, and culture. I am also convinced that the institution of slavery was in serious ferment within the Confederacy and that during the war black southerners began acting out their own liberation. Surely it is significant that nearly 200,000 black men were soldiers during the Civil War and that near its end the Confederate government took the bold, desperate step of recruiting black troops. The Museum of the Confederacy should speak to the experience of black Confederates, and indeed the museum has done so with exhibits and publications.

At some time in the future, historians will portray race and the American South in terms of fusion. Whatever is or was "southern" has been a blend of Native American, African, and European peoples and cultures—red, white, and black. Examples of this amalgam are endless—place names, songs, folk tales, speech, religious traditions, dance, dress, work rhythms, obvious blood kinship, and even more obviously Elvis Presley. The theme will be "confluence," and that insight is important.

But during the recent past in Richmond, Virginia, the theme has been conflict in a city in which the majority of residents are African American. Here are some examples.

On Monument Avenue, home to statues of Confederate icons Jefferson Davis, Robert E. Lee, Stonewall Jackson, and J. E. B. Stuart, is now a statue of Arthur Ashe. When Ashe was growing up in Richmond, he could not play tennis on public courts, and his statue provoked rancor on both sides of a racial divide.

On the James River in 1999, some of Richmond's promoters proposed a mural portrait of Robert E. Lee to grace one of the panels of a floodwall. A member of the City Council called Lee a "Hitler" and a "Stalin" and demanded that his portrait not appear on the floodwall.

To the site of the Tredegar Iron Works, a place of industrial import to the Confederacy and now home to the National Park Service's Richmond Battlefield Park, in 2003 came a statue of Abraham Lincoln with his son Tad, commemorating Lincoln's visit to Richmond in April 1865. Hue and cry accompanied the unveiling, and overhead flew an airplane towing a banner, "Sic Semper Tyrannis." Translated "Thus Always to Tyrants," this Latin motto of the Commonwealth of Virginia is also the line John Wilkes Booth screamed as he leapt onto the stage at Ford's Theatre after shooting the president.

Near the statue, in the renovated gun foundry of the Tredegar Iron Works, is now the National Civil War Center at Historic Tredegar, another museum to divert visitors from the MOC. In accord with its name, the "National" institution attempts to tell the "whole" story—Union, Confederate, and African American. In a fantasy world of cultural tourism and enlightened public history, the National Civil War Center and the Museum of the Confederacy should complement each other. Indeed some of the artifacts on exhibit at the Tredegar are on loan from the MOC.

Unfortunately we do not live in a fantasy world of cultural tourism and enlightened public history. The Museum of the Confederacy lives in Richmond, which was once the capital of the Confederacy. And it is in jeopardy again, beset by a trinity of troubles, most of which involve location, legacy, and race.

The most pressing manifestation of the MOC's difficulties at this moment is money, or the lack of it, rather, from admissions, contributions, and endowed income. In fact the perfect storm—convergence of all possible negative factors—arrived in the form of an anticipated half-million-dollar budget deficit to greet the then new President S. Waite Rawls III. This deficit was only the latest and greatest among several, covered each year with withdrawals from unrestricted funds in the MOC endowment. But these unrestricted funds were about exhausted, and a desperate request for a one-time grant of $700,000 from the Commonwealth of Virginia for 2006–7 produced only an insulting $50,000 in appropriations.

Once more, those who cared about the Museum of the Confederacy needed to become creative. Waite Rawls responded to the crisis with a flurry of proposals for the future of the museum:

—Move the White House.
—Move the museum.
—Move the White House and the museum.
—Move within Richmond.
—Move outside of Richmond, maybe outside of Virginia.
—Forge a "strategic alliance" with another institution, perhaps the Virginia Historical Society, possessed of greater space and deeper pockets.

These extreme solutions certainly attracted public attention, if nothing else. Many were the machinations before and behind the scenes. Rawls admits to twenty serious proposals from places in Virginia to provide a new home for the MOC.

The plan that emerged and now seems to foretell the immediate future of the Museum of the Confederacy calls for the White House to remain in place. The present museum building, too, will remain as a headquarters for staff and repository for research materials, at least for the next five years and maybe beyond that time. The artifacts and collections within the museum, however, will move to sites within a "museum system." Three sites, to be constructed or renovated, will "take the Museum to the people." These sites will be Appomattox Court House, Fort Monroe (at the tip of the peninsula between the James and

York rivers), and within the Fredericksburg area. The facility at Appomattox might open as soon as 2011; Fort Monroe and Fredericksburg would follow.

Rawls has described the "museum system" scheme as an epiphany during a drive home to Richmond from Appomattox. About 150,000 people visit Appomattox each year—in the two-lane boondocks on the way to nowhere—to see where Robert E. Lee surrendered to Ulysses S. Grant. Less than a third of that number come to MOC, to see an incredible collection of treasures in a major metropolitan center. Perhaps there is a lesson here about accessibility and "destination tourism." Maybe it is time to take these wonders on the road.

In the meantime the museum survives. Rawls has been hard at work selling the institution. Contributions have increased. The MOC has operated with a balanced budget for a couple of years. And the museum has continued to do what it has been doing since 1896, in the words of the mission statement, "to serve as the preeminent world center for the display, study, interpretation, commemoration, and preservation of the history and artifacts of the Confederate States of America."

The MOC has and is taking advantage of digital communication and presentation as well. The last new thing is "Vodcast"—video podcasts available for downloading onto iPods or other portable digital players.

In addition the MOC boasts an outstanding, talented, and dedicated staff. Let me mention two of them I have come to know. John Coski has the title "historian and director of library and research." He does much more, and he has written the definitive work on an important (especially for the MOC) topic, *The Confederate Battle Flag: America's Most Embattled Emblem* (Harvard University Press, 2005). Abdur Ali-Haymes is museum operations assistant. He began coming to the MOC as a very young boy, had a career in the U.S. Army, and returned to the museum. In the spring of 2008 he escorted three fourteen-year-old boys and their fathers from Seattle on a tour of the White House. I tagged along, and I can honestly state that he led the most outstanding tour of a historic site that I have ever experienced.

This is exciting history, because no one now knows how it will end. The Museum of the Confederacy hangs in the balance. I can imagine best and worst case scenarios. Waite Rawls has a plan. John Coski and Abdur Ali-Haymes with other skilled professionals are doing their best in challenging circumstances.

Here is a situation comparable to that early hour on May 2, 1863, near Chancellorsville when Robert E. Lee told Stonewall Jackson, "Well, go on," or on the evening of April 6, 1862, near Shiloh when Ulysses Grant said to William T. Sherman, "Yep, lick 'em tomorrow though." It is June 5, 1944. The polls have just closed on November 4, 2008. Fate lies in the balance. No one knows what will happen.

Tension persists. Waite Rawls has said that he is trying to find a balance in the operations of the MOC. He hears "many critics who THINK IT IS a shrine to the Confederacy and an equal number who WISH IT WERE such a shrine."

The museum has and is an extraordinary corpus of stuff and staff. This is powerful material about a crucial experience. It is volatile, too. The sacred relics of a would-be nation dead for nearly 150 years still move people to passion. The museum inspires enlightenment, and it incites illness.

So I return once more to that parking deck overlooking Shockoe Valley for closure and one final metaphor. People coming from the museum and from the Medical College of Virginia Hospital mingle in this dim space of the deck. In one sense the two institutions, museum and hospital, are alike. Most of their patrons depart more healthy than they were when they arrived. But some do not.

NOTE

This essay depends, in large measure, upon personal experience and conversations. Some of the documents I consulted perhaps twenty years ago were then in the "brown room," a basement space into which people had stacked papers in as orderly a fashion as possible. This circumstance explains why I have supplied no notes. I believe this topic is especially appropriate to this collection because Jon Wakelyn and I discovered together in graduate seminars that the history of history is at once important and fun.

JON L. WAKELYN'S CONTRIBUTION

XXXXXXXXXXXXXXXXXXXXXXXXXXXXXXXXXXXXXXXXXXXX

JANE TURNER CENSER AND ROSEMARIE ZAGARRI

J on Wakelyn's impact on the field of history extends beyond his scholarly research, writing, and editing. Like a stone dropped in a pond, his contributions have radiated outward to influence a much larger circle of students and colleagues whom he touched in various ways over the course of years.

After receiving his Ph.D. in 1966 from Rice University, where he studied under Frank E. Vandiver, Wakelyn taught briefly at Washington College in Chestertown, Maryland. In 1970, he came to the History Department at the Catholic University of America, where he quickly rose from assistant professor to associate professor. In recognition of his scholarly merit, he was appointed ordinary (full) professor in 1977. Over the years, he assumed a number of administrative posts, serving as CUA's associate dean of the School of Arts and Sciences from April 1975 to September 1978 and as department chair from September 1987 to August 1993. For two semesters in the early 1990s, he took his expertise abroad as a visiting professor at St. Patrick's College in Maynooth, Ireland. Then after more than a quarter-century at Catholic University, Wakelyn moved to Kent State University, where he served first as department chair and then as professor of history until his retirement in 2006.

Because of the breadth of Wakelyn's vision, it has sometimes been difficult to categorize his scholarly field. A major unifying aspect of his academic career has been its focus on the South, especially the South of the early nineteenth century and the Confederacy. There he has concentrated on ideas and activities, most often of the educated and politically active. Whether political slogans, literary creations, or religious credos, the important ideas shaping life in the nineteenth-century South have drawn Wakelyn's close scrutiny. As a scholar of the South, Wakelyn has been sympathetic to but critical of its people and their actions. This view is apparent in much of his writing, but the collection of his essays that appeared in 2002, *Confederates against the Confederacy: Essays on Leadership and Loyalty,* most clearly reveals these aspects and in many ways sums up his scholarly interests and rounds out his contribution to southern history.

Jon Wakelyn's first years in the historical profession hinted at the role he would play as a chronicler of the southern mind, especially the radical South Carolinian ideology that culminated in secession. At Rice University, Frank Vandiver, a scholar widely known for his expertise in military history, supervised Wakelyn's dissertation, which focused on William Gilmore Simms, one of the nineteenth-century South's best-known poets and writers. In the book that emerged from the dissertation, *The Politics of a Literary Man: William Gilmore Simms,* Wakelyn found a fresh new angle. Rather than examine why Simms did not write the great American novel, Wakelyn considered the Carolinian's career as a political newspaperman and politician. In particular, Wakelyn scrutinized how Simms, a Unionist in the 1820s and 1830s, hurled himself across the political spectrum to join those who advocated secession and an independent southern nation. While chronicling Simms's ill-starred career as a political newspaperman and his short stints as a state representative, Wakelyn dwelt on Simms as a public intellectual. Here in addition to the newspaper work, Wakelyn followed Simms's social criticism, explored themes in the Carolinian's fiction, and examined his role in literary Charleston and beyond.[1]

This wide-ranging examination of Simms offered a new view of his political evolution. Wakelyn emphasized the popularity that the author gained in South Carolina for his diatribes against English travel writers Frances Trollope's and Harriet Martineau's antislavery observations. The 1832 review in which Simms blasted Trollope in some ways foreshadowed the longer, more intense review of Martineau that he wrote in 1837. In both accounts, the southern author stalwartly defended slavery in ways that later became commonplace among southern partisans. "Realizing that the best defense was a good offense," Wakelyn pointed out, "Simms centered his attack on Miss Martineau's book around her avoidance of the many Northern social problems, including the position of the free Negro and the white laborer in Northern society."[2] Wakelyn's study provided modern scholars with a helpful new interpretation of a thwarted Old South thinker as well as the manner in which intellectuals in the Old South operated. In this way, he helped to open a fruitful new direction on intellectual life in the South.

Although sympathetic to Simms, Wakelyn was thoroughly aware of the extent to which the novelist hewed to the nationalist southern line. Calling Simms a "historical propagandist," Wakelyn examined the author's attempt to create "a readable and usable past" through the authorship of histories and biographies. Moreover, by the 1840s, Simms was writing history thoroughly subordinated to his goals of defending his section in past and present. Wakelyn called this history "almost escapist, revealing an attachment to the simpler, more ordered, and conservative past of his people." In his historical accounts Simms confronted a theme that Wakelyn has explored in other contexts: the role of the leader. Whether the subject was Andrew Jackson, Francis Marion, or Christopher Gadsden, Simms admired men of loyalty and heroism, especially military heroism.[3]

As a creative mixture of intellectual and political history, with a focus on Carolina thinkers, Wakelyn's first book paralleled the research that William Freehling and Drew Faust were undertaking at the time. These studies of the political and intellectual ideas of elite Carolinians also set the stage for the thorough ongoing examination these men and women later received from Michael O'Brien as well as Elizabeth Fox-Genovese and Eugene Genovese.[4]

Other works that Jon Wakelyn produced early in his career showed not only his interest in political and intellectual history but also his familiarity with the social history and social-science history that formed such an important intellectual current in the 1970s and 1980s. Indeed he adopted this latter methodology in his first reference publication, a biographical dictionary of political and military leaders of the Confederate period.

The *Biographical Dictionary of the Confederacy* appeared in 1977 as the first of many reference works which he wrote or oversaw as an advisory editor. The book included information about 651 political and military leaders of the breakaway southern nation, compiled through a social-science approach. Not content merely to present information about important figures, he also indicated his criteria for inclusion of the leaders he studied. Careful to obtain information in a variety of categories that could be used for comparison, he used his introduction as a prosopography, a way to profile the leaders. Surveying loyalties according to birth cohorts, he indicated that "unionist state leaders who made an impact at their secession conventions were growing old, while the secessionists were in the prime of life." Thus Wakelyn's research followed similar patterns that

William Barney was finding for Alabama and Mississippi political leaders in the secession crisis.[5]

Interested in Confederate soldiers, politicians, and bureaucrats as a leadership class, Wakelyn in his *Biographical Dictionary of the Confederacy* examined patterns of service during the war and after its close. In so doing, he found an overextended elite—in part because some died in battle or in office and had to be replaced, in part because they circulated among posts in state and central government. Thus, Wakelyn's dictionary had an interpretative side often absent in reference works. And most likely it was the combination of care about the leaders chosen, coverage, and interpretation that helped to win a coveted American Library Association Outstanding Book Award for 1978.

In addition to the dictionaries he edited or oversaw, Jon Wakelyn also produced two other important reference studies, *Southern Pamphlets on Secession, November 1860–April 1861,* which was published in 1996, and *Southern Unionist Pamphlets and the Civil War,* which appeared in 1999. These will stand as a major contribution to generations of students and scholars and the profession of history. As with his other reference works, Wakelyn set out the universe of possibilities and explained why the pamphlets presented were chosen. Among the southern pamphlets on secession, Wakelyn chose 20 of the 120 available, and his appendices provided information about those not selected. His introduction sketched the context for the production of these pamphlets in the Upper and Lower South, pointing out how their low price and portability made them an ideal form of communication in the period. Indicating how southern ministers were some of the first to tackle the question of secession during the crisis of 1860–61, Wakelyn examines their views as well as those of southern politicians. Thus, he illustrated that in fact some Unionists and secessionists were in dialogue during the pamphlet deluge of early 1861. Yet Wakelyn not only sketched the context in which the pamphlets were produced, but also indicated similarities and differences in the arguments used by Upper and Lower South writers and Unionists and secessionists. In the end, he tellingly argued, "But all of the slave state pamphleteers, however they disagreed over what to do, claimed that slavery was central to their culture, its past definition and its future life."[6] Not surprisingly this volume drew plaudits not only for its "superbly selected" documents, but also its "insightful introduction."[7]

For the volume of southern Unionist pamphlets, Wakelyn again showed the social scientist's sensibility as he carefully indicated the representativeness of those twenty-two pamphlets chosen for inclusion (out of a possible sixty). Spanning the period of the Civil War, they originated in the border states as well as the Confederacy. In his thoughtful introduction, Wakelyn declared that they indicated the "complexity of life in the beleaguered Confederacy." He also argued how important the issue of governance was to these southern dissenters who, in the end, almost all disavowed slavery. Pushing his story toward the Reconstruction of the South that would have to follow the war, Wakelyn also indicated that these Unionists rejected a return to the antebellum status quo but also worried about the kind of peace that would be possible. As one scholar asserted, not only were the Unionist pamphlets "an admirable job of editing," Wakelyn's assembling and publication of them performed "an important service for the profession."[8]

After the publication of the *Biographical Dictionary,* Wakelyn also edited in the 1980s several different collections of essays, which charted future directions for research. In *The Southern Common People: Studies in Nineteenth-Century Social History,* Wakelyn and his co-editor Edward Magdol compiled a series of articles, most previously published, about working folk, black and white. Dividing their collection into antebellum and postbellum sections, they combined classic commentary from earlier in the twentieth century by distinguished historians such as Frank Owsley, Guion Johnson, and W. E. B. Dubois with excellent articles published during the previous five years. The combination produced a volume that for the antebellum period included such provocative essays as that by Forrest McDonald and Grady McWhiney positing a distinctive way of life and outlook for the southern herdsman and one by Ira Berlin on the status differences among free people of color in the upper and lower South. For the postwar period, the editors chose important pieces that explored social structure and paired them with path-breaking examinations of organizations that fought for common folks, such as the Farmer Alliances and the Knights of Labor. They also included Lawrence Goodwyn's cameo of the physical assault on biracial Populism in a Texas county and David Montgomery's evaluation of Goodwyn's book on Populism. All in all, the articles featured in this book previewed the social histories that these scholars and those following them would write in the 1980s and 1990s.[9]

Similarly, two other books edited by Wakelyn in the 1980s highlighted the work of younger scholars and showed new directions for research. As a faculty member at Catholic University of America, he along with Randall Miller of St. Joseph's produced a pioneering volume on the various Catholic constituencies of the antebellum South. Wakelyn's own article in the volume surveyed

Catholic elite southerners. Noting that the Catholic Church did not condemn slavery, he found various coteries of successful slaveholding Catholics and indicated some of the differences in various states' Catholic communities. In both Upper and Lower South, he found acculturated elites who fit in well with their communities. Indeed, they like the Catholic clergy tended to accept the politics of their local area; Upper South Catholics were far more Unionist than those in the Deep South.[10]

In *The Web of Southern Social Relations: Women, Family, and Education,* Wakelyn and his fellow editors, Walter J. Fraser and R. Frank Saunders Jr., published the essays that had been presented at a symposium at Georgia Southern. Covering almost three centuries, these articles presented the latest research on southern women, families, and educational practices. Indeed, the areas sketched in this volume have been fruitfully followed by a generation of researchers in the last twenty-five years. Wakelyn's own contribution, "Antebellum College Life and the Relations between Fathers and Sons," explored the social and educational functions played by colleges. In his exploration of the contentiousness between fathers and sons that often arose over issues of authority, Wakelyn presaged some of the questions that later scholars have taken up in their examination of masculinity in the South.[11]

Wakelyn's most recent collection of essays, *Confederates against the Confederacy: Essays on Leadership and Loyalty,* has returned to many of the important ideas apparent in his writings. Highlighted in this book are themes in southern history that have driven his research over the past four decades. Early in his career, in his examination of Simms, Wakelyn took an interest in various forms of leadership, especially military leadership. In one chapter of *Confederates against the Confederacy,* he examines a group seldom studied: the speakers of the various state legislatures within the Confederacy. Finding them reactive, he argues that these political leaders as a group failed to provide support for the central government, in large part because of their localist vision.[12]

Wakelyn also returned to his measuring of loyalty to or disaffection with the short-lived government of the Confederate states and gauging its effect on the outcome of the war. Going beyond his work on the Unionist pamphlets, he became one of those who argued that dissent and disaffection crippled the effectiveness of the southern independence effort. Wakelyn mainly followed the careers of white dissenters, especially those with wealth or political authority, such as Mary Boykin Chesnut, who recorded the divisive gossip swirling in the government circles that she frequented.

Wakelyn's continuing interest in ideas also is apparent. His article on James Henry Hammond, whom he pronounced a "cautious but committed secessionist," followed the Carolinian into the Civil War, noting that Hammond was "too conservative to be a Confederate." Indeed Hammond chafed against the southern government's orders to grow food crops in place of cotton and, in the end, never was able to have faith in that government. Wakelyn also details the careers of numerous Upper South politicians who had been dubious about secession and remained either skeptical or hostile about the Confederate government and its war with the North.

In the way that Wakelyn has been in the swirl of scholarly exchange for the last thirty-five years, this collection of essays shows his awareness of the relevant questions of the day and his ability to help shape the scholarly debate. Like William Freehling, he has been instrumental in creating a more nuanced view of the South, even the South of the Confederacy.[13] Their emphasis on the loyalty and disloyalty manifested has enriched our knowledge of the period.

In addition to this significant record of scholarly publication, Jon Wakelyn has augmented our historical understanding in many intangible ways. Throughout his entire career, Wakelyn has been actively engaged with the larger profession. For almost a decade he dedicated his time to the Washington Historical Society as it attempted to carve out an identity for the city's local history in a place overshadowed by the history of the federal government. In the early 1990s, he served on the important, but controversial, committee to draft a curriculum establishing national history standards. At times he was called upon to offer his expertise and advice to other history departments by acting as an external reviewer. To all of these activities, Jon brought his characteristic energy, enthusiasm, and decisiveness.

These traits also made him a superb teacher and mentor. Generations of undergraduates flocked to his courses on slavery, antebellum America, and the Civil War. His combination of rigor in the classroom and excitement for his subject led Catholic University to award him its Outstanding Teacher Award in 1983. In addition, he supervised eleven Ph.D. students and numerous M.A. theses. Inside and outside the classroom, Wakelyn encouraged his students to think like historians and to meet his rigorous intellectual demands.

His doctoral students, in particular, remember Jon as an outstanding mentor. According to Charles Ritter, a Wakelyn student who became a professor at Notre Dame College in Baltimore, Jon was "very caring but exacting; he did not let me get away with anything." He was also incredibly generous and loyal to his graduate students. Michael Connolly, assistant professor of history at Purdue University North Central, observed, "If you were 'his student,' he looked after you like a father—helping you with classwork, advising you with various university problems, sending you to talk to the right people." His mentoring did not end with graduation. Wakelyn often invited former students to collaborate with him with on joint publications or editing projects.

Wakelyn has had a keen eye for identifying historical talent. Over the years as the editor of various historical series, he encouraged many scholars to submit and publish their works. While chairing the History Department at Catholic University, he hired young historians who practiced the latest kinds of social history, women's history, and cultural history. In the department, he sought to promote a high level of civilized discussion and scholarly exchange. As a frequent researcher at the Library of Congress, he interacted with his fellow Americanists in the Washington area. And with local younger scholars, he mixed trenchant criticism and encouragement. He not only nurtured the careers of individual historians but also built a larger sense of intellectual community.

Wakelyn's infectious intellectual curiosity led him to make another kind of scholarly contribution. He has been the editor, or co-editor, of three series of scholarly works: Contributions in American History, published by Greenwood Press; the American Biography Series, published by Harlan Davidson; and the Shades of Blue and Gray: Civil War Studies, published by the University of Missouri Press, which have collectively published over 150 books. As a series editor, Wakelyn aggressively sought out good work and solicited authors for his series. His editorial imprint can be found in books as diverse as a historiography of American urbanism, a treatise on the music of the Civil War, and a biography of Mae West. These editorial endeavors have allowed Wakelyn to remain engaged with the newest historical scholarship and to shape emerging debates in the field.

For many years, Jon Wakelyn used to say that, when he retired, he was going to be a "Professor at the Library of Congress." His recent return to the Washington, D.C., area has made this dream a reality. He can now can continue to do what he has always loved, historical research and writing. Professor Alan Kraut of American University, Jon's friend and collaborator, puts it this way: "Jon is a consummate historian. He loves the whole ball of wax—not just the research and writing, but the teaching, the mentoring, the conference-going, everything. He's an old-fashioned gentleman-scholar, in the best sense." Jon will join the faculty at American University in fall 2009 as a historian in residence. The pond still ripples with his impact.

NOTES

1. Jon L. Wakelyn, *The Politics of a Literary Man: William Gilmore Simms*, Contributions in American Studies, no. 5 (Westport, CT: Greenwood Press, 1973).

2. Ibid., 62.

3. Ibid., 115.

4. See, for examples, William W. Freehling, *Prelude to Civil War: The Nullification Crisis in South Carolina, 1816–1836* (New York: Harper & Row, 1966); Drew Gilpin Faust, *A Sacred Circle: The Dilemma of the Intellectual in the Old South, 1840–1880* (Baltimore: Johns Hopkins University Press, 1977); Drew Gilpin Faust, *James Henry Hammond and the Old South: A Design for Mastery,* Southern Biography Series (Baton Rouge: Louisiana State University Press, 1982); Michael O'Brien, *Conjectures of Order: Intellectual Life and the American South, 1810–1860* (2 vols., Chapel Hill: University of North Carolina Press, 2004); and Elizabeth Fox-Genovese and Eugene D. Genovese, *The Mind of the Master Class: History and Faith in the Southern Slaveholders' Worldview* (Cambridge, UK: Cambridge University Press, 2005).

5. Jon L. Wakelyn, *Biographical Dictionary of the Confederacy* (Westport, CT: Greenwood Press, 1977), 27; William L. Barney, *The Secessionist Impulse: Alabama and Mississippi in 1860* (Princeton, NJ: Princeton University Press, 1974).

6. Jon L. Wakelyn, ed., *Southern Pamphlets on Secession, November 1860–April 1861* (Chapel Hill: University of North Carolina Press, 1996), xxix.

7. A. James Fuller, Review of *Southern Pamphlets on Secession* in *Journal of Southern History* (1997).

8. Jon L. Wakelyn, ed., *Southern Unionist Pamphlets and the Civil War* (Columbia: University of Missouri Press, 1999), xii; James Huston, Review of *Southern Unionist Pamphlets and the Civil War* in *Journal of Southern History* (2001).

9. Edward Magdol and Jon L. Wakelyn, eds., *The Southern Common People: Studies in Nineteenth-Century Social History,* Contributions in American History, no. 86 (Westport, CT: Greenwood Press, 1980).

10. Jon Wakelyn, "Catholic Elites in the Slaveholding South," in *Catholics in the Old South: Essays on Church and Culture,* ed. Randall M. Miller and Jon L. Wakelyn (Macon, GA: Mercer University Press, 1983), 211–39.

11. Jon Wakelyn, "Antebellum College Life and the Relations between Fathers and Sons," *The Web of Southern Social Relations: Women, Family, and Education,* ed. Walter J. Fraser Jr., R. Frank Saunders Jr., and Jon L. Wakelyn (Athens: University of Georgia Press, 1985), 107–26.

12. Jon L. Wakelyn, *Confederates against the Confederacy: Essays on Leadership and Loyalty* (Westport, CT: Praeger, 2002).

13. William W. Freehling, *The South vs. the South: How Anti-Confederate Southerners Shaped the Course of the Civil War* (New York: Oxford University Press, 2001).

SELECTED WORKS BY JON L. WAKELYN

XXXXXXXXXXXXXXXXXXXXXXXXXXXXXXXXXXXXXXXXXXXXX

The Politics of a Literary Man: William Gilmore Simms (1973)
Biographical Dictionary of the Confederacy (1977)
The Southern Common People: Studies in Nineteenth-Century Social History (1980)
Catholics in the Old South: Essays on Church and Culture (1983)
The Web of Southern Social Relations: Women, Family, & Education (1985)
American Legislative Leaders, 1850–1910 (1989)
Southern Pamphlets on Secession, November 1860–April 1861 (1996)
Leaders of the American Civil War: A Biographical and Historiographical Dictionary
        (1998)
Southern Unionist Pamphlets and the Civil War (1999)
Confederates against the Confederacy: Essays on Leadership and Loyalty (2002)
Birth of the Bill of Rights: Encyclopedia of the Antifederalists (2004)
The Anti-Federalists: A Biographical Dictionary with Collected Speeches and Writings
        (2004)
America's Founding Charters: Primary Documents of Colonial and Revolutionary Era
        Governance (2006)

CONTRIBUTORS

ORVILLE VERNON BURTON is university distinguished professor of humanities and professor of history and computer science at Clemson University, and director of the Clemson CyberInstitute. Burton has authored or edited fifteen books and more than one hundred articles. His most recent work is *The Age of Lincoln* (Hill and Wang, 2007), which won the Chicago Tribune Heartland Literary Award for Nonfiction and was selected for the Book of the Month Club, History Book Club, and Military Book Club. Recognized for his teaching, Burton was selected nationwide as the 1999 U.S. Research and Doctoral University Professor of the Year (presented by the Carnegie Foundation for the Advancement of Teaching and by the Council for Advancement and Support of Education). In 2004 he received the American Historical Association's Eugene Asher Distinguished Teaching Prize, and was appointed an Organization of American Historian Distinguished Lecturer for 2004–10.

JANE TURNER CENSER is a professor of history at George Mason University, where she has taught for over twenty years. The most recent among the five books she has written or edited is *The Reconstruction of White Southern Womanhood, 1865–1895* (Louisiana State University Press, 2003). Her essays and prize-winning articles have appeared in numerous journals, including the *Journal of Southern History, Comparative Studies in Society and History, Southern Cultures,* and *American Quarterly.*

MICHAEL J. CONNOLLY earned his M.A. and Ph.D. at The Catholic University of America, studying under Jon L. Wakelyn. Connolly has taught previously at Franklin Pierce University and St. Anselm College in New Hampshire, and is currently an assistant professor of history at Purdue University North Central in Indiana. He is author of *Capitalism, Politics, and Railroads in Jacksonian New England* (University of Missouri Press, 2003) and serves as list editor for H-New England.

PAUL D. ESCOTT is Reynolds Professor of History at Wake Forest University. A native of St. Louis, he received his B.A. degree cum laude from Harvard College and earned his M.A. and Ph.D. degrees from Duke University. His previous books include *After Secession: Jefferson Davis and the Failure of Confederate Nationalism* (Louisiana State University Press, 1978), *Slavery Remembered: A Record of Twentieth-Century Slave Narratives* (University of North Carolina Press, 1979), *Many Excellent People: Power and Privilege in North Carolina, 1850–1900* (University of North Carolina Press, 1985), and *Military Necessity: Civil-Military Relations in the Confederacy* (Praeger, 2006). Recently he published *"What Shall We Do with the Negro?": Lincoln, White Racism, and Civil War America* (University of Virginia Press, 2009).

JUDITH F. GENTRY received her Ph.D. at Rice University where she, along with Jon L. Wakelyn and Emory M. Thomas, studied under Frank E. Vandiver. Gentry is currently a professor of history at the University of Louisiana at Lafayette. Gentry has written extensively on Confederate economic issues, and her article "A Confederate Success in Europe: The Erlanger Loan," *Journal of Southern History* 36 (1970) won the Mary Hayes Ewing Publication Prize in Southern History. Her most recent work, coedited with Jane Allured, is *Louisiana Women: Their Lives and Times* (University of Georgia Press, 2009). She has served on the Board of Advisory Editors of the Jefferson Davis Papers and wrote the introduction to the ninth volume. She was an advisor and was interviewed on camera for the Civil War and Reconstruction parts of the prize-winning documentary *Louisiana: A History*, aired in 2003 by the Louisiana Public Broadcasting System. She has served as president of the Louisiana Historical Association and of the Southern Association of Women Historians and served on the National Council of the American Association of University Professors.

HERMAN HATTAWAY is a professor emeritus of history and religion studies at the University of Missouri–Kansas City. He has a Ph.D. from Louisiana State University, where his major professor was T. Harry Williams. Hattaway's name is on the cover of nineteen books: he wrote or co-wrote nine of them and he wrote forewords or commentaries for the other ten. Hattaway is best known for his books *Jefferson Davis, Confederate President* (University Press of Kansas, 2002), coauthored with Richard D. Beringer; *General Stephen D. Lee* (University Press of Mississippi, 1976); and *Shades of Blue and Gray: An Introductory Military History of the Civil War* (University of Missouri Press, 1997), which was the impetus for the Shades of Blue and Gray series by the University of Missouri Press. *How The North Won: A Military History of the Civil War* (University of Illinois Press, 1983), co-written with Archer Jones, is Hattaway's magnum opus.

LEONNE M. HUDSON received his bachelor's degree at Voorhees College and his M.A. and Ph.D. degrees at Kent State University. He authored *The Odyssey of a Southerner: The Life and Times of Gustavus Woodson Smith* (Mercer University Press, 1998) and edited the volume *Company "A" Corps of Engineers, U.S.A., 1846–1848, in the Mexican War* (Kent State University Press, 2001). He has published several articles and numerous book reviews. He is an associate professor of history at Kent State University and a former colleague of Jon L. Wakelyn.

CLAYTON E. JEWETT received his M.A. and Ph.D. degrees from The Catholic University of America, where he studied under Jon L. Wakelyn. Jewett teaches history at Baylor University, is the coeditor of the Shades of Blue and Gray series published by the University of Missouri Press, and serves as the head coach of the Baylor Men's Rugby Team. He is the author of *Texas in the Confederacy: An Experiment in Nation Building* (University of Missouri Press, 2002), *Rise and Fall of the Confederacy: The Memoir of Senator Williamson Simpson Oldham, C.S.A.* (University of Missouri Press, 2006), and coauthor of *Slavery in the South: A State-by-State History* (Greenwood Press, 2004). His current project is a biography of Texas Civil War Governor Pendleton Murrah.

ALAN M. KRAUT is university professor of history at American University. He received his Ph.D. in history from Cornell University. Specializing in United States immigration and ethnic history and the history of medicine in the United States, he is the prize-winning author or editor of eight books and many scholarly articles. Among his awards is the Theodore Saloutos Prize from the IEHS for the best book in immigration or ethnic history, which he received for his 1994 volume, *Silent Travelers: Germs, Genes, and the "Immigrant Menace"* (Basic Books). His volume *Goldberger's War: The Life and Work of a Public Health Cru-*

sader (Farrar, Straus & Giroux, 2003) has been honored with the Henry Adams Prize from the Society for History in the Federal Government, the Arthur J. Viseltear Prize from the American Public Health Association, and the Watson Davis and Helen Miles Davis Prize from the History of Science Society. His research has been supported by the Rockefeller Foundation, the National Endowment for the Humanities, the Smithsonian Institution, and the National Institutes of Health. He chairs the Statue of Liberty–Ellis Island History Advisory Committee and is a consultant to the Lower East Side Tenement Museum. He regularly serves as a historical consultant on PBS and History Channel documentaries. He is the past president of the Immigration and Ethnic History Society. He is an Organization of American Historians Distinguished Lecturer and is a fellow of the Society of American Historians.

DAVID E. KYVIG received his Ph.D. from Northwestern University and is distinguished research professor emeritus at Northern Illinois University. His book *Explicit and Authentic Acts: Amending the U.S. Constitution, 1776–1995* (University Press of Kansas, 1996) received the 1997 Bancroft Prize and Henry Adams Prize of the Society for History in the Federal Government. His book *The Age of Impeachment: American Constitutional Culture since 1960* (University Press of Kansas, 2008) was a *Choice* Outstanding Academic Title for 2008.

KENNETH NIVISON holds a Ph.D. from The Catholic University of America, where he studied under Jon L. Wakelyn. Nivison is an assistant professor of history at Southern New Hampshire University. His current book project is *Proving Grounds: New England Colleges and the Making of Civil War Leadership*. He resides in Manchester, New Hampshire, with his wife and son.

DANIEL E. SUTHERLAND received his Ph.D. from Wayne State University, where he studied under Grady McWhiney. Sutherland has been the Douglas Southall Freeman Professor at the University of Richmond, a visiting fellow at Wolfson College, University of Cambridge, and currently is a professor of history at the University of Arkansas. He is the author or editor of thirteen books about the nineteenth-century United States. His book *Seasons of War* (Free Press, 1995) received both the Douglas Southall Freeman Award and the Laney Prize. His most recent publication is *A Savage Conflict: The Decisive Role of Guerrillas in the American Civil War* (University of North Carolina Press, 2009).

EMORY M. THOMAS took his B.A. with Honors from the University of Virginia and his Ph.D. from Rice University, where he studied with Jon L. Wakelyn and Judith Gentry. He is Regents Professor Emeritus at the University of Georgia. He once taught Latin at the secondary level, played on what was then the longest losing streak in major college football, and defended Cincinnati and Dayton against the "Evil Empire" from 1965 to 1967. More recently he has taught and written United States history. Among his eight books are *Robert E. Lee: An Album* (W. W. Norton, 2000), *Robert E. Lee: A Biography* (W. W. Norton, 1995), *Travels to Hallowed Ground: A Historian's Journey to the American Civil War* (University of South Carolina Press, 1987), *Bold Dragoon: The Life of J. E. B. Stuart* (Harper & Row, 1986), and *The Confederate Nation, 1861–1865* (Harper & Row, 1979). Thomas has held a Senior Fulbright Lectureship at the University of Genoa, the Douglas Southall Freeman Chair at the University of Richmond, and was the Mark W. Clark Distinguished Visiting Professor of History at The Citadel. He is also the subject of a Festschrift, *Inside the Confederate Nation: Essays in Honor of Emory M. Thomas* (Louisiana State University Press, 2005).

BERTRAM WYATT-BROWN, Richard J. Milbauer Emeritus of History, University of Florida, and visiting scholar, Johns Hopkins University, is the author of ten books, the best known of which are *Southern Honor: Ethics and Behavior in the Old South* (Oxford University Press, 1982), which was a finalist for a Pulitzer Prize, and *The House of Percy: Honor, Melancholy, and Imagination in a Southern Family* (Oxford University Press, 1994). Wyatt-Brown earned his Ph.D. from Johns Hopkins University and is a previous recipient of a Guggenheim Fellowship and an NEH Fellowship. He served as president of the Southern Historical Association from 2000 to 2001. He is currently working on a number of projects, including "Honor and America's Wars" and "Who Owns the Dead? Hazards of Biography and Memoir."

ROSEMARIE ZAGARRI earned her M.A. and Ph.D. degrees at Yale University and currently is professor of history at George Mason University. Jon Wakelyn was her colleague at The Catholic University of America and the series editor for her book, *A Woman's Dilemma: Mercy Otis Warren and the American Revolution* (Harlan Davidson, 1995). Her most recent work is *Revolutionary Backlash: Women and Politics in the Early American Republic* (University of Pennsylvania Press, 2007).